Development
of Perception
in Infancy

DEVELOPMENT OF PERCEPTION IN INFANCY

THE CRADLE OF KNOWLEDGE REVISITED

Martha E. Arterberry

and

Philip J. Kellman

OXFORD
UNIVERSITY PRESS

OXFORD

UNIVERSITY PRESS

Oxford University Press is a department of the University of Oxford. It furthers
the University's objective of excellence in research, scholarship, and education
by publishing worldwide. Oxford is a registered trade mark of Oxford University
Press in the UK and certain other countries.

Published in the United States of America by Oxford University Press
198 Madison Avenue, New York, NY 10016, United States of America.

Library of Congress Cataloging-in-Publication Data
Names: Arterberry, Martha E., author. | Kellman, Philip J., author. |
Arterberry, Martha E., The cradle of knowledge.
Title: Development of perception in infancy : the cradle of knowledge
revisited / Martha E. Arterberry and Philip J. Kellman.
Description: 1 Edition. | New York : Oxford University Press, 2016. |
Includes bibliographical references and index.
Identifiers: LCCN 2015044393| ISBN 9780199395637 (pbk. : alk. paper) |
ISBN 9780199395651 (epub) | ISBN 9780199395644 (UPDF)
Subjects: LCSH: Perception in infants.
Classification: LCC BF720.P47 A78 2016 | DDC 155.42/237—dc23
LC record available at http://lccn.loc.gov/2015044393

9 8 7 6 5 4 3 2 1
Printed by Webcom, Canada

For our families

Contents

Preface

In 1998, we published *The Cradle of Knowledge: Development of Perception in Infancy.* In that book, we drew on infant perception research to evaluate a number of philosophical issues regarding perception and the origins of knowledge. We discovered a great deal about the early capacities of young infants, and we were able to clarify some age-old questions. At the same time, many questions remained unanswered. Our goal for this book is to revisit these philosophical issues and outstanding questions more than 15 years later. As will be shown, many advances have been made in the intervening years. Moreover, new areas of inquiry have been tackled. At this juncture, we see the field standing firmly on an understanding of the basic capacities of infants at different ages (e.g., acuity, motion detection, and intermodal perception) and asking what infants do with this information—perceive people, objects, and events.

Our treatment this time is much the same as before. We first introduce each topic from philosophical and historical perspectives, and then we evaluate each issue relying on research with infants. When possible, we address mechanisms of change, in addition to describing what infants can do when. Our theoretical perspective continues to be informed by the work of J. J. and E. J. Gibson. From such a perspective, we focus on the information available for perception, when it is used by the developing infant, the fit between infant capabilities and environmental demands, and the role of perceptual learning.

We are grateful to many people who devoted their valuable time to comment on this book as it evolved and to the team at Oxford University Press for their help through the publication process. Much of this work was written while MEA was on sabbatical at Northwestern University. She thanks Colby College for the sabbatical leave, and Sue Hespos of the Department of Psychology at Northwestern University for her collegiality and enthusiasm.

Introduction

More than three centuries ago, the philosopher John Locke (1690/1971) recounted the query he received from his friend William Molyneux:

Suppose a man born blind, and now adult, and taught by his touch to distinguish between a cube and a sphere .... Suppose the cube and sphere placed on a table and the blind man to be made to see: ... [could he] by his sight, before he touched them ... distinguish and tell which is the globe, which the cube? (pp. 121–122)

Locke and Molyneux answered in the negative. In their view, only by learning to interpret the sensation of vision and associating them with touch could visual sensations become connected to a notion such as *form*.

How we obtain knowledge through the senses has long intrigued philosophers and scientists. Many have sought to understand the nature of perception by asking how it begins, and their answers have anchored conceptions of human nature and formed the foundations of theories of knowledge.

It is striking that Molyneux posed his question about what untutored perception might be capable of in reference to an *adult*. Given that the experiment was imaginary, why not ask about perceptual responses un-influenced by a lifetime of thinking and learning; why not ask about a human infant? Apparently, the idea of assessing perception in the helpless human infant was considered too far-fetched even for thought experiments. In this regard, not much had changed in 1947 when Austin Riesen wrote, "The study of innate visual organization in man is not open to direct observation during early infancy, since a young baby is too helpless to respond differentially to visual excitation" (p. 107).

The study of human perceptual development turned out to be possible after all. Researchers have discovered windows into the human infant's perceptual world. Although unable to speak, point, or locomote, even newborn infants respond in subtle ways that reveal aspects of their sensory and perceptual experiences. Through diverse and often ingenious efforts, researchers have exploited these responses to reveal perceptual competence, test hypotheses about processes, and infer neural mechanisms. Some of the answers they have uncovered would have surprised Lock and Molyneux, as they have surprised modern researchers.

Why do we care about how perception develops? The reasons are those that have kept these questions in the forefront of intellectual debate for centuries.

The beginnings and workings of perceptual knowledge bear on fundamental questions of both epistemology and psychology: What links ideas in our minds to external reality? Are perceptual processes that connect the mind to the world inherent in the mind or are they constructions from experience? Today, we know these questions unfold at several interacting levels. How does energy carry information and how can it be extracted by perceptual systems? To what extent has sensitivity to structured information, and the neural circuitry that carries out perception, developed through the evolution of perceptual systems, and how much does perception become organized through experiences of the individual? Do the basic processes of perception differ across individuals depending on their personal histories?

It is sometimes argued that questions of nativism versus empiricism are misguided—that all development is an interaction between organism and environment. Perceiving organisms must of course eat and breathe, and their perceptual systems will deteriorate if not stimulated. These interactions with the environment, however, do not answer questions of whether organisms come equipped innately or maturationally to pick up information and represent their environments in meaningful ways. The study of perceptual development can and, as we will see, often has answered such questions.

We also care about perception as a prerequisite to understanding other aspects of human cognitive and social development. The developing infant's interactions with the physical and social worlds are both enabled and constrained by what can be perceived. What has recently been learned about perception, we suggest, requires a new account of development. The discovery that human beings begin the path of development at quite a different place than previously suspected has many consequences.

Finally, the study of perceptual development sheds light on the character of perception itself and its place in the mind. Early in the 20th century, the Gestalt psychologists contended that relationships are most important in perceiving and that intrinsic mechanisms in the nervous system respond to these. Still today, this lesson is not fully appreciated. Students of cognitive science, neuroscience, and psychology often think in terms of sensation (or basic filtering of stimulus energy attributes) and cognition—general inferential processes that "recognize" or "make sense of" sensory inputs. However, a wealth of evidence points toward autonomous perceptual mechanisms that stand between sensation and cognition. More than half of the cerebral cortex appears to be dedicated to perceptual information processing. This massive allocation of brainpower may serve primarily to extract stimulus relationships and produce abstract, meaningful descriptions of reality. There may be no better way to acquire an appreciation of the character and function of perception than by studying its development.

In writing this book, we have stayed close to the methods and data of scientific research on infant perception. A simpler and neater story could have been told with fewer details; no doubt such a story would have better suited some purposes.

On the other hand, the story of infant perception research is one in which experimental findings are replacing centuries of conjecture about the origins of the mind. Like conjecture, interpretation of data has pitfalls, and these are not easy to prevent or remedy without keeping in view the methods and results on which conclusions and generalizations depend.

1 Views of Perception and Perceptual Development

INTRODUCTION

Perception forms the portal between reality and knowledge. It is the gateway through which matter and energy in the physical world lead to ideas in the mind. An enigmatic bridge, it appears as biological activity from one end and conscious awareness from the other. In the theater of the mind, it is the opening scene.

In giving us contact with the world, human perception is proficient and unobtrusive. The world simply appears to be there, in all its dimensions and detail, from even a brief glance. To walk, we place our feet on some surface whose location and solidity are obvious. To grasp, we reach to where an object is located. We turn toward a speaker, knowing before turning where and often who the speaker is. The accuracy and transparency of perception mislead the casual observer, and sometimes the expert, into thinking that knowing through the senses is uncomplicated.

In the development of the individual, perception is pivotal. Learning about the physical and social worlds and acquiring language rely on the products of perception. To the extent perceptual ability is lacking at the beginning of life, these tasks must be postponed. Developing perception becomes the central task of early development, as many theorists have suggested (e.g., Piaget, 1954).

In seeking to understand perceptual development, we encounter several key questions. How does perception get started? It is easy to demonstrate that the senses function from birth. But do they reveal a world of objects, situations, and events? Or do they serve up at first only the "blooming, buzzing confusion" suggested by William James (1890)? When perceptual knowledge is attained, how does the process work? To explain how a quantum of light absorbed by a photoreceptor in the eye initiates an electrical signal in the nervous system involves many complexities. Equally mysterious, however, are processes that determine from many rays of light—each carrying no information about how far it has traveled—the position, size, and shape of an object several hundred feet away. Moreover, perceptual abilities are not static; they change with development and experience. Which of these changes depend on simple growth or the maturation of new mechanisms, and which depend on learning to interpret the inputs to the senses or acquiring skill in selecting information? How do perceptual changes cause and result from changes in other cognitive and motor abilities? To begin to pose such questions, we need first to consider the character and function of perception.

ASPECTS OF PERCEPTION

One reason the study of perception is so fascinating and complex is that it involves questions of fundamentally different kinds. We can discover these different aspects by considering almost any perceptual phenomenon and asking what needs to be explained.

Issues of Representation and Process

Consider the display in Figure 1.1A. We see five objects varying in shape and color. The same five areas are rearranged in Figure 1.1B. Now things look different. We notice three objects, not five, and the objects have acquired some interesting qualities and relationships. The circle on the left has become translucent; we can see part of another object through it. The circle on the right is pierced by the middle object. The middle object is seen as a whole despite having two visible parts separated by a gap on the right and a differently colored part on the left.

This example illustrates that perceptual experience is not a simple inventory of stimulus inputs. Both Figure 1.1A and Figure 1.1B may be straightforwardly described as containing five regions of certain colors at certain positions on a flat surface. Indeed, this is exactly the type of description used by the computer on which the displays were created to send instructions to the printer. There is no depth, nothing transparent, and no interpenetrating objects. Your perceptual system handles these inputs very differently, mapping the five simple regions into three objects, one of which is translucent and one pierced by another.

In this example, the transformations between the stimulus inputs and what is perceived depend on relationships in the stimulus. As the Gestalt psychologists argued long ago, perception is not merely a response to local stimuli; it depends on *patterns* in space and time. A crucial part of the task of understanding perception is finding out what dimensions, features, and relationships we extract from the inputs. We seek to determine how these are represented and what further processing is required to produce the objects, scenes, and events of our experience. These questions address the level of *representation and process* in the study of perception.

We might set out to study perception in the infant or the adult with this goal alone. By manipulating stimulus inputs and measuring what is perceived, we can obtain data allowing us to build theories about perceptual processes. This task is central but not sufficient. One limitation is that in pursuing this task alone, we would end up with a catalog of curiosities. On receiving stimulus pattern *a*, the visual system engages processes *b* and *c*, leading to our perceiving *d*. We would lack a deeper understanding of our catalog of transformations. We could say nothing of why a visual system should take pattern *a* and end up with percept *d*.

Issues of Ecology

Let us look again at Figure 1.1. It is remarkable that this arrangement of color patches on a piece of paper should evoke the perception of one object passing through another, or five patches making three objects. But consider the following: If three

A

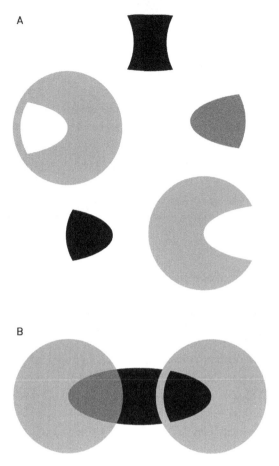

B

FIGURE 1.1

Organization in perception. The five visible areas in part A appear as three perceived objects in part B. Source: Created by P. J. Kellman.

objects were positioned in space in the proper way, and if one were translucent, then the projection to the eyes could be the same as what we get from the picture. Where one object passed behind the translucent one, that part of the display would appear different in surface lightness, whereas its boundaries maintained their continuity with those not covered by the translucent object. In other words, the percepts rendered by the visual system are physically plausible—that is, they could be caused by a suitable physical arrangement in the world, given the laws of optics.

A stronger claim can be made. The technology for placing precise arrangements of ink on paper is a relatively recent human invention. In the natural world, the one in which animals evolved over millions of years, if your eyes received the patterns in Figure 1.1, you would almost certainly be confronting an arrangement of a translucent object and two others—the scene your visual system says is there. To make such a claim, we need to know a great deal about the ecology—about what goes on in the physical world and how it produces patterns of light sent to our eyes. Stated informally, it would be very improbable for five separate physical objects to come together in such a way that their boundaries displayed the continuity we see in Figure 1.1. Moreover, certain lightness relations in the scene are exactly right for a translucent surface, and certain positional relations are exactly right for one object penetrating another, but these relations would be quite coincidental otherwise.

We now see that our understanding of perception must involve—in fact, must begin with—the study of the world to be perceived. We call this the *level of ecology* in the study of perception. Although sensation and perception have been studied systematically for several hundred years, a clear understanding of the importance of this level has emerged only in the latter part of the 20th century (Gibson, 1950, 1966, 1979). The first stop on the road to understanding perception is a rigorous analysis of the *task* of perception—what is to be perceived—and the ways in which environments make *information* available to accomplish the task.

Issues of Biological Mechanism

To capture, represent, and transform information requires mechanisms of considerable complexity. How does perceptual processing take place in the nervous system? This is the question of the level of *biological mechanism*. When we consider nonbiological information-processing systems (machines) along with biological ones, we might prefer Marr's (1982) label—the *level of hardware implementation*. In some ways, this level requires the least introduction. Everyone knows that to understand vision, for example, we need to know about the retina, about rods and cones, and about where optic nerve fibers project in the brain. If one develops a vision problem, the facts of biological mechanism are most relevant to its causes and treatment.

Although we may speak of this level as a single category, it encompasses various levels of its own. Each sense involves specialized receptors and associated neural mechanisms designed to bring to the receptors a particular form of energy from the outside world. In vision, for example, the lens and cornea refract incoming light rays onto the retina, and several different muscle groups allow the eyes to be pointed, focused, and converged, to optimize the pickup of information. Beyond the receptors, neural structures are wired to register key features in energy patterns; these in turn feed into various neural streams specialized for extraction of higher-order information. Still other neural mechanisms must integrate information from different processing streams and different senses to produce our coherent experience of objects and events.

MULTIPLE LEVELS IN THE STUDY OF PERCEPTION

We have now introduced three levels important in understanding perception—the level of *ecology*, the level of *representation and process*, and the level of *biological mechanism*. Table 1.1 indicates the kinds of questions asked at each level. In this section, we take a closer look at each level to sharpen the issues within and between levels that guide our study of infant perception.

Table 1.1 Three Levels of Analysis in the Study of Perception

Level of Ecology	Level of Representation and Process	Level of Biological Mechanism
What is the perceptual task?	How is information extracted? How is information represented?	What biological mechanisms accomplish the extraction, representation, and processing of visual information?
What information is available for perceiving?	What computations are performed?	
What constraints simplify the task?		

The Level of Ecology

What are the tasks of perception, and what information is available to do these tasks? Gibson (1966, 1979) noted the central importance of these questions and argued that answering them requires study of the way environments interact with energy to provide information. In vision, he called this enterprise *ecological optics*. The term *ecological* designates facts at a level relevant to perceiving organisms. Not every fact about the physical environment is relevant. We are concerned with the physical world within certain spatial and temporal ranges. In spatial terms, our concerns lie primarily between approximately one-tenth of a millimeter and 10,000 meters. In this range, the texture and topography of surfaces and the shapes and sizes of objects are relevant to our activities. At one end of this range, we may be concerned with minute variations that make a surface rough or smooth or with tiny markings on visible surfaces. At the other end, we can set and maintain a course with reference to distant mountains. The physical distances between stars and the distances between molecules, in contrast, may be preconditions for our existence but are not ecologically relevant for guiding behavior. Our perceptual concerns are likewise confined in time. Organisms may apprehend and react to changes or events in the environment unfolding in milliseconds or hours but not to those occurring in nanoseconds or centuries.

Within these ranges, what sorts of information about the physical world are important? Complex perceptual systems belong exclusively to mobile organisms, and we can understand much about perceptual function from that simple fact. In the first place, the task of moving through the environment requires selectivity and guidance. We need to know about surfaces of support in the world, about footholds and drop-offs, and about obstacles and passageways. To maintain posture and balance as we locomote, we need ongoing information about our own position relative to surfaces of support and to gravity. Next, there are the aspects of the physical world—including objects, events, and the spatial layout—that we need to apprehend if we are to do anything useful by moving. Objects, which are coherent, bounded, material units, often are inanimate, such as rocks, plates, and pillows. Many of their properties are important to our interactions with them, including their forms, sizes, rigidity, and composition. Other entities we perceive, such as people, cats, and spiders, are animate and may pose danger or provide protection, comfort, and companionship. With those of our own species, it is important that we perceive emotion, demeanor, action, and intention, as well as spoken language. Analogous to the boundaries in space that specify surfaces and objects, we perceive *events*—sequences of motion or change that are in some sense coherent and separate from other goings on.

This brief description of the subset of the physical world relevant to perception is illustrative, not exhaustive. Certain ways of thinking about perception lead to the possibility that its full scope is surprisingly wide. Besides surfaces, objects, people, and events, connections among physical events—causality—and among social ones—social intention—might be detected by perceptual mechanisms rather than constructed from learning about the world. After understanding more about perception and its development, we will be in a better position to consider these possibilities.

Ecology and Information

What about the *optics* in *ecological optics*? Information, like objects and events, must be appropriate to spatial and temporal scale. Thus, Gibson argued that ecological optics is not fundamentally concerned with trackings of single rays of light or the absorption of quanta by molecules emphasized in traditional geometric and physical optics. Instead, we attempt to identify information produced by interactions of volumes of light with objects and surfaces at a scale relevant to perceiving organisms.

Marr (1982) emphasized the need for formal *computational* accounts at this level. How can the objects and events of the physical world be determined mathematically from informational variables available to the perceiver? Often, obtaining a unique and accurate answer requires the use of *constraints*. A constraint is an assumption about the way the world works that may be incorporated into perceptual computations to restrict their possible outcomes. The most powerful constraints derive from general and enduring features of our physical world. For example, objects in our world have spatiotemporal continuity. In order to move from one place to another, they must pass through positions in between. Objects do not appear at one place, vanish, and materialize some distance away. A perceptual system that incorporates this premise will exclude percepts of discontinuous objects that would otherwise be compatible with available information.

As another example, consider perception of object size. What information is there for perceiving size? The projection of a viewed object takes up a certain portion of our field of view; we call this *projective size* or *visual angle*. Projective size is a poor guide to physical size because it varies with viewing distance. However, there is an invariant relation between physical size, projective size, and distance: The ratio formed by the object's real size and its distance is the tangent of the visual angle. Figure 1.2 illustrates. The projection of the object onto the eye can be obtained by drawing straight lines from points on the object through the nodal point[1] of the eye to the retina. If distance can be registered, a perceptual processor

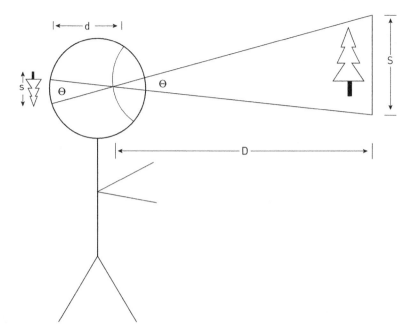

FIGURE 1.2

Size and distance relations. S is the real object size, D is its distance from the observer, s is the projected size at the retina, d is the distance from the nodal point of the eye to the retinal surface, and Θ is the visual angle projected by the object. The inverted tree to the left of the eye depicts the retinal image. Source: Created by P. J. Kellman.

that incorporates this relationship can compute a real size from visual angle, available at the eye of the observer, and register distance. This mathematical relationship concerning size and distance is a fact about the world in which we live—that is, a fact about optics and projective geometry. An important part of the study of perception is to determine when such relationships are incorporated as constraints in perceptual processing. Such constraints may be inborn or maturational, presumably resulting from evolution under consistent conditions (Gibson, 1966; Johansson, 1970; Shepard, 1984). On the other hand, some theorists have suggested that constraints may be discovered through learning by the individual (Goldstone, 2003; Helmholtz, 1885/1965; Wallach & O'Leary, 1982).

This example of size perception can be extended to illustrate the importance of thorough ecological analysis. Although it was long believed that physical size could be recovered perceptually only by using distance information, Gibson (1950) noted a relational variable that offers size information without using distance. On a textured surface whose texture elements are relatively uniform in size, the visual array projected to the eye contains a *texture gradient*. The projective sizes of texture elements decrease as the surface extends father away from the observer. Gibson noted that an object resting on a textured surface will occlude the same number of texture elements no matter what its distance. Object size, then, might be perceived in relation to texture element size. Seeing two objects at different distances as being the same size might not require using equations about size and distance; rather, they can be directly compared to the texture elements at their location.

The relation between projective size and distance applies equally to viewed surface texture and viewed objects, allowing us to obtain size by their relation without using distance information. The usefulness of this relation also depends on the fact that, due to gravity, most objects in our environment rest on ground surfaces.

The example underscores the primacy of the level of ecology in understanding perception. Many advances in understanding perception have come from the discovery of stimulus relationships (e.g., decreasing texture size with distance) that provide more direct information about some physical property (e.g., depth) than do simple variables. If we have limited or misleading notions about information, we may not understand what is detected and computed by perceptual systems. Even where many details are known about the neurophysiology of perceptual systems, an understanding of which details are relevant and what brain mechanisms need to extract and compute depends on a clear ecological or computational account of perception.

The Energy World

We have thus far said little about the role of *energy* in sensation and perception. In terms of function or tasks, we have emphasized not perception of energy, such as seeing light, but perception of physical structure, such as objects and surfaces. In terms of means, we have emphasized the pick-up of information. But how does information become available? We are able to perceive only because the material environment around us is awash with energy. We are constantly immersed in seas of acoustic vibrations, electromagnetic waves, chemical and temperature gradients, and much more. Only some of this energy is available to our senses. It is sobering to realize that while standing in your living room, thousands of cellular telephone calls, air traffic control transmissions, commercial radio and television broadcasts, and wireless Internet traffic are passing undetected through your body.

Energy links the physical world of material structures and events to the perceptual world in which objects and events are represented. We see a table not by direct contact but by means of the light it reflects. Due to the evolution of specialized systems for receiving them, we are sensitive to certain forms and ranges of energy.

There is no question that perception begins with energy interactions at sensory receptors. This first step, however, has given rise to many misconceptions about perception. One is that we can understand perception by understanding local responses to energy. Another misconception is that what we *perceive* is energy. Perceiving properties of energy is in fact a means, not an end. Perception informs us more about matter than energy, by means of patterns in ambient energy. In the final outputs of perception—what we experience or represent—our knowledge about energy per se is generally poor. For example, in a lighted room, we perceive the layout of surfaces of varied reflectance, but we have little or no sense of how much light, in absolute terms, comes to the eye from each surface (Gilchrist, Delman, & Jacobsen, 1983).

It is so intuitive that what we hear is sound and what we see is light that to suggest otherwise may be shocking. But these notions are arbitrary, as we can readily grasp by thinking about the casual chains involved in perception. Consider the following: Causal interactions of objects with light send patterns of light to the eyes. A pattern of light as it hits the retina is the last step in the causal sequence of sight that lies in the physical world, *outside* of our biology. Perhaps this fact underlies the idea that what we see is light. But the causal chain continues. Light goes no further into the nervous system than the retina, where it gives rise to electrical signals. Significantly, no one would claim that seeing occurs in the retina; it occurs in the brain. The light is left behind as subsequent electrical events take place en route to later destinations in the nervous system, where perceptual representations and conscious experiences are produced. In this causal chain from objects to light patterns to electrical signals to perception, what should lead us to single out light as the thing that is perceived? It makes no more sense to say we see light than that we see electrical signals in the retina.

The causal chain of perception carries information about all of the steps. Patterns of cortical activity contain information about light patterns *and* about retinal electrical patterns *and* about objects in the world. Singling out one of these as what we perceive is arbitrary, except on functional grounds. In the use and evolution of these causal sequences in biological systems, the important properties extracted are usually far along the causal chain: objects, spatial layout, and events. Sometimes a property of energy is a salient output of perception, such as when a sound is loud enough to cause pain. What we most often find in the descriptions we obtain from perception, however, are behaviorally important aspects of the physical world's material structure, not its energy characteristics.

Explaining perception, then, must include accounts of the catching of energy by receptors. But it requires much more. As our description makes clear, perception is determined by events that occur both earlier and later. Perceiving what is in the world is possible because interactions of energy with objects produce patterning across space and time. These patterns in spatial temporal relationships are often not even definable in terms of local receptor activity. Discovering and specifying precisely patterns in energy that provide information to perceptual systems is our task at the level of ecology.

The Level of Representation and Process

The function of perception is to provide accurate representations of the world to organisms and to guide their action. These representations and the processes that derive them comprise what we labeled the *level of representation and process*. Much of what needs to be explained in perception is what these representations contain and how well they correspond to the physical world. In the study of infant perception, we compare the scope, accuracy, and detail of the infant's perceptual world to the physical world as well as to the perceptual world of adults.

In calling the outputs of perceptual processes *representations*, we use the term broadly. We certainly mean to include characterizations of the outputs of perception as *descriptions* of the environment (Marr, 1982; Pylyshyn, 1973). We do not mean to imply, however, that the outputs of perception are always accessible to consciousness. Some theorists view the outputs of perception as leading to the adjustment of ongoing action in perception–action loops, rather than as comprising explicit descriptions to be thought about, remembered, and so on (Gibson, 1966; Turvey, Shaw, Reed, & Mace, 1981). A standing person, for example, makes periodic postural adjustments to compensate for detected sway. The visual or vestibular registration of sway is seldom conscious. For our purposes, registration of knowledge about the environment (or self) will count as part of the perceptual world, whether or not it is conscious or accessible to other cognitive processes. Although the differences among these cases are interesting, they are not particularly well illuminated by studies of infant perception. It is often tractable to test an infant's registration of some aspect of the environment, but it is much more difficult to distinguish whether it has been registered implicitly or made explicit in the infant's awareness.

The first step in understanding representation and process is some account of infant perceptual competencies. Much of our focus is on research revealing these. What aspects of the environment are perceptible by infants? Which of the multiple sources of information used by adults are usable by infants? Prior to the 1960s, these questions were sources of speculation and controversy but not of experimental research. In this book, we show that these questions have been answered to an impressive extent in many perceptual domains.

Direct Versus Algorithmic Perceptual Processing

How to characterize representation and process in perception has been controversial. Marr (1982) argued that perceptual processes are "algorithmic," in the sense that the outputs of perceptual processes depend on a sequence of representations and operations on them. Our label is more neutral about the character of perceptual processes. Some processes seem aptly described as algorithmic. In other instances, perception may involve not a sequence of representations but, rather, a more direct mapping from stimulus relations onto perceptual outcomes, as emphasized by Gibson (1966, 1979) and others (Cornman, 1975; Epstein, 1982; Hochberg, 1974; Johansson, 1970; Runeson, 1977; Turvey et al., 1981). A related issue is whether perception must be described as inferential in the sense of requiring assumptions about the world to constrain the possibilities consistent with the input (Fodor & Pylyshyn, 1981). An example may help illustrate these issues in understanding the character of perception.

Consider an object approaching an observer at a constant velocity. The size of the object's optical projection increases as it comes closer. Knowing when the object will contact the observer, however, might seem to require calculation. At a certain instant, the object projects a certain size on the retina of each eye. If the object is familiar, its distance may be calculated using the same geometry we considered previously. The real size of the familiar object is retrieved from memory. Distance to the object may be computed from the projected size (visual angle) and the real size. Another distance calculation taken after a known time interval could be used to calculate velocity. Then, if velocity is constant, the *time to contact* could be derived from the object's last position and its velocity. This algorithmic approach would require acquiring, storing, and comparing projective sizes and distance estimates along with accurate timekeeping. The sensed visual angles, as well as the distance estimates, are intermediate representations used to obtain the final result. The inferential character of the process is less obvious.

Lee (1974) provided an alternative analysis of this problem. Omitting mathematical details, the main result is that time to contact is specified directly by a higher-order optical variable. This variable is a ratio of the optical position of the approaching object's boundary and its first temporal derivative (*optical velocity*). The latter refers to the rate at which a contour or feature changes position on the retina. The upshot is that a ratio of two variables available at the observer's eyes mathematically specifies time to contact, without any need for computations involving distance and object size.

Now suppose a sensory system is wired so as to function as a detector for this higher-order variable. The only mental representation involved with such a detector might be its output—that is, time to contact. Indeed, empirical evidence suggests that perceptual systems in a variety of species do extract this information, and it is used to guide important behaviors (Lee & Reddish, 1981). It is in this sense that perception may be direct: Properties of the world may be detected by perceptual mechanisms sensitive to relational variables in the stimulus; computations on intermediate representations may not be required.

Studies of infant perception have not settled the question of whether perceptual processes are algorithmic or direct. Such studies suggest that the answer may vary across perceptual domains. We need to ask the question of representation and process separately for different perceptual abilities.

The Level of Biological Mechanism

The study of the machinery in the nervous system that allows us to extract, represent, and transform information is a rich and multifaceted enterprise. Studies of sensory psychophysics seek to define the range and limits of sensitivity of sensory systems to particular dimensions of energy, such as the range of frequencies the auditory system can detect. Taking a developmental stance, we seek to characterize changes in these sensitivities and theorize about their causes in neural maturation, learning, attention, motor development, and so on. Correlated with these efforts is direct investigation of physiological mechanisms underlying sensation and perception in animal subjects. Some of these studies address truly perceptual issues, such as how we detect and represent the positions of objects in space, whereas others are concerned with limits of sensory receptivity that constrain the pickup of information. Some research is undertaken in the hope of understanding and treating defects of perception. This concern involves almost solely the level of biological mechanism. If you wish to build a computer vision system, you will want to understand ecology and the representations and algorithms used in human visual perception. If your vision becomes cloudy, however, you should consult an ophthalmologist.

One of the fundamental insights of the study of information processing is that the levels we have discussed are not reducible to each other. The specialist who understands algorithms for computing depth from differences in images given to the two eyes probably does not also perform cataract surgery, and vice versa. Neither is using concepts and relationships that will ultimately be replaced by the other's. One important reason is that hardware implementation (biological mechanism) is not unique. Given a task, and a process for doing that task, there are many possible implementations. Thus, an account of perception can be scientific and precise at the ecological and process levels but reveal little about the details of the actual hardware.

The converse insight is sometimes less well understood. But it is one key to understanding perception and perceptual development, as well as information processing in general. That is, a detailed account of biological hardware alone does not explain perception. Accounts of ecology and process are not facts about neurons. They cannot be gleaned from ever more precise maps of neural firing and transmitter uptake. In fact, the reverse is true; choosing which observations of hardware are likely to be important rather than incidental requires knowledge of the task and the processes of perception (Chomsky, 1980; Marr, 1982; Putnam, 1975).

In this book, our primary focus is on ecology and process. This emphasis is in part due to the impossibility of treating all of the levels adequately in one book. A truly massive amount of information is available on biological mechanisms alone, and the research has varied goals. Our focus is *perceptual knowledge*—how perceivers come to know the world around them, what processes achieve this knowledge, and how they change over time. But this is a statement of emphasis and not exclusion. Most scientists who work in cognitive science and neuroscience at any level would agree that work at each level informs the others. Indeed, we have enjoyed several remarkable decades in which the facts at various levels connect and constrain each other far more than has previously been the case. Among the reasons are more precise quantitative theories about information and process, along with powerful new techniques for probing brain mechanisms. Accordingly, we have quite a bit to say about physiological mechanisms, but we stress those facts that clearly connect to the acquisition of perceptual knowledge, such as ways in which what we know at the biological level constrains information processing. Chapter 2 is devoted exclusively to this topic, and physiological aspects arise in our treatment of many other topics as well. Where our discussion of topics in the anatomy and physiology of developing sensory systems is less than comprehensive, the reader may consult several excellent sources (Daw, 2013; Møller, 2012).

STARTING POINTS OF PERCEPTION: TWO GENERAL VIEWS

We have seen that understanding perception involves three levels of inquiry—ecology, representation and process, and biological mechanism—and connections across levels. But we have not yet mentioned perhaps the most remarkable fact of all: The landscape is dynamic, not static. From the beginning of each human life (earlier, in fact), it is constantly forming and changing. These are the phenomena of development and learning. In this book, we examine early perception in various domains, such as object, space, motion, intermodal, and speech perception. In each case, we attempt to discover the starting points and paths of development of important perceptual abilities. In most cases, two general views compete to describe how perception begins and develops. One family of views—which we label *constructivism*—is empiricist in spirit, emphasizing the construction of perceptual reality through extended learning.[2] The other family of views—which we label *ecological*—encompasses a more nativist approach, emphasizing the role of evolution in preparing human beings to perceive. We introduce and examine each view in turn.

Constructivist Views of Perceptual Development

How might we know the world through our senses? The general answer given by constructivists has dominated theorizing about perception in philosophy and experimental psychology for more than two centuries. Constructivist views begin with the fact that sensory receptors, such as rods and cones in the eye, do not apprehend objects directly; each responds to a tiny region of impinging energy. As a result of their activation, receptors give rise to characteristic sensations, such as brightness at a particular location on the eye. Perception—knowing something about the objects and events in the outside world—consists, in constructivist views, of somehow making sense of these sensations. The process is like an inference: We must guess, hypothesize, or imagine what external objects might produce our sensations. Because many possible objects could give rise to particular sensations, the process can succeed only through learning. We learn which sensations co-occur and succeed one another, what visual sensations predict about tactile sensations, and so on. Drawing on memories and associations of past sensations, we construct a coherent interpretation of the causes of our sensations. This construction is the world we perceive. From this perspective, perceptual development must consist of an extended period of learning to interpret sensations before meaningful perception of coherent objects and events is possible.

Constructivist views about the building of perception out of sensation originated with British empiricist philosophers (Berkeley, 1709/1910; Hobbes, 1651/1974; Locke, 1690/1971; Reid 1785/1969). These views were further elaborated by key figures in early experimental psychology (Helmholtz, 1885/1965; Titchener, 1902; Wundt, 1862), by modern perceptionists (Hochberg, 1981; Wallach, 1985), and by developmental theorists (Harris, 1983; Piaget, 1954, 1976). The specific ideas of these theorists differ somewhat but share the main features of our schematic account.

The arguments for constructivism were originally logical ones. Two are particularly instructive for understanding both the constructivist stance and departures from it. We label these arguments the *ambiguity* and *capability* arguments.

The Ambiguity Argument

In his 1709 *Essay Toward a New Theory of Vision*, Berkeley (1709/1910) asked how we might possibly obtain reliable information through the visual sense. Berkeley pointed out that the projection of an object onto the retina of a single eye is inherently ambiguous; an infinite number of variously sized and shaped objects in the world could give rise to the same retinal image. If visual patterns are ambiguous, some nonvisual information is needed to disambiguate them. Berkeley suggested that the nonvisual information was provided by the oculomotor cues of accommodation and convergence. *Accommodation* refers to changing of the thickness of the lens to bring images at different distances into focus. *Convergence* is the turning inward of the eyes so that the two eyes image the same point in space. In each case, the muscular contractions required to accomplish the task would correlate with physical distance to the target, and these muscle sensations might also start out as meaningless but could come to signify depth by association with experiences of reaching for and contacting objects.

The Capability Argument

The growth of experimental physiology in the 19th century gave rise to perceptual theorizing rooted in knowledge of basic sensory capacities. Progress in sensory physiology centered on basic elements, such as individual sensory receptors and electrical conduction in individual nerves. An almost inevitable consequence was a strong emphasis on local activity in sensory nerves in attempting to explain perceptual knowledge. Particularly influential was the formulation advanced by Johannes Müller (1838/1965). Müller, often considered the father of experimental physiology, was concerned with the physiological basis for differences in sensory qualities across the senses. When the eye is stimulated, normally by light but also by pressure or other means, we have sensations of brightness and color. As the example illustrates, characteristic sensations are a function less of the external stimulus than of the particular sensory apparatus affected. Müller called this idea the *specific energies of nerves*. The qualities possible in each sense derive from specific properties of the particular sensory nerves. (We now know that the nerves themselves do not differ in the various sensory systems; Müller's insight accordingly is transferred from the nerves themselves to the separate brain areas to which different sensory nerves project.) Müller's notion of specific nerve energies is profound in making clear that sensations inhere in the observer and not the world.

It suggests a way of thinking about perception, however, that is less fortunate. Consider a few of Müller's doctrines (Müller, 1838/1965):

I. In the first place, it must be kept in mind that external agencies can give rise to no kind of sensation which cannot also be produced by internal causes, exciting changes in the condition of our nerves.

III. The same external cause also gives rise to different sensations in each sense, according to the special endowments of its nerve.

V. Sensation consists in the sensorium's receiving through the medium of the nerves, and as the result of the action of an external cause, a knowledge of certain qualities or conditions, not of external bodies, but of the nerves of sense themselves; and these qualities of the nerves of sense are in all different, the nerve of each sense having its own peculiar quality or energy.

VIII. The information thus obtained by the senses concerning external nature, varies in each sense, having a relation to the qualities or energies of the nerve. (pp. 27–33)

We recount Müller's doctrines in detail to give a sense of the logic of a sensation-centered view. Any sensory effect could have multiple causes and moreover reflects more the properties of the nerve affected than anything else. Taken together, we can call these doctrines the *capability* argument. By their nature, the senses have only the capability of producing one kind of product—sensations. These characteristic sensations of each sense reside in the observer, not in the world.

Taking the capability argument at face value, it becomes baffling how we might move from having sensations to having knowledge about the external world. To the philosophically unsophisticated, it seems that perception puts us in contact with objects and events in the outside world. Given the capability argument, this cannot really be so. At best, we construct, guess at, or imagine the world. We do so by cataloguing, associating, and reasoning about sensations. Achieving perceptual knowledge must consist of inferring the causes of our sensations. We might even be predisposed to do this. In Müller's (1838/1965) words, "The imagination and reason are ready to interpret the modifications in the state of the nerves produced by external influences as properties of the external bodies themselves" (p. 27).

The ambiguity and capability arguments are not entirely distinct. Berkeley's (1709/1910) claim that a ray of light striking the retina carries no information about how far it has traveled can be viewed as a capability argument. However, the arguments are somewhat different. Berkeley's argument concerns the patterns (images) coming to the eye, irrespective of the sensory apparatus from the retina on. The capability argument is an argument about sensory mechanisms. It is in the nature of the sensing process that all the observer can really acquire are sensations, and these are results of specific neural activity within the observer.

In subtle or overt form, this inference from the capabilities of individual receptors or neurons to explanations of perceptual capacity still characterizes much work in sensory physiology and perception. It also characterizes some descriptions of perception by cognitive scientists. Specifically, it is often assumed that the senses deliver some raw or uninterpreted data that is then worked into meaningful form by cognitive processing, incorporating expectations and prior knowledge ("top-down" processing) to obtain the result.

Constructivism: Dissent and Modernization

Problems with the classical constructivist view have often been noted. Kant (1781/1902) questioned how our representations of the world could ever originate from sensory input alone. The fact that we have coherent experience presupposes modes of mental organization, such as the dimensions of space and time, into which our sensory experiences are arranged. A different sort of dissent came from the physiologist Hering (1861–1864), who emphasized the functioning of the two eyes as an integrated system that apprehends depth directly. Binocular disparity—differences in retinal positions in the two eyes stimulated by a target—might allow direct detection of depth without learning. Hering's claims attack both the capability argument, because the perceptual system can be seen as responding to relationships rather than local stimulation, and the ambiguity argument, because the characterization of the visual stimulus in terms of single retinal images is considered to be mistaken.

Despite these dissents, extreme constructivist views dominated experimental psychology until the early 20th century. At that time, the Gestalt psychologists mounted a comprehensive attack on the notion that percepts are built up from local sensations. Their demonstrations and arguments suggested that *patterns* are fundamental to perception, whereas sensations are incidental. Form or pattern, they asserted, is not a sensory concept at all. The Gestaltists made this point using a variety of demonstrations of *transposition* phenomena. Consider a square made of solid red lines. From the constructivist perspective, the total experience of viewing the square is the collection of various sensations of discriminable locations and the redness and brightness at each. Thus, "the whole is the sum of the parts." The Gestaltists noted that one can easily change all of the sensations, however, while preserving the form of the square. A square constructed from black dots, changed in size and positioned elsewhere on the retina, is nevertheless a square (Figure 1.3). Thus, "the whole is different from the sum of the parts." A melody illustrates the concept for temporal patterns. One can change the constituent notes while preserving the melody, as long as certain relationships among the notes are preserved. Conversely, presenting the original sensations in jumbled order destroys the original form.

Despite its telling arguments and demonstrations, the Gestalt critique was unsuccessful at dismissing constructivist views of perception's origins. Part of the problem was the lack of a successful alternative view. Perceptual organization, the Gestaltists suggested, resulted from the activity of field forces in the brain, a notion that received little support and has since been abandoned. In addition, constructivist views evolved to meet some objections while retaining their emphasis on learning in perception. The modified views elaborated Helmholtz's (1885/1965) notion that experience might lead not only to stored sensations but also to the

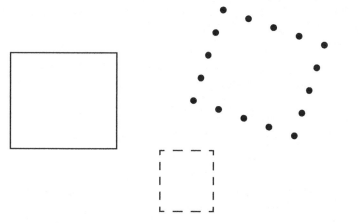

FIGURE 1.3

The three objects are perceived as squares despite changes in elements that define the shape, size, and orientation. Source: Created by M. E. Arterberry.

abstraction of perceptual rules that could be used in the interpretation of future sensory impressions (Brunswik, 1956; Hochberg, 1978). Brunswik, in particular, argued that the Gestalt laws of perceptual organization could be learned by experiences with objects. Such neo-Helmholtzian views have remained influential to the present time (Harris, 1983; Hochberg, 1981; Nakayama & Shimojo, 1992; Rock, 1983).

Ecological Views of Perceptual Development

A different perspective on perceptual development—an ecological view[3]—starts from radically different premises about perception. Its basic ideas were elaborated by J. Gibson (1966, 1979) and E. Gibson (1969, 1984; see also Johansson, 1970; Shepard, 1984). Here, we develop an ecological view that is generally consistent with the viewpoint elaborated by both J. Gibson and E. Gibson; however, some particulars are closer to the positions elaborated by Johansson (1970), Braunstein (1976), and Shepard (1984).

A basic premise of ecological views is that the perceiving organism is awash not only in energy but also in information. Ambient energy is structured by its interactions with objects, surfaces, and events. These interactions are lawful, resulting in a detailed correspondence between patterns in ambient energy and the structure of the environment. The specificity of the patterning of energy by the physical layout makes the environment knowable via detection of structure in the array of energy (J. Gibson, 1966). A second major premise is that perceptual systems evolved not to allow the organism to have meaningless sensations but, rather, to pick up information in energy patterns. The focus is on the perceiving apparatus as an integrated system for information extraction rather than on activity at single receptors or even simple summing of such activity in multiple locations. Receptive elements and individual nerve fibers are parts of larger devices whose circuitry is set up to extract useful information.

The organism is considered to be *actively* involved in the pursuit of information. Take the visual system as a case in point. More than a passive array of retinal receptors, it is an active, highly coordinated, information-seeking system. Ciliary muscles change the shape of the lens, focusing light on the retina. The two eyes turn inward or outward to place the same point in space at the center of each. The eyes may turn as a unit to follow the moving stimulus or focus on a particular feature of an object. The head may also turn, or the observer may move her body to improve her view of a scene. These attunements are closely linked to events in the environment and the perceiver's behavior. The organism's behavior allows it to actively extract information, and this information in turn guides ongoing behavior (J. Gibson, 1966).

On this view, perceptual development begins with meaningful contact with the world, although some perceptual systems may mature after birth, and skill in picking up particular information may improve with practice. This developmental starting point differs conspicuously from that in the constructivist account. If perceptual systems have evolved to pick up meaningful information, perceiving objects and events may not require a long learning period. Perceptual systems may no more have to "learn to interpret" sensations than they have to learn which portion of the electromagnetic spectrum interacts informatively with objects. Perceptual systems may be richly structured devices specialized to take patterns as inputs and produce meaningful and functionally useful descriptions of objects and events as outputs.

To be plausible, ecological views must incorporate some answers to the ambiguity and capability arguments of constructivism. Let us consider these answers. As before, we use visual perception as our example because it has been most central in debates about these issues.

Answering the Ambiguity Argument

Berkeley's (1709/1910) analysis of ambiguity is technically correct if one considers only the information available in a momentary image projected on a single retina. Human perception, however, does not work that way. First, as Hering (1861–1864) described, the two eyes can work together as a system to detect depth from differences in the optical projections to the two eyes. More important, perhaps, the best information available to perceivers is extended in time, and perceptual systems are equipped to utilize such information (J. Gibson, 1966). Looking with a single eye through a peephole, a three-dimensional scene may be indistinguishable from a photograph or photorealist painting. When the observer views a real-world scene or photograph while walking, however, the optical transformations across time differ drastically. Assuming the environment to be at rest, the pattern of optical changes furnishes unequivocal information about the three-dimensional spatial relationships in the scene, with the relations between optical transformations and the real scene specified by the laws of projective geometry. It has been claimed that this *kinematic* information given by observer or object motion is fundamental to ordinary perception. The momentary retinal image considered by Berkeley may be a degenerate input to perceptual systems (J. Gibson, 1966, 1979; Johansson, 1970).

The reply to the capability argument is complementary to the reply to the ambiguity argument. J. Gibson (1966) argued that perceptual systems are geared to detect structure in ambient energy rather than properties of the energy itself (e.g., intensity or wavelength of light). Although the separate senses have their characteristic sensations, "sensation is not a prerequisite of perception, and sense impressions are not the 'raw data' of perception—that is, they are not all that is given for perception" (J. Gibson, 1966, p. 48). Perceptual systems actively extract higher-order information from incoming stimulation. The specialization of perceptual systems to detect information about the environment (and about the self) is the result of evolution (J. Gibson, 1966; Johansson, 1970; Shepard, 1984). Over evolutionary time, perception has come to exploit enduring regularities or constraints of the physical world.

The ecological rejoinders to constructivism undermine the *logical* case for learning in perceptual development. Empirical investigations become central. Does perception give a meaningful representation of the world from the beginning? Can available information that is abstract and extended in space and time be used by naive perceivers? Despite available information and the possibility of evolved mechanisms of information pickup, the meanings of sensory patterns might nevertheless be learned, and the most optimal information might not be utilized. Moreover, the facts might differ for different perceptual abilities: Development might conform to the ecological view for some capacities and fit a constructivist account in other cases. We cannot decide by logic alone; we must pursue these questions by observation and experiment.

PERCEPTUAL CHANGE

Perception changes with age. Details of surface texture obvious to an adult are invisible to a 2-month-old infant. The same infant makes no use of differences in the projections to the two eyes, although these specify vivid depth to a 5-month-old. Through the lifespan, perceptual change continues. A student pilot peers out the window, unable to locate the airport in the midst of roads, buildings, and streams, while her instructor spots it effortlessly. Perceptual skills attained through experience underlie expert performance in many domains (Kellman & Massey, 2013).

Less apparent is what exactly changes. How does the infant perceiver differ from an older child or adult? What is the role of learning? Of maturation? Is there only one kind of perceptual learning or several? Are processes of change in early perceptual development similar to or different from the perceptual changes that occur later in life as adults develop expertise in particular domains?

One class of change—perceptual change due to *maturation* of the nervous system—may be unique to the first year of life. We will encounter many examples, including visual acuity and stereoscopic vision, in Chapters 2 and 3.

Against this backdrop of maturing sensory capacities, we attempt to assess the role and characteristics of learning in perception. Investigators of every theoretical persuasion agree that learning changes perception. What is hotly disputed are the nature and implications of the changes. In particular, from the two general views of perception come two different answers—answers that imply radically different understandings both of the learning process and of the experienced perceiver. J. Gibson and E. Gibson (1957) called these opposing views of perceptual learning *differentiation* or *enrichment* theories. These two notions of perceptual change will be useful as landmarks as we consider early perceptual development. We explore them in turn.

Enrichment: Perceptual Learning in the Constructivist View

Enrichment describes the notion that meaning must be added to the raw data brought in through the senses. What we mean by *meaning* is reference to the environment. Thus, perception can furnish knowledge about the environment (or misunderstandings of the environment from misperception). Sensation does not implicate an external world. The notion of enrichment is a necessary companion to classical ideas about the starting point of perception. If the senses deliver to the observer only meaningless sensations, some process must add meaning for knowledge of the outside world to be attained.

Different possible enrichment processes have been proposed. Constructivist views have often emphasized associations based on contiguity in space or time and also similarity. Such associations apply both to current stimuli and to stored memories of earlier sensations. For example, when the observer is presented with an apple, the various locations at which red is sensed are linked by contiguity in time and space and by similarity. These sensations can call up earlier ones, based on similarity and perhaps recency in time. Association with sensations of touch has often been accorded special status, as in Berkeley's (1709/1910) famous dictum, "Touch educates vision."

Knowledge of an external object is composed of a combination of current sensations and those called up from memory. In structuralist psychology, the former was called the *core* and the latter the *context*; meaningful perception was held to be possible only by adding the context to the core (Titchener, 1902). One of the most famous accounts of perceptual knowledge as enrichment was given by Helmholtz (1885/1965) and has become known as Helmholtz's rule: "Such objects are always imagined as being present in the field of vision as would have to be there in order to produce the same impression on the nervous mechanism " (p. 152).

The world we perceive comes about as an act of imagination using current sensations and associated ones from memory. Helmholtz also emphasized another aspect of enrichment—namely the abstraction of general rules from experience. He contended that perceptual experience leads inductively to the formation of abstract perceptual rules. These rules, in turn, function as premises in inference-like perceptual processing; thus, perception has the character of *unconscious inference*.

The most detailed view of enrichment, and the one most influential in theories of infant development, is Piaget's theory (1952, 1954, 1976). Reality is constructed out of sensorimotor experience. At first,

there is not involved, it goes without saying, any interest of the child in the objects themselves that he tries to watch. These sensorial images have no meaning, being coordinated neither with sucking, grasping or anything which could constitute a need for the subject. Moreover, such images have neither depth nor prominence .... They therefore only constitute spots which appear, move, and disappear without solidity or volume. They are, in short, neither objects, independent images, nor even images charged with extreme meaning .... Still later ... the visual images acquire meanings connected with hearing, grasping, touching, with all the sensorimotor and intellectual combinations. (Piaget, 1952, pp. 64–65)

Unique in Piaget's analysis is the idea that interpretation of sensations comes about not merely from association with other sensations but with *action*. Connecting self-initiated movements and their sensory sequences forms the basis of the growth of knowledge about oneself and the world.

Differentiation: Perceptual Change in the Ecological View

Ecological views suggest that meaningful contact with the environment is possible without the necessity of enrichment. There is no stage in development in which the senses yield an uninterpreted product; perception is always directed to the external environment. Ecological views do not, however, assert that perception is unchanging through the lifespan. In fact, perceptual changes with experience are dramatic, both in early development and in later life. The type of change is what Gibson and Gibson (1955) termed *differentiation.* The environment provides a wealth of information, far too much to be extracted all at once. Moreover, the new perceiver lacks skill in information extraction. With experience, perceivers develop selective skills. Perceptual learning considered as differentiation learning is the development of precision and speed in the pickup of information.

In her classic work *Principles of Perceptual Learning and Development,* E. Gibson (1969) described these changes: With experience in a particular domain comes increasing specificity of discrimination, more optimal deployment of attention, and discovery of higher-order perceptual structure. E. Gibson and Pick (2000) further emphasize that the active perceiver discovers invariants of events, objects, layouts, and *affordances,* or the properties of events, objects, and layouts as they relate to the perceivers' capability for using them. Perceptual development, then, is the process of learning meanings for what can be perceived and learning the information that distinguishes one event, object, or layout from another.

An interesting feature of perceptual learning is that it sometimes seems to occur without explicit reinforcement or even feedback. Mere exposure may be sufficient. E. Gibson also advanced an interesting conjecture about the content of perceptual learning. Learning primarily consists of learning *distinctive features.* These are attributes within a stimulus set that are relevant to distinguishing members of a set. What is interesting about this claim is that not all aspects of objects are said to be learned from exposure to the objects. Rather, the contrasts among members of a stimulus set come to the fore in perceptual learning. This idea makes interesting predictions about exposure to particular stimulus sets and transfer of what is learned.

PROSPECTUS

In what follows, we examine experimental research on the development of perception to determine the ecological and constructivist foundations of perceptual competence, the character of perceptual processes, and the sources of change. Research in infant perception has already shed considerable light on these issues. We will find that some claims of constructivist and ecological views must be abandoned or modified, whereas others have received strong support. There may even be some hope of reconciling key ideas from conflicting general views of perception into a single coherent whole. We return to these issues in Chapter 12, after we have more thoroughly explored the infant's perceptual world.

NOTES

1. The *nodal point* is the point of intersection of all rays that pass through the optical system of the eye undeflected. Other rays of light leaving in slightly different directions from a given object point will arrive at the same image point, but they will get there by being deflected due to refraction by the eye's optics.
2. In other domains of cognitive development, constructivism may have other connotations and contrast strongly with, rather than subsume, associationist accounts.
3. Although the terms are similar, it is important to distinguish the *level of ecology* in the study of perception from *ecological views of development.* The level of ecology refers to facts and concepts about how physical environments make information available for perception. It is theory-neutral in the sense that any theory of perception must include analyses at this level. Ecological views of perceptual development embrace the idea that perceptual mechanisms have evolved to pick up information about functionally important properties of the environment. The closeness in terminology reflects a shared emphasis on lawful relations in the physical world as crucial to understanding both how perception works and how it evolved.

2 Physiological and Sensory Foundations of Perceptual Development

INTRODUCTION

More of the human brain is devoted to perceptual information processing than to any other function. Vision alone, it is estimated, involves more than 30 different areas and 40–50% of the entire cerebral cortex. Adding other senses, it appears that the bulk of cortical processing serves functions of perception.

Even so, the whole brain weighs only several pounds and could be held in our two hands. Thinking of the brain this way, as a small object, we might suspect that focused scientific effort would readily reveal how it works. Unfortunately, inspection at a finer grain gives us a different view of the difficulty of the task. Neurons—the units of information transmission in the brain—number approximately 100 *billion*. Their functions are realized in their connections with other neurons, and these *synapses* number approximately 10^{14}, or approximately 1,000 for every neuron. Connectivity on such a scale makes possible awesome computational power but also makes the task of describing in detail how computations are carried out in the brain a daunting challenge. Most visual areas, for example, are known to be connected to each other, and the hypothesis that each is connected to every other cannot be ruled out by existing data. It is no wonder that the human brain has been claimed to be the most complex device in the known universe.

When we seek to understand the brain early in life, we add to this complexity the dimensions of growth and change. Whereas some plasticity can be found at later ages, never are the changes so extreme and rapid as in the infancy period. Before birth and beyond, the vast neural machinery of perception is under construction. Its status at any given age inevitably decides the potentials and limits of perception in the infant.

Based on their status at birth, animal species are classified as *altricial*, meaning helpless and immature at birth, or *precocial*, comparatively mature, mobile, and functional at birth. In such a classification, *Homo sapiens* is designated as altricial. Although not born with its eyes closed, as are kittens and many other altricial species, the human newborn is nonetheless relatively immobile and long dependent on its parents for care. These are just the outward manifestations. On the inside, the newborn has an incompletely developed brain, and other parts of its nervous system continue to mature for some time after birth.

Yet the extent of postnatal development should not obscure the fact that much perceptual machinery is already in place at birth (Stiles, Brown, Haist, & Jernigan, 2015). Compared to other altricial species, humans are perhaps unique in that all sensory systems become functional before birth (Gottlieb, 1971). The newborn opossum, by comparison, is born without eyes or ears (the eyes open approximately 55–79 days postnatally). Gottlieb considers humans and other primates as "unique in having combined the precocial pattern of sensory development with the altricial pattern of motor development" (p. 118).

In this chapter, we consider aspects of physiological development and sensory limitations that make possible and constrain the acquisition of perceptual knowledge. The division of labor between this chapter and our later topics comes from distinguishing two types of questions and research on infant sensory and perceptual development.[1] In later chapters, our primary focus is on perceptual knowledge—knowledge of objects, spatial layout, and events. Our present concern is with sensory limits and changes in them caused by physiological development. These outer boundaries of receptivity, such as visual acuity, do not directly reveal what is perceived and represented, but they place constraints on it. Sensory maturation in human infants has implications for early perception, for development in general, and, as a practical matter, for attempts to study infants' capabilities.

THE HUMAN INFANT'S NERVOUS SYSTEM

Linking the infant's physiology to sensory and perceptual functioning is a difficult undertaking. We are limited by what is known about physiology and perhaps even more by our modest knowledge about how structures and events in the nervous system carry out perceptual processing. On the behavioral side, measures of sensory and perceptual function in infants are somewhat blunt instruments. The result of these compounded uncertainties is that our conclusions about specific physiological limitations on perception must be tentative. More encouraging is the fact that progress is occurring rapidly in all of the domains relevant to understanding brain and behavior. As a result, hypotheses about neural links to perception, and their developmental patterns, are becoming more plausible, precise, and testable than they were even in the recent past.

Neural Development

Soon after conception, development of the nervous system begins. Cortical neurons begin to form at 10 weeks of gestation and are completed at approximately 18 weeks (Casaer, 1993). Once neurons form, they migrate, under the guidance of chemical gradients and of glial cells (discussed later), to genetically programmed sites in the nervous system. Formation of the cortical layers occurs from the deepest layer out toward the surface of the cortex (Jacobson, 1991). On reaching their destinations, neurons begin a branching process that allows each to form 1,000 or more connections with other neurons. Dendrites, the parts of a neuron that receive signals from other neurons across synaptic junctions, grow in treelike fashion, earning the colorful name *dendritic arborization*. Different brain areas follow different timetables. For example, differentiation of the visual cortex occurs between 25 and 32 weeks of gestation (Purpura, 1975), whereas differentiation of the cerebellum, a structure that controls movement, begins much later and continues to almost 3 years of age (Casaer, 1993).

Synaptic Development

Neuronal interactions occur primarily by chemical activity across synapses. Across these gaps, branches from a neuron's axon may trigger the electrical discharge of another neuron. Synapse formation in the human cerebral cortex increases greatly after neuronal migration is nearly complete in the second trimester of pregnancy (Huttenlocher, 1994). Most occurs after birth, however, especially in a burst of activity between 2 and 6 months of age. During this time, the number of synaptic contacts increases by a factor of 10, reaching a total number that is approximately double that typically found in young adults (Figure 2.1). The overproduction of synapses is corrected by a synapse elimination process that begins at approximately 1 year of age and is completed by 10 years (Huttenlocher, 1994).

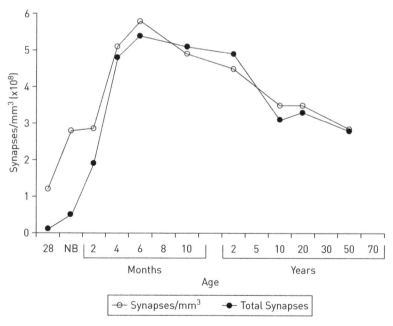

FIGURE 2.1

Changes in synaptic density across the life span. "28" indicates density estimates at 28 weeks of gestation, and "NB" indicates density in newborn infants. Source: Redrawn with permission of Elsevier from Huttenlocher, P. R. (1990). Morphometric study of human cerebral cortex development. *Neuropsychologia, 28,* 517–527; permission conveyed through Copyright Clearance Center, Inc.

At least in the visual cortex, this elimination process results from a pruning of unstimulated dendritic connections rather than by programmed neuronal cell death (Huttenlocher, 1990).

Animal studies suggest that both synaptic growth and pruning are related to experience. Increases in synapses have been reported for young animals reared in complex environments and adults in some circumstances (Greenough, Black, & Wallace, 1987; Holtmaat, Wilbrecht, Knott, Welker, & Svoboda, 2006). Synapse increase is correlated with an increase in skills such as maze learning and memory (Bailey & Kandel, 2009; Greenough, Volkmar, & Juraska, 1973; Greenough et al., 1987; Holloway, 1966). Conversely, particular kinds of stimulation and the acquisition of specific behavioral patterns may be accomplished by selective pruning of synaptic connections and probably selective neuronal death as well. One example is the formation of ocular dominance columns in the visual cortex. For binocular vision, the brain must keep track of which information comes in through which eye. In the monkey, there are originally overlapping inputs from the two eyes in binocular areas. Eventually, a sorting occurs into alternating bands ("columns") of cells, each responsive to only the left eye or the right eye. It is likely that this formation of ocular dominance columns results from altering of synaptic connections based on visual experience (Baroncelli et al., 2010; LeVay, Wiesel, & Hubel, 1980; Lou, Wu, Lui, & Li, 2011). If both eyes receive normal visual input, a competition process leads to the normal alternating bands. If one eye is denied visual experience, it ends up represented by narrow bands, whereas the experienced eye's projections terminate in wider bands (LeVay et al., 1980).

Myelination

In the central nervous system, neurons are interspersed with 10–50 times as many *glial cells*, which do not carry information but act as a support system. Among their many functions, they add structure, separation, and insulation and remove debris (Hirrlinger & Nave, 2014). Certain kinds of glial cells are responsible for the process of *myelination*, the covering of an axon by a glial cell membrane, which greatly increases the conduction speed of the neuron and lowers its action potential threshold. With its new *myelin sheath*, the neuron's conduction speed increases from approximately 2 m/sec to 5 m/sec.

Increased myelination during the first months of life facilitates sensory responses and complex motor patterns (Dubois et al., 2008). Myelination may be especially important in tracts connecting separate brain areas. Casaer (1993) mentions a number of developmental milestones that occur at approximately the same time myelination occurs between separate brain sites.

Functional Regions of the Brain

At birth, the nervous system is more mature toward the periphery and less mature centrally. This may in part account for why infants are equipped with a large number of reflexes but few intentional movements within the first few weeks of life (Brandt, 1979).

Gottlieb (1971) reviews evidence of an invariant sequence of the development of sensory systems in a number of mammalian species. The evidence suggests that earliest sensitivity emerges in the tactile sense, usually somewhere in the head region, followed by vestibular sensitivity, auditory sensitivity, and visual sensitivity. The significance of this pattern is not clear. However, it is intriguing that the ordering appears to go from proximal to distal: Sensitivity is first to direct contact and body orientation and is followed by the senses of audition and vision that are used to detect more remote stimuli. The order suits the priorities of the developing organism, which will be able to withdraw from a noxious stimulus (e.g., a heel stick during a routine blood draw in the neonatal nursery) or reorient itself (e.g., raise the head) long before it can crawl or walk toward or away from a remote object or event. Perhaps this functional interpretation of the order of appearance of sensory systems is most likely. As Gottlieb states, "On logical grounds, evolution is a consequence of nature's more successful experiments in ontogeny" (p. 106). We normally think of developmental patterns as being consequences of evolution, but in fact the success of certain patterns in the individual's development determines which developmental patterns persist.

In humans, all four of these systems—visual, auditory, tactile, and vestibular—appear to be functional before birth but with varying levels of maturity. We consider these, as well as the gustatory and olfactory systems and motor development, in the following sections.

VISUAL SYSTEM ANATOMY AND PHYSIOLOGY

Exquisite specialization for detecting spatial variation is the hallmark of the mammalian visual system. From a point on an object, reflected light sets out in many directions, yet the optics of the eye capture this light and ensure that rays reaching the eye from a single point end up focused on a unique point on the retina, while light from other directions is placed elsewhere. The close packing in the retina of approximately 7 million cones and approximately 120 million rods serves not only to catch most entering light but also to preserve information about its direction of origin. This information makes possible the detection of changes in the input across the plane of the retina and ensures that they correspond to spatial changes in the optic array outside. The changes in the optic array often derive from important differences in objects, surfaces, orientations, and arrangements in the world. Systematic linkages from patterns in objects, space, and events to patterns in the optic array and patterns in the observer's nervous system make it possible to obtain knowledge of the world through the senses. Optimizing the extraction of this knowledge is the incredible engineering of the eye: Adults resolve spatial details. For example, in Vernier acuity—discriminating the misalignment of two vertical lines—adults can perceive misalignments that are 20–30 times smaller than the diameters of individual retinal receptors. These feats of spatial precision are only in progress in the newborn, and in the case of Vernier acuity, adult levels may not be reached until 5 years of age (Zanker, Mohn, Weber, Zeitler-Driess, & Fahle, 1992; see also Brown, Adusumilli, & Lindsey, 2005).

The Eye

From birth to early adulthood, the human eye grows approximately 50% in axial length (distance from the front of the eye to the retina at the back). The fastest growth in eye size occurs during the first year, with axial length changing from approximately 16 mm to approximately 20 to 21 mm, making up about half of the difference between the newborn and adult size of approximately 24 mm. Because the size of the image on the retina increases with eye depth, we would expect newborns' visual acuity to be worse than that of adults by one-third, given this factor alone. Some other basic optical factors that might affect visual sensitivity, such as pupil size, transparency of the ocular media, and transmittance of the lens, probably do not significantly limit early vision relative to adult characteristics.

At the retina, however, we find a number of factors that make newborns' vision dramatically worse than that of adults. For adults, fine detail and color are detected primarily in the fovea, a 1- to 2-degree central region of the visual field. Visual acuity in the fovea is 2.5 times better than at 10 deg out in the periphery and 8–10 times better than at 40 deg out. In the newborn, however, the fovea is strikingly immature. Newborns' cones, the photoreceptors in the fovea that provide color and high spatial resolution, are spaced about 4 times further apart than those of adults (Yuodelis & Hendrickson, 1986).

More limitations are evident when we examine individual photoreceptors. In adults, the cone is a long, thin structure that has an *inner segment* that catches quanta of light and funnels it (using the same principles as fiber optics) to the *outer segment*, where it can be absorbed by molecules of photopigment to trigger an electrical signal. Compared to those of adults, infant cones are much shorter, and the inner segments have a much more bloated shape. Analysis of the shape of the infant's inner segment suggests that it would not function as an effective waveguide; therefore, light reaches the outer segment to initiate a photochemical response only if it is aimed directly at the aperture of the outer segment (Banks & Bennett, 1988).

The probable effects on visual efficiency of the spacing and shape of newborns' cones were calculated by Banks and Bennett (1988). Whereas adult cones catch approximately 65% of the light hitting the foveal area, the neonate's arrangement catches only 2%. Thus, most light hitting a newborn's fovea never contacts a photoreceptor.

The Visual Cortex

Visual processing of spatial detail, crucial for pattern, object, and event perception, is carried out in cortical visual areas. Projections extend from the optic nerve leaving the eyes to the lateral geniculate nucleus in the thalamus (a subcortical relay station) to the visual cortex. Another important visual pathway is entirely subcortical, extending primarily from the peripheral visual fields to the superior colliculus in the midbrain. This pathway appears to subserve rapid orienting to stimuli appearing in peripheral vision but does not process much pattern detail.

Anatomical observations indicating that the visual cortex is not fully mature at birth (Conel, 1939–1963), in addition to several aspects of infant visual performance, have led to the hypothesis that the newborn's visual processing is entirely subcortical (Bronson, 1974). For example, newborns show saccadic eye movements to track slow-moving stimuli and orient more readily toward stimuli in the temporal (near the ear) than the nasal (near the nose) visual fields, characteristics that could be controlled by subcortical orienting mechanisms. Moreover, brain electrical responses to properties that are known to be processed in the visual cortex, such as edge orientation, are weak or absent in the first 6 weeks of life.

The notion of the "decorticate" newborn fit the bulk of behavioral and electrophysiological evidence at the time it was suggested. In extreme form, however, it is contradicted by several lines of behavioral evidence showing perceptual competence and implying some cortical function. Several aspects of visual performance that would require cortical involvement have been clearly documented. Habituation effects, when a stimulus is shown repeatedly over time, transfer from one eye to the other (Slater, Morison, & Rose, 1983), and newborns are able to transfer information, such as surface texture, from one modality (e.g., touch) to another (e.g., vision; Sann & Streri, 2007).

As discussed later, a number of basic sensory functions, such as sensitivity to orientation, direction of motion, and spatial phase, all appear weak at birth and much more robust 6–8 weeks afterward. None of these functions, however, appears entirely absent, even in tests at the earliest ages. Perhaps the best way to view early infants' visual behavior is primarily as being controlled subcortically in the earliest weeks of life, with some cortical interactions with subcortical pathways (Braddick & Atkinson, 2011). The cortical activity may involve at first only certain layers of cortex and processing functions that mature earliest. In particular, it is possible that for the neonate, more detailed pattern information may be taken in than can be used to influence attentional behavior. This hypothesis may help to reconcile the absence of certain electrophysiological responses and the weakness of certain sensory sensitivities in the newborn with some rather remarkable indications of perceptual competence that we explore later.

BASIC VISUAL CAPABILITIES

Our immediate concern is to consider the sensory consequences of the infant's immature fovea and visual cortex. The incomplete maturation of the infant's nervous system constrains early visual sensitivity in numerous ways, limiting resolution of spatial and temporal detail as well as sensitivity to contrast, orientation, motion, depth, and color.

Spatial Resolution

A common way to assess spatial resolution is in terms of *minimum separable acuity*, the smallest spacing between pattern elements that can be resolved. When the whole pattern consists of parallel dark and light stripes of constant widths, we can characterize spatial resolution in terms of *spatial frequency*—the number of black and white stripe pairs per degree of visual angle. Such patterns, often referred to as *gratings*, may contain gradual variation from black to white following a sinusoidal pattern (sine wave gratings) or abrupt changes from homogenous dark stripes to light ones (square wave gratings). Grating acuity is characterized by the highest frequency distinguishable from a solid gray pattern having the same luminance as the average of the black and white pattern. It is often convenient to assess an adult's vision by having the subject identify letters of different sizes. Tested this way, acuity is usually described in terms of the Snellen scale, a ratio comparing what the participant sees at 20 feet (or 6 m) to the distance required for similar spatial resolution by a standard observer with good vision. Thus, 20/40 means the observer's resolution at 20 feet is the same resolution as the standard observer would have at 40 feet. In spatial frequency terms, 20/20 vision corresponds to a resolution of stripes of approximately 1 min of arc (~30 cycles/degree (c/deg)). (Holding your thumb approximately 10 inches away from your face, you could resolve approximately 75 black and white bands within the width of your thumbnail at this resolution.)

Newborns have far worse visual acuity than adults, perhaps approximately 1 or 2 c/deg, or 20/400. Acuity improves in almost linear fashion to near adult levels during the first 8 months of life (Norcia & Tyler, 1985). Several different methods have been used to estimate infant visual acuity, and results have varied somewhat with method (for reviews, see Kellman & Arterberry, 1998, 2006).

A Methodological Digression

The topic of visual acuity and its measurement presents a convenient opportunity to introduce methods for measuring infant perception. These basic methods and variants of them have produced the findings we discuss in later chapters. The methods differ in the kinds of infant responses measured by the experimenter. We can distinguish four categories of methods:

- *Stimulus-specific behavior*: A few classes of stimuli produce characteristic behaviors. Some of these behaviors are reflexes, whereas others appear to be functionally appropriate, voluntary actions, such as reaching or crawling. A characteristic response to a stimulus can allow us to infer, at minimum, that the observer detects the stimulus. If the stimulus evokes an adaptive response, we may be able to infer that the stimulus conveys meaningful information about the environment. When a person walking alters her path to avoid a pothole, we infer that she detected the existence and location of the hole. A similar close coupling between certain stimuli and characteristic behaviors allows us to infer what the infant perceives. Unfortunately, this method is limited in scope because of the modest behavioral repertoire of young infants and the protracted development of motor skills. One reflexive action that has been used to study visual acuity is the *optokinetic nystagmus* (OKN) reflex. OKN is elicited when an observer looks at a large, repetitive moving pattern: It consists of a rhythmic sequence of slow tracking eye movements followed by saccadic jumps of fixation back toward the straight-ahead direction.

- *Visual attention responses*: Some of the most successful behavioral methods exploit general exploratory behavior and characteristics of infant visual attention. *Preferential looking* (PL) methods rely on infants' tendency to look at any pattern in preference to a blank field or to one pattern over another. A variant of this method is the *forced-choice preferential looking* (FPL) method, in which infants are presented with two displays and a naive observer judges which one the infant prefers, using any aspect of the infant's behavior. *The habituation and recovery* method relies on infants' tendency to look more at novel stimuli after repeated exposure to a particular stimulus or class of stimuli.
- *Conditioned operant behavior*: Operant methods rely on conditioning and discrimination-learning paradigms. After a response is trained (reinforced) in the presence of a particular stimulus, the experimenter can test for generalization of that response to variations in the stimulus.
- *Physiological measurements*: In these methods, sensory or perceptual response is inferred from measured physiological variables, such as electrical activity in the brain or heart rate. Typically, the measure charts a change from baseline activity, such as a *visually evoked potential* (VEP) or an *event-related potential* (ERP).

Visual Acuity Discrepancies

Estimates for visual acuity vary depending on which method is used for assessment—OKN, PL, or VEP—with VEP providing the highest estimates. This discrepancy in acuity estimates across methods is difficult to interpret. Atkinson (2000) suggests that some of the discrepancy is due to differences in stimuli. For example, acuity estimates are higher if a larger screen is used compared to a smaller screen. However, stimulus differences across studies cannot account for all of the difference. This discrepancy highlights a major issue regarding physiological indices of sensory and perceptual function: What does the measurement mean? For VEPs, there is evidence that the electrical signals come from an early stage of cortical processing. If so, then reliable evoked responses to a display indicate that the signal has made it through the optics of the eye, through the geniculostriate pathway at least to the visual cortex. Regardless of what other questions there may be, reliable VEP results indicate which signals are passed to a certain point in the nervous system.

But what do measured VEPs mean with regard to what the infant sees? If we knew that the VEP is a physiological marker of sensory experience, then we could accept VEP estimates of acuity. Lower sensitivity indicated by behavioral measures would be due to infants' inconsistent attention or their weaker preferences for barely visible stimuli. Suppose instead that we knew that the VEP comes from a neural process before sensory experience emerges; then it would vouch for an intact optical–neural pathway to some point, but it would not estimate visual acuity. Behavioral estimates of acuity would then be preferable for deciding what infants see. Unfortunately, we do not know enough about the VEP to decide.

We have the same problem with behavioral measures, but the directionality is different. With physiological measures, we cannot be sure that a *positive* response indicates that something has been *perceived*. With behavioral measures, we can be comfortable that a positive response indicates perception at some level. On the other hand, a *negative* result in behavior is almost always uninformative. Perception is not the same as action, nor does it always lead to action. An infant may detect a stimulus but fail to show an overt response. In this regard, a good physiological measure may have advantages, in showing that some internal response to a signal did or did not occur at some level of the nervous system.

Peripheral Acuity

Our discussion of visual acuity has characterized acuity presumably involving foveal vision. What about visual acuity in the rest of the visual field? For adults, acuity drops off steeply going from fovea to periphery. For the infant, however, the fovea at birth is less mature than the peripheral areas of the retina. Sireteanu, Kellerer, and Boergen (1984) investigated the development of infants' acuity in the peripheral visual field. Based on measurements of the first eye movement from a central to a peripheral target, they estimated infants' acuity at approximately 10 deg from the fovea. Sireteanu et al. found an increase from 1.6 c/deg to 3.2 c/deg between 2 and 4 months of age but no change from 4 to 11 months. For comparison, adult peripheral acuity is approximately 10 c/deg (Frisen & Glansholm, 1975). When foveal acuity was measured using VEP, incremental changes in peripheral acuity were seen between 10 and 35 weeks of age, and central acuity was always higher than peripheral acuity (Allen, Tyler, & Norcia, 1996). Thus, from birth to adulthood, acuity will become 6–12 times better in the fovea but only 2 or 3 times better in the periphery.

Implications of Spatial Resolution for Perception

Despite variations in methods and their attendant theoretical uncertainties, available acuity estimates provide strong clues about the level of visual detail in the infant's visual world. Newborn acuity is approximately 1 to 2 c/deg or 20/400 Snellen. With grating acuity at the low end of this range, the newborn could resolve a stripe width of 20 min. Missing would be much textural detail of distant surfaces; small text would pose a problem if the infant could read. Acuity would not, however, pose much of a problem for detecting the layout of surfaces in ordinary environments, the shapes of common objects, or fine texture of near objects. At a viewing distance of 20 inches, for example, a texture element 1/8 inch in diameter would be resolvable. The hole in a small letter "o" in ordinary book print should be resolvable from 10 inches away. Interestingly, there is evidence that deletion of high-frequency (fine-detail) information has little effect on adult pattern recognition (Ginsburg, 1978). Similarly, von Hofsten (1983) notes that an infant's acuity, although far inferior to that of an adult human, is approximately the same as that of an adult cat. If cats could read, their acuity might prove something of an impediment, but their perceptual–motor behavior is quite good. There are additional considerations raised by the young infant's contrast sensitivity (discussed next), but grating acuity in and of itself does not pose a major obstacle to early perception, perceptual development, or attempts to study them.

Contrast Sensitivity

Acuity measurements provide information about the visual system's ability to resolve detail under conditions of high contrast. Another basic determinant of visual sensitivity is *contrast*—the range of luminance in a pattern. One standard measure is Michelson contrast, defined as

$$\left(L_{max} - L_{min}\right) / \left(L_{max} + L_{min}\right),$$

where L_{max} and L_{min} designate the maximum and minimum pattern luminances, respectively. This measure ranges from 0 to 1, increasing with the difference between the darkest and lightest areas in a display.

Contrast threshold, the minimum contrast needed to detect a pattern, varies with spatial frequency. An adult contrast sensitivity function (sensitivity = 1/ threshold value) is shown in Figure 2.2A. Several well-known features of this function can be recognized. Sensitivity is highest in a middle range of spatial frequency, with the optimal frequency (detectable with least contrast) at approximately 3 to 4 c/deg. Above 10 c/deg, sensitivity decreases steeply and cuts off at approximately 30 c/deg for adults, corresponding to the limit of visual acuity.

Compared to the contrast sensitivity of adults, that of newborns is not impressive. Figure 2.2B shows data from several laboratories (Atkinson, Braddick, & Moar, 1977a, 1977b; Banks & Salapatek, 1978, 1981; Pirchio et al., 1978). Sensitivity increases during the first 6 months, especially for high spatial frequencies. The low-frequency falloff is not consistent at 1 month but steepens between 2 and 6 months. With age, the range of detectable spatial frequencies, and thus acuity, increases, and peak contrast sensitivity shifts rightward, matching the adult peak at 3 to 4 c/deg by approximately 3 months. These results have been found with both moving and static gratings, although infants appear to be more sensitive to moving as opposed to static gratings of low spatial frequencies (Atkinson et al., 1977a).

Implications of Contrast Sensitivity for Perception

Banks and Dannemiller (1987) note that although infant contrast sensitivity is poor relative to that of adults, it is quite sufficient to detect many of the intensity variations in common objects and spatial layouts. To use their example, under normal illumination, a human face often gives contrasts of 0.7 to 0.8 between skin

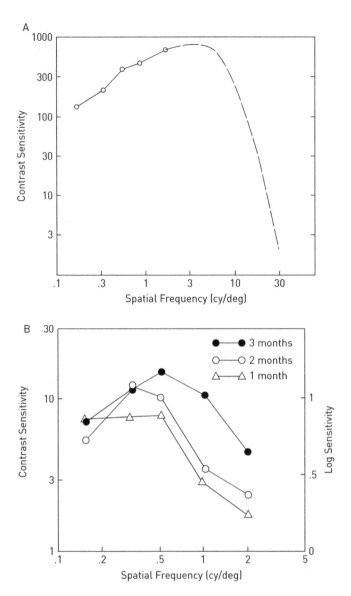

FIGURE 2.2

Contrast sensitivity functions for (A) adults and (B) 1-, 2-, and 3-month-old infants.
Source: Redrawn with permission of Association for Research in Vision and Ophthalmology
from Banks, M. S., & Salapatek, P. (1978). Acuity and contrast sensitivity in 1-, 2-, and 3-month-
old human infants. *Investigative Ophthalmology and Visual Science, 17,* 361–365; permission
conveyed through Copyright Clearance Center, Inc.

and hair. Sensitivity at threshold for a contrast of 0.7 would be 1.428; 1-month-olds
exceed this sensitivity throughout most of the range of spatial frequencies they can
detect. As we concluded regarding acuity, these limitations of early vision would
be expected to affect pickup of fine spatial details. Minute textural variation and
subtle gradations of intensity may not be visible to the young infant. Perception
of ordinary objects and events in well-lit environments is not greatly limited by
contrast sensitivity.

Another point to keep in mind is that poor contrast sensitivity does not imply that above threshold, contrasts are less noticeable for infants than adults. Due to the possible operation of a compensation process, *contrast constancy*, it is likely that apparent contrasts remain in correspondence with actual (physical) contrasts more than would be expected from the infant's contrast sensitivity function (CSF) (Banks & Dannemiller, 1987). The infant's threshold may be higher, but above this threshold, the appearance of different contrasts may be similar for adults and infants.

Mechanisms of Development in Contrast Sensitivity and Acuity

An elegant means of quantifying early visual capacities, tracking changes, and inferring the mechanisms of developmental change is the *ideal observer* analysis (Geisler, 1984, 2011), pioneered in the study of infant vision by Banks and colleagues (Banks & Bennett, 1988; Banks & Dannemiller, 1987; Banks, Geisler, & Bennett, 1987; Banks & Shannon, 1993). In this method, known sources of optical error (spherical aberration, chromatic aberration, diffraction due to the pupil, clarity of the optical media, and errors in image focusing) are quantified. Added to these effects are estimated effects due to immaturities in neonates' photoreceptors and their cumulative effects on vision. The resulting estimates are compared to estimates of infant visual performance obtained from experiments. In general, these analyses suggest that infants' acuity and contrast sensitivity in the first 6 months of life fall well below the levels that should be possible given limitations that are known. Ideal observer estimates predict, based on preneural mechanisms, a 1.3 log unit (20-fold) decrease in contrast sensitivity and a 0.6 log unit (4-fold) decrease in grating acuity. Observed data show larger decrements. Because infants' contrast sensitivity is worse than predicted by the ideal observer model, infants' limited vision is not due solely to optical and photoreceptor immaturities. Skoczenski (2002) suggests that post-receptor mechanisms, specifically intrinsic neural noise from random addition of action potentials in the visual cortex, account for infants' poor performance. Ideal observer analysis of changes in contrast sensitivity in infant macaques confirm this post-receptor hypothesis, suggesting maturation of cortical circuits as the likely reason for protracted development (Kiorpes, Tang, Hawken, & Movshon, 2003).

Orientation Sensitivity

It is now well established that initial cortical processing of visual input involves neural units selective for orientation, retinal position, and spatial frequency. Each of these dimensions of selectivity is crucial for the extraction of information for perception. Orientation in particular would seem to be required for all later processing concerned with recovering object boundaries, form, and texture. Indeed, adults show differential responsiveness in the visual cortex to vertically, horizontally, and concentrically organized patterns (Aspell, Wattam-Bell, Atkinson, &

Braddick, 2010). For infants, orientation sensitivity is weak in the earliest weeks of life (Braddick, 1993; Lee, Birtles, Wattam-Bell, Atkinson, & Braddick, 2012).

Using visual evoked potentials, one might expect to pick up a cortical electrical response to periodic alternations of orientation of a grating stimulus. Starting at 3 to 4 weeks of age, infants show VEP responses to stimuli that reverse in orientation at 3 reversals per second (r/s), whereas slightly older infants, approximately 8 weeks of age, respond to faster reversal rates (8 r/s; Braddick, 1993). These reversal rates are still well below adult responsiveness (Pei, Pettet, & Norcia, 2007). Moreover, infants' latency in orientation-reversal VEP does not reach adult levels until 50 weeks (Lee et al., 2012). These characteristics of orientation responses seem to be paced maturationally; preterm infants of the same gestational age showed responses similar to those of full-term infants, suggesting that duration of visual experience is not relevant (Birtles et al., 2007).

Habituation studies of newborn orientation discrimination were conducted by Slater, Morison, and Somers (1988). After habituation to a high-contrast square-wave grating (a striped pattern) oriented 45 deg from the vertical (Figures 2.3A or 2.3B), 3-day-old infants were presented with a pair of displays containing two patterns, one matching the orientation seen during habituation and one shifted 90 deg (45 deg from the vertical in the opposite direction; Figures 2.3C and 2.3D). To control for possible responding to local stimulus features (e.g., the black area

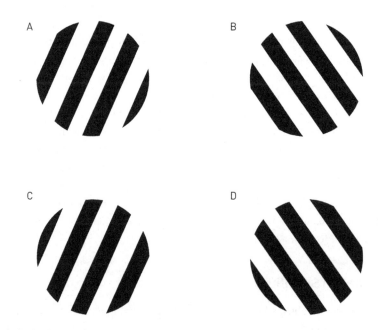

FIGURE 2.3
Stimuli used to test infants' orientation sensitivity. Infants were habituated to one of the four grating patterns shown. After habituation, infants habituated to (A) or (B) were tested with patterns (C) and (D), whereas infants habituated to (C) or (D) were tested with (A) and (B).
Source: Redrawn with permission of SAGE Publications from Slater, A., Morison, V., & Somers, M. (1988). Orientation discrimination and cortical function in the human newborn. *Perception*, *17*, 597–602.

being located at the upper left), the phase (position of black and white stripes) was reversed in the test displays from what it had been during habituation (e.g., compare Figures 2.3A and 2.3C). On the first test trial, infants looked on average 77% of the time at the stimulus in the novel orientation; 15 of the 16 infants looked more at the novel stimulus. In the world of habituation studies, this result is impressive in terms of both the strength of the response (77% novelty preference) and the consistency across infants (94% looked longer at the novel pattern).

The findings from behavioral studies with newborns appear to be at odds with the findings from VEP measures. VEP studies suggest that infants might be "orientation blind" before 3 to 4 weeks of age; however, according to behavioral studies, newborns have some sensitivity to orientation. It is sobering to find infants acting with so little regard for the electrophysiological data. It turns out the solution to this puzzle may be based on methodology and stimulus characteristics. Atkinson et al. (1988) found that when tested with dynamic patterns, as is often the case for VEP studies, newborn infants do not show orientation sensitivity. However, when newborns were tested with static patterns in a habituation paradigm that allow simultaneous comparison of stimuli of different orientation, they did show orientation sensitivity. This discrimination was tenuous because infants showed a preference for the novel stimulus only on the first test trial.

Implications of Orientation Sensitivity for Perception

Very young infants do demonstrate orientation sensitivity from birth with certain types of stimuli. Clearly, some maturational process operates to improve orientation sensitivity from rudimentary beginnings to full function. Likely candidates are maturation of higher cortical mechanisms and myelination of visual areas (Baker, Norcia, & Candy, 2011; Braddick & Atkinson, 2011; Lee et al., 2012).

The behavioral studies directly demonstrating infant orientation sensitivity have important implications. As discussed later, behavioral studies of form perception indicate impressive early, if not innate, abilities that are difficult to explain without assuming sensitivity to contour orientation. A second implication is a lesson that arises often in infant perception research: Negative results are largely uninformative. Failure to observe an ability might indicate that infants lack it, but it might instead indicate their inattention, their lack of preference among discriminable stimuli, domination of their fixation by some other stimulus attribute, and so on.

Temporal Aspects of Vision

Information carried by motion or change is crucial to visual perception of the environment's stable properties, such as the three-dimensional layout, as well as changes or events occurring within it. Early sensitivity to motion and change would be a prerequisite for the infant to tap this reservoir of dynamic information. Conversely, early immaturities or limitations in temporal processing would constrain early perception in important ways.

The basic sensitivities that allow access to the world of changes and events include detection of motion, its direction, and its speed. They also include temporal resolution, or the ability to resolve the onsets and offsets of stimulus changes.

Temporal Resolution

Analogous to the ability to resolve changes in luminance that unfold across a spatial dimension, temporal resolution is an important aspect of a visual system. For a light blinking on and off, there will be some rate of flicker too fast to resolve visually, and a constant light (more or less the average of the light and dark episodes) will be seen. The highest frequency at which the flicker is detectable is called the *critical flicker frequency* (CFF); for adults, the CFF varies with factors such as stimulus contrast but is approximately 60 Hz (cycles per second) under the best conditions.

To study infant CFF, a spatially homogenous display with a given frequency of flicker is paired with another display that presumably appears as unchanging. Choosing the brightness of the unchanging display poses a challenge. Suppose that the flickering display is not detectable as such by the infant's visual system but that the averaging characteristics of the infant's system are unknown. It would be difficult to be confident that the brightness chosen for the unchanging display matched the brightness of the flickering display. In the absence of such a match, a visual preference might be observed based on the difference in perceived brightness. A clever way of avoiding this problem has been employed in CFF studies with infants (Nystrom, Hansson, & Marklund, 1975; Regal, 1981). The "unchanging" comparison stimulus is in reality a flickering display whose frequency is well above the adult's CFF, presumably undetectable as flickering by infants. Whatever the temporal averaging characteristics of the infant's system, the two displays should match in the event that no flicker is detected in either one.

Nystrom et al. (1975) obtained CFF estimates using a visual preference procedure with 6- and 10-week-old infants. Unpatterned flickering stimuli of 1, 5, 10, and 20 Hz were all preferred to the 100-Hz comparison stimulus. Nystrom et al. also tested all possible frequency pairs among their stimuli. In all cases not involving the 100-Hz stimulus, they found preferential fixation of the higher frequency. Regal (1981) studied infants longitudinally as well as cross-sectionally at 1, 2, and 3 months of age. On average, CFFs were estimated at 41 Hz at 1 month of age, 50 Hz at 2 months, and 51 Hz at 3 months. Under similar conditions, adult CFFs averaged 53 Hz. These results indicate that temporal resolution of these high-contrast stimuli is adult-like by 2 months and not drastically different at the earliest age tested (1 month). With lower frequencies, sensitivity in infants is lower than that in adults by approximately one to two orders of magnitude (Teller, Lindsey, Mar, Succop, & Mahal, 1992).

A more comprehensive description of temporal properties of early vision is given by measurement of infant temporal contrast sensitivity functions (tCSFs). As for visual acuity, the temporal resolution is also affected by the contrast of the stimulus. Thus, to fully understand temporal resolution, we need a tCSF that is

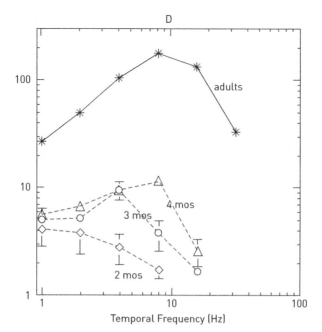

FIGURE 2.4

Contrast sensitivity plotted as a function of temporal frequency for infants and adults.
Source: Redrawn with permission of Elsevier from Rasengane, T. A., Allen, D., & Manny, R. E.
(1997). Development of temporal contrast sensitivity in human infants. *Vision Research, 37,*
1747–1754; permission conveyed through Copyright Clearance Center, Inc.

derived by varying both Hz and contrast. Figure 2.4 shows adult and infant thresholds as a function of contrast (Rasengane, Allen, & Manny, 1997). Most notable is
how different the young infant tCSF is from that of adults. At 4 months, the shape
of the function begins to approximate that of adults, showing maximum sensitivity at midrange frequencies; however, performance is still suppressed. Similar
developmental trends have been found in macaques, with sensitivity to low and
high frequencies developing at different rates (Stavros & Kiorpes, 2008).

Implications of Temporal Aspects of Vision for Perception

Temporal resolution in the human visual system reaches adult levels earlier in life
than spatial resolution and appears to be reasonably good from the beginning of
life. Because processing of temporal change underlies perception of motion and
events, one possible consequence is that visual perception of motion and events
might be comparatively advanced and proficient relative to detection of fine spatial
detail. Indeed, this appears to be the case, as discussed in later chapters.

Motion Detection

Infants detect and attend to motion from birth. Their range of perceptible velocities is smaller than in adults but adequate to process most ordinary events. We

defer much of our discussion of visual sensitivity to motion and its underlying mechanisms until we examine motion and event perception in Chapter 6.

One major sensory limitation deserves mention here, however. A requirement for extracting useful information about objects and events is *directional sensitivity*. Motion direction is likely encoded by mechanisms in the visual cortex. This sensitivity is weak or absent in the first several weeks of life. VEP responses to direction reversals are not found until 6 to 8 weeks of age, with responses to slower (5 deg/sec) velocities emerging earlier than responses to faster (20 deg/sec) velocities (Wattam-Bell, 1992). Similar findings are obtained using behavioral measures, specifically FPL, in which one condition paired a display with a region of dots moving in a consistent direction with another display having random dot motion (Figure 2.5). Whereas 15-week-olds showed robust preferences, 8- to 11-week-olds showed only weak evidence of sensitivity, although they did look more at the coherent motion at the slowest velocities tested (Wattam-Bell, 1992).

Studies using FPL and habituation methods with 1-month-olds found no evidence that infants of this age can discriminate a field containing regions of coherent dots moving in opposite directions from a field containing dots moving in a uniform direction (Wattam-Bell, 1996a, 1996b). One-month-olds do discriminate

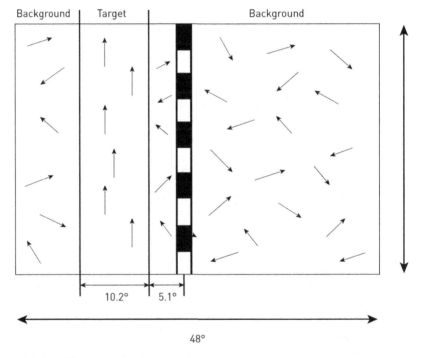

FIGURE 2.5

Display used to study infants' directional sensitivity. The two display panels differed by the presence of a vertical strip of coherently moving dots in the center of the left-hand panel. All other motions were random in direction. The center column of rectangles was used to attract infants' attention to the center of the display and disappeared during each trial. Source: Redrawn with permission of Elsevier from Wattam-Bell, J. (1992). The development of maximum displacement limits for discrimination of motion direction in infancy. *Vision Research, 32,* 621–630; permission conveyed through Copyright Clearance Center, Inc.

motion from nonmotion: They responded differentially to stationary dot fields and a moving field of dots (moving at velocities of 10 deg/sec and greater), and they showed some ability to distinguish coherent from incoherent motion patterns. Wattam-Bell (1996b) argued that the latter two tasks could in principle be done without directionally sensitive mechanisms, and that the results involving the opposite-direction versus uniform-direction fields are a better test for directional sensitivity. This ability appears to be present by 6–8 weeks (Wattam-Bell, 1996b).

This developmental pattern has been replicated. Banton, Dobkins, and Bertenthal (2001) found thresholds for differences in direction of 17 deg in 18-week-olds and 22 deg in 12-week-olds; findings were indeterminate for 6-week-olds. These results are consistent with the possibility that directional sensitivity first emerges at 6–8 weeks of life (Wattam-Bell, 1992, 1996a, 1996b). Before this time, infants may be sensitive to motion or temporal change at least, but they may not extract information about direction.

The possibility that directional sensitivity is absent at birth seems paradoxical given that even newborns will track, using saccadic eye movements, a moving stimulus. In order to tease out this apparent discrepancy, Mason, Braddick, and Wattam-Bell (2003) directly compared infants' directional sensitivity as measured by OKN and FPL. Within the same infant, they identified a lag in directional sensitivity when measured using FPL compared to OKN (Figure 2.6). From 8 to 27 weeks, there was no change in thresholds for OKN, but there was significant improvement for FPL measures. These findings suggest that OKN and early visual tracking may depend on subcortical mechanisms (Atkinson & Braddick, 1981; Mason et al., 2003). It is plausible, then, that the young infant possesses directional sensitivity implicitly in largely reflexive tracking mechanisms but that directionally sensitive mechanisms that contribute to perceptual representations (i.e., those in the cortex) begin to mature 6–8 weeks after birth.

Many of infants' most sophisticated early perceptual achievements that we explore later in this book depend on information carried by motion. It is surprising that directional sensitivity seems so poor at the beginning. We consider further its implications for particular perceptual abilities when we explore object and motion perception in Chapters 5 and 6.

Oculomotor Function

Aslin (1993a) aptly summarized the importance of oculomotor adjustment (accommodation and convergence) in human vision:

The mature human visual system has evolved the capacity to (1) select a small portion of the retinal image for close attention; (2) optimize the quality of the retinal image by adjusting its posterior focal distance to match the plane of the retinal receptors; and (3) direct and maintain the two foveas on the object of attention despite changes in object distance. The ability to adjust the optics and binocular alignment of the eyes to match an object's viewing distance affords great efficiency in gathering detailed information about a real-world scene. (p. 30)

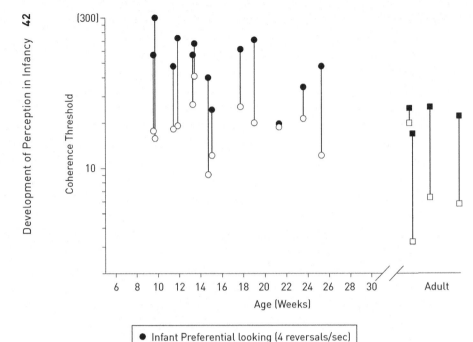

FIGURE 2.6

Directional sensitivity, measured by OKN and FPL, in the same infants and adults. The vertical line connects the values for the same individuals. Source: Reprinted with permission of Elsevier from Mason, A. J. S., Braddick, O. J., & Wattam-Bell, J. (2003). Motion coherence thresholds in infants—Different tasks identify at least two distinct motion systems. *Vision Research*, *43*, 1149–1157; permission conveyed through Copyright Clearance Center, Inc.

Accommodation

Accommodation refers to changes in the shape of the lens as a function of object distance. The purpose of these changes is to focus on the retina what is being viewed in the real world. The earliest study of infant accommodation suggested that newborns' eyes had a fixed focus of approximately 19 cm but that accommodation improved through the first 3 or 4 months to nearly adult levels (Haynes, White, & Held, 1965). A limitation of this study was the use of a fixed-size target. Given newborns' relatively poor visual acuity, the decreasing image size at farther distances may have been inadequate to drive an accommodative response (Banks, 1980). Further research equating target visual angle at different distances and using a variety of ingenious methods has revealed that despite larger errors than adults, even newborns are capable of reasonably accurate accommodation and adjustments in the appropriate direction for targets within a range of approximately 75 cm or less (for a review, see Aslin, 1993a). Other estimates indicate reasonably accurate responding up to 150 cm (Howland, Dobson, & Sayles, 1987).

Convergence

Convergence is the coordination of the two eyes to allow focusing on near or far objects. The eyes need to turn toward each other increasingly more as objects get closer. Early studies of convergence found that even in newborns, convergent eye movements in target-appropriate directions were present. The accuracy of convergence was reported to be variable but improving within the first few months of life. Newborns studied by Slater and Findlay (1975) showed convergence in the appropriate direction with target distances between 12.5 and 50 cm. Accuracy was good between 25 and 50 cm but not at 12.5 cm. Aslin (1977) investigated 1-, 2-, and 3-month-olds' ability to converge and diverge to a target moving in depth. He found that infants at all ages generally exhibited divergence when the target moved away and convergence when the target approached, but with age, the frequency of making a convergent or divergent movement in the appropriate direction increased. The youngest infants showed least accurate convergence for targets at the nearest viewing distance (12 cm). In a study with targets between 25 and 200 cm, infants even at the youngest age tested (26–45 days) showed appropriate slopes relating convergence to target position (Hainline et al., 1992). Convergence has been estimated to be good at 6 to 7 weeks and adult-like by 8 to 9 weeks of age (Horwood & Riddell, 2013).

Implications of Oculomotor Function for Perception

Within the first few months, infants can accurately accommodate and converge their eyes with varying target distances. These functions are somewhat more error-prone than for adults, and variations occur with drowsiness and attentional fluctuations (Atkinson, 1984; Banks, 1980). For convergence, accuracy is initially poor at very near distances (<15 cm) but surprisingly adult-like beyond. Basic oculomotor adjustments begin early in infancy to guide and enhance the pickup of visual information. Their role may extend even further. The muscular adjustments that accomplish accommodation and convergence provide distance information for adults and may possibly do so for infants. We consider this possibility when we examine space perception in Chapter 3.

Binocular Depth Perception

Binocular disparity arises due to the separation of the two eyes, resulting in differences, or disparities, in the two retinal images. This disparity can be used as a cue to depth. Sensitivity to binocular disparity, or *stereopsis*, seems to be absent in the first several months of life. It emerges at approximately 16 weeks on average, with stereoscopic acuity rapidly approaching adult-like levels (Brown, Lindsey, Satgunam, & Miracle, 2007; Held, Birch, & Gwiazda, 1980). A precursor to stereopsis, at approximately 8 weeks, is binocular rivalry, suggesting that the necessary cortical foundation is developing at this time (Kavšek, 2013). Critical to the development of stereopsis is experience with overlapping images from the two eyes; this experience fundamentally alters neural connections in the visual cortex. If the eyes are not properly aligned or vision is poor in one eye, perhaps due to a congenital cataract, stereopsis does not develop (Hussin, 2009). As with visual acuity, contrast also impacts stereopsis; adults show infant-like levels under low-contrast conditions (Brown et al., 2007). We consider the details of the development of binocular depth perception in Chapter 3.

Color Vision

Color is one of the most captivating aspects of visual experience. More than any other basic visual attribute, color seems to be involved with emotional and aesthetic responses. Surprisingly, the functional importance of color vision remains unclear. Consider watching a movie in black and white. The perception of people, objects, spatial layouts, and events works well despite the absence of chromatic information. So what does color add? It is likely that adding chromatic variation to a scene (or evolving color vision mechanisms to take the species' rather than the filmmaker's perspective) improves detection of differences, aiding perception of object boundaries and surface texture. Adjacent surfaces that may not differ in their effects on a single visual mechanism may present differences to a system based on three visual mechanisms of differing sensitivities across the wavelength dimension.

Whereas they may enhance detection of differences, biological color vision systems are not good detectors of specific wavelengths. (Any color experience may be the result of various combinations of wavelengths of light.) Moreover, the light from a surface that reaches the eye depends both on the surface absorptive and reflective characteristics and on the wavelength composition of the light source. Thus, the spectral composition of light reflected from a particular patch of a surface does not by itself specify any property of the surface or the illuminant. Comparisons across regions in natural scenes may allow detecting a surface's characteristics apart from illumination changes, due to *color constancy* mechanisms. Whether color is most important for enhancing differences in the visual input or for revealing particular surface properties through constancy mechanisms remains an interesting topic of discussion.

Inquiries into infant (and other species) color sensitivity began more than 100 years ago (for review, see Bornstein, 2006), but research before 1975 did not provide much in the way of a definitive statement regarding color vision's origins. The study of infants' color vision is difficult because researchers must distinguish infants' responses to colored stimuli from responses to other aspects of such stimuli, such as lightness.

To understand how researchers have solved such problems requires some background. Perceived qualities of color are responses to the physical dimension of *wavelength* or frequency of light. Wavelength refers to the distance between successive crests in waves of light. Because light waves move at a constant velocity, this distance between successive wave crests is inversely related to the frequency of waves passing a given point in a unit of time. Electromagnetic radiation spans a vast spectrum of frequencies, most of which do not give rise to any visual sensations. Specifically, the visual part ranges from wavelengths of approximately 400 to 700 nm.

Wavelength and Color Sensations

The relation between wavelengths and color sensations is rather complex. Single wavelengths of light cause particular color experiences; for example, a wavelength of 484 nm will appear as blue, and one of 680 nm will appear to be a slightly yellowish red. The converse relation is much more complicated and often misunderstood. When we experience a particular color, it does not imply anything about the presence of particular wavelengths of light. Many different combinations of wavelengths can give rise to *metamers*—indistinguishable color sensations. In other words, as visual perceivers, humans are not very good wavelength detectors.

These facts about color vision derive from the underlying mechanisms. *Cones*, the photoreceptors responsible for color vision, come in three types. They differ in terms of their *photopigments*, which are light-sensitive substances that absorb light. Each photopigment absorbs light across a range of wavelengths, described by its *absorption spectrum*, the probability of absorbing quanta of light at different wavelengths. Neural impulses produced when cones absorb light provide the signals on which color sensations are based. When a photoreceptor produces a neural signal, that signal carries no information about what wavelength caused it. Thus, a cone receptor and its neural consequences do not encode wavelength. The color sensations experienced by an observer depend solely on the patterns of activity across the three cone types. The three types of cone receptors—S, M, and L cones— can be distinguished in terms of whether their peak absorption probability falls in the short-, middle-, or long-wavelength part of the visible spectrum. Whereas it can be said that the best stimulus (most probable absorption) for a cone type lies at a particular wavelength, any combinations of light that produce equivalent effects on the three mechanisms will be indistinguishable.

Isolating Color Sensitivity

The study of color vision is complicated by the fact that stimuli vary along several dimensions. In addition to chromatic *color* or *hue*, there is *brightness* (related to light intensity) and *saturation* (roughly, how much the purity of a color is reduced by mixing with broadband light; pink is a desaturated red). Isolating responses based on these separate sensory qualities with infants is difficult. Infants might discriminate two stimuli differing in hue, for example, on the basis of some attribute other than hue, such as a brightness difference. Teller and Bornstein (1987) provide an analogy: In a black-and-white photograph, one can still tell the difference between a red ball and a white ball based on the different shades of gray. Thus, to show color perception, we need to rule out responsiveness based on differences in brightness, or shades of gray.

Matching displays in brightness for a particular adult does not guarantee that the displays will be matched in brightness for an infant. Several procedures have been devised to separate infants' responses to hue from responses to brightness. One is to estimate the infant's *spectral sensitivity function*, the relative sensitivity across the wavelength continuum. Then, differently colored lights can be matched for brightness, theoretically leaving only a hue difference as a basis for discriminating between them. Unfortunately, it is difficult to be precise about the infant's spectral sensitivity function, and it may vary across individuals as well. Nevertheless, matching chromatic stimuli for approximate brightness is usually a starting point for infant color vision research. From this starting point, brightness of the stimuli can be varied while holding only a hue contrast constant so that discrimination across the array of stimuli can be based only on hue—that is, there is no consistent brightness difference that could govern responses. In the study by Peeples and Teller (1975), stimulus luminance was varied above and below the matching brightness level. Eight-week-olds discriminated a red from a white stimulus at all luminances. Because small steps of luminance variation were used, we can infer that the red and white stimuli had matching luminance for at least one stimulus pair.

Early Color Sensitivity

What do these kinds of studies indicate about when infants first perceive color? By 2 to 4 months of age, infants' color vision is similar to that of adults (for review, see Kellman & Arterberry, 2006). Results with 8-week-olds suggest that most color vision mechanisms function by this age, although some deficiency in the short-wavelength cone receptors (S cones) has been suggested (Adams & Courage, 2002; Teller, Peeples, & Sekel, 1978). Before 8 weeks, however, infants do not pass many tests of color vision at which 8-week-olds succeed, and it is generally accepted that newborns are functionally color deficient. A great deal of recent work has addressed the nature of the younger infant's limitations in sensing color, and the evidence supports deficiencies in all three cone types (Adams & Courage, 2002; Suttle, Banks, & Graf, 2002).

"My Baby Likes Red"

Researchers of infant perception often hear parents assert that their child prefers red over other colors, and some of the earliest studies of infant vision have shown color preferences (e.g., Spears, 1964). If such early color preferences exist, they may provide insight into basic issues about human color sensitivity. Although the physical dimension of wavelength has no abrupt categorical boundaries, our perceived color qualities do. Moving up the wavelength scale from 400 nm, monochromatic (single wavelength) lights all have a bluish, and initially a reddish, component. The reddish aspect disappears by approximately 478 nm. As wavelength increases further, a greenish component enters, making the lights blue-green and then green-blue until 505 nm. At that point, the blue is gone, and the hue is uniquely green.

These observations relate to qualitative experiences of color. The studies we have considered so far tested discriminability of colors. Other research has attempted to address the categorical nature of color experience in infancy. Do infants share the color categories of adults, or are these categories fashioned in part by learning or perhaps culture? Bornstein, Kessen, and Weiskopf (1976) tested infant categorization of color using a habituation paradigm. Four-month-old infants were habituated to displays of one wavelength. Following habituation, infants were presented with three test displays. One display had the same wavelength as the habituation display (e.g., a blue of 480 nm). The two other test displays varied from the habituation display by the same wavelength difference (e.g., 450 and 510 nm). In this example, 450 nm is also perceived as bluish by adults, but 510 nm is perceived as green. Bornstein et al. found that looking time increased to the displays that crossed a categorical boundary more than to displays of a different wavelength that were within the same color category. This result was replicated by Franklin and Davies (2004), who also found adult-like categorical perception of blue-purple and pink-red. Moreover, infants show different ERP responses to within and across color category boundaries, as do adults, and older infants show latency differences in eye movements depending on whether color stimuli are within or between color categories (Clifford, Franklin, Davies, & Holmes, 2009; Clifford et al., 2012; Ozturk, Shayan, Liszkowski, & Majid, 2013). Later in this book, we present other examples of categorical perception, suggesting that this is a fundamental ability not limited to color.

Do infants prefer some colors over others? An attempt to compare infant and adult color preferences was conducted by Bornstein (1975). He asked adults to rate the pleasantness of wavelength patterns that are typically described as one hue (e.g., unique blue; called a prototype) or a combination of hues (e.g., blue-green; called a mixture). Bornstein's adult participants generally rated unique hues as more pleasant than combination hues (e.g., compare R-B to B and R in Figure 2.7A). He then presented 4- and 5-month-olds with paired stimuli, where one member of the pair was a unique hue and the other a combined hue. With some exceptions, infants fixated unique hue stimuli longer than combination stimuli (Figure 2.7B), and their preferences, based on looking time, matched the adult ratings (compare the open circles to the closed circles in Figure 2.7A; see also Teller, Civan, & Bronson-Castain, 2004; Zemach, Chang, & Teller, 2007).

It is apparent that among unique hues infants have preferences for some colors over others, although there is some disagreement regarding which hues infants prefer most. For example, Bornstein (1975) found strongest preference for red and blue compared to yellow and green (see ordering of prototypes in Figure 2.7B), whereas Taylor, Schloss, Palmer, and Franklin (2013) found a stronger preference for red and yellow compared to green and blue depending on lightness, and Franklin, Bevis, Ling, and Hurlbert (2010) found strongest preference for red and least for green. These findings are consistent with categorical perception of color stimuli and indicate some special status of unique hues. Parents may be correct when asserting their baby likes red, but their baby may also like blue as opposed to violet, yellow as opposed to orange, and green as opposed to blue-green.

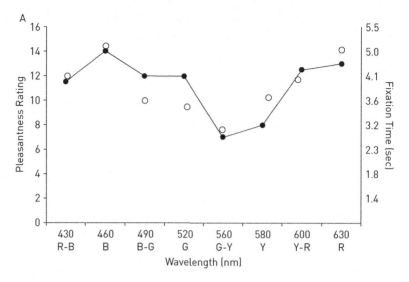

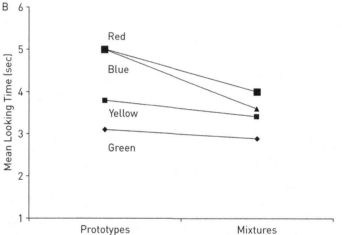

FIGURE 2.7

(A) Relation between infants' fixation times and adults' pleasantness ratings for different hues. Wavelength is given on the c axis in nanometers, with letters indicating the appearance of single wavelength stimuli (R, red; B, blue; G, green; and Y, yellow). Open circles plot infant fixation times; closed circles plot adult pleasantness ratings. (B) Infants' fixation to prototype (unique) versus mixture (combined) hues. Source: Redrawn with permission of Elsevier from Bornstein, M. (1975). Qualities of color vision in infancy. *Journal of Experimental Child Psychology, 19,* 401–419; permission conveyed through Copyright Clearance Center, Inc.

Color Constancy

Our discussion of color has so far focused on infant responses to chromatic varia- tion. An issue of higher order is that of color constancy, the tendency for an object's perceived color to remain the same across variations in illumination. As noted pre- viously, the spectral composition of light at the retina is determined jointly by the wavelength composition of the illuminant and by reflective characteristics of a sur- face. The experience of an object appearing the same color when viewed outdoors in sunlight and then viewed indoors under incandescent light may seem mundane.

From the perspective of perceptual science, it represents quite a puzzle (Brainard, Wandell, & Chichilnisky, 1993). The problem is that the wavelength composition of sunlight and that of incandescent light are very different; as a result, the wavelengths entering the eye from a given surface change greatly depending on the illuminant.

To our knowledge, Dannemiller and colleagues (Dannemiller, 1989; Dannemiller & Hanko, 1987) carried out the first studies of infant color constancy. Using cathode ray tube displays, they simulated changes in both the reflectance properties of surfaces and the spectral composition of the illuminant. Twenty-week-old infants who were habituated to objects viewed with one illuminant generalized habituation to the same objects with a changed illuminant. In contrast, 9-week-olds did not show this behavior; they dishabituated to the change in illuminant, suggesting a failure of color constancy at this younger age. Yang, Kanazawa, Yamaguchi, and Kuriki (2013) similarly found evidence of color constancy in 4½-month-old infants, using a FPL task in which they were able to test each infant under controlled luminance conditions. The reasons for the developmental change in color constancy remain to be investigated.

Implications of Color Vision for Perception

By 2 months of age, the visual world of the infant starts to appear in color, and it closely approximates that of adults by 4 months. Moreover, young infants and adults appear to share color preferences for central colors and perceive the visual spectrum categorically. Using color to identify an object despite variations in illumination, namely color constancy, is an ability that appears somewhat later, at approximately 4½ to 5 months. Presumably, the encoding of color serves young perceivers in the ways that have been hypothesized for adults—aiding in segmenting the world into objects and highlighting textural features of surfaces, allowing them to be recognized or discriminated. As discussed later, however, there is still development in the use of color for some object identity tasks (Bremner, Slater, Mason, Spring, & Johnson, 2013; Woods & Wilcox, 2010). Perhaps infants' early sensitivity to color also allows them the rich aesthetic and emotional responses to color that, although somewhat mysterious, contribute uniquely to human visual experience.

THE AUDITORY SYSTEM

Newborns can hear. Even before birth, by approximately the seventh prenatal month, development of peripheral mechanisms for hearing is nearly complete (Bredberg, 1968). As we consider in Chapter 7, researchers have known for several decades that newborns often look in the direction of a sound (Wertheimer, 1961). But how well do infants hear? How do the limits of the infant's auditory world compare to those of the adult? In this section, we take up these questions and introduce three additional methods—auditory brainstem response, observer-based psychoacoustic procedure, and the operant head-turn procedure.

Absolute Thresholds

The human infant's sensitivity to sound falls short of adult levels. Absolute thresholds—the minimum physical energy detectable—are as much as 50–60 decibels (dB) higher than adult norms (Eisele, Berry, & Shriner, 1975). Because the decibel scale is logarithmic (i.e., its units are equal ratio steps), this represents a major difference in the sound pressure level needed to trigger a sensory response. A 60-dB difference corresponds to a 1,000-fold change in sound pressure. This difference means that an adult can detect a whisper, whereas a newborn can detect just an average speaking voice.

Sensitivity varies by frequency. Figure 2.8 shows audibility curves across frequency for infants 3, 6, and 12 months old and adults reported by Werner and Bargones (1992). The curves, indicating relative sensitivity across frequency to pure tones (single frequencies), are similar in shape. These results were obtained using the *observer-based psychoacoustic procedure* (OPP), a variant of the forced-choice preferential looking procedure used in vision research (Olsho, Koch, Halpin, & Carter, 1987). As with FPL used with visual tasks, in the OPP an observer may use any aspect of the infant's behavior to determine whether an infant is being presented with a sound. Following a judgment, the observer receives feedback regarding his or her accuracy.

Approximately half of the difference between infant and adult auditory sensitivity is made up in the first 6 months, with improvement continuing into middle childhood (Elliott & Katz, 1980). Some insight into the mechanisms underlying

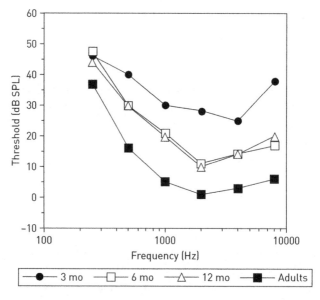

FIGURE 2.8

Average absolute thresholds for pure-tone stimuli for adults and 3-, 6-, and 12-month-old infants. Source: Redrawn with permission from Werner, L. A., & Bargones, J. Y. (1992). Psychoacoustic development of human infants. In C. Rovee-Collier & L. Lipsitt (Eds.), *Advances in infancy research* (Vol. 7). Norwood, NJ: Ablex; permission conveyed through Copyright Clearance Center, Inc.

these behavioral findings comes from studies measuring absolute thresholds using the *auditory brainstem response* (ABR). The ABR consists of low-amplitude electrical potentials generated by the activation of the auditory nerve and structures in the auditory brainstem, a subcortical part of the auditory pathway. These potentials occur within 10 msec following the onset of an auditory stimulus (Moore, 1982). The measure requires no overt behavioral response. Using ABR, Kaga and Tanaka (1980) found click-evoked thresholds in newborns within 15–20 dB of adult thresholds. The pattern of responses and the rate at which the growing child reached adult threshold levels were different from those found with behavioral measures. At low frequencies (500 Hz), adult response levels were reached by 1 month of age. This finding suggests that the rather slow progression of low-frequency sensitivity toward adult levels found in behavioral studies reflects changes occurring beyond the brainstem in the auditory system, probably cortical processing. Medium- to high-frequency sensitivity (4,000 Hz) reached adult levels between 3 and 7 months in the ABR studies. Most interesting, very high-frequency stimuli (8,000–12,000 Hz) produced thresholds at adult levels before 3 months, and thresholds at 16,000 Hz were on average 10 dB better than those of adults at both 1 and 3 months of age (Klein, 1984; for review, see Saffran, Werker, & Werner, 2006).

Superior infant ABR responses to very high frequencies may be related to hearing loss for high frequencies that occurs from childhood to adulthood. Whereas the child may hear sounds up to 20,000 Hz, adult limits are lower, cutting off at approximately 15,000 Hz (Moore, 1982). It is nevertheless unclear what to make of the discrepancies between behavioral and electrophysiological measures. Werner and Bargones (1992) sought to directly compare thresholds using ABR and OPP measurements. Participants were presented with 1,000-, 4,000-, and 8,000-Hz tone pips lasting 5 msec. Infant and adult ABR thresholds were approximately the same at each frequency. Behaviorally, adult thresholds were on average 15–20 dB lower than their ABR thresholds, but infant behavioral thresholds were 15–30 dB higher than their ABR thresholds. Werner and Bargones suggest that this discrepancy may be due to the maturation of neural structures in the primary auditory pathway beyond the brainstem (auditory cortex) or to nonsensory factors (e.g., attention or motivation). Further work by Bargones and Werner (1994) provided evidence in favor of the attentional hypothesis: Adults may be much better than infants at selectively attending to a single frequency. This finding dictates caution in making the claim that infants hear less well than adults, but the magnitude of the sensitivity difference and its persistence until later in childhood suggest that development leads to improvement in both attention and auditory sensitivity.

Differential Sensitivity and Frequency Resolution

Sounds of a single frequency are rarely presented in contexts outside of auditory threshold experiments. Instead, sounds follow one another, consist of multiple frequencies, and differ in intensity or loudness. Adults discriminate intensity changes between sounds as small as 1 or 2 dB, whereas infant sensitivity is weaker, ranging between 3 and 12 dB at 7–9 months (Sinnott & Aslin, 1985). Adults also detect smaller frequency differences than infants, but not by much. With frequency signals between 1,000 and 3,000 Hz, Olsho and colleagues (Olsho, Schoon, Sakai, Turpin, & Sperduto, 1982a, 1982b) found that 5- to 8-month-olds discriminated approximately a 2% change; adults discriminated a 1% change. Infants discriminated higher-frequency tones (4,000–8,000 Hz) as well as adults.

Most environmental sounds contain combinations of frequencies. Frequency resolution is the observer's ability to perceive the individual components in a complex sound. An excellent paradigm for studying frequency resolution is *masking*; a threshold for one stimulus is obtained in the presence of a competing stimulus or masker. Studies using masking suggest that infants' frequency resolution thresholds are 10–15 dB higher than those of adults, but they are qualitatively similar. When the background noise level increases by 10 dB, both infant and adult thresholds increase approximately 10 dB (Bull, Schneider, & Trehub, 1981).

Early audition researchers noticed that humans perceive the parts of a complex sound more easily if the components have dissimilar frequencies (Moore, 1982). This phenomenon has been conceptualized in terms of the *critical band* notion. A certain range of frequencies close to a target frequency will exert a masking effect, making detection of the target frequency more difficult. Frequencies outside of this critical band will exert a much reduced or negligible masking effect. Schneider, Morrongiello, and Trehub (1990) determined the critical band for 6-month-olds, 2-year-olds, 5-year-olds, and adults. They found that masked thresholds for all ages increased with bandwidth up to a critical width. Further increases in bandwidth did not result in increases in threshold. They also found that the size of the critical band did not change substantially with age. Thus, infants as young as 6 months have a critical band that is similar to that of adults, and changes in auditory filter width cannot explain differences found between adult and infant auditory thresholds.

Temporal Resolution

As we listen to music or speech, we process exquisitely subtle and complex information about duration and rhythm in auditory signals. Prerequisite to extracting such information is the capacity to assign boundaries in time to particular sounds and intervals between them. Such temporal resolution abilities are heavily involved in speech perception, auditory localization, rhythm perception, and the detection of signals in noise.

A task typically used to determine temporal resolution is gap detection. What is the smallest space between stimuli that can be detected? Adults have very good gap detection abilities, noticing gaps as small as 2–5 msec (Werner, Folsom, Mancl, & Syapin, 2001; Werner, Marean, Halpin, Spetner, & Gillenwater, 1992). Three- to 6-month-old infants show similarly precise gap detection as adults when tested using electrophysiological measures (ABR and cortical electroencephalography, EEG) with stimuli within the same frequency ("same channel"; Trainor, Samuel, Desjardins, & Sonnadara, 2001; Werner et al., 2001). Gap detection across frequencies ("between channel"), which is more analogous to the context of speech perception, is much more difficult for infants than for adults. Adult between-channel thresholds remain low, approximately 5 msec, whereas 6-month-old infants' thresholds are elevated by a factor of 10–50 msec (Smith, Trainor, & Shore, 2006; Werner et al, 1992). This difference cannot be attributed to different methods. When tested for within-channel gaps using behavioral methods, infants detected gaps as small as 11 msec (Trehub, Schneider, & Henderson, 1995).

Few studies have addressed the development of temporal resolution. One study was carried out by Morrongiello and Trehub (1987), who compared 6-month-old infants' temporal resolution to that of 5½-year-old children and adults. Adults discriminated changes as small as 10 msec, 5½-year-olds discriminated changes of 15 msec, and infants discriminated changes of 20 msec. Performance was not affected by whether duration of the noise (burst) or the silence was varied. Thus, infants' temporal resolution is not as precise as that of adults, but it is not too bad either.

Implications of the Auditory System for Perception

The infant's auditory capabilities begin before birth but do not reach adult levels for some months afterward. Absolute sensitivity, analogous to visual acuity, is much worse than that of the adult, but the ability to discriminate among frequencies is good. Temporal resolution abilities also lag those of older children and adults. It is not clear whether these immaturities limit the young infant's ability to acquire information or guide behavior. Adults' absolute sensitivity may be greater than needed for the learning tasks faced by the infant. For an adult, detecting the sounds of events out of sight, far away, or of very low intensity may have adaptive value, but these may be irrelevant or worse for a young infant. Remote sounds that cannot be matched to visible events may actually be a distraction or impediment to some early learning. Evaluating such a conjecture would require a more detailed analysis of the developmental tasks of early infancy as well as an ecological survey of sound sources in the infant's environment. What we can say with greater confidence is that the infant comes into the world already an able auditory perceiver but becomes an even better one later.

THE SOMATOSENSORY SYSTEM

A variety of senses whose receptors lie in the skin comprise the somatosensory system. This system makes possible sensitivity to touch, pain, temperature, and more. Judging from infants' responses to hot liquids, a pin prick, or a soft stroke on the cheek, one might suspect that newborns' somatosensory system is well-developed, and indeed it is.

The somatosensory system begins to develop during the sixth prenatal week with the appearance of synapses between sensory fibers and receptive neurons in the spinal cord (Okado, 1981). Development of the system approaches completion between the 20th and the 24th week of gestation, although full myelination is not completed until much later in childhood (Kostovic & Goldman-Rakic, 1983).

Touch

The relative maturity at birth of this system is easily seen in behavior. Infants typically respond to noninvasive touch with increased movement and increased heart rate. Touch contributes to the regulation of infant state, reduction of stress responses, and can play a role in eliciting and maintaining attention (Feldman, Singer, & Zagoory, 2010; Jean & Stack, 2012). Infants are also sensitive to the location of touch. Alert neonates will turn their heads reliably toward a tactile stimulus applied to the mouth on 93% of trials, toward an air puff on the cheek on 75% of trials, and toward a stroke on the forearm on 65% of trials (Kisilevsky, Stach, & Muir, 1991). Moreover, infants show an integrated constellation of behaviors to a tactile stimulus. When stroked on the forearm, infants first move the stroked limb, then the head, and then the eyes to the side of stimulation (Dodwell, 1983). In addition to indicating the locus of tactile stimulation on the body, the somatosensory system provides information about objects in the world. As discussed in Chapters 8 and 9, infants can determine properties of objects, such as surface characteristics and substance, from oral or manual contact within the first month of life and from active manual manipulation later in the first year when more sophisticated motor skills emerge.

Pain

Another important aspect of somatosensory sensitivity is pain. Do infants, as do adults, experience radically different sensory and emotional qualities from a stroke on the arm and a pin prick? The question of whether young infants experience pain has been of considerable interest from both theoretical and practical perspectives. Some medical procedures have been performed on infants without anesthesia based on the belief that infants are incapable of feeling pain. Given that infants' somatosensory system is well-developed neurologically and that infants display clear emotional behavior to pain stimuli, it might be more reasonable to use anesthesia. Indeed, this has now become common practice even though its use continues to be debated (Gunter, 2002; Lago et al., 2009).

Making a scientific case that an infant feels pain is nevertheless difficult. The difficulty points to one of the deepest issues in studying sensation and perception. The qualities of our sensations or the contents of our knowledge are known to each individual internally. In scientific research, we never measure these directly. We can measure only behavior of some kind. We interpret the participant's behavior as indicating the presence of a particular sensation or percept when it gives us a simpler explanation of the observed behavior than we would have otherwise (Hochberg, 1968). The problem is worse in studying infants because they have a limited range of behaviors and in particular cannot give verbal reports. (Interestingly, the Latin root of the word infant—*infans*—means "one unable to speak.") Thus, we have less to go on in making the inference of sensory awareness or perceptual knowledge. As we have already briefly discussed, for many perceptual and sensory variables, experimenters can arrange circumstances that reveal perceptual knowledge. If an infant reliably looks more at one of two stimuli differing only on one dimension, the experimenter can infer that the infant is sensitive to the difference along that dimension. Pain presents one of the most difficult cases for this kind of inference because a pain stimulus is normally accompanied by some other sensory event (i.e., touch). A response indicating detection of the stimulus may not necessarily reveal that pain as opposed to mere touch was registered. Some of these complications exist in pain research with adults as well (Stevens & Johnston, 1993).

Regardless of the difficulty in interpreting pain research, investigators have attempted to identify behavioral and physiological responses to invasive stimuli (Anand & McGrath, 1993). Most newborns experience a number of procedures soon after birth, some of which are invasive (e.g., an injection of vitamin K into the abdomen, heel stick for blood sampling, and circumcision), and these provide opportunities to study pain perception in very young infants. Compared to noninvasive procedures, such as the application of a disinfectant to the umbilical stem, full-term infants react to invasive stimuli with a common facial expression similar to a pain expression seen in adults. This expression includes tightly shut eyes, nasolabial furrow, open lips, and a cupped, taut tongue (Grunau, Johnston, & Craig, 1990). Accompanying this grimace is a rapid-onset, high-pitched cry. Preterm infants also show similar responses to invasive procedures, depending on gestational age. Intensity of the characteristic facial "pain expression" increases with gestational age; infants between 25 and 27 weeks of gestation do not show different facial expressions between invasive and noninvasive procedures (Craig, Whitfield, Grunau, Linton, & Hadjistavropoulos, 1993). All of these observations are consistent with the idea that young infants, sometime after 27 weeks of gestation, experience pain.

Implications of the Somatosensory System for Perception

The somatosensory system is functional at birth even though the system may not reach maturity until 3–8 years of age. Young infants can locate the source of touch and obtain information about objects from oral and manual exploration. Sensitivity to pain is found in newborns and even preterm infants.

GUSTATION AND OLFACTION

Gustation (taste) and olfaction (smell) function almost inseparably. As a case in point, the distinctive flavors of an apple or an onion derive from a combination of taste and smell information. Most people know, however, that strictly speaking taste is defined as the activity of certain chemoreceptors ("taste buds") located on the tongue, sensitive to only four basic sensations: sweet, sour, salty, and bitter. Even so, it comes as a surprise to most that tested with eyes shut and nose pinched closed, a person given a piece of raw onion will judge it to be a piece of an apple.

Four Taste Sensations

Research on the development of taste has centered around the four taste sensations. The adult form of the taste bud is present in the fetus at 13 weeks of gestation. To study taste perception, researchers typically monitor the infant's facial expressions following the placement of a substance in the infant's mouth or monitor the amount of intake of substances with different tastes. Obviously, inferring particular sensations from facial reactions or other responses is subject to the same difficulties discussed in relation to pain. Some understanding of infant taste can be gleaned, however, from differences in response to different stimuli. Studies with newborns suggest that at birth infants can discriminate at least three of the four basic taste sensations—sweet, sour, and bitter (for review, see Oster, 2005). Infants' sensing of (or preference for) saltiness develops within the first few months of life. When a large amount of salt is placed in the mouth, newborns show no particular facial expression (Rosenstein & Oster, 1988), but they ingest more plain water than a salty solution (Beauchamp, Cowart, Mennella, & Marsh, 1994). By 4 months, infants prefer salty concentrations over water. A similar change is found for bitter tastes. Newborn infants do not reject solutions laced with urea (although they do show a negative facial expression), whereas infants between 14 and 180 days of age do so (Kajiura, Cowart, & Beauchamp, 1992).

Olfactory Sensations

In contrast to taste, there are no primary olfactory sensations. Typically, to study smell, a cotton swab saturated with an olfactory stimulus is placed under an infant's nose, and a response, such as respiration changes, heart rate, leg withdrawal, or general activity, is measured. Studies of this sort indicate that newborns have a functional sense of smell. They show changes in respiration to anise acid (licorice), asafetida (garlic), acetic acid (vinegar), and phenylethyl alcohol (Engen & Lipsitt, 1965). Also, olfaction thresholds decline across the first few days of life, most pronouncedly so between the first and second day (Lipsitt, Engen, & Kaye, 1963).

The discrimination and location of odors have been tested in the context of infants' ability to recognize their mother's breast pads. Macfarlane (1975) found that infants at 5 days of age will turn their head toward a used breast pad from their mother when it is paired with a clean one. By 6 days of age, infants show evidence of discriminating their mother's smell from that of another woman by preferentially turning toward their mother's used pad. Formula-fed infants also show the ability to discriminate their mother's odor from a neutral odor (Porter, Makin, Davis, & Christensen, 1991). The chemical composition of breast fluids is similar to the chemical composition of amniotic fluid, and infants may be preattuned to respond selectively to their mother's unique olfactory cues (Porter & Winberg, 1999). However, learning may also be a part of the process. In naturally occurring circumstances (namely, breast-feeding), the odor is that of their mother, of course, but young infants can learn to prefer other odors during feeding as well (Allam, Marlier, & Schaal, 2006).

Infants' senses of taste and smell are fairly functional at birth. These senses work together to provide infants with information about what substances they may or may not want to ingest. Moreover, smell may help infants recognize familiar objects and people in their environment.

MOTOR DEVELOPMENT

A main theme of this book is that much perceptual knowledge precedes action in early infant development. Compared to the development of perceptual systems, development of motor skills is slow. This observation reverses the traditional formula that perceptual knowledge originates from sensorimotor activity (e.g., Piaget, 1954). Of course, perception and action do have important interactions, as discussed in Chapter 9, but initial perceptual competence appears well before the infant can crawl or walk, reach, or grasp in a coordinated manner. For example, many young infants' visual capabilities are close to adult levels by 6 months of age, whereas self-locomotion, such as crawling, may be just beginning at this time.

A fundamental tenant of Gibson's ecological approach to perception is that we act in order to perceive and we perceive in order to act (J. Gibson, 1979). The interconnection of perception and action is obvious in adults. For example, you hear a sound behind you and you turn your head to look and/or you move closer to interact with the object making the sound. For infants, the interconnectedness may not be as obvious; however, infants do move their eyes toward sounds, they crawl around barriers to find objects, and they orally and manually explore objects. Because we discuss perception–action relationships in detail later, we restrict ourselves to a few topics here—a discussion of eye movements and some general observations on the development of body movements.

Eye Movements

Among the earliest coordinated motor movements are eye movements. We previously discussed an example of a reflexive eye movement present at birth: OKN. Here, we focus on intentional eye movements. We can distinguish in adults two types—saccadic and smooth-pursuit eye movements. *Saccadic eye movements* occur when a target is detected in the periphery and a large eye movement is executed to place the target on the fovea. Aslin and Salapatek (1975) describe adult saccades to a peripheral target as having high velocity and brief latencies and as being ballistic in nature (Figure 2.9A). *Smooth-pursuit eye movements*, in adults, are continuous or smooth tracking movements whose rate varies with the velocity of the target. Smooth pursuit allows the viewer to maintain the projection of a moving target on the fovea.

Although saccadic eye movements are present at birth, they do not take the form of adult saccades (Aslin & Salapatek, 1975). Whereas adults' initial saccades

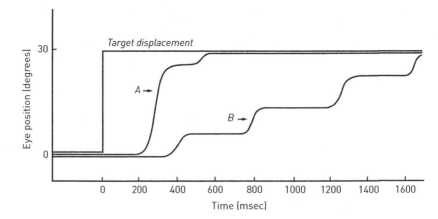

FIGURE 2.9

The time course of a saccadic eye movement to a target by (A) an adult and (B) a 2-month-old infant. Source: Reprinted with permission of Elsevier from Aslin, R. N. (1987). Motor aspects of visual development in infancy. In P. Salapatek & L. Cohen (Eds.), *Handbook of infant perception: From sensation to perception* (Vol. 1). Orlando, FL: Academic Press.

are matched to target distance, infants' initial saccades may cover only a fraction of the distance to the target, and subsequent saccades tend to be matched to the initial saccade in amplitude (Figure 2.9B). Bronson (1990) found that the average accuracy of infants' saccades remains unchanged between 3½ and 8 weeks of age but improves by 11–14 weeks.

In contrast to saccadic eye movements, smooth-pursuit movements are difficult to detect until approximately 2 months of age (Aslin, 1981). Infants younger than 2 months can track a moving object, especially if it is moving slowly, but they ordinarily make a series of saccades to follow the target. Evidence suggests that smooth-pursuit movements can occur in infants younger than 2 months, but these have low gain—that is, they lag behind the target (von Hofsten, 2004; von Hofsten & Rosander, 1996). Between 2 and 3 months, smooth pursuit improves substantially, especially for slower moving targets, and by 5 months infants' eye movements are predictive in that they lead the target rather than follow it (von Hofsten & Rosander, 1997). This developmental story is applicable only to horizontally moving targets. Pursuit of vertical targets is more difficult, even for infants up to 12 months of age and adults (Gronqvist, Gredeback, & von Hofsten, 2006; Gredeback, von Hofsten, Karlsson, & Aus, 2005).

Body Movements

Human motor development reflects two general principles. First, development proceeds in a *cephalocaudal* direction—that is, it progresses from head to foot. Motor skills involving the head, neck, and arms appear before those involving the lower torso and legs. Motor development also progresses in a *proximodistal* direction—that is, development advances from the center of the body outward.

Coordinated movement of the trunk and shoulders appears before coordination of the arms and hands.

Initially, many infant movements may be actions guided by reflexes rather than under voluntary control. At birth, head control is limited to moving from side to side while infants are lying on their back. By 4 months, almost all infants can keep their head erect while being held or supported in a sitting position. Coordinated arm movements begin to emerge at approximately 4 months of age, and manipulation skills become increasingly specified to object properties up to 12 months of age, as discussed in Chapter 9.

The first form of self-produced locomotion is rolling. By 5 months, 90% of infants are able to roll over, and many are already on their way to some type of crawling. The average age for standing and beginning of walking is 11½ months of age, and 90% of infants are walking well by 14½ months of age (Bayley, 1969).

Implications of Motor Development for Perception

In comparison with sensory development, motor development is delayed. This delay is extremely important for understanding the relations of perception and action, as discussed later in this book. It casts doubt on theoretical views asserting that perception first arises through action (such as Piaget's (1952, 1954) ideas of the sensorimotor construction of reality or Berkeley's (1709/1910) "touch educates vision"). It suggests instead that the development of activity is preceded and guided by perceptual knowledge. However, the effects inevitably flow in both directions. As motor skills develop, infants can more readily obtain information through their own actions. When one can reach, crawl, and walk, the world becomes more accessible and increasingly rich in opportunities for exploration.

The later development of infants' motor abilities has profoundly influenced views of early perception. Because infants do not *do* much, they have been thought not to *know* much. Advances in the study of infant perception have depended crucially on investigators devising methods to exploit the few response capabilities of young infants. In turn, these methods have allowed us to discover a surprising repertoire of perceptual competence hidden within the relatively immobile infant.

CONCLUSION

The starting point for perception for infants varies depending on the system, with the visual system showing many immaturities early in life. Development across the first few months of life may be directed by neurological maturation and changes in the sensory organs (e.g., cone migration and changes in the shape of the eye). At the same time, young infants cannot do much motorically, nor are they required to do much. Thus, their perceptual systems may be viewed as matching the demands placed on them for perceiving, interacting with, and understanding their world. Later in this book, we discuss a number of early competencies by very young infants, including newborns, that seem nothing short of amazing given the physiological and sensory foundations for these processes.

NOTE

1. This chapter is slightly encyclopedic and includes a number of topics not strictly necessary for understanding the material in later chapters. The reader interested in particular topics in infant perception might read this chapter selectively.

3   Space Perception

INTRODUCTION

No ability is more fundamental to human perceptual and cognitive development than spatial perception. If objects and events did not come coherently organized in a three-dimensional framework, the world would appear chaotic and mysterious. If two dimensions, up–down and left–right, were given but there was no depth, the idea that physical objects routinely come into and leave existence would be inescapable. Lack of a coherent spatial order was surely on the mind of William James when he characterized the world of the newborn as a "blooming, buzzing confusion" (James, 1890).

As discussed in Chapter 1, the question of how space perception originates occupies a central place in perceptual theory. Logical arguments about the need for learning in perception were developed around issues involving space, particularly the "third" or depth dimension (Berkeley, 1709/1910; Helmholtz, 1885/1965; Piaget, 1954). Likewise, the ecological view's revised analyses of the information for perception centered on kinematic and stereoscopic information about space (Gibson, 1966; Johansson, 1970). The possibility that perceptual systems might have evolved to utilize such information is illustrated by visually guided, spatially oriented behavior in the newborns of some nonhuman species (Hess, 1956; Walk & Gibson, 1961). However, neither the theoretical claims about the information available for perception nor studies of other species can tell us how human spatial competence emerges. The issues require experimental research with human infants.

Researchers have taken up this challenge, and in this chapter we consider what they have discovered about the origins of human spatial perception. We focus on perception of the three-dimensional locations and relationships of objects and surfaces. A number of other spatial topics involving object properties, such as configuration and orientation, are treated in later chapters on pattern and object perception. Vision is primary, but other senses also contribute to spatial perception. We treat vision here; some aspects of auditory and haptic space perception are treated in later chapters.

ECOLOGY OF SPATIAL PERCEPTION

The Task of Spatial Perception

What spatial aspects of the environment are important to human functioning? For upright, mobile organisms, maintaining posture and guiding locomotion are high priorities. Effective locomotion requires detecting the arrangement of obstacles and spaces between them and becomes even more critical at higher speeds, such as when running. In addition to locomotion, other actions require spatial information, from the simplest reaching and grasping to the expert activities of a neurosurgeon or a pilot landing a jet airplane on a heaving aircraft carrier at night. Both ordinary and extraordinary activities depend on accurate perception of distance and size, and many involve coordinating space, time, and motion. Beyond immediate action, spatial perception serves to establish representations of the environment that guide action in the future and form the bases of thought.

Important for understanding early spatial perception in *Homo sapiens* is that human infants do few of these things. On average, a human infant does not crawl until 6 or 7 months, does not walk until approximately 1 year, and does not even reach effectively until 4 or 5 months. On attaining these milestones, the infant still remains relatively incompetent in finding its own nutrition or escaping danger. As discussed later, however, spatial perception begins much earlier. What is its function before complex action systems emerge? Spatial perception, and early perceptual ability in general, may serve to advance cognitive and motor development. Despite the lack of motor skill, the infant can learn a great deal about the physical and social environments, and over time the infant can guide the emerging action skills through accurate perception.

Another function of early spatial perception might be to guide perceptual learning. As described in Chapter 1, two varieties of perceptual learning might occur—*differentiation learning*, more precise extraction of information with experience, and *enrichment*, the learning of new stimulus variables that come to specify spatial properties by correlation with already usable information. Some evidence in adult perception is consistent with the idea that new depth cues can be acquired by the latter kind of learning (Wallach & O'Leary, 1982). As we consider early spatial abilities, we discuss some sources of spatial information that may involve this kind of learning as well as those that depend on inborn mechanisms or neural maturation.

Information and Constraints in Spatial Perception

Space has three dimensions. To the physicist, space is normally isotropic, meaning its properties are the same in all directions. Visually, however, the three dimensions of space are not created equal. The optics of the eye map inputs from different radial directions onto different retinal locations. The ordering of targets in the environment from above to below the observer is preserved in the retinal projection, as is the ordering from left to right (see Figure 1.3). Not given is the third dimension—the distance to an object reflecting light to the eye. Much of what needs to be explained in space perception involves distance. Not only is perception of distance important in its own right but also it is connected to many other perceptual properties, such as size.

Sources of information about depth and distance are remarkably numerous. Albert Yonas, a leading investigator of the development of depth perception, has remarked that "God must have loved depth cues because she made so many of them." Some order can be imposed by noticing that most depth cues in biological vision systems involve one of three different solutions to the problem of distance. We call them *parallax information, information based on assumed physical equality,* and *oculomotor information.* We also mention two other depth information sources that do not fit neatly into this categorization: *interposition* and *familiar size.*

Parallax Information

Parallax refers to differences in the optical projections of an object imaged from different positions. This information is the basis of triangulation: By measuring the direction of the moon from two widely separated locations a known distance apart, its distance from earth may be estimated. The same type of information is exploited in more than one way in human vision. *Binocular disparity* refers to differences in the projections to the two eyes from features in the environment (Figure 3.1).

When we look at a point, that point is imaged in the center (the fovea) of each eye. Other points at approximately the same distance from the observer will project to corresponding retinal locations. Points at different distances will project to disparate (or different) locations in the two eyes, and the magnitude of disparity increases with distance from the fixated point. Disparity from points nearer than the fixation point can be distinguished from that due to points farther than it by the direction of disparity. *Crossed disparity* characterizes nearer points. The projection from a point closer than the fixation point will be more to the left in the visual field of the right eye and more to the right in the visual field of the left eye. You can easily demonstrate crossed disparity (Figure 3.1B) to yourself. Hold up the index fingers of your two hands in a line extending in front of your nose, one at a distance from your nose of approximately 8 inches and the other at arm's length. Focus on the farther finger. You will notice that the nearer finger (keep fixating the farther finger) appears as a double image. Now, close your left eye. You will notice that the right image in the double image of the near finger has vanished, meaning the right eye sees the left image (and the left eye saw the right image, before you closed it). This is what is meant by crossed disparity. *Uncrossed disparity* (Figure 3.1A) refers to cases in which the more leftward visual position is in the left eye, and the more rightward is in the right; such disparity comes from points farther away than the point of fixation. Again, hold up your two fingers, but this time focus on the nearer finger. You will notice the farther finger appears as a double image. This time, when you close your left eye, the left image vanishes. Because the left eye sees the left image and the right eye sees the right image, we have uncrossed disparity. The visible double images in this exercise help to make the point but are not necessary for the registration of disparity. For disparities below a certain amount, the visual world appears fused—that is, double images

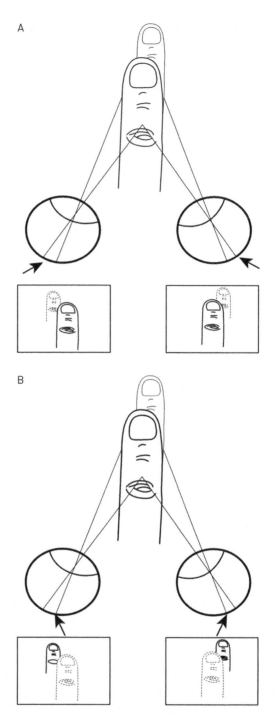

FIGURE 3.1

Illustration of binocular disparity: uncrossed (A) and crossed (B) binocular disparity. The upper illustration depicts the physical viewing situation; arrows indicate the foveae of each eye. The rectangles in the lower diagram show the image given to each eye. The solid figure is seen as fused; dotted figures are visible as double images. Source: Created by P. J. Kellman.

disappear and you see only one object at a distance. (Interestingly, both fused and visibly double images provide depth information.)

The relation between angular disparity and depth intervals in the world is not fixed. A given depth difference in the environment gives decreasing binocular disparity as a viewer moves farther away (disparity is inversely proportional to the square of distance). In combination with absolute distance information to some reference point in the environment, binocular disparity can provide highly accurate absolute depth intervals (Wallach & Zuckerman, 1963); however, its usefulness is dependent on other conditions, such as distance, illumination, and movement (Kane, Guan, & Banks, 2014).

The same geometry underlies *kinematic information* about depth, except that parallax comes not from simultaneous use of two eyes in separate positions but, rather, from the changing position of the observer over time. A moving observer sees a constantly changing sample of the optic array. These transforming optical projections carry structural information about the spatial layout of the environment (Gibson, 1966, 1979; Johansson, 1970, 1975).

Kinematic information is multifaceted. Gibson (1966) proposed the term *optic flow* to describe the transforming optic array given to a moving observer. Certain properties of the global flow field indicate the observer's motion through space, guide locomotion, and control posture (Crowell & Banks, 1993; Johansson, von Hofsten, & Jansson, 1980; Warren & Wertheim, 1990). These topics are discussed in-depth in Chapters 6 and 9, which are dedicated to motion perception and perception and action. Several more local sources of spatial layout information from motion are taken up in this chapter. Figure 3.2 illustrates four of these. *Optical expansion* and *contraction* can indicate relative motion between a target and the observer. For example, the projection of a moving object headed directly for the observer symmetrically expands over time, and, as discussed in Chapter 1, such a situation provides optical information about the time to contact between the target and the observer. There is evidence that adult humans are sensitive to this information and that it, or related information, guides locomotive behavior in a variety of species (Lee, 1974). *Motion parallax* or *motion perspective* refers to differential optical change for points at different distances during observer motion. It can indicate relative and possibly absolute distance from the observer under some conditions (Rogers & Graham, 1979). *Accretion and deletion of texture* refers to the gradual revealing or concealing of background texture when an object moves in front of a farther surface (or when an observer moves and views stationary surfaces at different depths). This form of information gives information about depth order (what is closer and what is further away). Finally, the continuously changing optical projection of an object, given by object or observer motion, carries information about its three-dimensional form, allowing perception of *structure from motion*. This topic is treated when we consider object perception in Chapter 5.

Parallax information, underlying both binocular and kinematic space perception, is preeminent in human spatial perception. A primary reason is its high *ecological validity*. The mapping between parallax information and

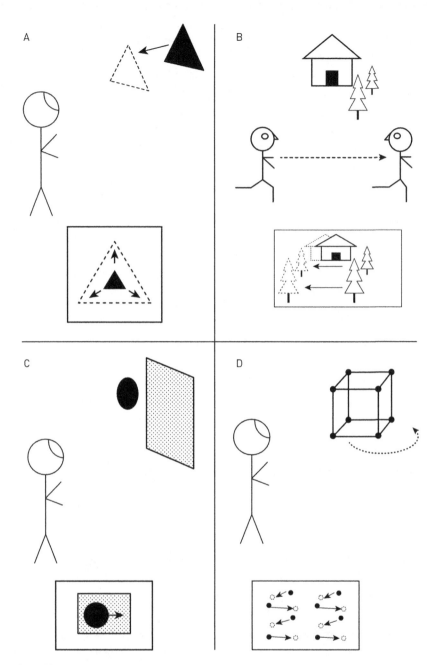

FIGURE 3.2

Depictions of four types of kinematic information about spatial relations. Top illustrations show the physical situation being viewed; bottom illustrations show the optical information available at the eye. (A) Optical expansion: As an object approaches the observer, its projection at the eye expands symmetrically. (B) Motion perspective: As the observer moves, the relative positions of viewed objects change in the projection to the eye, with nearer objects displacing more than farther ones. (C) Accretion and deletion of texture: Relative motion of an object and a farther surface leads to progressive occluding of background texture elements at the object's leading edge and revealing of texture elements at its trailing edge. (D) Structure from motion: The rotation cube produces relative motions of its visible points in the projection to the eye; relations among these motions vectors specify the object's three-dimensional structure. Source: Created by P. J. Kellman.

three-dimensional arrangements is ordinarily unambiguous, at least in terms of depth order. To present parallax relationships without their normal causes in the three-dimensional layout, one must go to great lengths. A stereoscope or special glasses at a movie theater may be used to present different images to the two eyes, or a virtual reality setup can give observer-contingent changes to simulate kinematic information.

Information Based on Assumed Physical Equality

The pictorial cues to depth give information in a static, monocular view. Several naturally occurring examples are shown in Figure 3.3. A number of these cues rest on similar foundations. Projective geometry dictates certain distance-dependent changes in images; for example, the visual angle projected by a given physical extent decreases with distance. Working this geometry backward, if two physical tokens (objects and spaces) can be assumed to have the same real size, then differences in their projective size can be used to order them in depth. This describes the depth cue of *relative size*. Due to *linear perspective*, the image of converging lines may indicate lines in the world, such as railroad tracks, that have constant separation but extend away in depth. *Relative height*, an often neglected and quite powerful cue, rests on the fact that more distant objects generally appear higher in the visual field (Epstein, 1966; Gibson, 1950). Here, it is assumed that both objects rest on the ground and that the ground surface is generally flat. When these assumptions are met, relative height is a consequence of the fact that we ordinarily view our environment from some height above the ground surface. Gibson described the rich information in *texture gradients*. If it can be assumed that the physical tokens along a ground surface (pebbles, cornstalks, cobblestones, etc.) are stochastically uniform, then the decreasing projective size of texture elements can indicate depth. Moreover, uniform surface texture may offer a direct means of size perception: Two objects may be perceived to be the same sizes despite differing distances from the observer because they will occlude the same number of texture elements. Finally, *shading* rests on the fact that surfaces identical in their light-reflecting properties will appear brighter or darker, depending on their orientation to the light source. Variation in luminance can thus be used to perceive surface topography.

Information based on assumed physical equality is not as fundamentally rooted in the physics and geometry of our world as is parallax information. It is easy to display these pictorial cues to depth in situations in which no depth exists, such as in paintings and photographs. In addition, it is not very difficult to find in ordinary environments violations of the assumed physical regularities on which these cues rely. For example, regular gradients of texture are common, but at the seashore, the average size of sand, shells, and pebbles decreases with distance from the water's edge. Many variations in surface luminance come from variation in surface reflectance rather than from differences in surface orientation. In all of these cases, pictorial depth cues may be inaccurate indicators of the spatial layout.

FIGURE 3.3

Examples of pictorial depth cues. (A) Linear perspective: The trees converge in the image. Also present is familiar size and relative height: The known size of the trees provides information for depth, and the smaller trees are farther away. Also, the trees closer to the horizon and higher in the picture plane (relative height) are farther away. (B) Texture gradient: Visible texture elements decrease with their distance. Also present is linear perspective. (C) Shading information provides information about contours of the tree bark and the deeper hole in the trunk. Source: Photographs courtesy of M. E. Arterberry (A and B) and M. K. Arterberry (C).

Oculomotor Information

Berkeley (1709/1910) proposed that visual information could be interpreted by association with muscular adjustments required for focusing the image (*accommodation*) and that converging the two eyes could provide information about the third dimension (*convergence*). Both of these adjustments should produce muscular sensations correlated with distance.

The physical facts that make these adjustments necessary are simply that (1) light moves in straight lines and (2) most surfaces (all matte surfaces) scatter incident light in all directions. Convergence depends only on the former: To view the same point in space, each eye must turn so that the fovea, the nodal point of the eye, and the target point are collinear. Accommodation is necessary because the closer a target, the more the eye admits a sheaf of light rays traveling in slightly different directions. Should these light rays from the same target point contact different retinal receptors, directional information would be lost. To get these divergent rays to focus on the same retinal location, more refractive power is needed for nearer targets. Changes in the thickness of the lens provide the variable refractive power.

Experimental appraisals of accommodation and convergence as distance information for adults have varied. Some early experimental work suggested a weak or negative relationship between accommodative strength and perceived nearness (Heinemann, Tulving, & Nachmias, 1959). A comprehensive review of spatial perception in the early 1970s suggested that accommodation and convergence were at best weak cues (Hochberg, 1971). Later studies led to a revival of these cues (von Hofsten, 1976; Wallach & Floor, 1971). These studies found that oculomotor cues, especially convergence, can provide accurate information.

Both accommodation and convergence are effective only at short ranges, up to 2 to 3 m in adults. The similar geometry underlying both cues dictates that as distance increases, the adjustments required decrease drastically. Taking convergence as our example, consider two points 20 and 21.5 cm distant from the observer (directly in front of a point midway between two eyes). Assuming the observer's eyes are 6.5 cm apart, the difference in convergence angles for fixating these two points is approximately 0.63 deg. In other words, changing convergence angle by 0.63 deg when viewing a target 20 cm away points the eyes at a location 21.5 cm away. For comparison, suppose the eyes start out fixating a target 3 m away. Changing the convergence angle by 0.63 deg in this case changes the fixated location by more than 1.5 cm. How much more? Now the eyes aim at a location 3000 m away.

Other Depth Information Sources

Not all known depth cues fit into the taxonomy we have given. One important exception is the pictorial cue of *interposition* (Figure 3.4). Interposition, or overlap, thus gives us depth ordering. It does not give metric information about depth intervals or distance from the observer. Interposition is slightly more intricate

FIGURE 3.4

A natural example of interposition. The alligators are in front of the rock, and the leaves are above the alligators. Note also the cast shadow created by the leaves. Source: Photograph courtesy of M. K. Arterberry.

than it may first appear. Why do we see one object as going behind another? One idea is that the area whose boundaries change direction at the intersection is seen as behind. Thus, so-called *T junctions* might be the informational basis of interposition (see Figure 3.8B). This notion is serviceable for most cases, but counterexamples exist (Ratoosh, 1949). The ecological regularity underlying interposition is that occlusion of one object's bounding contours by another object normally produces T junctions. These junctions are less likely to occur from other causes.

A second cue that does not fit into our taxonomy is the depth cue of *familiar size*. If the physical size of an object is known, then the size of its retinal projection in a given instance may be used along with remembered real size to determine its distance. There is evidence for the effectiveness of this cue for adults, especially when conflicting information is eliminated (Ittelson, 1953; but for conflicting views on the effectiveness of this cue in adult distance perception, see Hochberg & Hochberg (1953) and Predebon & Woolley (1994)).

SPACE PERCEPTION ABILITIES AND PROCESSES

How does space perception get started? Which parts, if any, of the adult's arsenal of information sources can infants use? For convenience, we organize our discussion around four classes of information, based both on their ecological roots and on similarities in the mechanisms by which they are processed. For example, parallax information underlies both kinematic and stereoscopic information, but here we separate these because they appear to be processed separately. The four classes are kinematic information, stereoscopic information, oculomotor information, and pictorial depth information.

An interesting conjecture regarding the development of space perception is that it may reflect the differing ecological validity of different information sources. Both kinematic and stereoscopic information, as noted previously, are less subject to ambiguity than are the pictorial depth cues. Early learning about the environment might be best served by reliance on only the most accurate sources of information, even if this means that some perceptual situations will be indeterminate (Kellman, 1993). We consider this conjecture in space perception and later in other domains in which perception can depend on multiple sources of information.

Kinematic Information About Space

Kinematic information is arguably the most important source of spatial information for adults, given its precision and informativeness for spatial layout, guidance of locomotion, and skilled action. Kinematic information is also noteworthy in being unambiguous under reasonable constraints (Lee, 1974). For example, the depth ordering of viewed objects given by motion perspective when an observer moves his or her head back and forth is unequivocal, as long as the objects also do not move contingent on the observer's movement. From the standpoint of ecological validity, infant perceivers might be expected to be equipped with mechanisms sensitive to kinematic information early in development. One might make the opposite prediction from other considerations. Much kinematic information is provided by observer motion rather than object motion. Because human infants do not self-locomote until approximately the second half of the first year of life, one might expect mechanisms sensitive to kinematic information to arise at that time or later.

Kinematic Information for Approach

The optical projection of an approaching (or "looming") object expands symmetrically as the object comes closer to colliding with the observer. This kind of optical change carries information about the object's time to contact, and adults use this information skillfully, whether when braking to avoid an obstacle while driving or trying to catch a ball (Schiff & Oldak, 1990). Studies with other species indicate that optical expansion patterns elicit unlearned defensive responses (Schiff, 1965); for example, fiddler crabs and frogs run (or hop) away from looming stimuli. Early studies of human infants 1 to 2 months old suggest that optical expansion displays trigger a defensive blinking response. In one study, Nanez and Yonas (1994) presented 4- to 8-week-old infants with an expanding or contracting field of dots on a screen. Infants blinked more and showed more backward head pressure to the expanding pattern than the contracting pattern. Moreover, blinks and head pressure were more likely to occur at the end of the looming trajectory, providing evidence of a defensive response. Ten- to 14-week-old infants showed similar responsiveness to the looming stimulus with a slightly elevated blink rate and change in head pressure.

Not all instances of retinal expansion are looming objects. As we move through our environment, we approach openings or apertures. The external contours of these apertures expand similarly to a looming object, but the expansion patterns mean something different—access rather than obstacle. Being able to determine the difference between an approaching object and aperture is important, and infants between 3 and 5 months of age can do so. Schmuckler and Li (1998) presented infants with identical expansion patterns except that one specified an object (it covered the background along the external edges as it approached) and one specified an aperture (it revealed the background in the middle as it approached). Infants blinked more to the approaching object than to the aperture (Figure 3.5). Unfortunately, Schmuckler and Li did not report whether there were age differences, so it is not known whether the youngest infants performed as well as the older infants in making this distinction.

There are several candidates for variables that infants may use to determine the spatial location of a looming stimulus and the timing for contact. As the stimulus approaches, the visual angle changes, as does the speed of the stimulus. Lee (1976) quantified this variable as *tau*, the inverse of the relative rate of angular expansion (see also Hecht & Savelsbergh, 2004). Functionally, the perceiver needs to determine accurately the time when the approaching stimulus will hit him or her (or the time to contact). Which variables infants respond to has been investigated by Kayed and colleagues (Kayed, Farstad, & van der Meer, 2008; Kayed & van der Meer, 2000, 2007). Infants approximately 5 months old (the youngest age tested) appear to rely on visual angle, blinking when a constant visual angle is achieved regardless of speed of approach. This strategy, however, resulted in inaccurate timing of the response when objects were accelerating. Slightly older infants, between 6 and 7 months, use a timing strategy, such that they blinked more accurately in accordance with time to contact. The timing of this shift appears to vary across

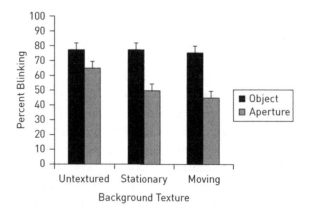

FIGURE 3.5

Percentage of blinking to approaching obstacle and aperture as a function of background condition. The untextured background was homogeneous. Stationary and moving backgrounds consisted of color cartoon images, one static and one moving, respectively. Source: Reprinted with permission of SAGE Publications from Schmuckler, M. A., & Li, N. S. (1998). Looming responses to obstacles and apertures. *Psychological Science, 9,* 49–52.

infants: In a longitudinal study, five infants already used a timing strategy at 22 weeks, whereas six switched to a timing strategy between 22 and 30 weeks (Kayed & van der Meer, 2007).

Motion Parallax

Researchers have long suspected that infants are sensitive to motion parallax early in life. In classic studies, Walk and Gibson (1961) tested depth perception using a visual cliff, a glass surface through which animals could see a surface below. Newborns of several species refused to crawl or walk onto the "deep" side of the cliff, and Walk and Gibson noted that these animals made lateral head movements that probably indicated use of motion parallax. Unfortunately, humans cannot be tested in the standard visual cliff situation until they begin to crawl (~6 months of age), and they do not conspicuously show lateral head movements even then.

The first study with human infants that reported experimental results related to the development of motion parallax was conducted by von Hofsten, Kellman, and Putaansuu (1992). They presented 14-week-old infants with an array of three vertical rods in a horizontal row, perpendicular to the line of sight. The infants were placed in a chair that moved laterally side to side, and the middle rod moved a small amount parallel and in tandem to the chair, creating the illusion that it was farther than the other two rods. After habituation, infants saw two displays: One was spatially similar in that it consisted of three aligned stationary rods; the other had three stationary rods with the middle rod displaced backward 15 cm, which gave the moving infant the same optical change patterns as in habituation. Infants generalized habituation more to the spatially different display having the same optical change as in habituation (i.e., the one with the middle rod set back), suggesting sensitivity to motion parallax information.

Similarly, Nawrot and Nawrot (2013) showed that motion parallax may be functional as early as 12 weeks of age. In a habituation study, infants aged 8–20 weeks were habituated to a corrugated surface composed of random dots, in which half of the display appeared to be closer than the other half based on the relative motions of the dots. Following habituation, the test display showed a depth reversal in terms of which half of the display was closer. Infants at 12 weeks showed a clear pattern of dishabituation to the depth reversal, and in another study the authors found some infants responding as early as 10 weeks (Nawrot, Mayo, & Nawrot, 2009).

Whether infants are using motion parallax information to perceive depth remains an open question, however. It is possible that in looking time studies, infants responded to some change in the visual information, such as a change in direction of dot patterns, rather than a change in the spatial arrangement. One way to show depth perception is to ask infants to make a spatially appropriate response, such as reaching. Condry and Yonas (2013) capitalized on the design of von Hofsten et al. (1992). Six-month-old infants were moved in front of two identical objects, one of which moved in phase with the infants and one that moved out of phase with the infants. The out-of-phase object was perceived by adults to be the closer object (in reality both rods were the same distance away). Following 8–16 sec of continuous movement, infants were allowed to reach for the objects. Under monocular conditions, infants reached 66.3% of the time to the out-of-phase object. In contrast, under binocular conditions, infants reached only 50% of the time to the out-of-phase object. In other research, Yonas and colleagues (e.g., Yonas & Granrud, 1985a) demonstrated that when infants see a depth difference, they reach for the closer object or region of a display. Thus, Condry and Yonas concluded that infants at least by 6 months use motion parallax to perceive depth and to guide action. Unfortunately, reaching is not an effective measure at 3 months (the lower limit of its usefulness is approximately 4½ to 5 months of age), so it is suggestive that infants respond to motion parallax information before 6 months, and perhaps as early as 10–12 weeks, but we cannot draw a firm conclusion about younger infants' use of this information for perceiving depth.

Accretion and Deletion of Texture

Accretion and deletion of texture is a source of kinematic information for edges that arises when two opaque surfaces move past each other at different depths (Gibson, Kaplan, Reynolds, & Wheeler, 1969; Kaplan, 1969). During the relative motion of the surfaces, texture elements on the further surface become visible (accretion) or hidden (deletion) at the edges of the nearer surface. In surfaces composed of random dots, in which no other information is available, accretion and deletion of texture effectively specifies edges, form, and depth ordering of surfaces to adult observers (Andersen & Cortese, 1989; Kaplan, 1969; Shipley & Kellman, 1994).

Several studies have shown that infants are able to determine the external shape of objects. The typical study involves habituation to a shape (e.g., a cross, square, or butterfly) specified solely by accretion and deletion of texture and then testing for dishabituation to a new shape. Kaufmann-Hayoz, Kaufmann, and Stucki (1986) and Johnson and Mason (2002) showed that 3- and 2-month-olds, respectively, perceived the shape of the moving stimulus. These results suggest that accretion and deletion of texture effectively specified edges and shape at this young age. We cannot, however, make inferences about whether infants perceived depth ordering in these displays. Granrud et al. (1984) used reaching to directly assess infants' depth perception from accretion and deletion of texture. They presented 5- and 7-month-olds with moving displays of computer-generated random dot surfaces with vertical accretion and deletion boundaries specifying nearer and farther surfaces. Infants of both ages reached approximately 50% of the time to the areas specified as nearer and 35% of the time to areas specified as farther. (The remaining reaches were to edges or to two or more regions at the same time.) Infants as young as 3 months may respond to accretion and deletion of texture for depth perception. Recall the study by Schmuckler and Li (1998) that tested infants' blink rate to approaching objects and apertures. When accretion and deletion of texture was added to optical expansion information, infants' blink rate to the approaching aperture decreased significantly. This finding suggests that infants were better able to determine the depth ordering of the approaching aperture and the background surface and, as a result, to perceive the approaching aperture as not as threatening as an approaching object.

These results suggest that sensitivity to accretion and deletion information arises early in infancy. There is question, however, about the basis of infants' responding. Ordinary accretion and deletion displays might contain two kinds of information. In addition to the actual appearance and disappearance of texture elements, there are different relations between moving texture elements and the boundary between the two regions. On one side, elements remain in a fixed position relative to the boundary; this side is nearer than the other. On the other side, elements move closer or farther from the boundary over time; this surface is farther. Tests with adults show that the latter information (termed *boundary flow*) is usable as depth information when no accretion and deletion of texture is present (Craton & Yonas, 1990). Five-month-olds also respond to boundary flow information, by reaching to the closer of two surfaces, when no accretion and deletion is present (Craton & Yonas, 1988), and 2-month-olds perceive the shape of an object from the relative motion of dots, without accretion and deletion of texture (Johnson & Mason, 2002). Further work may be needed to determine whether accretion and deletion of texture alone can specify depth order. The data suggest that, at a minimum, accretion and deletion of texture enables infant perceivers to locate boundaries between regions. The boundaries required to compute boundary flow were not given in any other way in the studies by Granrud et al. (1984), Kaufmann-Hayoz et al. (1986), and Johnson and Mason (2002).

Stereoscopic Information

Stereoscopic depth perception is among the most precise forms of spatial information. For adults, it allows perception of absolute depth intervals, given some information about distance of at least one visible point (Wallach & Zuckerman, 1963). Evidence suggests innate foundations for stereoscopic depth perception. Cortical cells sensitive to particular disparities at birth or after minimal visual experience have been found in several species (Hubel & Weisel, 1970; Ramachandran, Clarke, & Whitteridge, 1977).

For humans, perception of depth from disparity appears in some infants as young as 2 or 3 months, with most infants first showing sensitivity in approximately the fourth month. Programmatic research on disparity thresholds was carried out by Held and colleagues (Birch, Gwiazda, & Held, 1982; Held et al., 1980). They longitudinally studied infants' visual preferences for a striped display containing stereoscopic depth differences over a flat display. Infants showed reliable preferences at 12 weeks for crossed disparities and at 17 weeks for uncrossed disparities. Improvement in stereoscopic sensitivity once it appears is strikingly rapid (Figure 3.6). Thresholds changed from greater than 60 min to less than 1 min of disparity in a few weeks.

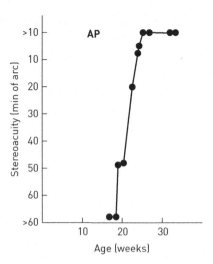

FIGURE 3.6
Stereoacuity estimates (in minutes of arc) as a function of age for an individual infant. This pattern of abrupt onset was found for 15 of 16 infants tested. Source: Redrawn with permission from Held, R., Birch, E., & Gwiazda, J. (1980). Stereoacuity of human infants. *Proceedings of the National Academy of Science, USA, 77,* 5572–5574.

Mechanisms Underlying the Onset of Stereopsis

The physiological basis of stereopsis is well understood, and its development is a good example of an experience-expectant process (Greenough, Black, & Wallace, 1987). Experience-expectant processes are common to all members of the species and evolved as a neural preparation for incorporating general information from the environment. In the case of stereopsis, the two eyes send projections to the visual cortex, and during the first few months of life ocular dominance columns develop (Hickey & Peduzzi, 1987). In these columns, neurons become specialized for input from one or the other eye. Development of ocular dominance columns is reliant on experience with overlapping images from the two eyes. Infants whose eyes are out of alignment (e.g., colloquially referred to as *cross-eyed* or *wall-eyed*; technically *amblyopia*) or who do not have vision from both eyes due to congenital cataracts do not develop stereopsis (Banks, Aslin, & Letsin, 1975; Maurer & Lewis, 1993). Interestingly, otherwise healthy infants who are born early (~2 months pre-term) develop stereopsis on average by 4 months post birth, which is 2 months of age based on length of gestation (Jando et al., 2013). If stereopsis were governed solely by maturational processes, preterm infants would not show sensitivity until 6 months. Thus, preterm infants, and their cortical structures, are able to take advantage of the visual information afforded by their early birth.

Disparity Sensitivity and Depth Perception

Do studies of early binocular function indicate that infants see stereoscopic depth or merely that infants can detect disparity differences? The issue is difficult to settle definitively. Indirect evidence derives from studies in which pre-stereoscopic infants look away from stereograms supposedly because they are unable to fuse the two images (Kavšek, 2013). The reasoning is that the unfusable or rivalrous stimuli are unpleasant because of the competing images from the two eyes (recall the double image of your finger in the previous demonstration of crossed and uncrossed disparity). Control conditions employed in several studies, and studies examining spatial behavior, also support the depth perception hypothesis. For example, Held et al. (1980) found that infants who showed clear preferences for vertical line displays containing horizontal disparity showed no such preference when the display orientation was rotated 90 deg to give 34 min of vertical disparity (a condition that induces binocular rivalry for adults). The result is most naturally interpreted as suggesting that ordinary preferential attention to disparity displays depends on perception of depth. On the other hand, it tends to suggest that disparities apart from stereopsis might affect infants' fixation.

A different approach to the problem is to search for differences in spatial behavior based on disparity sensitivity. Yonas, Arterberry, and Granrud (1987) found that only disparity-sensitive 4-month-olds were able to transfer information about object shape from kinematic to stereo information. In this study, infants were first habituated to a moving three-dimensional object. Following habituation, the familiar and a novel object were presented in a stationary stereogram. Disparity-sensitive infants looked significantly longer to the novel shape, whereas disparity-insensitive infants did not. Also, as discussed in more detail in Chapter 9, infants' ball catching significantly improves under binocular view between 5 and 7 months of age, most likely due to the contribution of sensitivity to binocular disparity (van Hof, van der Kamp, & Savelsbergh, 2006). On the basis of these results, it seems safe to conclude that the onset of disparity sensitivity in human infants closely corresponds to their ability to perceive stereoscopic depth.

Oculomotor Information

Accommodation

Accommodation refers to changes in the shape of the lens in order to focus images on the retina. Changes in the muscles that control the shape of the lens, called ciliary muscles, provide information for distance for adults. We discussed in Chapter 2 that when other limitations are avoided, infant accommodation is reasonably accurate; however, no research to our knowledge has directly assessed accommodation as a source of depth information in infancy.

Convergence

Chapter 2 presented evidence that convergence is operative within the first month of life and that infants show appropriate adjustments of their eyes to distances ranging between 20 and 200 cm. Moreover, convergence accuracy reaches adult levels by 8 or 9 weeks of age. If convergence is reasonably accurate, an important question is what could be the stimulus for eye movements leading to accurate convergence? Given the data on the development of stereopsis, binocular disparity does not seem to be a reasonable candidate before 3 or 4 months of age. Perhaps accommodation plays a role, given that its development appears to be slightly more advanced than convergence.

Under ordinary viewing conditions, it is likely that accommodation and convergence work together. Referred to as a *cross-coupling*, there is evidence of accommodative-driven convergence and convergence-driven accommodation. Infants between 3 and 6 months old show a linkage between the two. When convergence is induced by placing a prism in front of the eye, accommodative responses follow suit and the latency to do so is similar to that of adults (Bobier, Guinta, Kurtz, & Howland, 2000; Tondel & Candy, 2008).

Of interest is infants' use of convergence (alone or in combination with accommodation) for depth perception. One of the first studies to address this issue was conducted by von Hofsten (1974). He tested 5-month-olds' reaching behavior while they wore convergence-altering glasses. The results showed that reaches were shifted appropriately toward positions consistent with the convergence information. Thus, convergence can provide absolute distance information by 5 months.

Convergence may provide distance information much earlier, perhaps from birth, although the evidence is indirect. Kellman and von Hofsten (1992) studied 8- and 16-week-olds in a situation in which moving observers were tested for motion detection. The displays contained several stationary objects and a single moving object, with the moving object linked to the observer's moving chair (moving along a path parallel to it). Detecting motion in this situation requires distance information (Gogel, 1982). Infants showed evidence of accurate motion detection when they viewed the displays binocularly but not monocularly. Motion detection in the 16-week-old group may have been based on convergence, binocular disparity, or a combination of the two, but it is unlikely that disparity is present at 8 weeks. The best explanation for 8-week-olds' motion detection in this situation is that it is based on distance information furnished by convergence.

Results of other studies also indicate an early ability to extract distance information from oculomotor information (Granrud, 1987, 2006; Slater, Mattock, & Brown, 1990; Slater & Morison, 1985). These studies, discussed later, involve the use of distance information in the perception of object size and shape.

Pictorial Depth Information

Much of the groundbreaking work on the development of pictorial depth perception derives from a series of studies by Yonas and colleagues (for reviews, see Kavšek, Granrud, & Yonas, 2009; Kavšek, Yonas, & Granrud, 2012). Many of these studies used reaching as a measure, and they focused on isolating one source of depth information (e.g., interposition in the absence of shading). Displays in which pictorial information specified that one object or part of a surface was nearer to the infant than the other were presented under monocular (infants wore an eye patch) or binocular viewing conditions. If infants are sensitive to the pictorial cues available in the display, they should reach to the apparently closer object or part of the display under monocular conditions. Under binocular conditions, they should reach equally to the two objects or show no preference for one region of the display over another because binocular information overrides pictorial depth information.

The first study conducted by Yonas and colleagues demonstrates this method well (Yonas, Cleaves, & Pettersen, 1978). To test infants' sensitivity to linear perspective, they used the "Ames window," a trapezoidal window developed by Adelbert Ames (Ames, 1951; Figure 3.7A). When an adult views the Ames window with one eye from a sufficient distance, the window appears tiled in depth even though it is really perpendicular to the line of sight due to linear perspective and relative size. (Binocular viewing reduces or eliminates the effect.) In the study by Yonas et al., 5- and 7-month-old infants viewed the trapezoidal window monocularly or binocularly on different trials, and reaching to the two sides of the window was measured. Infants reached approximately equally to the two sides in the binocular condition, suggesting that any pictorial information was overridden by binocular information. Under monocular viewing, 7-month-olds reached significantly more to the larger side of the window—the side that was "apparently closer" if responding to the pictorial depth cues. Five-month-olds did not reach more to the larger side of the window. When linear perspective is combined with texture gradient information to create a receding surface in depth, a similar pattern emerges (Yonas, Granrud, Arterberry, & Hanson, 1986; Figure 3.7B). Seven-month-old, but not 5-month-old, infants reached more for the apparently closer of two objects that appeared to be sitting on the surface.

Isolating Pictorial Depth Information

Much of Yonas' early work focused on the development of sensitivity to different pictorial depth cues. The initial story was remarkably consistent: 7-month-olds but not 5-month-olds responded to the depth information. Here, we describe a few of these studies.

Familiar and Relative Size The depth cue of familiar size is unique in its importance for study learning effects in space perception. Familiar size works as follows: From the geometry of size and distance relations, the combination of a known object size and a given projective size can be used to compute the distance from the observer to the object (Figure 3.7C). What is special about this cue is that it requires specific learned information—the object's true size. Infants at 7 months of age do use this cue: They are able to use the size of a face to determine its distance, and they reach more to the larger of two faces (Yonas, Pettersen, & Granrud, 1982).

Showing that infants are able to use the known size of faces at 7 months of age to determine distance is, perhaps, not surprising given the fact that faces are common objects in infants' environment. There is plenty of opportunity to learn about the real size of faces and then to use that information for perceiving depth.

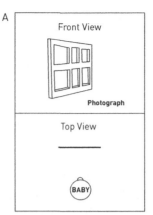

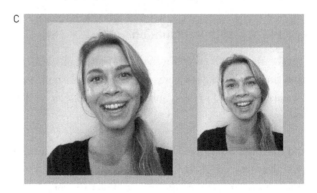

FIGURE 3.7

Displays used to test infants' pictorial depth perception used by Yonas and colleagues. The Ames window (A) contains linear perspective and relative size information creating the illusion that the window slants in depth. (B) An example of linear perspective and texture gradient information creating a surface slanting in depth such that the lower object appears to be closer than the higher object. The two different-sized faces in panel C provides the depth cue of familiar size. Source: Re-created with permission of Elsevier from (A) Arterberry, M. E., Bensen, A. S., & Yonas, A. (1991). Infants' responsiveness to static-monocular depth information: A recovery from habituation approach. *Infant Behavior and Development*, *14*, 241–251; and (B) Yonas, A., Elieff, C. A., & Arterberry, M. E. (2002). Emergence of sensitivity to pictorial depth cues: Charting development in individual infants. *Infant Behavior and Development*, *25*, 495-514. (C) After Yonas, Pettersen, and Granrud (1982), photograph of female courtesy of S. V. Champeau.

Surprisingly, infants do not need months of learning in order to use familiar size information. Granrud, Haake, and Yonas (1985) gave infants 5 min to play with two unfamiliar wooden toys, one smaller than the other. Following this familiarization phase, the infants viewed two toys that were the same shapes and colors as during familiarization but that now were of equal size (and displayed at the same distance). Seven-month-old infants reached more for the toy that was small during familiarization, suggesting that they perceived this object as nearer.

Relative size is similar to familiar size except that it does not rely on the known size of objects. Two identical objects, except for one being larger than the other, can induce the perception of depth. The larger object appears closer. When infants were presented with two identical discs, one large and one small, the same distance away, 7- and 5½-month-old infants reached significantly more to the larger object than the smaller object under monocular viewing conditions, but 5-month-olds did not (Yonas, Granrud, & Pettersen, 1985).

Shading Shading is a powerful cue to surface topography; Figure 3.3C gives an illustration. In a study by Granrud, Yonas, and Opland (1985), 5- and 7-month-olds were presented with a real surface containing a concavity and a convexity. They were also presented with a photograph depicting a concavity and a convexity. Classification of concavity and convexity from shading alone depends on the position of the light source; some species as well as human adults perceive such displays using the assumption that illumination comes from above (Hershberger, 1970). Granrud et al. assumed that infants would reach preferentially to an area that appeared nearer than the rest of the surface. Both age groups reached preferentially for the real convexity in both monocular and binocular conditions. Seven-month-olds viewing the photograph reached preferentially for the area specified to be convex by shading information, but only when they viewed the display monocularly. When viewing binocularly, they showed no reaching preference. Five-month-olds showed no reaching preferences to the photographic display under either monocular or binocular viewing. Similar results were found when infants were tested for sensitivity to *cast shadows* (Yonas & Granrud, 2006). These findings suggest that 7-month-old infants' visual system operates under the constraint that light comes from above (see also Corrow, Granrud, Mathison, & Yonas, 2011; Shirai, Kanazawa, & Yamaguchi, 2005).

Interposition and Line Junctions Figure 3.8A shows a display used to study the development of interposition (Granrud & Yonas, 1984). If infants perceive depth order from interposition, then in Figure 3.8A the leftmost part of the display would appear to be nearer than the middle, which in turn would appear to be nearer than the rightmost part of the display. The junctions between the lines are the key information here. At the intersection of the three surfaces, lines indicating the borders of each overlapping panel create a T junction. To adults, the stem of the T is the edge of the farther surface, and the top of the T is the edge of the closer surface (Marr, 1982). Granrud and Yonas (1984) presented 5- and 7-month-olds with the display depicted in Figure 3.8A and observed where they reached. Although the actual display was flat, 7-month-olds reached significantly more for the apparently closer (left) part of

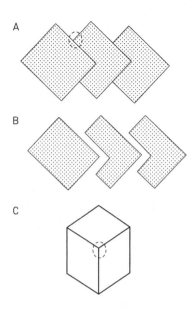

FIGURE 3.8

Interposition and wire figure: (A) depth display, (B) control, and (C) wire cube. Region highlighted by dotted circle shows T (A) and Y (C) junctions. Source: A and B redrawn with permission of Elsevier from Granrud, C. E., & Yonas, A. (1984). Infants' perception of pictorially specified interposition. *Journal of Experimental Child Psychology, 37,* 500–511; permission conveyed through Copyright Clearance Center, Inc.

Figure 3.8A; 5-month-olds did not. When infants were presented with control displays that disrupted the T junction information, such as separating the visible parts of the display (Figure 3.8B), infants' reaching to the left and right sides of the display was approximately equal.

Other types of line junctions in two dimensional displays provide depth information. For example, the *Y junction* facilitates perception of three-dimensional shape; it represents the intersection of three visible surfaces (see center region of Figure 3.8C). A clever way to test for sensitivity to Y junctions is the use of a wire figure that is concave (Corrow, Granrud, Mathison, & Yonas, 2012). In other words, the central vertex actually goes away from the viewer. Under binocular conditions, adults accurately report the display as concave. Under monocular conditions, adults report the display as convex. Infants' reaching to this display under both monocular and binocular conditions followed that of the adults: 5- and 7-month-olds reached significantly more to the central region under monocular view than under binocular view. This finding suggests that both age groups responded to the line junction information and perceived the display as convex when viewing it monocularly. (Note that this is the first study we have presented in which 5-month-olds have responded to pictorial depth information. We address this finding in more detail later.)

Together these findings suggest that by 7 months, and perhaps in some instances by 5 months, infants are responsive to line junction information for perceiving overlapping surfaces in depth and three-dimensional object shape. Additional work on perception of line junctions also shows that infants by 7½ months distinguish lines that represent edges and lines that are surface markings (Kavšek, 1999; Yonas & Arterberry, 1994).

Relative Height Like many pictorial depth cues, relative height is rarely found in isolation in natural scenes. For example, in Figure 3.3A, depth is depicted by linear perspective (converging lines created by the trees), familiar or relative size (decreasing size of the trees with distance), texture gradients (grass), and relative height. The key component to relative height is the position of objects relative to the horizon, but even against a blank or randomly textured background, higher objects are typically perceived by adults as being farther away (Epstein, 1966; Gibson, 1950; for review, see Sedgwick, 1986). Gibson posited that this is due to the fact that even a blank background suggests a terrain or floor. When infants are presented with a randomly textured surface with a clear horizon (like Figure 3.7B without the lines or black and white textured regions), both 5- and 7-month-olds reach more to the apparently closer (lower) object when viewing the display monocularly (Arterberry, 2008). Moreover, when ground texture is in conflict with ceiling texture (e.g., the ground specifies an object as closer, whereas the ceiling specifies the object as farther), 5- and 7-month-olds rely on the ground information for perceiving depth (Kavšek & Granrud, 2013). In contrast, when the horizon is removed by placing the objects against a homogeneous black field, only 7-month-olds are able to use the information from the relative height of the objects to perceive depth (Hemker, Granrud, Yonas, & Kavšek, 2010). Thus, we see the importance of a ground plane for perceiving depth and also development in the ability of infants to use height cues in the absence of information for the horizon.

Development of Pictorial Depth Information

The preceding discussion intentionally focused on studies using reaching as a measure to study infants' sensitivity to pictorial depth information. There is a difference between showing infants' attention to spatial information and using that information for perceiving depth. Reaching is an excellent measure for showing the latter. However, there are limitations with this measure. First, reaching cannot be used to study depth perception in younger infants because they are not very skilled at reaching (see Chapter 9). Second, reaching itself is developing between 5 and 7 months of age, leaving open the possibility that the observed 5 to 7 month shift in pictorial sensitivity (with a few exceptions) may be due to refinements in the control of reaching or the emergence of perceptual motor coordination. These hypotheses are vitiated by evidence that 5-month-olds do show clear reaching preferences to depth differences specified by binocular information (Granrud, 1986; Granrud, Yonas, & Pettersen, 1984). Furthermore, the same pattern of results has been found using a habituation method to test infants' perception of depth in the Ames window (see Figure 3.7A; Arterberry, Bensen, & Yonas, 1991).

Two studies using reaching as a measure found 5-month-old pictorial depth sensitivity (relative height and Y junctions; Arterberry, 2008; Corrow et al., 2012). Other studies relying on infant attention suggest that younger infants may be sensitive to some aspects of pictorial depth information at 5 months or younger. For example, Bhatt and colleagues showed 3-month-old infant responsiveness to line junctions and shading (Bertin & Bhatt, 2006; Bhatt & Waters, 1998); Shuwairi and Johnson (2013) showed 4-month-old infants' increased attention to impossible figures created by violations of line junctions and interposition. In light of findings such as these, Kavšek et al. conducted two meta-analyses on infants' sensitivity to pictorial depth information (Kavšek et al., 2009, 2012). One focused on studies that used reaching as a measure, and the other focused on studies that used attentional measures. When analyzing the reaching performance of 5- and 5½-month-old infants across 16 experiments (N = 475 infants), Kavšek et al. (2009) found evidence of sensitivity to pictorial cues; however, infants at this age were less consistently responsive than 7-month-olds, which is why it was difficult to document this sensitivity in many of the previous studies.

In their analysis of looking time studies, Kavšek et al. (2012) categorized the studies based on whether the researchers included controls or used methods, such as the transfer-across-cues paradigm, to assess whether infants were using pictorial depth information to perceive spatial layout. The transfer-across-cues method involves habituating infants to a layout or three-dimensional structure based on one type of cue (e.g., pictorial) and then presenting infants with the same and a different layout using another cue (e.g., binocular disparity; Arterberry et al., 1991). Studies that tested for the perception of spatial layout showed onset of sensitivity to be approximately 6 months of age. In contrast, studies without appropriate controls or methods sensitive enough to conclude infants' perceived depth showed early sensitivity (3–5 months of age). In these studies, it is possible that infants were responding to low-level proximal differences in the stimuli rather than perception of three-dimensional layout or shape. From this work, Kavšek et al. suggested that early attention to pictorial information, between 3 and 5 months, develops into the use of this information to perceive the three-dimensional world by approximately 6 months.

How might this progression look in an individual infant? A longitudinal study, in which the same infants were assessed every 2 weeks between the ages of 5 and 7 months for sensitivity to the depth cues of linear perspective and texture gradients, allowed for a finer analysis of the emergence of sensitivity to pictorial depth information both within and across children (Yonas, Elieff, & Arterberry, 2002). The resulting picture was one of variability. Of seven infants tested between the ages of 20 and 32 weeks, one showed sensitivity to the available depth information at 22 weeks, one at 24 weeks, two at 26 weeks, two at 28 weeks, and one at 32 weeks, the last date tested. Figure 3.9 shows the onset in one child. Thus, for most infants, the onset of pictorial depth sensitivity may occur between 22 and 32 weeks, and the timetable for full emergence may take 2–8 weeks. This level of variability discounts a strict maturational explanation for the development of sensitivity to pictorial depth information.

Development of pictorial depth sensitivity may be a product of perceptual learning. Each pictorial depth cue relies on at least one assumption that pertains to one or more regularity in the environment (Gibson, 1950). For example, light

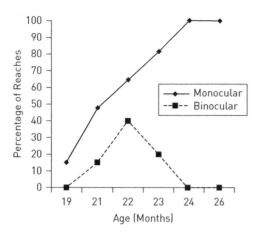

FIGURE 3.9

Percentage of reaching to the lower toy (see display in Figure 3.7B) by one infant tested monocularly and binocularly. Source: Redrawn with permission of Elsevier from Yonas, A., Elieff, C. A., & Arterberry, M. E. (2002). Emergence of sensitivity to pictorial depth cues: Charting development in individual infants. *Infant Behavior and Development, 25*, 495–514.

comes from above (shading), texture elements are regular in size (texture gradient), parallel lines converge with distance (linear perspective), and surfaces that cover other surfaces are closer (interposition). Infants may need to learn about these regularities and put them to use. Also, for the case for familiar size, infants need to learn the real sizes of objects in order to use this information to perceive depth. How infants may learn about regularities and about objects remains to be explained.

One possibility is that infants may learn to use these cues after they begin to move on their own around their environment. The importance of locomotion would be consistent with evidence in other species showing connections between self-produced locomotion and sensitivity to visual information about space (Held & Hein, 1963). Given the time frame of self-produced locomotion, which is approximately 6 months of age, and when the learning may be occurring (3–7 months), it is unlikely that learning is facilitated by crawling. Moreover, data support this claim: 7-Month-olds' locomotor status did not predict responsiveness to linear perspective and texture gradient information (Arterberry, Yonas, & Bensen, 1989).

Other learning accounts for the onset of pictorial depth perception remain possible. For example, infants might learn relationships between static, monocular patterns and depth relations given by motion or stereopsis. Moreover, it is possible that, like stereopsis, development of pictorial depth sensitivity is the product of both maturation and learning, with certain types of visual experience necessary for maturational processes to proceed. Further empirical work is needed to improve our understanding of the origins of pictorial depth perception. One experimental approach that might help to decide if roles of learning and maturation would be training studies, in which a new depth cue is presented along with already usable information about depth. Of interest in a study of this type is whether infants can use the information to which they already have sensitivity to aquire sensitivity to a new type of information. Alternatively, studying infants who do not have access to early visual experience, such as those born with cataracts, may shed light on the development of pictorial sensitivity.

Effects of Distance Perception on Object Perception

In addition to its direct value, information about distance affects perception of object properties, such as size, shape, and motion. Conversely, studies of perception of shape, size, and motion can provide windows into early spatial perception. This section considers several findings of this sort that have important implications for the development of space perception.

Size Constancy

To detect an object's size requires relational information. A given object's projection on the retina, or its retinal size, varies as a function of its distance from the observer. The specific relation was shown in Figure 1.3. If S is the real size of the object and D is the distance from the nodal point of the eye (where the rays cross), then

$$S / D = s / d, \tag{3.1}$$

where s is the projective size at the retina, and d is the depth of the eyeball from the nodal point to the retina. Since d is relatively fixed for a given eye, this relationship can be conveniently expressed as

$$S = sD / k, \tag{3.2}$$

where k is a constant. It is even more convenient to think of the retinal projection in terms of visual angle. For viewing distances large relative to the object's size,[1] the visual angle Θ is given by

$$\text{Tan } \Theta = S / D = s / d, \tag{3.3}$$

and

$$S = D \tan \Theta. \tag{3.4}$$

As Eq. (3.4) indicates, one way to achieve size constancy (perception of true size despite changes in retinal size) is to combine retinal size (or visual angle) with information about viewing distance (Holway & Boring, 1941).

How size constancy develops is a classic topic in infant perception research. For constructivist views of perception, size constancy is a paradigm case. Because real size depends on distance information and projective size, size constancy illustrates the need for inference in perception. Furthermore, if distance perception itself must develop by learning, size constancy might be predicted to be an elaborate developmental construction. Learning to interpret projective size in relation to distance would require scaffolding of learning to perceive distance in the first place. Against this background, the outcomes of infant size perception are nothing short of astounding.

In some of the earliest work on this problem, Day and McKenzie (1981) found evidence that 18-week-old infants are capable of perceiving size by taking distance into account. They habituated infants to an approaching and receding object (either a small or a large model of a head). After habituation, infants were tested with the same size object and another object of a different size, both moving within the visual angle range as the habituation object. For the most part, infants looked significantly longer to the object of a new size; however, the findings were more robust when infants were habituated to the large head. The use of the moving object desensitized infants to retinal image size such that in the test infants would have already experienced the retinal image size of both the familiar and the novel display. However, the desensitization does not allow us to know whether infants would normally respond to physical size or retinal image size. Granrud (2006) addressed this question in a study in which 4-month-old infants were presented during habituation with either a small disk placed 18 cm (18.9 deg) away or a large disk placed 50 cm (11.4 deg) away. Once habituated, infants viewed the small and large disks at 30 cm (18.9 and 11.4 deg, respectively) side by side. This placement created one test display with a novel physical size but a familiar retinal size and a second test display with a familiar physical size and a novel retinal size. Infants showed a novelty preference for the novel physical size, suggesting size constancy based on distance information combined with information about the real size of the object.

Slater et al. (1990) reported convincing evidence that newborn human infants have size constancy. Their conclusion rests on a pair of experiments that are worth considering in detail. In their first experiment, they measured newborns' visual fixation preferences to pairs of objects having identical shapes but different real sizes (cubes of 5.1 or 10.2 cm per side), positioned at two different distances (23–69 cm). In all cases in which the retinal size differed, infants showed clear preferences for the object of the larger retinal size. Moreover, in one pairing, in which the retinal sizes were equal, infants showed no preference. This experiment did not test size constancy but showed that infants spontaneously look more at objects with larger retinal sizes. In the second experiment, Slater et al. familiarized infants with an object of constant size—either the large or the small cube—positioned at six different distances over six trials. Then test trials were carried out in which the large and small cubes were presented together. The large and small cubes were positioned so that they had equal retinal sizes (i.e., the cube that was twice as large was placed twice as far away). Moreover, the cube shown in familiarization was placed at a distance where it had not appeared earlier, making the retinal size of both test objects novel. If infants had detected the constant size of the object shown during familiarization, they were expected to look longer at the object of novel size during the test trials.

All 12 infants did exactly that: They devoted an average of 83.8% of total test trial looking toward the novel-sized object. Because the design was counterbalanced, the large and small cubes were each used as familiarization objects. Hence, the larger object was novel for half of the infants, and the small object was novel for the other half. An additional helpful feature of the experimental design was that the test pair was identical to the one presented in the earlier visual preference experiment, at which time evoked no reliable preference. This comparison suggests that the strong preferences observed in the size-constancy experiment could be attributed to information obtained during the familiarization procedure. This remarkable result is supported by other research (Granrud, 1987; Slater & Morison, 1985).

Apparently, size constancy is an innate visual capacity. No visual ability more directly addresses the classical arguments of Berkeley, Helmholtz, and whole generations of philosophers and psychologists about the need for learning in perception. The human infant is built to use the geometry of projection, combining projective size and distance information, from its earliest days. This finding alone militates a radically revised view of perceptual development.

Shape Constancy

When a rectangle is slanted away from an observer (i.e., rotated around a horizontal axis), its projection on the eyes will be trapezoidal. Likewise, if a trapezoidal object is slanted so that its physically larger side is farther away from the observer by just the right amount, its projection will be perfectly rectangular. Under ordinary viewing conditions, adults detect the true shapes of surfaces despite their three-dimensional orientations. This ability requires combining projective shape information with distance or orientation information. Without three-dimensional spatial information, recovering the shapes of planar objects slanted in depth should be impossible.

Several researchers have documented evidence of shape constancy in infants between 6 weeks and 4 months of age (Bornstein, Krinsky, & Benasich, 1986; Caron, Caron, & Carlson, 1979; Day & McKenzie, 1973). In these studies, infants were presented with a shape, such as a square, slanted in depth. Infants recognized the object as familiar despite the trapezoidally shaped retinal image. This work also shows that infants are sensitive to fine degrees of tilt, as small as 10 deg (Bornstein et al., 1986). Slater and Morison (1985) tested newborn shape constancy. As in their study on size constancy, the researchers first tested for whether infants can detect a change in orientation or slant of the same shape. Using square and trapezoidal stimuli, infants were presented with pairs of a trapezoid and squares at different orientations ranging from 0 to 60 deg. Preference for the square was strong at 0 deg orientation (when it was frontal), and then it declined as orientation increased, or as the retinal image became more trapezoidal. This finding shows that newborns perceive small changes in orientation. They then tested newborns for shape constancy. Infants were familiarized to a square or a trapezoid at different slants. At test, they viewed the familiar stimulus at a novel slant and a novel stimulus. Infants showed a strong novelty preference: 71.9% of attention was directed to the novel stimulus compared to the familiar stimulus at a novel slant, implying that the infants perceived the constant real shape during the familiarization phase.

Depth Information for Size and Shape Constancy

The discovery of size and shape constancy in newborns answers some very old questions but also raises some questions that have not yet been answered. Achieving accurate size and shape perception in these experiments implies that at least one source of depth information is functional at birth. Moreover, this source of depth information must indicate absolute, not relative, distance from the observer to the target. Studies to date have provided no direct evidence of what this source might be. We can make inferences based on a process of elimination. In the experimental situation, projective size and viewing distance must combine to determine size. Likewise, distance information informs the perceiver of the degree of slant of a real object based on retinal image shape. Relationships of size and texture occlusion were not available because objects in these studies were suspended in midair in front of homogeneous backgrounds. In principle, newborns may have used accommodation as a cue for distance, but accommodation at this age may not have the necessary precision. In addition, it functions only weakly as a depth cue for adults. Motion parallax is unlikely given newborn infants require substantial head support, and they seldom make lateral head movements. What remains is convergence as the most likely source of absolute distance information underlying size and shape constancy. Its precision as a source of distance information for neonates is unknown, as is the precision of newborn size and shape constancy. How precisely must size be specified to produce the appropriate dishabituation patterns in the study by Slater et al. (1990)? On the assumptions that newborns correctly register projective size and that an object will not be seen to change its size unless a change in its distance is registered, Kellman (1995) calculated that infants must locate the object with an error not exceeding 2.5 deg of convergence angle. This level of accuracy is consistent with the work on convergence discussed in Chapter 2, albeit for slightly older infants.

CONCLUSION

Views of the origins of space perception have been dominated by Berkeley's legacy, almost to the present. Although varying in particulars, empiricist or constructivist positions have held that visual stimulation is inadequate to produce accurate depth perception and that reliance on other information, such as tactual sensations or action, is required to interpret vision. At the extreme, even the ability to detect spatial relations in two-dimensional images is sometimes theorized to arise from associative learning. The emerging picture of early space perception renders all versions of these views obsolete. Neurophysiological findings indicate that the visual system is hardwired to preserve two-dimensional spatial relations from retina to visual cortex, and studies of pattern perception (see Chapter 4) indicate that pattern sensitivity begins to operate very soon after birth. These discoveries alone might necessitate only minor repairs in the traditional view that space must be constructed from experience. However, our revised picture is most revolutionary regarding the third dimension. The experimental evidence is clear in showing that human beings live in a three-dimensional perceptual world from birth. Not only do newborns perceive visually in three dimensions but also their perceptual systems appear organized to combine distance information with other information to determine important object attributes, such as size, shape, and motion. These findings require a new view of spatial perception as fundamentally based on inborn and rapidly maturing neural machinery for extraction of information about objects and arrangements in the three-dimensional environment.

Neither our description of early competence nor the mechanisms underlying it are complete, however. Some of the astonishing experimental demonstrations of infant spatial knowledge need to be followed up by research that makes clear what sources of information underlie infant performance. This is particularly true in the case of size and shape constancy. These spatial abilities require some degree of metric information about space, as opposed to merely ordinal depth information. Convergence is emerging as the likely source of distance information in these cases. The evidence for convergence is largely circumstantial, however, and more direct evidence is needed. Berkeley may have been correct in suggesting the importance in space perception of the muscular information from convergence. Its power to specify depth, however, may be a result of inborn mechanisms and not learning.

Motion-carried information about space appears to operate very early, as shown, for example, by responses to kinematic information for approach. Further study is needed here as well to uncover the very young infant's full repertoire of responsiveness to kinematic information. Perhaps our clearest developmental picture of the emergence of a depth-processing system is seen in stereoscopic depth information. The rapid onset of stereoscopic acuity at approximately 16 weeks of age and evidence for biological mechanisms for binocular vision in other species and knowledge of cortical underpinnings in humans are all consistent with a maturational account of this important depth perception ability in humans. However, this maturational account relies on appropriate, expected experience, namely the overlapping images of the two eyes.

Emerging somewhat later than stereopsis is sensitivity to pictorial depth information. It is possible that infants' attention is directed early by pictorial depth information, at approximately 3 months of age, but use of this information for perceiving depth and guiding action emerges closer to 5 or 6 months of age. The processes underlying sensitivity to pictorial depth information still remain to be determined, but for some cues, perceptional learning must be a part of the explanation. For example, familiar size is not informative if one does not know the typical size of objects, and this knowledge can only be gained from experiences with objects.

The diversity of information sources contributes to the complexity of space perception. Adults use the full repertoire to comprehend spatial arrangements under varied circumstances, from viewing distant mountains to viewing a mosquito near the tip of one's nose. Our survey has revealed that the young infant perceives three-dimensionally but uses only a subset of tools available to the adult. Can we find any organizing theme in the progression of development? We previously raised the idea that the infant perceives less comprehensively than the adult but must perceive accurately so that early learning rests on a secure foundation. On this notion, the earliest appearing sources of information might be those that have the highest ecological validity. This notion is consistent with the relatively early emergence of kinematic and binocular information (convergence and stereopsis). Because they are based on differences in the optical projection to different observation locations (a moving eye at two different points in time or the observer's two eyes at a single point in time), their ecological validity is high. In contrast, pictorial depth information is far more ambiguous and arises later in development.

This attempt to connect developmental priority with ecological validity is conjectural. It is not clear how we might obtain definitive evidence for or against it. We might consider the conjecture to be strengthened if it fits the pattern of development in other perceptual domains having multiple sources of information. Object perception, discussed in Chapter 5, is such a domain, and we revisit the ecological validity conjecture there.

NOTE

1. The exact formula, required when Θ is not small (i.e., when distance is not large relative to object size), is $\Theta = 2 \arctan (S/2D)$.

4 Pattern Perception

INTRODUCTION

Space as we have considered it so far is the container and arranger of objects and events. At smaller scales, spatial variation also defines objects and their properties, such as their shapes, textures, and local features. Spatial variation in the optical projections to the eyes also conveys the topography of surfaces. Figure 3.3C illustrates the power of fine-grained spatial variation. Even on a flat piece of paper, the impression of complex bumps and crevices in a surface is vivid.

We see a different function of pattern variation in Figure 4.1A. Here, similarities and differences of pattern elements lead to the grouping of elements into surfaces and their separation from adjacent surfaces. Such processes allow the *segmentation* of scenes into objects, beginning with the discovery of edges, where surface properties change in an abrupt manner. This kind of variation guides attention, as can be seen in Figure 4.1B. A single element "pops out" if it differs from surrounding elements. In such cases, the time needed to detect the differing element does not increase with the number of surrounding elements (Neisser, 1964). The difference between the target and background elements in this example lies in a spatial relationship. Both types of elements are composed of identical vertical and horizontal line segments, but their spatial arrangement differs. Perception of such configural relations is perhaps the defining idea of *pattern perception.*

In this chapter, we examine the origins of human pattern perception abilities. Spatial structure in two-dimensional patterns has been the subject of many studies, and our inquiry must necessarily be selective. These studies have been conducted for many different reasons. Originally, much interest in two-dimensional pattern perception stemmed from a belief that three-dimensional object perception grows out of two-dimensional form perception. This idea turned out to be wrong, as discussed later. We treat sensitivity to two-dimensional pattern variables here and reserve for Chapter 5 research that bears directly on three-dimensional object perception. Our treatment of pattern perception may appear dated. This is because much of the early work in infant perception addressed questions pertaining to pattern perception. As a result, we focus primarily on the foundational studies that have produced many interesting and useful results. Later chapters discuss how our understanding of infants' perception in a number of areas rests on these important foundations.

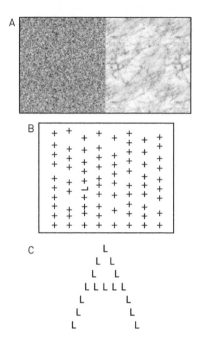

FIGURE 4.1

(A) Surface segregation by texture. (B) An illustration of attentional "pop out." The letter L is easily detected against the background texture plus signs. (C) A letter A is created by small L's, illustrating the difference between local (the L's) and global (the A) processing. Source: Created by M. E. Arterberry.

ECOLOGY OF PATTERN PERCEPTION

The ecology of pattern perception is multifaceted; important spatial relationships come in many varieties and contribute to many perceptual tasks. One unifying issue in the study of pattern perception involves the question of basic units or building blocks in perception. If we can perceive and represent an indefinitely large class of objects and patterns, these must somehow be constructed from sets of elementary constituents, limited in number. The key to understanding the flexibility and complexity of pattern and object perception might lie in the elementary pattern features and combination rules in early perception.

An early assault on this problem was Hebb's (1949) influential theory of cell assemblies and phase sequences. Complex perceptual structures were asserted to be based on neural connections built up from visual scanning of patterns in the outside world. The lowest level elements in this view were individual neural units coding specific locations. Basic features, such as an object corner, might emerge when eye movements along edges activate individual cells sequentially, causing them to become linked into *cell assemblies*. Later visual scanning of a whole shape might lead to the formation of connections among these cell assemblies into a shape representation.

In the 1960s, neurophysiological work made it clear that the visual system starts out with a richer encoding of spatial variables (Hubel & Wiesel, 1963, 1965).

Evidence that single neurons in the visual cortex are tuned to oriented edges, bars, and corners suggests that at least these spatial features need not be built through scanning or other experience. One interpretation of these findings was that they reveal innate building blocks of form perception. The possibility of such an elementary feature vocabulary was often embraced in models of pattern recognition for some time afterward.

As it turns out, the initial stage of visual filtering does not furnish directly the edges and corners of perceived objects. Instead, it appears to consist of an analysis, carried out in parallel across the visual field, of local orientation, contrast, spatial frequency, and motion. This analysis preserves spatial information but does not make it explicit. Indeed, the dominant view of this early stage of vision is that it performs in each local region a *Fourier* or *spatial frequency analysis* of the spatial luminance distribution. Any pattern of luminance can be uniquely analyzed as a combination of sinusoidally varying luminance components of different frequencies (the number of dark and light cycles per spatial unit), orientations, and amplitudes (contrasts). From these components, the original image could be reconstituted. Such a representation of the luminance distribution, however, could only be the input to perceptual analysis, not its result. A spatial frequency analysis does not make explicit objects, arrangements, or events in the external world.

Even the simple operation of locating object edges may not be accomplished by the outputs of single units in V1, the first visual cortical area. The fact that the visual system samples independently at different spatial frequencies means that a single abrupt edge of an object activates several different frequency channels. Figure 4.2 illustrates the situation. Detectors of different frequencies will signal the transition from dark to light at the position and orientation of the edge. These several responses are excellent raw material for edge detection, but edge detection would seem to require a subsequent mechanism that integrates information from these multiple channels (Marr & Hildreth, 1980; Olzak & Thomas, 1991). An even more daunting problem is that early visual analysis furnishes positions and orientations in the two-dimensional image and not the positions and orientations of features in the three-dimensional world. In short, the basic features needed for object perception or pattern recognition have to be synthesized further along in visual processing, and this may be done along different cortical pathways that then need to communicate with each other (Braddick & Atkinson, 2011; see Chapter 6).

This background, although incomplete, gives us some useful ways of thinking about the development of pattern processing by human infants. On the one hand, we might find that infants start out with the basic filtering operations of early vision, indicated by sensitivity to orientation and spatial frequency. They may lack mechanisms of perceptual organization that allow processing of relations, such as configuration, symmetry, or depth. On the other hand, higher-level mechanisms for relational perception might be included as part of the infant's initial vision package, in which case we should be able to find sensitivity to configuration, symmetry, and shape variables, and the infant would be much better equipped to process meaningfully the objects and structures in the outside world.

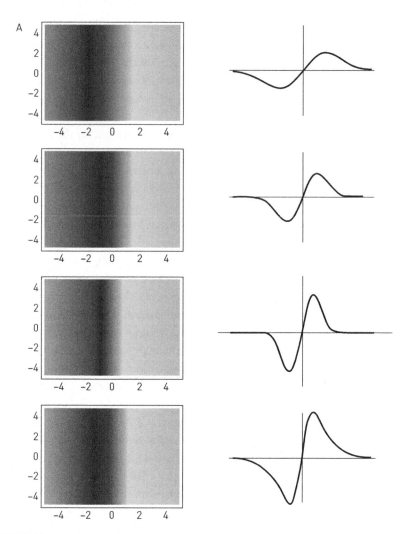

FIGURE 4.2

Relation of object edges, spatial frequency components, and spatial phase. (A and B) The top three shaded panels show luminance profiles that would activate cortical detectors of sinusoidal variations at different spatial frequencies. To the right of each panel is a graph of its luminance profile. (Luminance is given on the *y* axis for horizontal positions given on the *x* axis.) The bottom panel shows the sum of the three luminance profiles above. In panel A, the abrupt luminance edge shown at the bottom is the sum of the three different spatial frequency components shown above it. The bottom pattern would maximally activate vertically oriented channels at different frequencies all having the same spatial phase (i.e., positioning with respect to the edge). Panel B does not show a sharp edge, and activation of the several channels in this case should not signal a sharp edge. Source: Created by P. J. Kellman.

PATTERN PERCEPTION ABILITIES AND PROCESSES

Attention to Patterns

Infant attention is the means by which the experimenter accesses the infant's perceptual world. At minimum, an infant's attention must be attracted to the displays for most experimental methods to succeed. Beyond this, distinctive differences

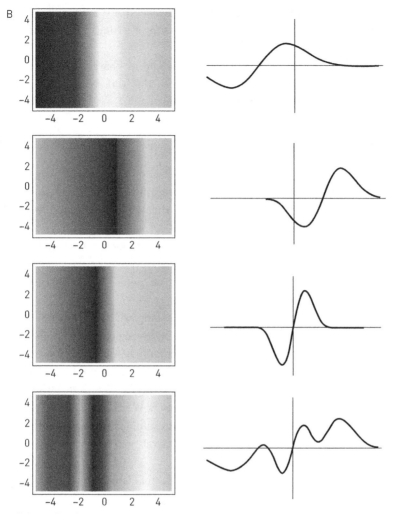

FIGURE 4.2 Continued

in infants' attention to various objects and events give us some idea of what game the infant is playing, so to speak. At any age, we can think of the infant as being involved with different perceptual tasks or having different priorities, determined by available perceptual capacities, knowledge (or lack of it), and motivation. We can gain some clues to these priorities and ask our own questions about perception by considering infants' attentional preferences.

Fantz, who developed the visual preference method (Fantz, 1958, 1961), conducted groundbreaking research on attentional preferences among patterns. He found that high-contrast stimuli were most effective in eliciting attention. Infants also preferred complex patterns and shapes. In descending order, infants most attended to a schematic face, newsprint, bullseye, red circle, white circle with black outline, and a gray circle. In general, curved lines and edges attract greater attention than straight ones, and multiple concentric circles (a "bullseye") are especially attention getting (Fantz, Fagan, & Miranda, 1975). The effectiveness of a high-contrast bullseye has led some to speculate that this stimulus preference might reflect an innate mechanism for facilitating eye contact between the infant and other people.

Since Fantz's early work, a number of investigators have attempted to understand what underlies infant pattern preferences. This work reveals important facts about infants' visual sensitivities and attention.

Pattern Complexity and Attention

Several studies have suggested that infants' attention varies with display complexity. In displays having multiple elements or repetitive features, such as checks in a checkerboard or turns in a random shape, attention increases with the number of features or elements up to some level and decreases with additional increases in complexity (Olson & Sherman, 1983). Preference for greater numbers of elements appears as infants get older. Likewise, in repetitive patterns, such as checkerboards, there may be an optimal size range or contour density that maximizes attentiveness (Karmel, 1974).

Studies of preferences related to pattern complexity provide rather indirect information about perceptual processes. An observed preference implies that the infant can see the difference between two stimuli; beyond that, it is difficult to determine whether preferences reflect differences in activation of local sensory mechanisms or whether they indicate perceptual organization—that is, experience of the pattern as having a shape or configuration. What we would like to know is whether infants' responses reflect only the barest function of early visual analysis or whether they reveal perception of configural relations. Several lines of research have sought to answer these questions.

Consider the patterns shown in the top half of Figure 4.3, used by Fantz and Miranda (1975) to study newborns' pattern preferences. Members of each pair were equated in terms of several variables (black and white areas, total length of contours, and element and angle numbers), except for the pair in column II. For example, in column I, the straight-edged square stimulus (second one from the top) was paired with the curved-edged "flower" stimulus above it. One-week-old infants preferred the curved member of each pair except for the pair in column IV, for which no reliable preference was shown. The investigators concluded that the preferences indicated form and contour discrimination by newborns.

Linear Systems Analysis

An alternative explanation is possible, however. Infants might distinguish the patterns based on any difference they pick up; perhaps there are differences between pattern pairs that do not require contour or form perception per se. Previously, we noted that a visual pattern may be analyzed as a set of sinusoidal luminance components having particular orientations, amplitudes, and frequencies. Moreover, it appears that the earliest cortical stage of visual processing may consist of this type of analysis (for review, see DeValois & DeValois, 1988). There are some interesting

| | FORM
TYPE I | FORM
TYPE II | FORM
TYPE III | FORM
TYPE IV |

0 5 10 15 20
SCALE (cm)

FIGURE 4.3

Curved versus straight-contoured stimulus pairs used to test newborn perception of form.
Source: Redrawn with permission of John Wiley and Sons, Inc. from Fantz, R. L., & Miranda,
S. B. (1975). Newborn infant attention to form of contour. *Child Development, 46*, 224–228;
permission conveyed through Copyright Clearance Center, Inc.

features of such an analysis that make it a plausible candidate for explaining what
happens in early visual processing and that also make it interesting to determine
the visual system's response to sinusoidal luminance patterns even if these were
not explicitly encoded in our nervous system. It is worth briefly describing these
features—the elements of *linear systems analysis*.

A linear system is one that obeys two constraints: *superposition* and *homogeneity*. Superposition can be defined as follows: For any inputs a and b and outputs $f(a)$
and $f(b)$, the system satisfies the relationship

$$f(a + b) = f(a) + f(b).$$

In words, the response to a combination of two inputs equals the sum of the
responses to each input separately. Homogeneity is the condition that

$$f(n \times a) = n \times f(a),$$

where n is any scalar (multiplier). That is, for an input multiplied by any quantity n, the system's response is the same as would be obtained by taking the system's response to the input alone and multiplying that output by n. Of the two conditions, superposition is more basic. (Except for some technicalities, homogeneity is derivable from superposition.)

An example of a linear system is a scale measuring weight. If two weights are placed on the scale at the same time, the measured weight should equal the sum of each measured separately. An example of a nonlinear system is a stack of some compressible items, such as lemon meringue pies. The height of 12 pies stacked on top of each other probably will not be 12 times the height of a single pie (and the whole experiment will make quite a mess).

The properties of linear systems make them easy to deal with mathematically. Moving from pies to visual displays, we are concerned with patterns of luminance distributed across space. We assume that in addition to being linear, the system is *shift invariant*, which means that if the input is shifted in space or time by a particular amount, the output is shifted by the same amount (for details, see Wandell, 1995). If a system meets these criteria, then it has the interesting property that any sinusoidally varying input will produce a sinusoidal output of the same frequency. The action of the system can alter only the amplitude (intensity at that frequency) and phase (position of the beginning of a cycle). Now here is the reason (one reason, at least) why we are interested in sinusoidal patterns. The mathematician Fourier proved that any complex pattern can be broken down into a unique set of sinusoidal components. If a system is linear, therefore, we need only know how it affects sinusoidal components at each frequency to characterize the system completely. That is, we can know the system's response to any complex pattern if we know its response to sinusoidal inputs of different frequencies, called the *modulation transfer function* of the system. The procedure consists of mathematically analyzing any input pattern into its amplitude spectrum (how much contrast at each frequency) and then altering the amplitude of each frequency component as specified by the modulation transfer function. At this point, we would have the output amplitude spectrum—a representation of the magnitude of response of the system to the particular pattern for various orientations and spatial frequencies. (To reconstitute the image passed through the system, we would also need the phase spectrum, which records the particular positioning of the amplitude components.)

To a reasonable approximation, human visual filtering through the first visual cortical area appears to satisfy the requirements of a linear system. This not only provides us with a powerful tool for understanding how an input pattern is encoded up to a certain point in visual processing but also suggests a hypothesis about early pattern sensitivity. It is possible that early in development only the outputs of this first stage of processing are functional. Thus, a pattern viewed by a neonate may produce activations in a population of detectors sensitive to various orientations and spatial frequencies. Instead of perceiving an organized pattern and responding to its configural features, an infant's attention on this view might be guided by gross features of the amplitude spectrum, such as the sum of activations of the various detectors stimulated by a pattern.

Evidence suggests that infant pattern vision starts out this way (Atkinson, Braddick, & Moar, 1977a; Banks & Ginsburg, 1985). Banks and Ginsburg investigated how a variety of experimentally observed infant pattern preferences might be explained by using simple measures based on the Fourier amplitude spectra of patterns, after filtering these in accordance with the infant's (estimated) contrast sensitivity function. Very simple indices, such as the maximum-amplitude component of a pattern and a total energy measure (summing the squared amplitudes of the components), turned out to be good predictors of published data on pattern preference for 1- to 3-month-old infants.

Attention to patterns based on component amplitude information does not require locating object edges. It is important to note that the predictive variables used by Banks and Ginsburg (1985) included no phase information. *Phase*, the relative spatial positions of the pattern components, appears to be essential for locating an edge rather than a collection of sinusoidal components. Figure 4.2 illustrates the role of phase relations in edge detection and shows that with different phase relations, patterns composed of the same spatial frequencies appear very different to adults. Direct tests of infants' discrimination of patterns having identical Fourier amplitude spectra but differing in phase were carried out by Braddick, Atkinson, and Wattam-Bell (1986). Before 2 months, they found no evidence of phase sensitivity. Both edge detection and classification would be difficult to accomplish without some sensitivity to phase.

Sensitivity to Configuration

Behavioral evidence on edge and pattern perception in the first months of life is not entirely consistent. Although pattern preferences seem to be predicted to a large extent by general activation measures obtained from linear systems analyses, there are other clues that edges and forms are perceivable by newborns.

Looking again at Figure 4.3, Fantz and Miranda (1975) found different results for the patterns in the bottom half of the figure. When all displays were enclosed by a white square, newborn pattern preferences disappeared. This effect appears to depend on the capture of attention by the outer contour of a pattern (Bushnell, 1979; Fantz et al., 1975; Haith, 1978). Such an effect would not obviously be predicted by characteristics of the Fourier transforms of these patterns. Instead, it might indicate some processing of pattern organization per se. On the other hand, it might imply some simple scanning rules that govern infant fixation (Haith, 1978). Indeed, the externality effect is one such example of infants' preferences being governed by scanning (and, as discussed later, attentional) rules.

The Externality Effect

Consider a display made of two shapes, one inside the other, such as a rectangle inside a circle. When infants younger than 2 months are presented with such a display, they seem to notice only the outer shape. Milewski (1976) labeled this phenomenon the *externality effect*. It was first identified in studies of infants' scanning by Haith, Bergman, and Moore (1977), Maurer and Salapatek (1976), and Salapatek and Kessen (1966, 1973). Infants at 1 month of age scan the external contour of a face, whereas 2-month-olds scan both internal and external features. Similarly, with simple geometric displays, 1-month-olds tend to restrict their fixations to the external edges of the display (Salapatek & Kessen, 1966, 1973).

Milewski (1976) investigated the externality effect using an operant paradigm in which visual displays were presented contingent on the infant's sucking on a nonnutritive nipple. Similar to the visual habituation paradigm, infants indicate a response to novelty by increasing their rate of sucking above a baseline. Moreover, infants' can become familiarized to or bored with a stimulus, and they indicate so by reducing their sucking rate. In the study, 1- and 4-month-old infants were familiarized with a line drawing of a circle embedded in a square. Following familiarization, infants were presented with a test display that had a novel external shape, a novel internal shape, both a novel external and internal shape, or no change. Four-month-olds responded to changes in all three change conditions with an increase in sucking amplitude. One-month-olds, on the other hand, responded only to the displays with novel external shape. Milewski suggested two possible explanations for this effect—attentional processes and poor acuity. To test for acuity limitations, Milewski presented another group of 1-month-olds with small and large single shapes. These were the same sizes as those used in the first study, but they were not compound figures. These infants responded to the changes in shape regardless of size. In another control study, Milewski tested for possible interference between contours of internal and external figures by increasing the separation between internal and external components. Still, with this increased separation, 1-month-old infants provided no evidence of discrimination of changes in shape. Based on further studies showing that 1-month-olds fail to detect a *change* in a small object adjacent to a larger one, Milewski (1978) concluded that infants have an attentional bias toward larger figures.

To study further these attentional issues, Bushnell (1979) used displays in which the internal element *moved* independently. In a habituation of looking procedure, 1- and 3-month-old infants were presented with compound figures in which the internal element either oscillated or flashed. He found that both age groups responded to a change in the internal figure. In addition, no differences were found in responsiveness of the groups that viewed a flashing element or an oscillating element. In another study, infants viewed compound displays in which the whole array oscillated. Under these conditions, 1-month-olds provided no evidence of detecting a change in the shape of the internal element. Thus, it appears that relative movement of the internal element draws attention to its shape.

Bushnell's (1979) data are also consistent with an object segregation hypothesis. Perhaps infants attend to object edges rather than textural variations within an object. Enclosure by a contour may be used as information that an area consists of one object. Differential motion of an internal area, however, might be a more powerful determinant of perceived segregation (see Chapter 5).

Ganon and Schwartz (1980) attempted to increase the salience of the internal target by making it more attractive without moving it. They used four compound figures—a bullseye or a 2 × 2 checkerboard embedded within either a triangle or a square. Using a design similar to that of Milewski (1976), Ganon and Swartz found that 1-month-olds discriminated the internal target. These results suggest that target salience can overcome the normal effects of relative size and position on infants' attention.

Global Versus Local Processing

The externality effect involves, at a minimum, two shapes, one embedded in another. Relatedly, one type of shape can be combined to make up another shape. For example, in Figure 4.1C, a large letter A is composed of small L's. A *global* response would be that the display is an A, whereas a *local* response would be that the display is a collection of L's. It is well documented that adults process such displays first globally; over time and with more effortful processing, the local features are processed.

Ghim and Eimas (1988) investigated infants' responses to such stimuli. Three- and 4-month-old infants were presented with large squares, diamonds, X's, and crosses made of small squares, diamonds, X's, and crosses. After familiarization with one shape, infants were tested for visual preferences for the familiar display and a novel display differing with respect to global form or constituent elements. Infants looked longer at the novel displays, suggesting that they are able to process and remember both local and global information available during familiarization. However, there is a global precedence, when both the global and local elements are changed. Following habituation (e.g., a square made of squares), Ghim and Eimas presented infants with a novel (a diamond) and familiar global shape (a square), both composed of novel local elements (diamonds). Infants showed a significant preference for the novel global shape. Colombo, Freeseman, Coldren, and Frick (1995) showed that individual differences may exist in the extent to which 4-month-old infants attend to local versus global features. Infants who quickly habituate (called "short lookers") process displays globally, showing an adult-like approach. In contrast, infants slow to habituate ("long lookers") process displays locally, thus perhaps explaining the longer looking times needed for these infants to process, and remember, complex displays.

Newborns have also been found to process both local and global elements in a display (Cassia, Simion, Milani, & Umilta, 2002). For example, in one study, infants were habituated to a cross made of small plus signs. Following habituation, one group saw the same cross made of plus signs and a cross made of small diamonds. Another group saw the same cross made of plus signs and a diamond made of plus signs. Both groups showed a significant novelty preference for the display with the change, whether it was at a global or a local level. Similarly to Ghim and Eimas (1988), Cassia et al. found a global precedence when local and global elements were placed in competition.

The findings with newborns, of course, are predicated on infants' ability to see both local and global elements. In everyday perception of young infants, it is likely they are responding to global features more so than local features given the ease of visibility of the larger, global, features. Combined with what we know about the externality effect, a progression from responding to outer contours or large objects to sensitivity to smaller or internal detail would be consistent with Eleanor Gibson's (1969) view of perceptual development and perceptual learning as a differentiation process, in which experience leads to extraction of finer detail.

Pattern Invariance and Change in Viewpoint

Global processing allows for attention to overall form. From one time to the next, forms are not always encountered in the same location or in the same orientation, nor are observers stationary. Thus, being able to perceive the equivalence of form or features across transpositions or changes in viewpoint is an important perceptual skill.

At the turn of the last century, Gestalt psychologists effectively criticized the dominant view of perception—that perceptions were aggregates of sensations. A cornerstone of their critique was the *transposition* argument: A form or pattern is not adequately defined as a set of sensations because the form can remain unchanged even if its constituent sensations change. Figure 1.4 illustrates several types of transposition. The "squareness" of the form remains despite changes in the retinal location of the form, whether it is large or small, whether it is made up of small circles or thin lines, or whether it is changed in orientation.

Although the Gestalt critique came bundled with a nativist view of how the nervous system apprehends form, arguments about the nature of form and about its origins in perceptual development are two different things. Form may be an abstraction, but a process to do the abstracting may or may not be within the perceptual repertoire provided to humans by evolution. A notion of form might involve relating some more elementary inputs, such as pattern features or even the eye movements required to scan a form (Hebb, 1949; Salapatek, 1975; Sutherland, 1961). Infants scan forms in systematic ways, such as fixating angles and contours (Haith, 1980).

Infant perception of form similarity across orientation was tested in a series of studies by Schwartz and Day (1979). Infants ages 9–14 weeks were habituated to a figure composed of three lines, creating an angle (a similar type of form is shown in Figure 4.4), and tested afterward for visual attention to the same form in a different orientation or a new form with a different angle between the lines. There was no reliable difference after habituation in looking times to identical patterns differing only in orientation. A pattern having dissimilar constituents (a new angle) in a similar orientation received the most dishabituation. Results of their studies led Schwartz and Day to conclude that pattern invariance is perceived by infants by 9–14 weeks. Moreover, their results also indicated that infants detect orientation differences as well as pattern identity.

Subsequent research by Slater, Mattock, Brown, and Bremner (1991) extended this work to newborn infants. Infants were habituated to simpler displays in which two black lines created an angle of either 45 or 135 deg (see Figure 4.4). During habituation, the orientation of the display varied, but the angle between

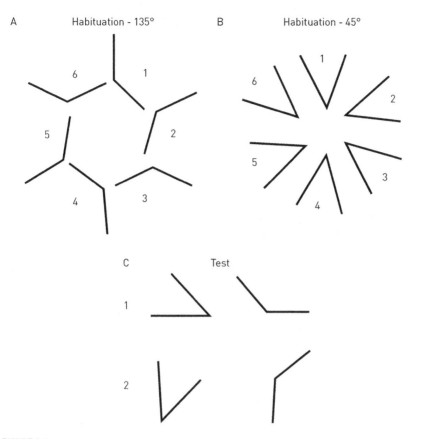

A   Habituation - 135°

B   Habituation - 45°

C   Test

FIGURE 4.4

Displays used to test newborn infants' perception of form similarity across changes in orientation. Half of the infants were habituated to set A and half to set B. (C) At test, infants saw either the two angles in set 1 or the two angles in set 2. Source: Redrawn with permission of Elsevier from Slater, A., Mattock, A., Brown, E., & Bremner, J. G. (1991). Form perception at birth: Cohen and Younger (1984) revisited. *Journal of Experimental Child Psychology, 51*, 395–406; permission conveyed through Copyright Clearance Center, Inc.

the lines did not. Following habituation, infants looked significantly longer to a display showing a new angle, suggesting that infants were able to abstract the angle between the lines across the different orientations.

Pattern invariance can also apply to three-dimensional objects. For example, at one point in time, you may view a coffee mug on your table and see that the handle is on the left of the mug. If you move around the table, the handle may be on the right side of the mug or not visible at all. Despite these variations, adults recognize the mug as the same mug. Infants are able to recognize three-dimensional objects across differing viewpoints by at least 3 months of age (Kraebel & Gehrardstein, 2006). In a mobile reinforcement paradigm, in which infants learn to kick their leg to make a mobile move and then are tested for recognition of the objects on the mobile, infants were initially trained to kick with one view (e.g., horizontal) of a multipart object. Following training, infants then saw a different view (e.g., vertical) of the same object, and they showed evidence of recognition by continuing a high level of kicking. This kicking rate was in contrast to when infants saw a new object: New objects result in a lower rate of kicking. To our knowledge, younger infants have not been tested, but based on the work of Cohen and Younger (1984), it would not be surprising if this ability also develops between 6 weeks and 3 months.

Symmetry

Well documented at least since the time of the Gestalt psychologists has been the special sensitivity of human visual processing to symmetry. Rubin (1915) noted symmetry as one factor influencing perception of ambiguous figure-ground displays (Figure 4.5). More generally, it has been argued that we tend to perceive the simplest, most symmetric organization consistent with the available information (Buffart & Leeuwenberg, 1981; Wertheimer, 1923/1958). Some phenomena that seem to involve a tendency toward symmetric perception may be explained by the operation of more local mechanisms (Kellman & Shipley, 1991; Marr, 1982); thus, the status of symmetry as a causal variable in perceptual organization remains unclear. For adults, however, symmetry is readily detected, and vertical symmetry may show cognitive advantages over other types of symmetry (Adams, Fitts, Rappaport, & Weinstein, 1954; Rossi-Arnaud, Pieroni, Spataro, & Baddeley, 2012). Even without knowing the exact mechanism, we can say that human vision exploits symmetry in detecting or encoding patterns.

Facility with symmetric patterns might be thought to arise from experience in perceiving and classifying objects. After all, animals are usually bilaterally symmetric, and plants may have symmetry along more than one axis. There are indications that sensitivity to symmetry is more deeply rooted in visual functioning, appearing quite early in infancy. Bornstein, Ferdinandsen, and Gross (1981) found that 4-month-olds habituated more quickly to a display having symmetry around the vertical axis ("vertical symmetry") than to a horizontally symmetrical or asymmetrical display. They also found that infants generalized habituation from one vertically symmetrical display to another, although they appeared less sensitive to horizontally symmetric displays. The advantage of vertical symmetry

 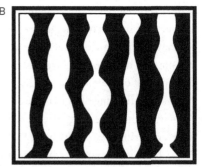

FIGURE 4.5
Symmetry in figure-ground organization. Symmetry black regions in panel A and white regions in panel B tend to be seen as figures rather than backgrounds.
Source: Created by P. J. Kellman.

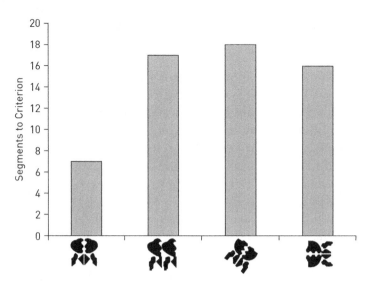

FIGURE 4.6

Habituation segments (each 10 sec) for varying in symmetry and orientation. Displays with fewer segments indicate that symmetry of the stimulus facilitated processing compared to those with more segments. Source: Redrawn with permission of Elsevier from Bornstein, M. H., & Krinsky, S. J. (1985). Perception of symmetry with infancy: The salience of vertical symmetry and the perception of pattern wholes. *Journal of Experimental Child Psychology, 39,* 82–86; permission conveyed through Copyright Clearance Center, Inc.

was explored further by Bornstein and Krinsky (1985). They recorded the number of 10-sec trials needed for 4-month-old infants' looking time to decline 50% from initial levels. Infants habituated significantly faster to vertically symmetrical patterns in Figure 4.6 compared to the other patterns shown in the figure, suggesting a processing advantage for vertical symmetry.

The pattern of greater sensitivity to vertical symmetry shown by infants is also characteristic of 3-month-olds, older children, and adults (Barlow & Reeves, 1979; Bornstein & Stiles-Davis, 1984; Humphrey & Humphrey, 1989; Mach, 1885/1959; Royer, 1981), and it also holds for 5-month-olds' manual haptic perception (Gantaz & Streri, 2004). It has been speculated that this advantage may be related to the bilateral symmetry of the visual system (Mach, 1885/1959). Another possibility is that an evolved sensitivity to vertical symmetry efficiently exploits informational redundancy in the natural world. In nature, vertical symmetry is most common— among plants, animals, and even the shapes of surfaces, such as hills and valleys. This predominance of vertical symmetry on the forms of nature is the handiwork of gravity, constraining biological priorities such as balance and locomotion, as well as geological phenomena, such as erosion.

Configural Processing of Faces

Some of the most systematic research on configurational perception has centered on face perception. The emphasis is natural given the importance of faces and observations that infants show strong preferences for faces and facelike stimuli.

Faces have a number of pattern features already discussed: They are compound displays with smaller elements (e.g., eyes) embedded in an external shape (e.g., the oval contour of the head), they are vertically symmetrical, and there are opportunities to perceive them across transpositions and/or viewpoints. Given young infants' limited acuity, limited perception of internal features, and apparent inability to respond to phase at 2 months, one might expect that face perception will also be immature in very young infants. Surprisingly, research has documented sophisticated face processing in newborns (Simion, Di Giorgio, Leo, & Bardi, 2011; Slater et al., 2011). The explanations for how infants do this range from attributing a special status to faces to which humans are innately attuned to identifying perceptual features that guide newborn attention and that also happen to be features of faces. This section briefly reviews the story of face perception research from a configural perspective; Chapter 10 addresses the importance of faces for social perception.

The story begins with Fantz and colleagues. In studies of newborns, facelike stimuli were among the strongest attractors of attention. However, a display with scrambled face parts did not fare much worse. Maurer (1985) cites 28 studies that investigated infants' preference for a normal face versus a face with the internal features rearranged or deleted. Before 2 months, infants do not show a preference for either type of display, but after 2 months of age, infants show a clear preference for a "normal" face over a "scrambled face." Many researchers concluded that for truly configurational perception, an important change appears to occur at approximately 2 months of age.

One explanation for these early preferences was suggested by several investigators applying linear systems analysis to early face preferences (Dannemiller & Stephens, 1988; Kleiner, 1987; Kleiner & Banks, 1987). The motivating question is whether observed preferences might be explained by the outputs of the earliest cortical stages of visual analysis—that is, the responses of units based on contrast, orientation, and spatial frequency. If so, early responses to faces would not imply social interest or even true pattern perception. As described previously, responses may be governed by some rule about the population of frequency detectors stimulated by the pattern.

A clever method for testing this possibility was devised by Kleiner (1987). She used two stimuli, a face and a lattice (bricklike pattern). Using the Fourier transform, she obtained the amplitude and phase spectrum of each. She then generated two new images combining the amplitude spectrum of the lattice pattern with the phase spectrum of the face and vice versa. These combinations have the effect of using the amplitudes (amount of contrast) for frequency and orientation components of one pattern but shifting their relative positions according to the phase relations taken from the other pattern (Figure 4.7, middle pair). To adults, the displays "looked" like the stimulus whose phase spectrum was used. For adults, the positional relations that create edges, corners, and other features are more crucial to pattern perception than having the correct amount of contrast for each amplitude component.

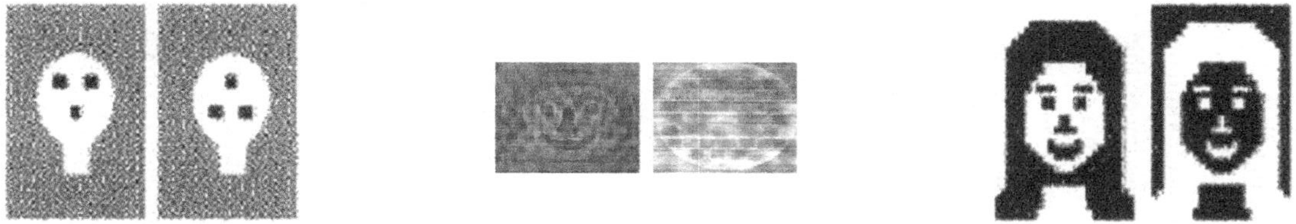

Age	Feature inversion			Phase and amplitude reversal			Contrast reversal		
	Config	Inversion	Neither	Phase of face	Amplitude of face	Neither	Positive contrast	Negative contrast	Neither
Newborns	9*	1	2	0	9*	3	0	0	12
6-week-olds	0	0	12	12**	0	0	3	0	9
12-week-olds	0	1	11	12**	0	0	12**	0	0

*$p < .05$. two-tailed binominal test. **$p < .001$. two-tailed binominal test. All other $ps > .1$.

FIGURE 4.7

Stimuli and preference results to test preferences in newborn, 6-week-old, and 12-week-old infants. Source: Redrawn with permission of SAGE Publications from Mondloch, C. J., Lewis, T. L., Budreau, D. R., Maurer, D., Dannemiller, J. L., Stephens, B. R., & Kleiner-Gathercoal, K. A. (1999). Face perception during early infancy. *Psychological Science, 10,* 419–422.

These unique displays allowed Kleiner (1987) to test two competing hypotheses—that infants' preferences for faces are based on their structure (because they look like faces) or that infants' preferences depend on the high-contrast values generated by faces in their amplitude spectra. On the latter hypothesis, pattern preference might be predicted by simple rules, such as the total energy in the amplitude spectrum or the strongest single component in the amplitude spectrum. Kleiner and Banks (1987) called this idea the "sensory hypothesis" and contrasted it with a "social hypothesis" positing that infants have some built-in sensitivity to the structure of faces. Kleiner and Banks presented amplitude and phase consistent and mixed stimuli to 2-month-olds and newborns. The linear systems model predicted 2-month-old infants' preferences; they preferred the displays with the phase spectrum of a face—that is, the display that looks facelike to adults. The results from newborns did not wholly support one or the other hypothesis. For the most part, displays containing the amplitude of a face garnered more attention supporting the sensory hypothesis; however, when shown one display composed of the amplitude and phase of a face (which looked like a face) and one display composed of the amplitude of a face and the phase of a lattice (which looked like a blurry lattice), newborns showed a strong preference for the former stimulus (a 69% preference). This finding is counter to the sensory hypothesis, which predicted no preference between these two displays, and it indicates some responsiveness to phase information by newborn infants.

At approximately the same time that Kleiner and Banks (1987) were pursuing the sensory hypothesis, Morton and Johnson (1991) highlighted one paper that did not fit the prevailing view. Goren, Sarty, and Wu (1975) found that when a facelike stimulus is moved in an arc over newborn infants, they will track it by moving their eyes and head. Interestingly, they track canonical faces farther and more reliably than scrambled ones or stimuli with no interior features. (Johnson, Dziuraweic, Ellis, and Morton (1991) replicated this effect.) Morton and Johnson (1991; see also Johnson, 2005) suggested that infants' face perception was guided initially by a subcortical process that relied on the general configuration of the face (two blobs for eyes and one for a nose were enough; see Figure 4.7, leftmost display). At approximately 2 months, face processing comes under cortical control, allowing infants to become more sensitive to the specific features of faces, which then facilitates infants' perception (and recognition) of specific faces.

One barrier to evaluating these explanations is the different methods and stimuli used to assess newborn face preferences. In an attempt to test these two explanations directly, Mondloch et al. (1999) conducted a forced-choice preferential looking study with three sets of stimuli: upright and inverted schematic stimuli like those used by Johnson and colleagues (left pair in Figure 4.7), two images that have phase and amplitude spectra in conflict (middle pair in Figure 4.7; the left display has the amplitude of a lattice and the phase of a face, and the right display has the amplitude of a face and the phase of a lattice), and two faces with contrast reversed (right pair in Figure 4.7). Moreover, they had two additional pairs of stimuli, one pitting vertical black and white bars against a gray patch to demonstrate that infants can show a preference (they should prefer the bars over the gray patch) and two pairs of black and white bars with contrast reversed, to which infants should show no preference. Twelve infants were tested at three ages: newborn, 6 weeks, and 12 weeks. As can be seen in the bottom of Figure 4.7, newborn infants preferred the schematic stimulus over its inversion, the amplitude stimulus over the phase stimulus, and showed no preference between the contrast-reversed stimuli. At 6 weeks, the schematic preference dropped away, preferences shifted to the phase stimulus (in the middle pair), but still there was no preference between the contrast reversed stimuli. Finally, at 12 weeks, a preference for the correct contrast display over the reversed contrast display was found. From these results, Mondloch et al. concluded that newborn preferences are influenced by the visibility of the stimulus and its resemblance to a face (a conclusion also reached by Valenza, Simion, Cassia, & Umilta, 1996). When the amplitude is the same (as in the left pairs in Figure 4.7), preference is for the schematic face. When amplitude is not equal, preference is for the display with the greater amplitude (which in this experiment was the lattice). The later preferences for the phase display at 6 weeks and the contrast reversed faces at 12 weeks were attributed to the role of emerging cortical processing and experience with faces.

Currently, there is no question that newborn infants perceive faces. How they do this is still debated, and the explanations continue to fall across a sensory–social continuum, although not all researchers use these specific terms. For example, Simion and colleagues (2011) suggest that certain features of displays attract newborn attention, such as top-heaviness (more features in the top half of a display compared to the bottom half) and congruency among features and external contours. And it happens that these features are characteristics of faces. Others appeal to quick learning processes, even perhaps starting in utero, to explain newborn face perception (Slater et al., 2011). Finally, an explanation building on the linear systems model suggests a role for binocular rivalry. Wilkinson, Paikan, Gredeback, Rea, and Metta (2014) suggest that newborns experience the two unfused images from each eye as a blurred image with a a small area of clarity resulting in a less blurry view of one eye of the person they are looking at, and this region attracts newborn attention. The support for their explanation is based on modeling, and although intriguing, it remains to be tested with human infants.

Together, the research suggests that preference for faces and facelike patterns is present at birth. How newborn infants perceive faces is still open to vigorous debate; however, it is clear that newborn face processing is rudimentary compared to later processing. This difference is likely governed by physiological constraints. It appears that overall activation levels in the cells of V1, where the earliest cortical visual processing occurs, strongly affect attentional preferences. By 6–8 weeks, sensitivity to true pattern characteristics appears to become more dominant. Nevertheless, we should not lose sight of the fact that newborn face perception is nothing short of amazing considering newborns' limitations in early vision and other aspects of pattern vision discussed in this chapter. Moreover, as discussed in Chapter 10, infants are not only perceiving faces but also may be recognizing their mothers, preferring attractive over unattractive faces, and perceiving eye gaze direction (Farroni, Csibra, Simion, & Johnson, 2002; Sai, 2005; Slater et al., 2000).

CONCLUSION

Infant sensitivity to surface and pattern arrangements forms a clear developmental pattern, consistent across the various lines of research. There is an early period, extending 6–8 weeks, in which pattern sensitivity can be documented but only by the most painstaking efforts of researchers. Following this period, infants exhibit a wide range of pattern perception abilities, including sensitivity to orientation, configuration, symmetry, and both internal and external features.

To this pattern of development, a maturational explanation is best suited. Various competencies that appear weak in newborns appear robustly after 6–8 weeks. The evidence seems incompatible with the idea that neural mechanisms for encoding configuration must be constructed from scanning or other associative operations, as has often been suggested (Hebb, 1949; Sutherland, 1961). Likewise, accounts based on learning by manipulation or locomotion cannot explain early pattern perception because infants in the first few months do not yet reach, crawl, or walk.

What do we know about mechanisms of change in the first 6–8 weeks of life? As discussed in Chapter 2, it has been argued that before approximately 2 months, the human infant processes visual information primarily subcortically. Subcortical processing allows directing the gaze based on stimulation outside the fovea, but true pattern vision requires the maturation of the visual cortex at approximately 2 months. At least some of the data we have considered indicate that the newborn can act to some degree in deploying visual attention to patterns that are processed in the visual cortex and beyond. However, the evidence is equally clear in indicating some deficit or bottleneck in such abilities.

The most frequently suggested bottleneck hypothesis is immaturity of visual cortical areas and of connections between cortical and subcortical structures (Braddick & Atkinson, 2011; Bronson, 1974; Johnson, 1990). Improved processing at 6–8 weeks is thought to reflect myelination of the retinocortical pathway. Explosive growth of synaptic connections is also underway by 2 months of age (Huttenlocher, 1994; Figure 2.1). Particularly important might be myelination of connections between interacting areas. Casaer (1993) hypothesized that

it is, however, not myelination such as which is important but rather whether centres in the brain which are intensively interacting are provided with fast signal-conducting pathways. The exciting developmental idea is the concept of myelination as highways connecting growing cities. (p. 106)

The evidence is on the whole consistent with the idea that improvements in overall speed or processing capacity allow more sophisticated use of previously established mechanisms. Chapter 3 presented evidence that newborns perceive true object size despite differences in distance and perceive planar shape despite different three-dimensional slants. These achievements require pattern processing of considerable sophistication. It is possible that future advances will allow us to identify particular information-processing components that are truly new at 8 weeks, but the current picture is consistent with the idea that a main effect of cortical maturation is to boost the power of abilities whose basic neural machinery is already in place. The human newborn is not merely a subcortical visual processor. Nor do configurational processing abilities appear de novo at 2 months as a result of learning or maturation. Rather, cortical maturation appears to provide the speed and capacity needed to make pattern processing more effective or, alternatively, to provide better voluntary control over attention that allows infants to demonstrate their abilities to experimenters.

One early motivation for studying two-dimensional pattern perception was that it would provide a window into the development of perception of three-dimensional space and objects. This goal has not been realized. There is no reason to believe that static two-dimensional displays are somehow simple or primary. In examining results showing pattern discrimination, we can be confident that one pattern differs perceptually from another. We may be curious, however, as to whether a figure is seen as separate from ground or whether a single two-dimensional view can evoke a percept of a three-dimensional object, as in adult perception. Little progress on these questions has come from studying pattern perception. These are different questions, and they must be asked in different ways. We turn next to these issues of object perception.

5 Object Perception

INTRODUCTION

It is an interesting exercise to glance around a room, close one's eyes, and then attempt to remember what one has seen. In a particular room, one may remember a lamp, television, sofa, some small pillows, a notepad, and a pair of shoes. It is striking that our inventory of the environment consists primarily of *objects*. Object perception reveals the physical units in the environment—where the world comes apart. It enables predictions about interactions and events. When a 2-year-old tugs your elbow, your hand is sure to follow, but the cup you are holding may not stay with your hand, and the coffee inside will surely not remain with the cup.

In obtaining knowledge about units in the physical world, vision is most important. The visual system is specialized for the extraction of spatial detail, and the interactions of light with surfaces allow us to gain precise and detailed knowledge from a distance. The packaging of much of this knowledge in terms of objects gives both a reasonable account of the physical world and an efficient vocabulary for cognition.

Any attempt to understand how object perception comes about quickly reveals that it is a complex and remarkable achievement. The physical linkages and three-dimensional arrangements of visible areas are not given by simple or obvious properties of reflected light. Rays of light do not cohere or connect to each other as do the parts of objects that reflect them. How we recover the structure of the environment from information in the light is the focus of studies of object perception.

ECOLOGY

The Relativity of Objects

From a great distance, the planet earth appears as an object, but ordinarily we experience it as an extended surface, not a bounded object. At the other extreme, a single molecule of a substance may be composed of a number of atoms, but neither the molecules nor the atoms are objects of ordinary perception. It appears that being an object depends on the observer and his or her attributes and purposes. Are objects, then, physical units, psychological units, or somehow both?

Objects are *ecological* units (Gibson, 1966, 1979): They depend on both the organism and the environment. Specifically, objects are physical units that exist in restricted niches in terms of spatial extent, temporal duration, and their coherence relative to physical forces. The relevant ranges of extent, duration, and cohesion depend on the organism's (in this case, human) capacities and behavior.

Spatially, objects, such as rocks, leaves, chairs, and shoes are bounded volumes of matter pertinent to the size and manipulative abilities of humans. In general, things that are large relative to the human body tend to be represented as surfaces rather than objects. It is interesting to consider that the objectness of certain things may change with growth and development. To an infant, a sofa may be large enough to be more or less a terrain feature, like a hill. The sofa is more object-like to adults large enough to lift and carry it.

Objects also have a temporal scale. The philosopher Nelson Goodman (1951) suggested that "an object . . . is an event with a relatively long temporal dimension" (p. 129). When we characterize an object as functionally coherent, we mean that during events such as moving or lifting, the entity retains its unity. But this coherence is conditioned on duration. The coffee mentioned previously coheres momentarily with the flying cup before making its dramatic exit. At the other extreme, it is unlikely that over centuries the ceramic cup will remain intact as a unit. What counts as an object is thus tied up with events: An object is a physical unit whose persistence in time is long relative to the duration of human actions.

The coherence of an object is considered relative to the forces involved in events. It is not an object if small biomechanical forces easily break it up; a clump of mashed potatoes is not an object. On the other hand, a ceramic cup is a perfectly good object because it survives ordinary human manipulation, even though it does not withstand being dropped on a hard floor. The relevant range of physical forces seems inescapably ecological. Perceived objects are the physical units that cohere through ordinary human activities.

There are ambiguous cases, perhaps best described as *partial* objectness. A tree rooted in the ground is neither freely moveable nor fully integral with the earth. Touching a countertop with quick-drying glue on one's fingertip, the fingertip and countertop may now cohere as strongly as the fingertip and the rest of the finger. These cases might suggest that our description of the environment in terms of objects is somewhat arbitrary. Many ambiguous cases nevertheless have a physical basis, in terms of homogeneity of composition, the nature of the forces producing cohesion, and so on. It would be a mistake not to consider the tree and its roots a coherent object because for many purposes (e.g., planting), it is one. And with the right solvent, one's finger may be unglued from the countertop.

We have not exhausted the issues involved in defining objects and their ecological basis, but we have created a serviceable framework. Objects are physically cohering, bounded volumes of matter at a scale and across the transformations relevant to human activity.

The Task of Object Perception in Infancy

Parallel to our remarks about the ecology of space perception, the functions of object perception early in life differ from those that emerge later. This difference in the functions of object perception in infancy and later on may have consequences for the emergence of object perception abilities (Kellman, 1993). Adults perceive objects from a variety of sources of varying ecological validity. The diversity of information sources may allow adults to act adaptively under the widest range of situations. In a given situation, some sources of information may not be available, but others will be. Some information may be tentative or somewhat uncertain, but the perceiver's need to make a rapid response may require using what is available. Moreover, ongoing perceptual activity may allow the adult to correct errors. For the infant, the situation is the opposite. There is little capability for split-second action and less opportunity for active exploration. Consequences of erroneous perception might be greater in infants, whose general knowledge is limited. These consequences will not involve ineffective action, but they will provide inaccurate data for the infant's developing comprehension of the world. The infant may not correct errors as well because its options for moving and exploring are limited. Evolutionarily, a premium may be placed on an ontogenetic sequence in which information of highest ecological validity comes to function earliest (Kellman, 1993). As discussed later, the order of emergence of object perception abilities is consistent with this conjecture.

Information and Constraints

Defining objects is one thing; perceiving them is another. The facts of object perception are remarkable and challenging. Following our definition, we might imagine that objectness is determined by acting on candidate objects. Does an object hold together as we move it? Does it separate from adjacent things? It is striking that these sensible tests for discovering objects play a negligible role for adult perceivers. We need not manipulate objects to perceive them. This faculty broadens our horizons of action and knowledge unimaginably. But it is mysterious. How are we able to partition the world accurately from information in reflected light (and in some cases from information in other ambient energy)? Perhaps this faculty depends on an earlier developmental stage in which objectness is determined by direct manipulation. On the other hand, at maturity, this faculty must be based on information of some sort, available when the perceiver views a scene at a distance. If there is information out there, might its use be hardwired in the nervous system rather than learned?

Understanding object perception and its origins involves understanding multiple achievements. Light reflected to the eyes does not explicitly indicate the physical linkages and three-dimensional arrangements in a scene. The optic array does contain information, but much must be done to make this information explicit. To get the kinds of representations—of objects—we obtain perceptually, we must accomplish several different tasks. As we examine these components of object perception, we will see that each, in turn, can be based on multiple sources of information. With this profile in hand, we can determine the young infant's status with regard to various object perception abilities. Infants get an early start down the road of object perception, but their vehicle is a stripped-down model compared to what adults drive. The picture of early competence and late-appearing abilities, moreover, reveals an intelligible overall pattern.

Edge Detection, Edge Classification, and Boundary Assignment

Projections to the eyes must contain information, or we could not perceive. What must be done to make that information explicit—to reach a representation that features objects, their boundaries, shapes, and so on? *Edge detection* is the first step. Which locations in the optic array might be object boundaries? Edge detection is based on locating various kinds of discontinuities in the optic array. Because objects are often made of different materials, luminance, color, and texture tend to be homogenous or smoothly varying within a single object but often change abruptly from one object to another. Boundaries are also given by discontinuities in depth and in motion (Gibson, Kaplan, Reynolds, & Wheeler, 1969; Julesz, 1971; Shipley & Kellman, 1994).

Not all discontinuities, however, correspond to object boundaries. In the case of luminance discontinuities, some are textural markings or shadows on surfaces. Also, depth and motion discontinuities may occur within a unitary object, when it is partly self-occluding. Edges once detected must therefore be classified into these functionally different categories, a process called *edge classification*. Next, there is *boundary assignment*. Visible contours most often correspond to a boundary of one object, whereas the surface on the other side of the contour continues behind (Koffka, 1935; Rubin, 1915). When one sees a tree in front of a house, the contour between the tree and the house bounds only the tree; the house continues behind. If there were a tree-shaped hole in the surface of the house, the boundary assignment would be reversed—that is, the house would be bounded, and an interior wall seen through the hole would pass behind. Boundary assignment is crucial to perceiving objects; it is an important part of the answer to Koffka's classic question: Why do we see things and not the spaces between them?

Depth and motion discontinuities at boundaries are some of the best sources of information for boundary direction. Of the two surfaces whose optical projections meet at the contour, the surface whose points have greater depth values (i.e., whose points are farther away) is the surface that passes behind at the boundary edge. During object or observer movement, accretion and deletion of texture specifies depth order, and once again, it is the nearer surface that "owns" the boundary.

Unit Formation and the Fragmentation Problem

Solving the riddles of edge detection and classification would be a major achievement but only a small step toward a full account of object perception. We have not yet introduced the most difficult problem—what might be called the *fragmentation problem*.

Spatial and Temporal Fragmentation

The spatial continuity and temporal persistence of objects contrasts with their fragmentary effects on our senses. Most objects are partly *occluded* by other objects. This problem was implicit in our description of boundary assignment. At each location where a boundary bounds one surface, another surface slips behind to destinations that are optically unspecified. A glance at the scene around you reveals the pervasiveness of these effects. For every object boundary you see, part of another object or surface is hidden at that location. How can the observer recover the structure of three-dimensional objects from optical input when virtually every boundary in the input specifies a location at which some part of an object or surface goes out of sight?

Somehow we manage. Consider the display shown in Figure 5.1. Without special effort or reflection, the display in Figure 5.1A may be seen to contain three large objects. Their shapes are shown in Figures 5.1B, 5.1D. A number of thin objects resembling blades of grass are intermingled with these objects. Each of the grasslike objects is also seen as a bounded object. With effort, we can count them and find that there are 12. Far more daunting is the task of counting the number of homogenous regions that connect to form each object. The shape in Figure 5.1C as it appears in Figure 5.1A is formed by combining 11 regions separated by occluding surfaces, the object in Figure 5.1D is formed from 8 regions, and the object in Figure 5.1B is formed from 5 regions. It is a revealing fact about the function of human visual perception that its outputs are complete objects and not the shapes of visible regions.

We have only scratched the surface of the perplexities in Figure 5.1A. Here are a few more. The regions we have been referring to as homogenous are really not in any simple sense; most have gradients of luminance (changing shades of

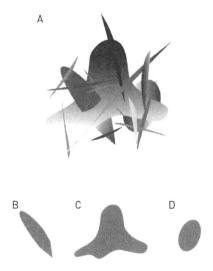

FIGURE 5.1

Example of perceptual unit formation despite spatial fragmentation. The unoccluded objects shown in panels B–D are readily perceived in panel A despite the numerous instances of partial occlusion and luminance variation. Source: Created by P. J. Kellman and redrawn with permission of Elsevier from Kellman, P. J. (1996). The origins of object perception. In R. Gelman & T. K. Au (Eds.), *Perceptual and cognitive development: Handbook of perception and cognition* (2nd ed., pp. 3–48). San Diego, CA: Academic Press.

gray). As is common in ordinary environments, widely separated and differently colored visible regions may belong to a single object. The perception of whole objects, rather than such separate regions, cannot be explained by familiarity; the shape shown in Figure 5.1C, for example, was designed to be unfamiliar and could hardly be considered more familiar than many smaller regions in the image. Not all areas of similar luminance are seen as connected. In the figure, there are several examples of object boundaries that traverse areas identical in luminance; these are *illusory contours*. One example is the midsection of the "blade of grass" at the top of Figure 5.1A. An even more curious phenomenon occurs for the object in Figure 5.1B. As it appears in Figure 5.1A, this object passes through the surface of another object. Seeing it as one object requires linking separated parts into a unit that pierces the other object.

The ubiquity of partial occlusion derives from very basic facts: Light moves in straight lines, most objects are opaque, and environments usually contain objects at different distances from the observer. Fortunately, human perceivers possess visual processes equal to the physical demands of occlusion: In Figure 5.1A, they turn the chaos of 45 projected regions into three objects and some stray foliage. In doing so, human perceivers are *interpolating contours* across gaps in proximal stimulation (Kellman, Garrigan, & Shipley, 2005). In other words, they are perceiving edges where none are physically specified, and they are doing it in such a way as to segment the visual array into discrete objects.

So far, we have described spatial fragmentation, but fragmentation occurs across time as well. As we move through an environment, the bits and pieces of objects that reflect light to the eyes and the occluded parts constantly change. Because visual acuity is relatively poor outside of the fovea, we also sample stationary environments over time with frequent changes of gaze. We may have a particular view of an object for 100 or 200 msec, or perhaps as long as several seconds, but seldom much longer. Human perceivers recover objects' continuity despite temporal fragmentation.

Information for Unit Formation

What information is available about connected objects in the world? Valuable types of segmentation and grouping information come from motion. Motion is closely related to the notion of an object (Spelke, 1988); to be an object is to maintain coherence during movement. A connected entity's parts are constrained; they may move only in certain ways while remaining connected. For three-dimensional rigid objects, projective geometry allows us to precisely characterize what optical changes can occur as the objects move through space (Braunstein, 1976; Johansson, 1970; Ullman, 1979). Nonrigid objects produce a greater variety of projective changes, but the class of transformations is still limited by the connectedness of the object. Conversely, certain optical transformations are not consistent with the possibility that two viewed areas are part of the same object.

A number of other stimulus relationships that play a role in perception of object unity were articulated by the Gestalt psychologists, who were the first to seriously wrestle with problems of unit formation (Koffka, 1935; Michotte, Thines, & Crabbe, 1964; Wertheimer, 1923/1958). Motion's role was expressed as a principle of *common fate*: Things are grouped together if they move together. Other principles apply to stationary arrays. The principle of *good continuation* holds that a straight or smoothly changing contour comprises a unit, whereas an abruptly changing one may not. *Good form* suggests that optical input is organized so that simple, symmetrical objects are perceived. Similar parts are unified according to the principle of *similarity*, and nearby things are grouped by *proximity*. These principles were explicitly applied to the problem of recovering unity of partly hidden objects by Michotte et al.

The Gestalt descriptive principles do not permit precise or quantitative predictions, and most of the key terms in the Gestalt laws resisted formal definition for most of the past century. These include the "good" in good continuation and good form and also the notions of simplicity, common fate, and similarity. Nevertheless, the principles contained important insights, most of which could readily be illustrated.

Two Processes in Unit Formation

Contemporary work has made progress in giving more precise form to the Gestalt principles. Kellman and Shipley (1991) proposed dividing information for unity into two categories—the *rich* or *edge-sensitive* and the *primitive* or *edge-insensitive* processes.

The edge-insensitive process elaborates Wertheimer's (1923/1958) idea of *common fate*. Visible areas that share certain geometric classes of motion relationship are grouped together. The class of rigid motions (motions that preserve interpoint distances in three-dimensional space) is certainly included, but certain nonrigid motions might be included also. The process is edge insensitive because the positions and orientations of the edges of visible parts play no role in determining their completion behind the occluding object. This information does not specify the exact form of the hidden parts under occlusion. For this reason, Kellman and Shipley (1991) labeled it the "primitive process" (cf. Hebb, 1949).

The edge-sensitive process depends on edge positions and orientations, both in stationary and in moving displays. Many of its formal properties, and some of its neural mechanisms, have been elucidated in recent years (Field, Hayes, & Hess, 1993; Kalar, Garrigan, Wickens, Hilger, & Kellman, 2010; Kellman & Shipley, 1991; Polat & Sagi, 1993; Shapley & Gordon, 1987; von der Heydt, Peterhans, & Baumgartner, 1984). The input–output relations in this process may be thought of as a mathematical formalization of the Gestalt principle of good continuation— that is, that segmentation and connection of parts depend on straight lines and smooth curves. Detailed models of the edge-sensitive process may be found elsewhere (Grossberg, 1994; Kellman & Shipley, 1991; Kellman et al., 2005). For our purposes, two points are most important. First, for adults, certain edge relationships support object completion (such edges are termed *relatable*), whereas others do not (Kalar et al., 2010; Kellman et al., 2005). Figure 5.2 gives some examples of

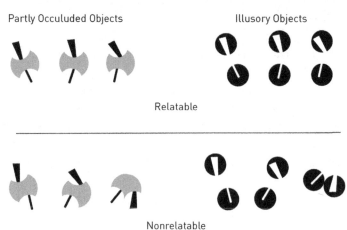

Relatable

Nonrelatable

FIGURE 5.2

Examples of relatable and nonrelatable edges. *Relatable edges*: In the upper left quadrant, edge relations of the visible black areas satisfy the geometric criterion of reliability, and they are seen as connected behind the occluder. In the upper right quadrant, the same contour relations produce illusory contour connections across gaps. *Nonrelatable edges*: When the same visible areas do not satisfy the criterion of reliability, they are not perceived as connecting across gaps. Source: Created by P. J. Kellman; after Kellman and Shipley (1991).

relatable edges and nonrelatable edges. The definition of edge relatability is a mathematical one, but it can be understood intuitively as expressing the constraints that boundaries constructed by the visual system are smooth (i.e., they contain no sharp corners), are monotonic (they are singly inflected), and do not bend through more than 90 deg. Second, the boundary interpolation process at work in occlusion cases is the same as in illusory figures (Kalar et al., 2010; Kellman, Yin, & Shipley, 1998; Ringach & Shapley, 1996; Shipley & Kellman, 1992).

Experimental evidence from adults supports the relatability criterion as a description of the edge-sensitive process (Kellman & Shipley, 1991; Kellman et al., 2005; Shipley & Kellman, 1992), although there may be additional constraints on unit formation. This account of unit formation emphasizes local edge tangents and their relations, rather than more global processes such as overall symmetry of resulting objects or familiarity of objects, in the process of boundary perception. It thus differs from both Gestalt accounts and empiricist or associationist accounts. In contrast with rather open-ended inference or hypothesis-testing accounts (Gregory, 1972; Rock & Anson, 1979), the process appears to be governed by more autonomous mechanisms, consistent with evidence that completion and illusory contour formation are based on early visual processing (von der Heydt et al., 1984).

Three-Dimensional Form Perception

Once unit formation is complete, objects are segregated from surrounding surfaces, and remaining aspects of object perception have to do with their specific properties. Of these, *three-dimensional form* is especially important because much of what we do with objects depends on their forms. Even in cases in which some object property other than form, such as edibility, is most important, it is by means of form that we recognize objects.

Adults perceive three-dimensional form from at least three different sources of information, and each of these stands as the canonical example for a theory of form perception. We often perceive—or recognize—the whole form of a familiar object from a single, static view. From past experience, we may know what a certain three-dimensional object looks like from a particular viewpoint. This means of perceiving form illustrates John Stuart Mill's (1865/1965) definition of an object as "the permanent possibilities of sensation." On this view, the object's three-dimensional reality consists of its various retinal projections from different viewpoints. With experience associating the various views, each comes to evoke the set of possible views as well as other object properties, such as the feel of the object.

The Gestalt theorists also emphasized form perception from a single view but for radically different reasons. Even unfamiliar objects could be perceived this way because the two-dimensional stimulation sets in motion organizational forces in the nervous system that lead to perception of simple, regular, three-dimensional forms. The proposed neurophysiology connected to these ideas seems implausible today, but we might still argue that form perception depends on unlearned organizational tendencies. On the other hand, Brunswick (1956) suggested that these tendencies might be acquired by experience with object regularities.

A third theory emphasizes the role of motion in form perception. Information given by continuously changing optical projections, often called *structure from motion* (Ullman, 1979) and originally called the *kinetic depth effect* (Wallach & O'Connell, 1953), enables perception of three-dimensional form. As an object rotates or as an observer walks around an object, the projection to the eyes deforms. The observer does not see a deforming two-dimensional projection, however. Rather, the transformations are seen as a three-dimensional object of unchanging shape that is rotating in space. As noted previously, for a rigid object, the particular set of transformations received at the eye can be deduced using projective geometry from the structure of the object and the relative motion between object and observer. However, the task of vision is the reverse—to recover the object's three-dimensional structure from the optical transformations received. Under reasonable assumptions, these transformations in principle allow recovery of three-dimensional object structure (Gibson, 1966, 1979; Johansson, 1970; Ullman, 1979).

ABILITIES AND PROCESSES

We now have in hand a sketch of the components of object perception and of the information and constraints that make each possible. Our taxonomy looks something like this: edge detection, edge classification, boundary assignment, unit formation, three-dimensional form perception. This breakdown is helpful in appreciating the multiple tasks involved in extracting objects and their properties from optical information. It does not represent a linear sequence of operations performed in perceiving objects. Although some steps logically precede others (e.g., edge detection precedes edge classification and boundary assignment), others may have a more complex relationship, such as unit formation and boundary assignment (Kellman & Shipley, 1991). Breaking object perception into these components does not constitute a sequential model but equips us to usefully examine the origins of object perception, which we now proceed to do.

Edge Detection

We can make some reasonable inferences about the early status of these abilities from other research. In Chapter 4, we reviewed infant sensitivity to differences among two-dimensional shapes and patterns. Taken at face value, discrimination between two shapes might be interpreted as implying at least edge detection. Similarly, infants' ability to detect a mismatched shape from a field of otherwise matching shapes (e.g., a "plus sign" in a field of L's; Adler & Gallego, 2014) suggests sensitivity to edges and the relations among the segments. Other research suggests that infants approximately 7 or 8 months old are sensitive to luminance changes specifying edges of objects and that they can discriminate the difference between edges and surface markings (Kavšek, 1999; Yonas & Arterberry, 1994). To define shape, it might be argued, an edge must be classified as a surface boundary rather than a shadow or textural marking. This conclusion is not obvious, however. Recall our discussion of linear systems analysis. A pattern could be detected in terms of its Fourier components, and any detectable difference in the amplitude spectra of two patterns might be a sufficient basis for distinguishing them.

Other research, however, suggests an early capacity for perceiving edges and much more. Newborn shape and size constancy strongly imply that newborns can detect and classify edges in at least some circumstances. If the planar shape of an object is perceived despite its three-dimensional slant, the perceiver must represent that object as bounded and situated in three-dimensional space. A similar argument can be made from the size constancy results. If real object size is perceived across a range of distances and projective sizes, as the newborn results suggest, the object's boundaries must be registered.

What is the basis for early edge detection? Both luminance edges and depth discontinuities (between object and background) were available in the studies of size and shape constancy. In other research suggesting edge detection, such as some studies of face perception and the externality effect, only luminance differences were present. Kinematic information also appears to specify edges as early as tested (Johnson & Mason, 2002; Kaufmann-Hayoz, Kaufmann, & Stucki, 1986).

There is currently little information on the limits of early edge detection abilities. Pattern perception research has typically used high-contrast boundaries. We can guess from our discussion of contrast sensitivity in Chapter 2 that much of the fine detail and many low-contrast edges perceptible by adults are not detectable by infants. On the other hand, adult sensitivity far exceeds the minimum required for normal perception of objects and events, and infant sensitivity improves quickly from birth to approximately 6 months.

Edge Classification

Early shape perception may imply edge detection, but edge classification is less clear-cut. Infants do appear to have an early capacity for classifying edges as object boundaries. Accretion and deletion of texture allows shape perception by 3-month-olds, but this result does not necessarily imply edge classification (Kaufmann-Hayoz et al., 1986). Other research indicates that 5- and 7-month-olds reach preferentially for the edges of objects specified by accretion and deletion of texture (Granrud et al., 1984). Moreover, as discussed later, relative motion of adjacent objects may also provide information for edges.

Strikingly, there is a possibility that luminance and chromatic edges do not specify object boundaries until a relatively late age. When a shape of one color (and lightness) is seen against a background of differing color, adults ordinarily see the (projectively) enclosed area as figure and the surrounding surface as ground (Rubin, 1915). It is not clear that this is the case for infants. Instead, they may see the shape as a differently colored region on a continuous surface rather than as a separate object.

Some observations made by Piaget (1954) may be the earliest indications of this perceptual limitation. When Piaget's child Laurent was 6 months, 22 days old, Piaget noted that

Laurent tries to grasp a box of matches. When he is at the point of reaching it I place it on a book; he immediately withdraws his hand, then grasps the book itself. He remains puzzled until the box slides and thanks to this accident he dissociates it from its support. (p. 177)

Piaget concluded that Laurent did not segment the array into separate objects when it was stationary. In other words, visible luminance edges may not be classified as object boundaries. Piaget estimated that such segmentation abilities may not arise until approximately 10 months of age.

Piaget's (1954) observations might be subject to other explanations. Later experiments, however, have supported his account. In displays with adjacent objects (one next to another), infants have trouble segmenting the two objects, even if there are color and textural differences. For example, 3-month-old infants are not surprised when two objects that are clearly perceived as two objects by adults based on differences in surface features or junction information move together laterally (Needham, 1999; Spelke, Breinlinger, Jacobson, & Phillips, 1993) or in depth (Kestenbaum, Termine, & Spelke, 1987).

Von Hofsten and Spelke (1985) addressed similar issues using infants' reaching behavior. Five-month-old infants were presented with displays consisting of a small, near object; a larger, farther object; and an extended background surface (similar to Piaget's matchbox and book only oriented vertically rather than flat on a table). In some conditions, the larger object moved, either rigidly with the background surface or with the smaller object. It was assumed that reaches would be directed to perceived boundaries of graspable objects (usually the one perceived as nearest in an array). Spatial and kinematic relations between the objects were varied, and infants' reaches were recorded. Much as Piaget (1954) had observed, when the array was stationary and the objects were adjacent (the smaller one touched the larger one), infants reached more to the edges of the larger, farther object. This result suggests that infants perceived the two objects as a unit and distinguished the unit from a large extended background surface (as Piaget had also noticed). Separating the two objects in depth, however, led infants to reach more to the nearer, smaller object. Motion also produced object segregation; when the larger object moved differently from the smaller object, more reaches were directed to the smaller, closer object. This clever manipulation excluded the possibility that infants merely reach for visible moving surfaces; motion of the larger, farther object increased reaching to the smaller, stationary one. The results support the idea that discontinuities in motion or depth segregate objects, whereas luminance discontinuities do not (see also Needham, 1999; Vishton, Ware, & Badger, 2005).

In summary, some sources of object boundary information have higher ecological validity: They more accurately indicate physical separation in the environment. Depth and motion discontinuities are less ambiguous than luminance and color changes. The latter may arise from object boundaries but also from textural variation on continuous surfaces. Together, these results make sense from a functional standpoint. Early edge classification appears to fit the theme that more valid information sources arise earlier in perceptual development.

Boundary Assignment

If an object is seen in front of another object or background, boundary assignment has occurred. The bounded object "owns" the visible contour; the other visible surface continues behind. Evidence that infants distinguish shapes, or figures from grounds, might indicate that they compute boundary assignment.

We may consider the Slater and Morison (1985) shape constancy result with newborns as suggesting both edge classification and boundary assignment, probably from discontinuities in depth at object edges. Much of the world and also observers are in motion, and accretion and deletion of texture appears to be a good candidate for reliable information; infants as young as 5 months reached for the surface specified to be nearer by texture accretion and deletion, suggesting not only boundary assignment but also perception of two surfaces in depth (Granrud et al., 1984). Defensive responding to a looming object may also imply boundary assignment. The infant might be reacting to a substantial object approaching, whereas if boundary assignment were reversed, it would be an approaching aperture. Indeed, that is what happens. Three- to 5-month-old infants show more defensive responses to approaching objects than apertures, and responsiveness to the looming object increases as more accretion and deletion of texture is present

(Schmuckler & Li, 1998; see Figure 3.5). In more complex scenes, the ability to detect and assign boundaries may come later in the absence of motion (Vishton et al., 2005; von Hofsten & Spelke, 1985).

Unit Formation

At this point, we know that from certain kinds of information, such as depth or motion, young infants parse the world into visible pieces. Each such piece may "own" some of its boundaries but be enclosed at others by occlusion boundaries—that is, boundaries belonging to some nearer object. What abilities do infant perceivers possess to sew together these visible pieces behind their occluders and arrive at representations resembling the real three-dimensional objects in the world?

To study infants' perception of unity under occlusion, Kellman and Spelke (1983) developed a method using habituation and recovery of visual attention. Suppose a partly occluded object such as that shown in Figure 5.3A (to us it looks like a rod behind a block) is shown on repeated trials during a habituation period. If infants perceive this display as containing a complete object continuing behind the occluder, then they should look significantly longer to the novel broken rod (the display that

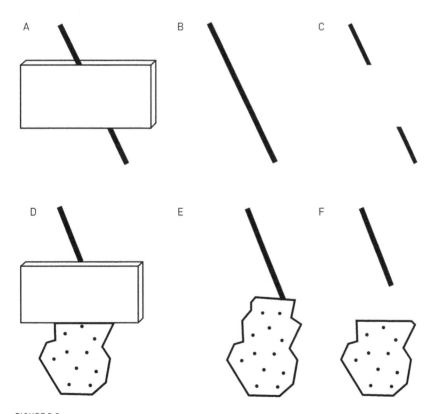

FIGURE 5.3

Habituation (A and D) and test stimuli (B, C, E, and F) used to test infants' perception of partly occluded objects. Source: Redrawn with permission of Elsevier from Kellman, P. J., & Spelke, E. S. (1983). Perception of partly occluded objects in infancy. *Cognitive Psychology, 15*, 483–524.

corresponds to the visible areas of the object present in the occlusion display) than to the complete object, even though the center region of the complete rod had not been seen previously. The two test displays are shown Figures 5.3B and 5.3C.

Using this method, perception of object unity and boundaries from both edge-insensitive and edge-sensitive processes was studied in 16-week-old infants. At 16 weeks, maturation of basic visual sensitivities has occurred, but skilled reaching and self-locomotion have not yet begun. Accordingly, unit formation abilities that depend on learning by association of touch or action with visual information should not yet be present.

Common Motion and Edge Relatability

An experiment conducted by Kellman and Spelke (1983) maximized the information available by providing common motion (which should be usable by the edge-insensitive process) and edge relatability (which should be usable if infants have the edge-sensitive process). Similar to Figure 5.3A, the occlusion display consisted of two visible, aligned parts of a rod that shared a common lateral translation behind the block. Infants were habituated to this display and tested afterward with two unoccluded test displays, presented in alternation. The complete test display contained a moving complete rod, and the broken test display consisted of two moving rod pieces separated by a gap where the occluder had been. After habituation, infants showed the pattern that would be expected if the occlusion display had been perceived as a unified object; they dishabituated markedly on the first test trial to the broken display but not to the complete display (Figure 5.4). This study indicated that some unit formation ability operates by 16 weeks of age but did not distinguish the edge-sensitive and edge-insensitive processes because information usable by both was present.

Isolating the Common Motion (Edge-Insensitive Process)

To determine which class of information determines infant unit formation, Kellman and Spelke (1983) used a display similar to that shown in Figure 5.3D. Protruding from behind the occluder was a black rod at the top and a red blob-shaped piece with black textural markings. The visible edges of these two parts are not relatable, nor are they linked according to similarity or any other Gestalt principle. During habituation, the visible parts moved side to side with a common lateral translation. Results were similar to those of the first study: Infants responded as if the two visible parts were connected behind the occluder. The broken test display that included only the parts previously visible in the occlusion display produced strong recovery of visual attention (Figure 5.3F). The complete test display, which was constructed by continuing the rod halfway down and the random blob halfway up, induced little recovery from habituation (Figure 5.3E).

The edge-insensitive process appears to operate at 16 weeks: Common motion alone specifies object unity. An interesting sidelight of these results is that they occur despite the fact that the specific form of the connection between the two

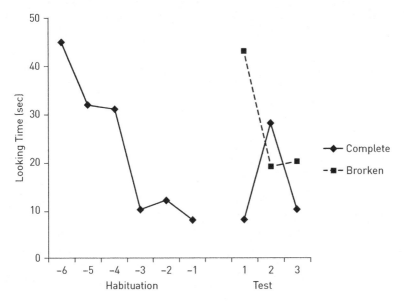

FIGURE 5.4

Results of an experiment testing unity perception from common motion and relatable edges. Four-month-old infants were habituated to two aligned, visible parts sharing a common lateral translation (either A or D pictured in Figure 5.3). Looking times are shown for the last six habituated trials (with the final one labeled –1) and the test trials. Test trials consisted of successive presentations of unoccluded complete and broken displays, with half of the subjects seeing the complete display first. Source: Redrawn with permission of Elsevier from Kellman, P. J., & Spelke, E.S. (1983). Perception of partly occluded objects in infancy. *Cognitive Psychology, 15*, 483–524.

differing visible parts is unspecified in the occlusion display. The edge-insensitive process indicates unity but not the specific form of the occluded region. The complete test display must contain some novel contours in the region that had been covered; however, this display evoked little dishabituation. It seems that visual attention in this situation is controlled more by unity or connectedness than by specific form—a conclusion supported by Craton (1996), Johnson, Bremner, Slater, Mason, and Foster (2002), and van der Walle and Spelke (1996).

Subsequent research sought to specify what motion relationships underlie the edge-insensitive process. Kellman, Spelke, and Short (1986) found that rigid translations along any axis, including translations in depth, lead to infants' perception of object unity. The use of projective geometric information in rigid translations in object perception is consistent with ecological theories of how perception works and how it gets started (Gibson, 1966, 1979; Johansson, 1970). An even more elegant story would be one in which infant perception utilized the full class of rigid motions—that is, rotations as well as translations. Some types of rotation, however, do not specify object unity until 6 months of age, and it is not clear when oscillation is effective. If the rod rotates around a central point behind the occluder (it moves like a pinwheel), infants do not perceive unity (Eizenman & Bertenthal, 1998). If a solid object rotates on a vertical axis such that it looks like it is spinning in depth behind the occluder, 4-month-olds, and possibly 2-month-olds, perceive the object as solid (Johnson, Cohen, Marks, & Johnson, 2003). Thus, it appears that the class of motions engaging the edge-insensitive process in the early months is not the full class of rigid motions. In particular, common direction of visible parts seems to be required. In contrast, for adults, the full class of rigid motions, as well as many nonrigid ones, supports object unity.

The Nature of Motion in Unit Formation: Evidence of Position Constancy

Further work shows that object motion, not retinal motion, is key. Optical events similar to those given by a moving object can arise from another source— movement of the observer. When a stationary observer views a rightward translating object, its image moves on the observer's retina. The same optical displacement can arise if the observer views a stationary object and moves to the left. The ability to distinguish between the optical transformations due to object motion and observer motion is crucial to perceiving the world as remaining stable when the observer moves—an ability called *position constancy*.

Many perceptual theorists have suspected that achieving position constancy requires extensive learning. Prior to experience, events of object and observer motion may be confused with one another (Helmholtz, 1885/1965). From experience, the observer becomes able to interpret particular optical changes as motion of an object or of the self. Helmholtz suggested that a useful source of information might derive from the fact that observer-induced optical changes tend to be reversible. One can make an object (optically) slide to the left by moving one's head to the right. A moment later, one can put everything back in place by moving one's head to the right. When objects move, the changes are not reversible by the observer's action.

Another possibility exits, however. J. Gibson (1966, 1979) noted that object and observer motion have different optical properties. Object motion produces changes between the object and its background that are in general different from what happens when the observer moves while viewing a stationary array. Given the ecological importance of distinguishing object and observer motion, it is possible that perceptual mechanisms sensitive to such differences exist even in young infants.

These questions—whether infants distinguish optical information for object and observer motion and, if so, which of these provides information for unit formation—were investigated by Kellman, Gleitman, and Spelke (1987). Infants sat in a moving chair that was moved back and forth along a wide arc. In a *conjoint motion* condition, shown in Figure 5.5A, the infant's chair and a partly occluded object were rigidly connected beneath the display table so that they rotated around a vertical axis in between. This condition contained real motion of the object in space but no physical displacement relative to the infant. If real object motion underlies unit formation, and if it is detectable by a moving observer, this condition was expected to lead to perceived unity. In an *observer movement* condition, shown in Figure 5.5B, the infant was moved in an arc while viewing a stationary occluded rod. If optical displacement alone can specify unity, infants were expected to

A

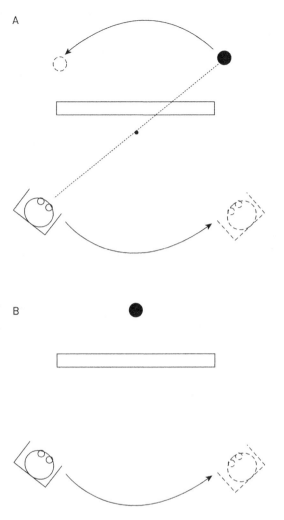

B

FIGURE 5.5
Top view of arrangement used to test infants' perception of unity under conditions of
observer and object motion. (A) Conjoint motion condition. (B) Observer motion condition. Source: Redrawn with permission of the American Psychological Association from
Kellman, P. J., Gleitman, H., & Spelke, E. S. (1987). Object and observer motion in the perception of objects by human infants. *Journal of Experimental Psychology: Human Psychology and
Performance, 13*, 586–593.

perceive a complete object in this condition. Infants' looking patterns revealed that
those in the conjoint movement condition perceived the unity of the rod (i.e., they
looked longer to the broken rod in the test trials). Infants in the observer movement condition looked equally to the two test displays, suggesting that they were
unable to perceive the unity of the two visible ends of the rod. Separate analyses,
based on looking time differences to moving and stationary displays, suggested
that infants in the conjoint motion condition perceived object motion during their
own motion, whereas infants in the observer movement condition perceived the
display as stationary. These results provided the first indication that young infants

can distinguish optical changes from object and observer motion and that they can perceive moving and stationary objects during their own movement.

Real object motion, but not optical change given by observer motion, supports the edge-insensitive process. The reliance of unit formation on real motion, not optical displacement in general, makes sense in terms of the ecological validity of the two kinds of information. When two visible parts move through space with an unvarying relationship, they are virtually certain to be connected. Such a rigid relationship between moving objects would not occur by chance for very long. Thus, rigid motion of object parts has very high ecological validity for specifying unity.

Development of the Edge-Insensitive Process

Is the edge-insensitive process an unlearned foundation of object perception? To address this question, we need to know how it operates earlier in life than 4 months of age. Researchers have used similar rod–block displays to test perception of unity in 2-month-olds and newborns. Johnson and colleagues (Johnson & Aslin, 1995; Johnson & Nanez, 1995) found that 2-month-olds perceived a rod moving behind a block as complete as long as the block was not too wide (26% of the rod occluded as opposed to 41%) and when all parts of the rod were visible over time (there were gaps in the block behind which the rod moved). Moreover, infants between 2 and 3 months of age are more successful at perceiving object unity if they visually attend to both ends of the rod and its path of motion (Amso & Johnson, 2006; Johnson, Davidow, Hall-Haro, & Frank, 2008; Johnson, Slemmer, & Amso, 2004). Thus, 2-month-olds are able to perceive object unity under some conditions; however, these conditions must allow for easy interpolation across the gap, either by showing the middle region of the rod across time or by reducing the size of the gap (see also Arterberry, 2001).

Newborn infants, in contrast to 2- and 4-month-olds, show a consistent preference for the complete rod following habituation (Slater, Johnson, Brown, & Badenoch, 1996; Slater, Johnson, Kellman, & Spelke, 1994; Slater et al., 1990). This finding suggests that they perceived the rod as broken during the habituation phase, even though the size of the rod and the depth separation of the rod and block were increased in comparison to those used with 4-month-olds and when the block height was reduced and texture was added to the background to increase the available information specifying the depth relations (Slater et al., 1994, 1996). The implications of these findings are that newborns are making their perceptual judgments based on the visible parts of the displays, and they cannot make judgments about the parts of the visual array that are occluded.

Although initially it appears that newborns begin life with an incorrect perceptual rule, assigning occlusion edges as object boundaries, it is more likely that newborns lack some basic visual sensitivity needed to detect common motion. It was noted in Chapter 2 that basic sensitivity to motion direction seems to be lacking before 6–8 weeks of age, probably due to immaturity of cortical areas (Braddick, Birtles, Wattam-Bell, & Atkinson, 2005). In occlusion situations, a newborn may detect motion but not the directional coherence of separate parts. If so, the visible areas may be perceived as separate bounded fragments. In other words, the fact that some parts of the array move and others do not may be detectable and may be used to segregate objects. Without perception of common motion direction, however, unit formation may not occur. This possibility was tested by Valenza, Leo, Gava, and Simion (2006). They presented newborn infants with displays in which the rod movement was specified by stroboscopic or apparent motion. In several experiments, the rod appeared to either move laterally (as would be the case for translation) or to oscillate back and forth behind the occluder. Following habituation, infants looked significantly longer to the broken rod, suggesting that they were able to use stroboscopic motion to perceive the common motion of the visible ends of the rod, and thus the unity of the rod behind the block, in the habituation phase.

Available evidence is consistent with the idea that the edge-insensitive (common motion) process is unlearned and, under typical viewing conditions, awaiting the maturation of directionally sensitive mechanisms to operate. The similar timing of the appearance of directional sensitivity and the edge-insensitive process, along with the difficulties involved if infants begin with an incorrect perceptual rule, cast doubt on, but do not exclude, a role for learning in the development of the edge-insensitive process (for a different interpretation, see Johnson et al., 2008).

The Edge-Sensitive Process

Perceiving unity under occlusion in stationary arrays depends on the edge-sensitive process, based on edge relatability (Kellman & Shipley, 1991; Kellman et al., 2005). Considerable evidence suggests that relatable edges do not evoke perceived unity for infants in the first half year of life. After habituation to a stationary, partly occluded rod whose visible parts are collinear (e.g., Figure 5.3A without motion), 4-month-old infants look equally to complete and broken test displays (e.g., Figure 5.3B and 5.3C; Kellman & Spelke, 1983). What do equal looking times, with some dishabituation to both test displays, mean? If the visible rod pieces in the initial display were perceived as two separate objects, we would expect greater dishabituation to the complete display. Equal dishabituation to both test stimuli suggests that the broken and complete displays are equally consistent with the initial display. It is also consistent with a lack of attention to those parts of the display (the visible ends of the rod) during habituation. This latter possibility can be ruled out. Kellman and Spelke found evidence that the visible parts are detected. When infants were presented with a broken test display with pieces that were too small to have been the visible parts in the habituation display, infants looked longer to these smaller-than-possible parts. Thus, it appears that despite the fact that infants attend to the rod when it is stationary, both a broken rod and a complete rod are consistent with the representation of the habituation display. If the rules about object interpolation are to arise later, perhaps by learning, it would seem far better that the perceiver start out "agnostic" rather than use an incorrect perceptual rule.

Infants' inability to use the edge-sensitive process may extend through the first half year of life (Arterberry, 2001; Spelke et al., 1992).

Illusory Contours Recall that the edge-sensitive process, responsible for perception of partly occluded objects, has been implicated as the process for underlying illusory contours and figures as well (Kalar et al., 2010). Thus, studies of illusory contours and transparency may be used to provide converging evidence regarding the origins of the edge-sensitive process. Under conditions of motion, the story of infants' perception of illusory contours closely matches that of perception of object unity. Three- to 4-month-old infants perceive illusory figures when the edges undergo common motion (Kavšek & Yonas, 2006; Otsuka & Yamaguchi, 2003; Sato et al., 2013). Moreover, younger infants may also perceive illusory contours under some conditions (Curran, Braddick, Atkinson, Wattam-Bell, & Andrew, 1999; Valenza & Bulf, 2007). When and how infants perceive static illusory contours is a more complicated story.

One of the earliest studies addressing infants' perception of illusory contours in static images was conducted by Bertenthal, Campos, and Haith (1980). Using a traditional Kanizsa (1979) display shown in Figure 5.6A, 5- and 7-month-old infants were tested for perception of the illusory square by comparing their levels of attention to a display similar to that shown in Figure 5.6B, in which all four of the inducing elements (e.g., the "pacmen") were rotated, or to a display in which only two of the pacmen were rotated. In these latter two displays, adults do not perceive an illusory figure. In a habituation paradigm, 7-month-olds showed significant dishabituation to the novel stimulus, showing discrimination of illusory and nonillusory displays. This finding occurred regardless of whether the illusory display or nonillusory display served as the habitation stimulus. In contrast, 5-month-olds looked significantly more to the novel test display only when habituated to the illusory display but not vice versa, calling into question how well or easily infants perceived the illusory figure during habituation and/or test.

Other research concurs with the idea of a later timetable for emergence of perception of static illusory contours (Otsuka & Yamaguchi, 2003). For example, in an electroencephalography (EEG) study, infants at 8 months but not 6 months showed gamma oscillation patterns similar to those of adults when viewing illusory versus nonillusory squares (Csibra, Davis, Spratling, & Johnson, 2000). Gamma oscillations are associated with neural binding of stimulus features initially processed separately. Also, 6-month-olds do not show typical "pop-out" effects with illusory figures as seen with adults (Bulf, Valenza, & Simion, 2009). In addition, older, but not younger, infants provide evidence of perceiving an illusory figure as an object in depth (Csibra, 2001).

The research discussed thus far suggests a later developing edge-sensitive process. However, a few studies suggest that infants perceive some aspects of static illusory contours earlier than 8 months. Many of these studies provide suggestive but qualified evidence (Bremner, Slater, Johnson, Mason, & Spring, 2012; Kavšek, 2002; Otsuka, Kanazawa, & Yamaguchi, 2004). The study by Ghim (1990) provides

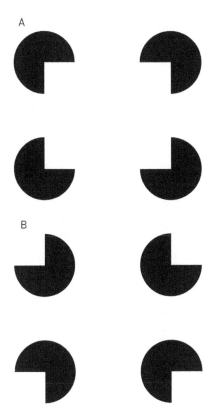

FIGURE 5.6

Two displays typically used to test infants' perception of static illusory contours. In panel A, the inducing elements (black circles) are orientated to create an illusory square. Panel B represents a symmetrical display, like panel A, but all of the elements have been rotated, eliminating any perception of an illusory figure. Rotating two of the four inducing elements in panel A also reduces the perception of an illusory square. Source: Created by M. E. Arterberry.

an example. In a series of experiments, Ghim tested 3- to 4-month-olds in a familiarization and preference paradigm for perception of illusory contours. She predicted that if infants perceived subjective contours, novelty preferences would be greater between a subjective contour display and a display without subjective contours. Some results were consistent with the hypothesis, but at least one outcome predicted by it failed to occur in each of five experiments.

It appears that development of the edge-sensitive process is protracted into the second half of the first year of life. Studies suggesting earlier sensitivity to edges and/or illusory figures have identified some conditions under which edges are interpolated across gaps, whether because of occlusion or because they are illusory contours. However, the evidence is weak, at best, for perception of complete forms in depth based on the edge-sensitive process before 7 to 8 months of age.

Origins of the Edge-Sensitive Process How does the edge-sensitive process develop? Both maturation and learning are possible contributors. An interesting possibility is that edge-sensitive mechanisms for boundary interpolation might be related to pictorial depth cues. In particular, the depth cue of interposition is closely connected to boundary interpolation under occlusion (Kellman & Shipley, 1991). Thus, the developmental story may be akin to the one for pictorial depth sensitivity, discussed in Chapter 3. Recall that Kavšek, Yonas, and Granrud (2012) suggested that early attention to pictorial information, between 3 and 5 months, develops into the use of this information to perceive the three-dimensional world by approximately 6 months. Similarly, infants' attention early in life may be directed to static information, such as partial edges and/or gaps between edges, which for older infants and adults specifies unit formation. Perception of transparency, a phenomenon that also relies on interposition and partial occlusion, also appears to fit this timetable (Kavšek, 2009).

The edge-sensitive process likely depends on a modular perceptual mechanism and not on a recognition process resulting from experiences with objects. The edge-sensitive process is innate in newborn domestic chicks. Regolin and Vallortigara (1995) used a filial imprinting technique to test newborn chicks' perception. Newborn chicks will follow and treat as a social partner the first moving thing they see after birth. In one experiment, newborn chicks were imprinted on a red triangle and tested after 3 days with two displays. In one, unoccluded, separate parts of the triangle were shown. In the other, the same parts were shown partly occluded. Chicks consistently chose to affiliate with the occluded triangle rather than the fragmentary display. The reverse pattern was found when chicks were imprinted with a fragmented display. The findings support the hypothesis that the edge-sensitive hypothesis is innate in chicks. These results in another species do not definitively determine the origins of the edge-sensitive process in humans, but they do make it plausible that the process could be the result of neural maturation.

Other considerations fit this hypothesis as well. Neurophysiological data from primates suggest that boundary interpolation processes are carried out surprisingly early in visual processing, certainly as early as V2 and possibly V1 (von der Heydt et al., 1984). It is imaginable, of course, that effects in V2 or V1 reflect some unknown feedback from higher levels, but there is no evidence that this is the case. Numerous psychophysical results indicate the operation of the edge-sensitive process in cases in which no familiar objects are involved (Field et al., 1993; Kalar et al., 2010; Kellman & Shipley, 1991).

Other indications that edge-sensitive unit formation is a perceptual module (Fodor, 1983) are the following: (1) Illusory contours and occluded contours are processed by the same mechanisms (Kalar et al., 2010; Kellman et al., 1998; Ringach & Shapley, 1996; Shipley & Kellman, 1992), (2) local edge relationships override familiarity (Kanizsa, 1979), and (3) the process obeys certain quantitative relationships (Lesher & Mingolla, 1993; Shipley & Kellman, 1990; 1992). If object completion depended on familiarity, these findings would all be unexpected. For example, equivalent strength of boundary completion in illusory and occluded figure cases would be surprising because occluded boundaries are orders of magnitude more common in ordinary visual experience than illusory ones.

In summary, characteristics of the edge-sensitive process in adults seem more consistent with a maturationally given perceptual mechanism than one derived purely from experience. On the other hand, the edge-sensitive process is absent or weak early in infancy, leaving open the possibility for a role for perceptual learning.

Summary: Unit Formation

Unit formation in adult visual perception appears to be governed by two separate processes, which we have labeled edge-insensitive and edge-sensitive. The edge-insensitive process utilizes motion, not edge, relationships and may operate in the earliest days of life. The edge-sensitive process is richer in specifying not only connectedness of objects but also the forms of hidden boundaries. This process appears to be delayed in development relative to the edge-insensitive process. The development of the two unit formation processes parallels their differing ecological soundness. If detected with precision, motion relationships are highly diagnostic of unity. Smoothness of object boundaries and connectedness of pieces that bear certain edge relations are common but not nearly universal characteristics of our physical environment. Accordingly, the edge-sensitive process, which is sensitive to edge relations given simultaneously or over time, is a robust and useful perceptual process but is not of the highest ecological validity. Moreover, to take advantage fully of this process may require perceptual learning on the part of the infant: For example, What regularities to attend to? How do objects behave when in full view and under occlusion? The development of unit formation, then, fits our characterization of perceptual development as beginning with the most secure information sources and progressing toward other useful but somewhat less trustworthy sources.

Three-Dimensional Form Perception

Each theoretical idea about the basis for three-dimensional form perception can be closely tied to a developmental account (Kellman, 1984). If an object's three-dimensional form is really a collection of stored two-dimensional views, then perceivers may initially have no notion of three-dimensional form at all. Form would develop from associated experiences of different views, perhaps closely connected to active manipulation of the object (Piaget, 1954). On this account, three-dimensional form perception awaits the results of a fabrication process that must take place for each object separately. An altogether different origin is possible if perceived three-dimensional form is a direct response to certain optical transformations. This view is often linked to the hypothesis of evolved neural mechanisms specifically sensitive to this kind of information (Fodor, 1983; Gibson, 1966; Shepard, 1984). The reason is that optical transformations and three-dimensional form are connected by physical and geometrical facts that have been unswervingly true and available throughout evolution. This kind of information does not depend on the particular types of objects that happen to be present in a particular setting or culture. It depends on the optics and geometry of projection of rigid objects. These are the kinds of regularity that evolution might have exploited in the adaptation of perceptual systems for mobile organisms (Gibson, 1966; Shepard, 1984). If so, sensitivity to this kind of information might be a basic property of the human visual system and not a product of learning.

A third developmental story, or rather two different stories, can attach to the idea that we use general principles to derive complete three-dimensional form from a single view of an object. On the Gestalt view, form can be perceived this way due to unlearned, organizational processes rooted in basic neurophysiology. A different account of the rules of perceptual organization was clearly articulated by Brunswik (1956) and anticipated by Helmholtz (1885/1965): The rules might be abstracted from an individual's experience with many objects. We noted previously that the idea of generating three-dimensional form by collecting various two-dimensional views has the unappealing consequence that the learning process must operate specifically for each object. However, adults often encounter unfamiliar objects and perceive their shapes, even from stationary views and under degraded conditions (Biederman, 2013). The ability to extract general principles from one's experience with objects might provide a viable account of some perceptual organization phenomena. Whether this view is best characterized as a differentiation account of perceptual learning or an enrichment account of perceptual learning is unclear. Obviously, this account would predict that three-dimensional form would not be present initially, whereas the organizational processes postulated by Gestalt theorists should operate as soon as the relevant brain mechanisms are mature.

Kinematic Information for Three-Dimensional Form Perception

Which account of the origins of three-dimensional form perception is correct? Wallach (1985) theorized that in every perceptual domain, such as form, depth, or motion, there is one primary source of information, usable innately and not modifiable by experience. Other cues are acquired later through correlation with the innate process. In form perception, he hypothesized that motion-carried information might be the innate process. This possibility motivated Wallach and O'Connell's (1953) classic studies of the *kinetic depth effect*. Specifically, Wallach and O'Connell wondered how knowledge of three-dimensional form can be available to congenitally monocular (stereoblind) observers; they lack binocular information about form. Pictorial information might specify three-dimensional form via learning, but what might guide the learning process? Thus, Wallach and O'Connell hypothesized an unlearned process of three-dimensional form perception based on the optical changes by motion.

That motion-carried information about form is most basic has been claimed on theoretical grounds. Adult speed and precision in detecting structure from motion suggest dedicated neural machinery, especially given the complexity of the information (Braunstein, 1976; Johansson, 1975). Indeed, we know a considerable amount about how the visual system processes motion and the dedicated areas of the cortex underlying this processing (Frisby & Stone, 2010). Another argument is rooted in developmental considerations: Kinematic information for form has the highest ecological validity. Mathematically, perspective transformations contain form under reasonable assumptions (Ullman, 1979).

For a stationary object viewed by a stationary observer, whole form may be predicted on the basis of simplicity, symmetry, or similarity to previously viewed objects. Such predictions depend on probabilistic facts about typical shapes of objects and vantage points that occur. It is difficult to quantify the validity of this information, but it does not approach the validity of kinematic information. If early perception is based on the most accurate information sources, we would expect kinematic information to be the original source of perceived form.

Evidence from infant research suggests that kinematic information does indeed play this role. The earliest competence in perceiving overall form appears to be based on kinematic information (Arterberry & Yonas, 1988; 2000; Kellman, 1984; Kellman & Short, 1987; Owsley, 1983; Yonas, Arterberry, & Granrud, 1987).

Testing infants' three-dimensional form perception presents a problem. A viewed three-dimensional object is seen from a particular vantage point or a set of such points. Each vantage point gives a particular two-dimensional projection to the eyes. To assess whether three-dimensional form is perceived, responses to these two-dimensional projections must be disentangled from responses to three-dimensional form. Suppose, for example, we habituate infants to a stationary three-dimensional object from a particular vantage point. If after habituation infants generalize habituation to this same display but dishabituate to a novel three-dimensional object, it may indicate that they detected the original three-dimensional form and discriminated it from the novel one. However, responses might instead be based on differences in the two-dimensional projections between the original and the novel object. This problem can be circumvented by exploiting the geometry of form and motion. Three-dimensional form information can be provided by rotation around various axes as long as there is some component of rotation in depth. One can therefore test for perception of the same three-dimensional form across rotation sequences that vary and that have much different two-dimensional appearances.

An experiment of this type tested 4-month-old infants using the two objects depicted in Figure 5.7 (Kellman, 1984). The purpose of the experiment was to assess early form perception for kinematic information and also from information in single and multiple static views. In the kinematic condition, infants were habituated to videotaped displays of a single object rotating in depth. Two different axes of rotation alternated over the habituation trials; the only constant throughout was the three-dimensional form. After habituation, infants were tested on alternating trials with the same object, moving around a novel axis of rotation, and a different object, also rotating around the same new axis. Changing the axis of rotation for the test trials ensured that the particular two-dimensional views and transformations were novel for both objects. Generalization of habituation to the same object would thus reflect perception of three-dimensional form and not a response to particular two-dimensional views. Indeed, infants' looking time showed this

Object 1   Object 2

ROTATIONS

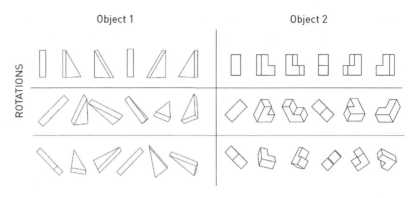

FIGURE 5.7

Objects and rotations used in experiments on infants' three-dimensional form perception. The two columns contain views of the same three-dimensional object. Rows indicate different axes of rotation. Source: Redrawn with permission of Springer from Kellman, P. J. (1984). Perception of three-dimensional form by human infants. *Perception and Psychophysics, 36*, 353–358.

pattern: They looked significantly longer to the novel than to the familiar object in the test phase. This pattern of results occurred regardless of which object or axes of rotation were used in the habituation and test trials.

For adults, even the line drawings of static views of the objects shown in Figure 5.7 are sufficient for perception of three-dimensional form. If infants were able to detect form from single views or sequences of static views, successful performance in the kinematic condition might indicate merely the use of one or more static views. To check this possibility, two other groups of infants were presented with sequential stationary static views taken from the rotation sequences. These two groups differed in the number and spacing of these views. One group had 24 views spaced 15 deg apart in the rotation sequence, shown at a rate of 1 sec per view; the other had 6 views spaced 60 deg apart, shown for 2 sec per view. Infants in both groups showed no evidence of three-dimensional form perception. Thus, in contrast to when the objects were in motion, infants presented with static views were unable to discriminate between the new views of an old object and views of a new object.

Motion Perspective in Form Perception

Interestingly, real motion of the object is not necessary for infants' perception of three-dimensional form. Recall that infants' perception of object unity from motion was dependent on real motion: Retinal motion from a stationary object produced by a moving observer was not sufficient for perceiving the rod as complete behind the block. The situation is different for the optical transformations that specify three-dimensional from. As an observer walks through an environment, *motion perspective* information provides the same optical transformations, relevant for three-dimensional form, that occur if the object rotates while the observer is stationary. If these transformations are the basis for early form perception, we would predict that there is nothing special about having the object move. Information could be given in principle by either object or observer motion. Kellman and Short (1987) tested this prediction that three-dimensional form should be perceivable by moving infants viewing stationary objects by using an apparatus in which the object was fixed and infants were moved in an arc around it. Infants were habituated to the same object supported along two different axes, and then they were tested with the habituation object and a new object supported along a third axis. The findings were the same as in the kinematic condition from Kellman (1984): Four-month-old infants looked significantly longer to the new object, indicating that they perceived three-dimensional form of a stationary object while they were moved around it.

Isolating Edge Transformations

Mathematical analyses of structure-from-motion information have focused on the positions of identifiable points (e.g., corners) at different times (Braunstein, 1976; Johansson, 1975; Ullman, 1979) or spatiotemporal changes in length and orientation of object edges caused by the object's rotation (Todd, 1982). However, the transforming optical projection of a rotating solid object also contains changes in brightness and texture gradients. Infant experiments using solid objects present both kinds of information, and they do not allow us to know the basis of performance. It might be possible that changes in brightness and texture are necessary for young infants to detect form (Shaw, Roder, & Bushnell, 1986).

Projective transformations of edges in the absence of surface gradients were tested by Kellman and Short (1987). Figure 5.8A shows examples of the wire figures, similar to those introduced by Wallach and O'Connell (1953), that were used in the study. Such objects contain edges but no surfaces connecting them. In rotation, the objects provide the same geometric transformations of surface boundaries as do solid objects but without transformations of surface brightness and texture. Lighting was arranged to eliminate visible shading changes even along the thin edges of the figures. As in the study involving solid figures conducted by Kellman (1984), 4-month-old infants were habituated to the same wire figure rotating around two different axes. Following habituation, they viewed the same figure rotating around a new axis and a new figure also rotating around the new axis. Infants generalized habituation to the same wire figure tested in a novel rotation, and they dishabituated to the new figure. Another group of infants were presented with static views; they provided no evidence of perceiving three-dimensional form from the static information. Thus, even without surface texture or changes in shading, infants appeared to be able to perceive three-dimensional form.

Later work showed that perception of three-dimensional form from kinematic information is possible at 2 months of age, and infants are able to do so with displays in which the edges are created from motion. Arterberry and Yonas (1988, 2000) presented 2- and 4-month-old infants with random dot displays, which when in motion specified either a cube or a cube with a corner missing. A static image of the actual display is depicted in Figure 5.8B. Figures 5.8C and D show schematic representations of the two displays when in motion (note that the edges and internal

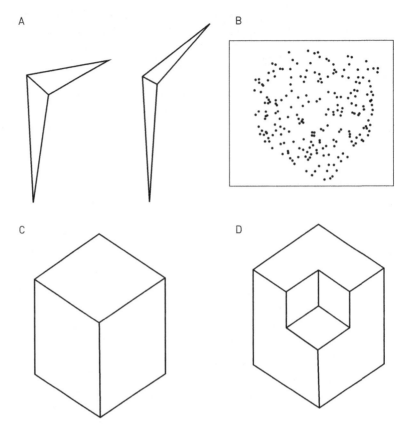

FIGURE 5.8

(A) Wire figures used to test form perception. (B) A static image of a random-dot display. When in motion, the relative motions of the dots in B created a complete cube (C) or a cube with a corner missing (D). Source: A, Redrawn with permission of the American Psychological Association from Kellman, P. J., & Short, K. R. (1987). Development of three-dimensional form perception. *Journal of Experimental Psychology: Human Perception and Performance, 13*, 545-557. B–D, Redrawn with permission of Springer from Arterberry, M. E., & Yonas, A. (1988). Infants' sensitivity to kinetic information for three-dimensional object shape. *Perception and Psychophysics, 44*, 1–6.

contours were created by the motion of the dots). Following the design of Kellman (1984), infants were habituated to one of the cubes oscillating around two different axes. Following habituation, infants were presented with the familiar cube oscillating around a new axis and a new cube also oscillating around the new axis. Infants of both ages looked significantly longer to the new cube. A second group of infants were tested in a control condition in which only the central region of the cube was visible. It is in this region that the proximal motion patterns differentiated the two shapes. The dots specifying the corner in the complete cube moved faster and farther than the dots specifying the indentation in the incomplete cube. Infants in this condition looked equally to the two test displays. Thus, infants as young as 2 months perceived three-dimensional form from kinematic information.

Perception of three-dimensional form in random dot displays occurs rapidly. Infants aged 4½ and 9 months recognized three-dimensional form specified by random dot displays after only 10–20 sec of familiarization (Hirshkowitz & Wilcox,

2013). By comparison, the 4-month-olds in Arterberry and Yonas's (1988) study were allowed to look a maximum of 60 sec on each habituation trial, and the infants looked on average 151 sec across six habituation trials. This comparison shows that infants may need only a small amount of time to perceive three-dimensional form from kinematic information but that infants prefer to continue to look at these moving displays beyond the minimum amount of time required to perceive form.

Moving three-dimensional objects are never fully visible at a single point in time. As an object rotates, it occludes parts of itself. If infants are not allowed to see a full rotation of a solid form, such as the objects used by Kellman (1984; see Figure 5.7), do they have expectations about what the full form should look like, including the back? Soska and Johnson (2008, 2013) sought to address this question. Infants were shown a three-dimensional form that pivoted 15 deg to the left and right. Following habituation to this form, infants viewed a full rotation of the solid form and a form whose front matched the view from the habituation phase but whose back was absent. Six-month-olds, but not 4-month-olds, looked significantly longer to the incomplete form, suggesting the younger infants were unable to extrapolate from the 15-deg views the full three-dimensional form.

Static Three-Dimensional Form Perception

In our discussion of kinematic information about form, we noted several control groups whose data suggested that 4-month-old infants do not extract three-dimensional form from static views of objects. This finding has emerged consistently (Kellman, 1984; Kellman & Short, 1987; Ruff, 1978). It is striking in its own negative way as the finding of early competence with kinematic information. Recall that adults readily perceive form from single or multiple static views. It would seem that we use this ability ubiquitously. Walk into a room and note the objects present. How few are rotating as we watch. Although we get some motion perspective information about objects as we move, we need not. We can see form by just glancing through the doorway of a room.

Although some studies suggest that this limitation may last well into the second half of the first year of life (Kellman, 1993; Ruff, 1978), there is evidence that form is perceived from static information. For example, infants recognize binocular static views of three-dimensional forms previously given kinematically (Owsley, 1983; Yonas et al., 1987). Also, 5-month-old infants given a limited number of static views of a three-dimensional form recognized the form in a different orientation and looked longer to a novel form (Mash, Arterberry, & Bornstein, 2007). Infants presented with only one view during familiarization did not treat the new form as novel. The findings suggest that perception of form based on static information is possible, but likely limited, at 5 months.

Nonrigid Unity and Form

Some of the most important objects in the infant's world are nonrigid. A person walking, a hand opening, and a pillow or the nipple of a baby bottle bending are examples of such objects. Perceiving nonrigid objects presents special challenges. We now discuss what is known about early unity and form perception in nonrigid objects.

We can define nonrigid objects as those having points whose separations in three-dimensional space change over time. If we manipulate a rock, all of its points remain in a constant relationship, despite the object rotating or translating in space. A human hand is different. When a closed fist opens, the point-to-point distance from a fingertip to the base of the wrist changes a great deal. Human movements can be considered jointed motions because changes are caused by operation of joints between relatively rigid segments. Elastic motions, such as bending, stretching, or squeezing a rubbery substance (or a jellyfish), are quite different nonrigid transformations. Analytically, it has been more difficult to describe processing constraints that allow recovery of nonrigid motions from optical information than is the case with rigid motion (Cutting, 1981; Hoffman & Flinchbaugh, 1982; Johansson, 1975; Webb & Aggarwal, 1982).

Perceptual systems are undeterred, however. Form perception includes nonrigid objects, even if these present more analytical challenges. These objects paradoxically retain identity despite form changes. Is it meaningful to say that some aspect of form is preserved for nonrigid objects? It is meaningful. A jellyfish does not have the same form as a walking person, for example. What is preserved across nonrigid motions are not metric properties, such as interpoint distances, but topological ones, such as the adjacency of points.

Since the pioneering work of Johansson (1950, 1975), most research on nonrigid motion has used displays composed of separated points of light in a dark surround. Johansson (1975) showed that the human form and events in which it participates can be perceived from motion information alone. He constructed films of people moving in which the only visible information came from small lights attached to the main joints of the body. Viewing these films, observers rapidly and effortlessly detect a person walking, a couple dancing, and various other events. Inverting the display hampers recognition of the human form (Sumi, 1984).

Infant perception of the human form from motion relationships was initially investigated programmatically by Bertenthal, Proffitt, and colleagues (Bertenthal, 1993; Bertenthal, Proffitt, & Cutting, 1984; Bertenthal, Proffitt, & Kramer, 1987; Bertenthal, Proffitt, Kramer, & Spetner, 1987; Bertenthal, Proffitt, Spetner, & Thomas, 1985). When 3- or 5-month-old infants were habituated to motion sequences of an upright walking person, they dishabituated to an inverted walker (Figure 5.9). Static views taken from the motion sequences did not support discrimination performance. These results, however, do not indicate whether infants actually perceived a person walking. Some evidence suggests that infants do detect the familiar form of the person in point light beginning by 5 months of age (Bertenthal, 1993). This conclusion derives from two stimulus manipulations that disrupt the appearance of a walking person for adult perceivers—inversion and phase shifting. Phase shifting means staggering the starting locations in the periodic motions of particular point lights. Both 3- and 5-month-olds discriminate normal from phase-shifted displays when they are upright. When inverted,

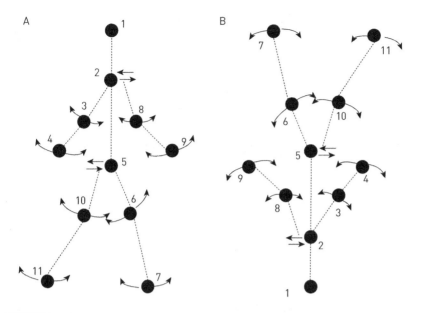

FIGURE 5.9

Array of 11 point lights corresponding to the head and joints of a person walking. The motion vectors drawn through each point light represent the relative motions of the points: Panel B is the inverted version of the display in panel A. Source: Redrawn with permission of the American Psychological Association from Bertenthal, B., Proffitt, D., & Kramer, S. (1987). Perception of biomechanical motions by infants: Implementation of various processing constraints. *Journal of Experimental Psychology: Human Perception and Performance, 13,* 577–585; permission conveyed through Copyright Clearance Center, Inc.

however, only 3-month-olds discriminate the two display types. The inference, albeit somewhat indirect, is that superior sensitivity to phase information with upright displays might be due to the fact that upright displays are perceived as a person walking and phase shifts disrupt that percept. Because inverted displays are not perceived as a person walking, proper phase relations are less salient. Following this inference, the results are consistent with the idea that these non-rigid motions are encoded as biomechanical motion by 5 months but not by 3 months.

Evidence of infants' perceiving point-light displays as a solid object derives from a study with older infants. Moore and colleagues (2007) presented infants with a point-light walker that passed behind or through a table. Both 6- and 9-month-olds looked significantly more to the event in which the walker passed through the table, something that would not be possible if both the table and the walker were solid objects (Chapter 6 discusses object permanence in more detail). Infants looked equally when a scrambled walker or an inverted walker passed through the table. Thus, as for adults, the point-light motions created the perception of a solid object, which to adults looks like a person.

Sensitivity to biological motion is present early. Newborns prefer biological motion to a random motion point-light display or a structured nonbiological solid shape created from moving point lights (Bardi, Regolin, & Simion, 2011;

Simion, Regolin, & Bulf, 2008). Newborns also show preferences for displays that are upright compared to inverted and displays that translate, regardless of whether they depict a walking human or a random motion (Bidet-Ildei et al., 2014; Simion et al., 2008). Finally, there is evidence that biological motion patterns are perceived with a gravity constraint (Bardi, Regolin, & Simion, 2014).

As with the work by Bertenthal and colleagues, these results do not indicate whether newborn infants actually perceived a person or nonhuman animal walking. What we can conclude is that humans enter the world prepared to attend to biological motion patterns. This preparedness facilitates infants' perception of important objects in their environment, such as their caregivers. Moreover, it supports Johansson's (1973) claim that detection of biological motion is an intrinsic capacity of the visual system. As perceptual expertise develops, perhaps by 5 months, infants come to see point-light displays globally as a person and not in terms of locally connected dots (Booth, Pinto, & Bertenthal, 2002).

What is developing? We can envision both learning and maturational explanations. At a general level, infants' motion sensitivity develops in the first few months of life (see Chapter 2 and 6). This development alone cannot account for the emergence at 5 months of perception of a person in a point-light display. Thus, perhaps with increasing experience with people and their movements, infants come to perceive them configurally (arms and legs that move with a particular relation to each other) rather than as composed of separate components (an arm or a leg). Also, neural development is implicated. Perception of biological motion in adults is governed by areas of the parietal cortex, specifically the superior temporal sulcus in the right hemisphere (Jokisch, Daum, Suchan, & Troje, 2005). Whether this neural organization is facilitated by experience with moving people or the product of a predetermined biological process independent of experience remains to be determined.

It is important to note that a point-light stimulus is ecologically bizarre. Whereas physical objects are ordinarily continuous, a point-light object is made of sparse, discontinuous points. Whereas normal objects have surface color and texture, point-light objects do not. Unless a visual system is built to process motion relationships, it is not obvious that these point-light collections should be encoded as anything other than noise. The recognition performance that may occur at 5 months presupposes that without any special training, normal events, such as a person walking, are encoded in terms of motion relationships that can be matched to the point-light displays. This is truly remarkable in the first half year of life or any other time because it indicates that the human visual system is built to be a device for extracting structure from motion.

Summary: Three-Dimensional Form Perception

Research on the development of three-dimensional form perception supports an ecological view (Gibson, 1966, 1979; Shepard, 1984). Recovery of object structure from optical transformations appears to depend on mechanisms present very early. Accounts attributing three-dimensional form perception to learning seem implausible given the developmental order in which kinematic and static information become useful. Can one argue that infants initially encode two-dimensional optical transformations and later learn their meaning in terms of three-dimensional form? No. Because three-dimensional form is not recoverable from static views before it is from dynamic information and before infants acquire skilled reaching and manipulation abilities, it is difficult to determine what the initial source of information about three-dimensional form might be.

CONCLUSION

As is the case of space, our view of early object perception has been conspicuously revised by research in recent years. Whereas Piaget believed that infants begin with incorporeal visual images devoid of meaning, we now believe that even the newborn begins on much more solid footing.

Viewed with a wide-angle lens, the pattern of early infant object perception abilities fits an ecological view: Perceptual systems evolved to provide meaningful contact with the environment and not to provide initially meaningless sensations. Highlighted in early object perception are sources of information that go beyond spatial relationships present in a single, static retinal image. Kinematic information given by moving observers and objects specifies three-dimensional objects and their arrangements better than any classical cues, such as pictorial information.

Shifting from a wide-angle to a telephoto lens, we see that neither the ecological perspective nor the traditional learning-oriented view captures the nuances of infant object perception. In every component of object perception, there are multiple sources of information, such as information carried by motion, information related to perceived depth, and information in static spatial (two-dimensional) relationships. Infants in every case respond to a subset of the information usable by adults. They show sensitivity to some information as early as tested, but they lack competence to use other sources until well into the second half of the first year. The pattern of competence and incompetence is not random. Kinematic information appears early, whereas information carried in two-dimensional spatial relationships appears later.

Initial stages of visual processing in the human visual system appear to be specialized for edge extraction (DeValois & DeValois, 1988; Marr, 1982). Although subject to maturation of neural areas, there is little doubt that edge detection is an unlearned ability. Evidence, direct and indirect, suggests that newborns detect edges from discontinuities in luminance, motion, and depth. However, limitations are obvious. For example, infants are limited in perceiving certain types of motion before 8 weeks, and stereoscopic depth information is unavailable before 16 weeks.

Edge classification in early infancy is accomplished from information carried by motion, such as accretion and deletion of texture, and from depth discontinuities. Early boundary assignment also appears to be based on depth and motion. Object boundaries for the most part seem not to be perceived initially from luminance and chromatic differences: Infants detect these but do not *classify* them as object boundaries until considerably later.

A similar combination of early capacities and limitations applies to perception of unity. The edge-insensitive process (dependent on motion relationships) is available, in limited form, at birth, but it quickly develops, perhaps due to the maturation of direction sensitivity in the visual cortex. During this same period, unit formation from the edge-sensitive process is absent.

Kinematic information is preeminent in three-dimensional form perception. For much of the first year, in fact, it appears to be the primary source of three-dimensional object perception. Perception of form from single, static views of objects seems routine for adults but largely outside of young infants' repertoire. Considering both unity and form, we may conclude that stationary environments often appear indeterminate to young infants. A disproportionate share of learning about objects' connections and three-dimensional forms must come from events in which objects or observers move. We conjecture, again, that the order of appearance of perceptual abilities closely parallels their ecological validity. This claim snugly fits early object perception. Adult perceptual systems exploit multiple sources of information for most object properties, but for infants, perceiving comprehensively is not nearly so crucial as perceiving accurately.

In our treatment of object perception, we have neglected the ultimate goal of perceiving objects: acting on or with them. Perception is intricately tied to action, and the tangibility and substance of objects have implications for what we can do with them. We consider substance in the next chapter, and we address infants' interactions with objects in Chapter 9.

6 Motion and Event Perception

INTRODUCTION

Perceptual systems are the property only of mobile organisms. It is an individual's motion through the environment, and the purposes served by moving, that makes perceptual knowledge crucial. Guiding this locomotion is perhaps the first priority of perception. Another is to detect and classify other moving things: Some of these may afford danger, some comfort; some may be nutritious, but others may be hungry.

Particular patterns and sequences of motion define *events*. Events involve objects, motions, and changes that are connected in *time*. They are coherent temporal sequences analogous to objects, which are spatially coherent units persisting across time. An event may involve patterns of change in a single object, such as a person walking, or complex sequences involving many objects. We do not attempt here a definitive characterization of events as ecological units, although such an attempt might be useful. Instead, we note a few common characteristics that should be sufficient to guide our discussion.

For an object, physical coherence of parts in space is defining. What links the momentary changes that comprise a unitary event? One link is physical momentum. The flight of a ball through the air is a single event, although the flight may last for many seconds. The ball's trajectory is caused by the initiating force, and it continues on a smooth path, subject to the influence of gravity. Momentum also connects separate objects. When a bowling ball collides into a set of pins, they fly in many directions, all caused by collisions with the ball and each other. Not all events are organized strictly in terms of physical causality. Social interactions, for example, may be partitioned into events in sensible ways. Actions united by a common purpose, such as eating dinner, may be events, although they may in turn be composed of many constituent events.

Perceptual events also are scaled ecologically, as are objects. A long, slow happening such as the movement of a glacier will not be a perceived event, nor will the vibrations of atoms, due to their size and speed.

It hardly needs to be said that these criteria and examples are heuristic in nature. Ambiguous cases can be generated easily. Such ambiguities should not obscure the fact that perceptual experience often does come packaged into events, whose parts cohere with each other but are clearly separable from other events. A compelling case for coherence and selective attention in event perception was made by Neisser and Becklen (1975). They produced videotapes of two superimposed events. In one event, three people tossed a ball to each other, and in another event, two pairs of hands played a hand-slapping game. Although the events appeared simultaneously on the same screen, viewers instructed to report particular occurrences in one event sequence (e.g., each throw of the ball) were unaware of the other event sequence (clapping hands). A similar demonstration involves asking participants to count the number of baskets that players make while playing basketball, and in doing so they fail to see a gorilla walk through the game. Although seemingly conspicuous and striking events, they are seldom noticed by observers monitoring one or the other of the ongoing event sequences. This phenomenon is called *inattentive blindness*, and it highlights the role of attention in perception (Chabris & Simon, 2010; Simon & Chabris, 1999).

The idea of event perception has also been important in understanding the information available for perceiving. As discussed in Chapters 1, 3, and 5, ecological views of perception and empirical research both suggest that information carried by motion or change plays an important role in perception of objects and space. Some theorists have gone so far as to argue that event perception is paradigmatic in perception (Gibson, 1979; Johansson, 1975). A motionless perceiver, receiving a stationary glimpse of the environment, is a degenerate or limiting case. Normal perception is inextricably bound up with ongoing action, and interactions among objects are of primary importance in our comprehension of the environment. Gibson (1966) noted a particularly interesting aspect of events—*dual specification:* Events provide information concurrently about *changes* occurring in the environment and *persisting properties* of objects and the spatial layout. We have discussed in previous chapters examples of how information carried by events specifies persisting properties of the world, such as object unity and form (e.g., a rod moving behind a block), depth (e.g., an approaching object), and spatial arrangement (e.g., accretion and deletion of texture). In this chapter, we focus on the other part of dual specification: perception of moving things, including motion of the self. We emphasize vision because it provides our most detailed access to motion and events.

Ultimately, abilities to perceive motion and events serve to support action in the world. For the young infant, however, responding to events is not primary. An infant's rapt attention to motion and events must serve a different function, helping him or her to develop an understanding of the physical and social worlds.

ECOLOGY OF MOTION PERCEPTION

Information and Constraints

Motion has a controversial history in perceptual theory. In structuralist psychology, motion was considered an inference from sensations of qualitative similarity, position, and time (Titchener, 1902). For example, a red circle seen at one place at one moment and then seen at another place might be inferred to have moved.

Researchers began to assault this view around the turn of the past century. Exner (1875), performing experiments on perceived succession of two sparks, discovered that at short succession intervals, observers lost the ability to perceive two separate sparks and instead reported a single entity moving. Exner argued that the ability to perceive motion below the threshold at which position and time could be distinguished indicated that motion was a perceptual primary and was not computed from registering position and time. The argument gained greater support from Wertheimer's (1912) stroboscopic motion experiments. With discrete flashes separated by a certain spatial interval, smooth motion of a single object was seen for time intervals between approximately 30 and 60 msec. If motion were a more general inference from time and position, there would be no reason to expect it to be confined so rigidly. Wertheimer offered an additional argument. One kind of motion, which he labeled *phi* motion, had a curious character. At temporal intervals longer than those required for smooth motion, observers reported a dual percept. On the one hand, they saw each light as being stationary and separate. At the same time, however, they saw something moving between them. Although the movement was clear, nothing in particular was seen as moving. For this reason, Wertheimer dubbed phi motion "objectless" motion. That motion can be perceived apart from moving things suggests that it is perceptually basic.

In the modern era, there seems to be little dispute over motion as a perceptual primitive, detected by dedicated mechanisms rather than constructed from other sensory products. This change in default assumptions about motion may be related to discovery of individual cortical cells whose firing is selectively influenced by location, direction, and speed of motion on the retina (Hubel & Wiesel, 1970) and by a particular visual cortical area, the medial temporal cortex (MT), that seems specially dedicated to processing motion signals (Allman, Miezin, & McGuinness, 1985; Mikami, Newsome, & Wurtz, 1986).

Currently, due to improvements in studying cortical responses in humans and cortical and single neuronal responses in primates, we know a significant amount about how motion is processed by the visual system. Before focusing on motion processing, we take a brief detour to elaborate on theories of both subcortical and cortical visual processing. First, as previously mentioned in several contexts, visual information can be processed via one or two visual systems: a cortical system and a subcortical system. The subcortical system consists of neural information from the eye passing to the superior colliculus and then on to ocular motor nuclei. This system is thought to guide orienting responses, and it may underlie some early perceptual processes. In the cortical system, information passes from the eye through the lateral geniculate nucleus and on to the visual cortex (Bronson, 1974). Research on humans, nonhuman primates, and other animal species has led to a detailed mapping of the visual cortex, identifying a number of areas specialized for processing specific types of perceptual information, such as color, orientation, and motion (Van Essen & Maunsell, 1983). The first stop in the visual cortex is labeled area V1. Other areas further along in processing are areas V2, V3, and V4, which are tuned, to varying degrees, to orientation, spatial frequency, and color. Area V5 or MT is specialized for motion.

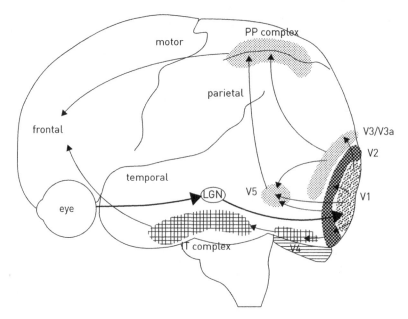

FIGURE 6.1

Schematic diagram illustrating the dorsal and ventral pathways. IT, inferior temporal region, the terminus of the ventral pathway; LGN, lateral geniculate; PP, posterior parietal region, the terminus of the dorsal pathway. Source: Reprinted with permission of Oxford University Press from Atkinson, J. (2000). *The developing visual brain*. Oxford, England: Oxford University Press.

In the cortical visual system, two pathways—the dorsal and ventral pathways— connect this early visual information to other areas of the cortex, and the pathways appear to govern different perceptual functions (Milner & Goodale, 2008; Ungerleider & Mishkin, 1982; Figure 6.1). The dorsal pathway, underlying vision for action, is involved in the ongoing real-time control of action by providing connections between the visual and parietal cortexes. The ventral pathway, underlying vision for perception, is involved in identification of objects and perceiving the relations among objects, such as in the case of scene analysis, by providing connections to the temporal cortex. Although there is debate about the exact functions of these pathways (Glover, 2004), there is little question that motion (area V5/MT) is involved in both acting on objects and identifying objects. Moreover, differential maturation of these regions may account for the some of the variation in the development of perception in infancy (Atkinson, 2000; Kiorpes, Price, Hall-Haro, & Movshon, 2012).

Multiple Stimuli for Motion Perception

Several types of situations can give rise to perceived motion. For a stationary observer, a target translating perpendicular to the line of sight produces a continuously changing projective location, or *optical displacement*. Motion can also occur for a moving target without retinal displacement if *optical pursuit* is engaged. In this case, although the visual input remains essentially unchanging, motion is signaled by the muscle commands controlling eye movements. A target that moves only parallel to the line of sight (toward or away from the observer) produces a different projective change—*optical expansion* or *contraction*. *Stroboscopic motion* occurs, as previously noted, when discrete—nonmoving—stimulus events have certain spatial and temporal relations. This type of motion is also called *apparent motion* because although there are temporal differences in the stimulus, there is no actual movement. Finally, *induced motion* of a stationary target may be perceived when its surrounding visible context is moved (Duncker, 1929).

Compared to the study of depth or object perception, systematic study of the development of motion perception is a relatively recent enterprise. Only some of the basic questions about the scope and limits of motion perception, and the effectiveness of particular stimuli, have been answered. Nevertheless, our understanding of the development of the perception of motion has been informed by our understanding of the neurological underpinnings of motion perception and findings from (primarily) electrophysiological studies, perhaps to a greater degree than many other areas of perception (Wattam-Bell et al., 2010).

MOTION PERCEPTION ABILITIES AND PROCESSES

Motion and Attention

If you want to attract an infant's attention, move something in front of his or her eyes. From the earliest days, infants orient to moving stimuli using head and eye movements (Haith, 1980). This power of motion to attract attention has been exploited by researchers who have added motion to their displays even when studying other aspects of perception.

It is not clear whether infant attention to motion reflects a response to motion per se or attention to what is most informative. From an earlier sensation-based perspective on perceptual development, the former idea—that infants are hardwired to attend to movement—would be more plausible. Such a tendency would facilitate learning about objects and events. The alternative is that information, not motion, attracts attention. As previously mentioned, infant perception of objects utilizes a subset of adult abilities; specifically, information carried by motion provides the earliest knowledge of object unity, three-dimensional form, and so on. As discussed later, infants also have early capacities to extract complex, functionally important relations from events, such as causal connections. Infants may attend to motion and events because these furnish the richest information about the environment. Which of these accounts of infant attention to motion is correct is not known.

Motion Characteristics

A moving object has a velocity that is composed of a direction and speed of position change over time. Both characteristics are important to observers. Research on early motion perception has been concerned with capacities and limits in perceiving these characteristics of motion, as well as the underlying mechanisms that make motion perception possible.

Directional Selectivity

An obvious point to make about motion perception is that direction is important. The radial motion present during optical expansion (looming) signaling an approaching object provides different information, and outcomes, than the motion produced by radial contraction. Relatedly, if you want to catch a moving object such as a ball, knowing in which direction it is traveling is crucial. Recall that we considered in Chapter 2 research suggesting that the ability to detect motion direction may not appear until 6–8 weeks of age. Before this time, infants may be "direction-blind" (Mason, Braddick, & Wattam-Bell, 2003).

The story, however, is more nuanced than presented in Chapter 2. There are different contexts under which direction of motion may be perceived. Consider the following examples: (1) a region moving against a stationary background or in a slightly different direction from another region (*relative motion*; Figure 6.2A), (2) one region moving in the opposite direction of another region (*shear*; Figure 6.2B), (3) elements moving in a circular direction (*rotational motion*; Figure 6.2C), and (4) all the elements in a field moving in the same direction

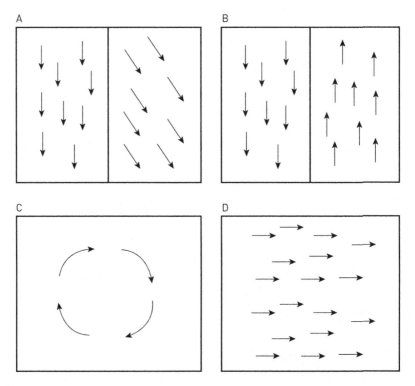

FIGURE 6.2

Four examples of motion: (A) Relative motion, (B) shear, (C) rotational motion, and (D) uniform or global motion. Source: Created by M. E. Arterberry.

(*uniform or global motion*; Figure 6.2D). Age of onset of sensitivity is not uniform across these different types of motions.

Sensitivity to rotational motion has been documented in 4-week-old infants, and there appears to be little change in sensitivity between 8 and 12 weeks (Kaufmann, Stucki, & Kaufmann-Hayoz, 1985; Shirai, Kanazawa, & Yamaguchi, 2008). Perception of shear, an extreme condition of relative motion, is absent in 3- to 5-week-olds; it appears to emerge between 6 and 8 weeks of age (Wattam-Bell, 1996a, 1996b). Moreover, both shear and relative motion show continued development in sensitivity between 8 and 20 weeks (Bertenthal & Bradbury, 1992). Sensitivity to uniform motion may be the last to develop. Both behavioral and visually evoked potential (VEP) studies have found no evidence of sensitivity to uniform motion before 8 weeks (Braddick, Birtles, Wattam-Bell, & Atkinson, 2005; Wattam-Bell, 1996a, 1996b). Once sensitivity emerges between 8 and 12 weeks, however, it appears to be relatively stable and adultlike in precision (Blumenthal, Bosworth, & Dobkins, 2013).

For a source of information that is most useful for adults as mobile perceivers acting an environment composed of moving objects, this relatively late and staggered onset is initially surprising. However, as discussed later, it is possible that studying motion in isolation of other information and in artificial tasks (perceiving motion for motion's sake as opposed to perceiving objects or depth) may underestimate infants' true capacities. Nevertheless, there is evidence that physiological maturation, particularly of the dorsal stream, may be a limiting factor (Braddick et al., 2005). Some suggest that early responsiveness may be based on subcortical processes, whereas later responsiveness relies on cortical maturation, particularly MT. Indeed, between 2 and 5 months, significant changes are seen in high-density electroencephalography (EEG) recordings at the occipital–temporal boundary where MT is located (Rosander, Nystrom, Gredeback, & von Hofsten, 2007).

Velocity Sensitivity

A number of researchers have tried to characterize infants' motion perception abilities in terms of the range of velocities that can be detected. Most studies have focused on the slowest movement that evokes perception of motion, and these estimates have varied with other stimulus variables. In an early study by Volkmann and Dobson (1976), a horizontally oscillating checkerboard pattern and a similar stationary pattern were shown in a visual preference procedure. One-month-olds showed weak preferences for the moving display, whereas 2- and 3-month-olds clearly preferred the moving display even at 2 deg/sec, the slowest velocity tested. To get an idea how slow this speed is, consider that when one views a computer screen from 18 in. (~46 cm) away, an ant crawling across the screen at 2 deg/sec will move approximately 0.3 in. (8 mm) in 1 sec and would take 40 sec to traverse a 12-in. (30-cm)-wide screen. This is a slow motion but well above velocity thresholds for normal adults. An even lower threshold was found by Kaufmann et al. (1985) using rotary motion, approximately 1.4 deg/sec at 1 month and 0.93 deg/sec at 3 months.

Somewhat higher threshold estimates have come from studies designed to distinguish different mechanisms underlying responses to moving patterns. Using vertical grating (dark- and light-striped) stimuli and a 75% preference as the threshold criterion, Aslin and Shea (1990) found velocity thresholds of approximately 9 deg/sec at 6 weeks and 4 deg/sec at 12 weeks. Dannemiller and Freedland (1989) estimated thresholds at approximately 5 deg/sec for 16-week-olds and approximately 2.3 deg/sec for 20-week-olds. However, they found no reliable motion preferences at 8 weeks. Dannemiller and Freedland (1991) studied *differential* velocity thresholds—the minimum difference in velocity that could evoke a reliable looking preference. They assumed that infants would preferentially fixate the display appearing to move faster. Twenty-week-old infants reliably distinguished a velocity of 3.3 deg/sec from 2.0 deg/sec but not from 2.5 deg/sec. Bertenthal and Bradbury (1992) found a slightly better threshold for 8-week-olds (1.2 deg/sec) and a threshold of 3.5 deg/sec for 13-week-olds. Although it is difficult to compare stimulus conditions and measurement techniques, these threshold estimates are much higher than velocity thresholds for motion detection in adults; the latter can be as small as 1 or 2 min of arc/sec when stationary reference points are visible (Kaufman, 1974). At 2 min of arc/sec, the ant crossing the 12-in. screen would take 40 min.

A Lower, or Different, Threshold for Motion Detection

Von Hofsten, Kellman, and Putaansuu (1992) suggested that threshold estimates obtained in visual preference studies of motion perception may greatly underestimate infant motion detection abilities. One concern is that a reliable difference between a moving and a stationary display in the visual preference method requires both that infants distinguish the displays and that the moving display attracts more attention. Very slow velocities might be detectable but not interesting. Another concern involves motion perspective. As discussed in Chapter 3, infants extract depth information from motion perspective. As you may recall from Chapter 3, von Hofsten and colleagues moved 14-week-old infants side to side in front of three rods. One of the rods moved contingent with the infants' motion. The findings suggested that infants perceived the middle rod as closer based on motion parallax information. This would not be possible, however, given the differential velocity thresholds suggested by Dannemiller and Freedland (1991). Von Hofsten et al. calculated that for a lateral head movement at 4 cm/sec, an observer with this threshold would not be able to distinguish a target at 69 cm (3.3 deg/sec) from one at 92 cm (2.5 deg/sec).

Von Hofsten et al. (1992) showed infant sensitivity to a differential velocity of .32 deg/sec, much lower than earlier estimates. There are two interesting differences, one methodological and one conceptual, between the studies of von Hofsten et al. and earlier motion threshold experiments. First, von Hofsten et al. used a habituation procedure, which might have overcome the detection versus interest problem we described in connection with preference measures. The second concerns the use of observer-contingent motion. It is possible that the smaller, observer-contingent motions studied by von Hofsten et al. are processed by a different perceptual system from larger, noncontingent motions. Contingent motions might be used by a motion perspective system to specify depth positions of stationary objects, whereas noncontingent motions (or larger motions) specify object motion. Further research is needed to explore the possibility of separate systems for processing optical change related to object motion and to depth.

Isolating Mechanisms Sensitive to Motion

Although the idea that motion is a perceptual primitive detected by specialized mechanisms is generally accepted, we may still question which particular responses by infants implicate motion mechanisms, such as detectors tuned to particular velocities. One complication in pinpointing such mechanisms is that the physical event of a continuously moving object produces multiple changes in a spatial array. It is possible that apparent detection of motion does not rely on motion-sensing mechanisms per se. Preferential attention to a moving pattern might indicate motion detection, but there are other possibilities. Positional change of the display or some part of it might be detected. If periodic stimuli are used, such as the changing checkerboard pattern used by Volkmann and Dobson (1976), the luminance at any point will change periodically. Responses might be based on this *flicker* rather than on motion per se.

Distinguishing mechanisms sensitive to velocity, position, and flicker in infant perception is possible due to research by Aslin and Shea (1990), Freedland and Dannemiller (1987), and Dannemiller and Freedland (1989). Using several combinations of temporal frequency and spatial displacement with random black-and-white check patterns, Freedland and Dannemiller found evidence that preference for a moving pattern over a static one is influenced by both spatial displacement and temporal frequency. The influence of temporal frequency is consistent with a velocity-sensitive mechanism but also with a flicker-sensitive mechanism. Aslin and Shea used vertically moving luminance (square wave) gratings to distinguish velocity- and flicker-sensitive mechanisms. These may be separated experimentally using stimuli of several spatial frequencies and velocities. A response based on velocity, for example, might be expected to change if velocity is doubled and spatial frequency halved. A flicker-sensitive mechanism, however, should remain unchanged by this manipulation because the temporal frequency (rate of dark–light changes at a single location) remains the same. Aslin and Shea's results indicated that the motion preferences of 6- and 12-week-old infants depended on velocity. Dannemiller and Freedland tested 16- and 20-week-olds using a display that eliminated the flicker in particular spatial positions that is characteristic of spatially repeating, moving stimuli. Their display contained a single moving bar flanked by stationary reference bars. Velocity of the moving bar, not the extent of displacement, best predicted infants' visual preferences, suggesting that infants' preference patterns were best explained by a velocity-sensitive mechanism. These results converge reasonably well in indicating true motion-sensitive (i.e., velocity-sensitive) mechanisms in the infants' visual system; however, whether young infants respond to motion or flicker is still under debate (Armstrong, Maurer, Ellemberg, & Lewis, 2011).

Velocity Perception and Reaching

An interesting application of infants' velocity perception is their anticipatory reaching for moving objects. Infants reach in a predictive way for objects moving through their field of view. This behavior appears at approximately the same time (~4 months of age) as directed reaching for stationary objects (von Hofsten, 1980). In one experiment, the moving object was attached to a 74-cm rod that rotated in a horizontal plane around a fixed point. At its closest point to the infant, the object was 14 cm away. Starting points and velocities were varied, and infants were scored for touching or grasping the object. Careful analysis of the timing and spatial properties of reaches suggests that infants reached with precision of approximately 0.05 sec and with no systematic timing error. Accurate reaching was observed for even the fastest-moving objects (60 cm/sec); additional observations on several infants showed accurate reaching for objects moving at 120 cm/sec. For various reasons, it is difficult to work back from these remarkable results to specific conclusions about the precision of infants' velocity perception. Moreover, ball catching may rely both on motion perception and on binocular depth information: Catching improves at approximately 5 to 6 months of age under binocular compared to monocular viewing conditions (van Hof, van der Kamp, & Savelsbergh, 2006).

The capacity to utilize spatial motion information in this task is impressive. Assuming that the development of reaching to stationary objects depends on maturation in the motor system, the findings also support the idea that accurate three-dimensional and event perception abilities precede skilled motor behavior. Given that predictive reaching and reaching for stationary objects appear at approximately the same time, the ability to perceive objects and events with considerable precision must already be in place.

Origins of Multiple Stimuli for Motion Perception

Wallach (1985) suggested that only optical displacement—the change in position of an object's projection to the retina—provides innate information for motion. Other cues, such as perceived motion during pursuit eye movements, might be learned by correlation with optical displacement. His argument was based on the adaptability of cues other than image displacement under conflict conditions. In experiments with adults, when different motion cues gave conflicting indications, other cues were recalibrated, whereas optical displacement was not. These findings offer useful insights into perceptual adaptation processes, but they may not provide evidence about which cues arise from learning. Some useful clues, however, are available from studies of infants.

Optical Displacement

The previous discussion of direction- and velocity-sensitive mechanisms is relevant to a consideration of the origins of optical displacement. All the stimulus conditions used in the studies we discussed could plausibly produce optical displacement.

Thus, the results may be taken to describe the development of motion perception from this stimulus. At the same time, none of the experiments controlled infants' fixation position. Thus, the infants may have tracked a particular moving feature in these displays.

Optical Pursuit

There is evidence that infants detect and attempt to follow moving stimuli from the earliest age; Chapter 4 discussed the fact that newborns will track a moving face stimulus. Chapter 2 noted that when an observer fixates a repetitive display—for example, a pattern of alternating black and white stripes, moving continuously— there is a characteristic, indeed involuntary, response called optokinetic nystagmus (OKN). In the "slow" or tracking phase, the observer follows, with some lag, a feature of the display up to some extreme point; then, in the "fast" phase, the gaze jumps back to approximately the center of the field, and the cycle begins again. In adults and children, this response is almost always accompanied by perceived motion.

Several studies have demonstrated that the OKN response to motion is innate (e.g., Maurer, 1975). In these studies, the moving pattern ordinarily fills the visual field—that is, the participant is placed within a moving cylinder. In one study, 93% of infants, all younger in age than 5 days, showed the response. Infants' following responses tend to be saccadic—that is, made up of small jumps rather than continuous smooth pursuit eye movements. OKN responses to uniform motion changed little between 6 and 18 weeks of age (Banton & Bertenthal, 1996).

The existence of the OKN response is consistent with detection of motion by neonates because OKN is ordinarily accompanied by perceived motion in children and adults. (This is true even in cases of motion sickness, in which the perceived motion is illusory.) On the other hand, OKN may be a reflexive response mediated subcortically and triggered by motion-like stimuli but may not reflect true motion perception (Braddick et al., 2005).

Similarly, perception of motion is suggested by the fact that smooth pursuit eye movements can sometimes be detected in infants younger than 2 months of age and can readily be found in infants older than 2 months (Shea & Aslin, 1990). These early eye movements lag behind the target (von Hofsten, 2004). By 9 months, infants' smooth pursuit of circularly moving targets is quite good, even when the target moves behind an occluder (Gredeback, von Hofsten, & Boudreau, 2002). One might infer perception of motion based on optical pursuit, but the inference is indirect.

Optic Flow

We considered in Chapter 3 research investigating whether infants detect and respond to the approach of objects from optical or *radial expansion*, sometimes called looming. The weight of the evidence supports the notion that optical expansion signals object approach to infants and that infants can distinguish between an approaching object and aperture.

Optical expansion and contraction information, or *optic flow*, also provides information about our position in space. Changing retinal patterns can alert us to a change in posture, whether it is an intentional change or not. Try standing with both your legs and your arms crossed and close your eyes. You will feel your body sway (and you may need to take a step to reorient yourself to avoid falling). Doing this task with your eyes open is much easier. You may still need to make small adjustments in your posture, but you are not likely to be in danger of falling over. Optic flow alone can induce the observer to perceive him- or herself in motion, and this fact has been used in tests of the roles of visual and vestibular inputs in postural control with both adults and children. Moreover, the moving observer can discern important properties of his or her locomotion, such as heading, from optic flow.

Controlling Posture For adults, control of posture is crucial for standing and walking, and complex postural manipulations are required to perform actions such as reaching, lifting, and throwing. For infants, motor development proceeds slowly; not until 3 to 4 months does an infant possess enough neck strength to hold his or her head steady when upright, and not until approximately 6 months do many infants become able to sit up without support. As advances in motor skills emerge, so does infants' sensitivity to optic flow.

Most often, these studies use a "moving room." A chamber with three walls and a ceiling is either suspended from the ceiling or mounted on wheels such that the room can be moved to present flow fields to a stationary observer (the floor does not move; Figure 6.3). In this situation, the participant is presented with conflicting information for postural stability. Whereas kinesthetic information

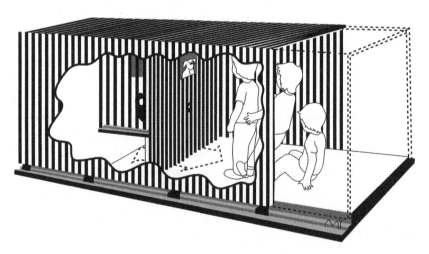

FIGURE 6.3

Moving room used to test postural stability. The side walls can move independently of the center wall, isolating changes in optic flow in the central and peripheral visual fields. Source: Redrawn with permission of the American Psychological Association from Bertenthal, B. I., Rose, J. L., & Bai, D. L. (1997). Perception–action coupling in the development of visual control of posture. *Journal of Experimental Psychology: Human Perception and Performance, 23*, 1631–1643.

(e.g., from the legs and feet) and vestibular information indicate that the observer is stationary, visual information indicates that the participant is moving, usually forward or backward. Adults tested in this situation show effects of this informational conflict. For example, Lee and Lishman (1975) found that adults responded to the change in flow field by adjusting their posture. When the walls moved backward, participants perceived themselves as swaying forward and thus adjusted their bodies backward to correct for the apparent sway. Further work with adults identified the importance of the location of the flow (Brandt, Dichgans, & Koenig, 1973; Held, Dichgans, & Bauer, 1975; Johansson, 1977; Stoffregen, 1985, 1986). Optic flow in the periphery is more effective in inducing the perception of self-motion and results in greater postural compensation.

At what point in development is optic flow information used in the control of posture? To answer this question, Lee and Aronson (1974) studied infants who had just begun standing. Children ranging between 13 and 16 months of age were placed in a moving room. Lee and Aronson found that 82% of the responses (staggering or falling down) were directionally appropriate to compensate for the visually specified position change. Others found similarly appropriate responses to changes in optic flow in standing or sitting infants, and, like adults, peripheral flow was more effective than central flow in eliciting postural adjustments (Bertenthal & Bai, 1989; Butterworth & Hicks, 1977; Schmuckler & Gibson, 1989; Stoffregren, Schmuckler, & Gibson, 1987).

It is likely that the coupling of vision and posture is present at birth. Jouen, Lepecq, Gapenne, and Bertenthal (2000) tested 3-day-old infants for postural changes in response to optic flow. They manipulated the direction and speed of peripheral flow and measured changes in head pressure. Neonates' head pressure responses were tied to velocity in a lawful manner (Figure 6.4), and their responses were remarkably consistent with reactions seen later in development. Similarly, Barbu-Roth and colleagues (2009, 2014) showed that changes in optic flow elicit newborn's stepping reflex. These findings suggest the early importance of visual information in maintaining posture. Moreover, the findings suggest that visual information may dominate kinesthetic and vestibular information when these are in conflict.

Heading Patterns of optic flow provide information for heading. When we approach a centrally located object, the flow field expands symmetrically (radially) on the retina. If we are approaching an object not in our direct path of travel, the flow is asymmetrical. Heading can be determined by the asymmetrical flow patterns, and adults are very sensitive to this information (angles of less than 1 deg; Royden, Crowell, & Banks, 1994).

In the first 6 months of life, infants can use flow information to perceive heading, but this ability is not nearly as precise as in adults. Three- and 5-month-olds discriminate heading changes of 22, 45, and 90 deg but not 12 deg (Gilmore, Baker, & Grobman, 2004). When this sensitivity approximates adult levels is not yet known, nor do we know whether infants younger than 3 months perceive heading changes. The relative difficulty in discriminating heading changes is

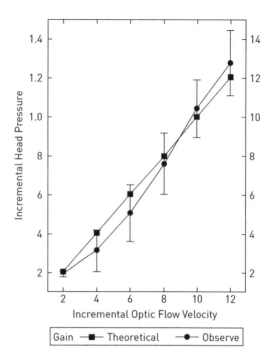

FIGURE 6.4

Theoretical and observed adjustment in posture as a result of changes in optic flow by newborn infants. Source: Reprinted with permission of Elsevier from Jouen, F., Lepecq, J., Gapenne, O., & Bertenthal, B. I. (2000). Optic flow sensitivity in neonates. *Infant Behavior and Development, 23*, 271–284; permission conveyed through Copyright Clearance Center, Inc.

surprising given infants' sensitivity to optic flow specifying an approaching or receding object. The protracted development of perceiving heading may be due to the lack of experience with self-produced motion; heading is less important if one does not have to worry about one's movement through the environment. Infants experience passive movement, and in this context, someone else has to worry about heading. Alternatively, as infants are carried, they may not be attending to the relevant information, an explanation akin to that of Held and Hein (1963). In their study, one kitten moved through a patterned space while yoked to a gondola carrying another kitten (this kitten experienced the same visual input but did not move him- or herself around the environment). The self-locomoting or active kitten showed more appropriate visually guided behavior than the passive kitten.

Neurophysiological development may also play a role here. Infants' electro-physiological responses to expansion flow show increasing efficiency between 5 and 12 months of age (van der Meer, Svantesson, & van der Weel, 2012). Moreover, flow fields can be decomposed into a combination of vector fields, including expansion, rotation, and translation. Adults show different VEP responses to these different types of motion; 24-week-old infants do not (Gilmore, Hou, Pettit, & Norcia, 2007). Instead, infants respond equivalently to expansion, rotation, and translation, suggesting local processing of the motion signal.

Stroboscopic (Apparent) Motion

Stroboscopic motion in infant perception has been studied using the OKN response. Tauber and Koffler (1966) reasoned that if infants could perceive stroboscopic motion, then they might exhibit an OKN response to a stroboscopic motion pattern. They created a display of black and white stripes in which the positions of white stripes shifted stroboscopically (lights turned on and off). Of the newborn infants tested, 64.7% showed a clear OKN response, leading the researchers to conclude that perception of stroboscopic motion is innate. The findings, however, could also suggest that lights turning on and off trigger the OKN reflex, without the perception of motion.

The displays in Wattam-Bell's (1992, 2009) studies of motion sensitivity used dots displaced by differing amounts per frame in different conditions. Using a forced-choice preferential looking procedure, Wattam-Bell assessed how much of a displacement infants could tolerate. If the displacement was perceived as coherent motion, the display appeared to have regions moving in different directions (shear), which was predicted to be more attractive to infants than a display with dots all moving in the same direction. In both studies, Wattam-Bell found that older infants were able to tolerate larger increases in displacement (e.g., .32 deg at 12 weeks vs. 7 deg at 24 weeks; Wattam-Bell, 2009). The available data are thus consistent with perception of motion in stroboscopic motion displays from an early age.

Conclusion: Motion Perception

A variety of information sources appear to support perceived motion in infancy, and infants engage in a variety of tasks based on motion information. The timing of onset of sensitivity to motion is not uniform, nor is our understanding of motion sensitivity complete (Table 6.1). For some types of motion, the evidence is slightly sketchy, and for others, such as rotation, we do not know for certain the age of onset because to our knowledge younger infants have not been tested. Researchers' efforts to chart the development of motion perception are hampered by the fact that showing a response to particular stimulus conditions is easier than proving that the response implies perception of motion (as opposed to position

Table 6.1 Approximate Age of Onset for Different Types of Motion Perception

Age	Motion Type
Neonate	Symmetrical radial expansion (looming)
	Stroboscopic (apparent) motion
1 month	Rotational motion
2 months	Relative motion
	Shear
	Optical pursuit
3 months	Uniform motion
	Asymmetrical expansion (heading)

change or temporal modulation). Our story is also incomplete because one stimulus for motion perception in adults—induced motion—has not yet been tested in infants, as far as we know, and there is much still to learn about the development of the neural circuitry underlying motion perception.

We can conclude that during the early months of life, infants do not perceive motion with the same level of precision as adults. In fact, infants' ability to perceive direction of motion is weak or absent until approximately 8 weeks. Where motion detection can be demonstrated earlier, infants' thresholds for detecting velocity appear to be much higher than those of adults, and the evidence is mounting regarding neurological constraints on infants' perception of motion. Nevertheless, the infant at 8 weeks of age and onward can detect all but the slowest motions of nearby people and objects; newborns can perceive an approaching object.

We have identified two reasons why motion is fundamental in perception. It plays an important role in perception of persisting properties of objects and the spatial layout. It is also important because we often need to perceive particular motion characteristics of moving objects, such as trajectory and velocity, and we need to monitor our own motion through the environment. We have said little so far of the most important reason why motion perception is fundamental: It is an integral part of perceiving *events*.

ECOLOGY OF EVENT PERCEPTION

It has been a long time since perceptual theorists debated whether motion was a product of perception or inference. In the meantime, the scope of perception has expanded. In ecological and computational views, perception's products are not sensory but abstract. The outputs of perception may include abstract descriptions of relationships in the physical world, as basic as where a moving observer is heading or as complex as causal relations between objects.

This is a radical idea. Functional descriptions of the environment—not just abstract representations of solid objects, surfaces, and spatial relations but descriptions of their actions and relations over time—may come from perception. Some of the earliest insights along these lines appeared in Michotte's (1963) book, *The Perception of Causality*, in which he marshaled theoretical and empirical evidence supporting the notion that causal impressions were produced by perceptual mechanisms sensitive to particular spatial and temporal relationships (also see Scholl & Tremoulet, 2000). Another well-known example is Johansson's (1975) demonstration that a person walking or other events, such as two people dancing, could be perceived rapidly and compellingly from a motion picture showing only the motions of tiny lights attached to the persons' main joints (recall Figure 5.9). Here, the local sensory inputs are impoverished. The points of light are not connected; the images are void of any surfaces or volume, much less the sensory information that would normally be available from a person involved in an action in a well-lit environment. However, the relations in the point-light motions, in as little as two motion picture frames, give striking and immediate impressions of persons and their actions (Johansson, 1975).

Abstract properties of physical objects may also be products of event perception. Consider notions related to substance, such as solidity and weight. These might seem to be haptic or kinesthetically known properties of objects. According to a sensation-based view, in fact, it might seem impossible that such properties could be perceived visually from reflected light; not so, however, according to an event perception view. Runeson (1977) argued that kinematic patterns in events specify the properties of objects. For example, adult participants in his experiments viewed other people lifting a covered box containing varying weights and estimated the weight on each trial. Participants' estimates were as accurate when they viewed someone else lifting the box as when they lifted it themselves. Complex relationships in the viewed biomechanical event of a person lifting something can specify material properties such as weight (Runeson & Frykholm, 1981).

Further work by Runeson and Frykholm (1983) extended these ideas to social perception. In their experiments, professional actors lifted covered boxes and attempted to convey the impression that the boxes contained either more weight or less weight than they really contained. Participants in this study viewed the actors and the lifting events. On the whole, participants correctly detected the true weights in the boxes, the deceptive intention of the actors, and the intended weight. Again, the authors explained their data in terms of information about physical (and social) dynamics available in visually perceived events.

Each of these examples of perceiving abstract physical properties from relationships in the input could be the subject of a long discussion. For example, we might ask whether the studies done so far show these abilities to be truly perceptual. These are empirical questions. The crucial point is that nothing in the definition or processes of perception rules out this possibility. Perception is often a response to higher-order relationships. Far from being incidental, the dependence of perception on relationships and on information given over time may be fundamental (Gibson, 1966, 1979; Johansson, 1970; Shepard, 1984). Related to this view is a particular idea about what results from perceiving: Perception yields knowledge about objects and events and not merely swatches of color, high-pitched sounds, or other sensory data. This idea stretches ordinary conceptions of perception's limits. The idea that the human nervous system has mechanisms that take sound frequency information as input and produce experiences and representations of pitch is uncontroversial. The idea that the human nervous system may take patterns of motion as input and produce experiences and representations of causation, animacy, or social intention is a newer idea and far more controversial. From an ecological standpoint, however, the idea that organisms have evolved mechanisms that extract important and abstract properties of objects and events from patterns in energy is fundamental.

The boundary between what is perceived and what is conceived or reasoned is difficult to resolve on philosophical grounds; it is probably an empirical issue (Fodor, 1983). We might ask what criteria can be used to establish that events are perceived. Among criteria that have been proposed for perceptual mechanisms are their strict dependence on particular stimulus relationships (Fodor, 1983; Michotte, 1963; Wertheimer, 1912), their speed, automatic engagement, dependence on specific neural mechanisms, and *information encapsulation*—that is, insulation of processing from general knowledge and beliefs (Fodor, 1983). Studies of infants may be among the most important sources of data for deciding these issues. Finding that some ability is tied to specific information and operates in early infancy raises the possibility of a perceptual account. Next, we examine several topics in event perception. For each, the data suggest that early capacities use stimulus patterns to obtain descriptions of functionally important environmental events.

EVENT PERCEPTION ABILITIES AND PROCESSES

Perceiving Object Permanence

Theories that focus on events in perception open the possibility that more of human knowledge is perceptual than has previously been assumed. Few would quarrel with the idea that extracting information about the movement or stationary positions of objects is part of perception. However, consider *object permanence*. Human adults appear to have several core beliefs about physical objects, including the belief that an object experienced at different times has continued to exist in the interim. Stated this way, the principle appears to be part of our cognitive structure, not a product of perception.

The view of object permanence as a cognitive achievement is a cornerstone of Piaget's account of development. For Piaget, the ability to represent an object as enduring when it is outside of sensory contact is an important benchmark of a changing representational system, one that appears at approximately 9 months of age. This age fits with certain highly replicable observations made by Piaget. Young infants who readily reach for a certain object will not search for it when it is hidden—for instance, if it is covered by a cloth. At approximately 9 months, the children will search for the hidden object (Piaget, 1954).

Many researchers have questioned Piaget's interpretations. Infants' lack of active search when an object is hidden may be due to limitations in planning and carrying out action (Diamond & Goldman-Rakic, 1983), representation (Bremner & Bryant, 2001), or problem-solving abilities (Munakata & Stedron, 2002; Shinskey & Munakata, 2003).

These criticisms are especially important in light of a different analysis of object permanence proposed by Gibson (1966) and Gibson, Kaplan, Reynolds, and Wheeler (1969). The continued existence of a viewed object that goes out of sight may not be a matter of assumptions or inferences but, rather, a matter of perception. Certain optical transformations occur when an object passes behind another object; specifically, there is a progressive shrinkage of the visible area (Michotte, Thines, & Crabbe, 1964), and there is deletion of the object's texture at the occluding edge (Gibson et al., 1969; Kaplan, 1969). Perceptual mechanisms may map these transformations into representations of object persistence. Figure 6.5 illustrates these two forms of information. Figure 6.5A shows a sequence of frames that when shown to adult participants give the impression of an object slipping

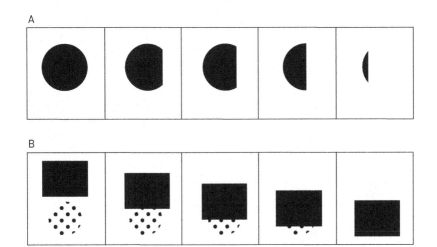

A

B

FIGURE 6.5
Progressive occlusion and accretion and deletion of texture. (A) Example of progressive occlusion. When the frames shown are viewed in a motion sequence, an unchanging disk is seen slipping behind the surface through a slit.(B) Accretion and deletion of texture. As the occluder covers the object, visible texture of the object is deleted, specifying that the object persists and goes behind the occluder. Source: (A) After Michotte, Thines, and Crabbe (1964); (B) created by P. J. Kellman after Gibson, Kaplan, Reynolds, and Wheeler (1969).

behind the surface through an unseen slit. Figure 6.5B illustrates the information of accretion and deletion discovered by Gibson et al.; the rectangle progressively covers the texture on the more distant circle. Different transformations specify an object going out of existence. Three examples are an object shattering into pieces on impact with a surface, an effervescent tablet dissolving in water, and a sandwich being eaten bite by bite. Although for convenience we have described the events and not their optical consequences, each of these events produces optical changes unlike the case of progressive occlusion.

To avoid possible limitations of young infants' abilities to plan and execute searches for hidden objects, researchers have designed tasks that assess infants' expectations in other ways (called the *violation of expectation* procedure). Baillargeon, Spelke, and Wasserman (1985) habituated infants to a screen, hinged to the display case floor, that rotated toward and away from the observer through 180 deg. After habituation, with the screen down in the forward position, a box was placed in its path. Two test events were then shown. In the "possible" event, the screen rotated back, gradually occluding the box until the box was no longer visible; the screen continued backward and stopped where it would have been obstructed by the box, resulting in a 112-deg rotation of the screen. In the "impossible" event, the screen continued back through the space in which the box would have been (180-deg rotation). (Habituation and test events are diagrammed in Figure 6.6.) Infants looked reliably longer at the impossible event, suggesting that they were surprised by the action of the screen in this event. A control experiment, in which the box was placed to the side of the screen, verified that the main result was not due to an intrinsic preference for the 180-deg event over the 112-deg

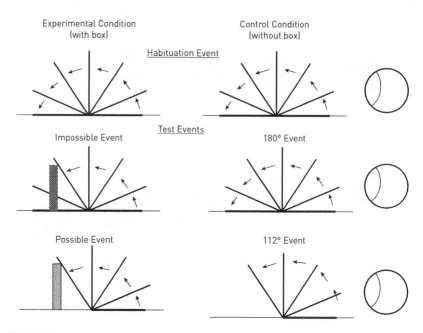

FIGURE 6.6

Habituation and test events used in an object permanence experiment. Source: Redrawn with permission of the American Psychological Association from Baillargeon, R. (1987). Object permanence in 3½- and 4½-month-old infants. *Developmental Psychology, 23,* 655–664.

event. Similar results were found in other experiments with infants as young as 3.5 months (Baillargeon, 1987).

These findings suggest an early capacity to represent the existence of an object that is out of sight. What is less often mentioned is that the persistence of the object may be *perceived*, at least initially. The optical transformation of gradual covering, as well as accretion and deletion of any visible texture on the hidden object, specifies the continuation of the object behind a nearer object (Gibson et al., 1969). To our knowledge, all of the studies showing a capacity for object permanence early in life use this sort of optical transformation (for review, see Baillargeon, 2008). Gibson et al. identified other optical transformations that result, for adults, in perceived annihilation of the object. There is also evidence that 5-month-old infants discriminate different ways of going out of sight (e.g., by occlusion, darkening of the room, or fading), and with age infants show predictive tracking to objects' location of reappearance if they undergo successive occlusion compared to implosion (Bertenthal, Longo, & Kenny, 2007; Charles & Rivera, 2009). The studies of early object permanence may be interpreted in an event perception framework as indicating the early appearance of perceptual mechanisms that produce representations of persistence from certain optical transformations.

According to this view, is there any cognitive (nonperceptual) component to representing a fully hidden object? We believe there is. It is likely that a perceptual mechanism produces a representation of an object that persists as it is being covered and momentarily afterward. If we leave for 2 days, return, and expect the object to still be under the cover, we are reasoning rather than perceiving. Time may be one important dimension separating representations resulting from perception from those requiring additional cognitive apparatus.

Perceiving Substance

Our world is made up of objects, surfaces, and other substances such as water and sand. Objects vary in their solidity and cohesiveness. For example, some objects are firm (e.g., a wooden block), and others are flexible (e.g., a sponge). There are other substances that we would not normally call objects; liquids and sand are two examples. The ability to distinguish among these substances, based on properties such as rigidity and cohesiveness, is provided by perceptual information. Motion information, in particular, is helpful (Todd, 1984; Ullman, 1979). The way objects move and the way they cohere during movement (imagine dropping a block, sponge, or water) provide information that discriminates object properties and their affordances, or what can be done with them (Gibson, 1979). For example, a block is a much better object choice for banging on a table to make a noise than a wet sponge or sand (and less messy too).

Very young infants discriminate rigid from elastic substances (Walker, Owsley, Megaw-Nyce, Gibson, & Bahrick, 1980). In a study by Gibson and Walker (1984), 1-month-olds were allowed to orally explore either a rigid or a spongy (elastic) cylinder for 60 sec (after which it was removed from the infants' mouths). Then infants viewed two cylinders, one rigid and one elastic. Infants looked significantly longer to the novel cylinder, suggesting they were able to recognize as familiar the visual transformations for rigidity (or elasticity, depending on their familiarization condition), and they were attracted to the novel movement.

Similarly, infants can make use of motion characteristics to make predictions regarding objects of different substances. Hepsos, Ferry, and Rips (2009) presented 5-month-olds with a single glass containing either a blue solid or a blue liquid. In both cases, the blue substance filled approximately one-third of the glass. During habituation, the infants saw one glass containing either the solid or the liquid tilted to the left, right, and forward. In this event, the liquid moved as the glass was tilted, but the solid did not. During test, infants saw two pouring events. In one event, the liquid was poured into a second glass. In the second event, the solid was "poured" into a second glass (actually it tumbled out of one glass into the other). Infants looked significantly longer at the novel event (the solid event if habituated to the liquid event or the liquid event if habituated to the solid event), suggesting that the movement of the solid or liquid in habituation set up expectations for the substance properties during a pouring event. In a second experiment, infants reacted differently to a rod being inserted into a solid compared to a liquid, with more looking in the solid condition. Relatedly, infants as young as 3 months perceived quantity from sand-pouring events as long as the different events varied in quantity along a 1:4 ratio (Hespos, Dora, Rips, & Christie, 2012). As with object permanence, there is rich perceptual information specifying the properties of substance, and we find that infants in the first half year of life respond to this information.

Perceiving Causality

Previously, we mentioned Michotte's (1963) proposal that causal impressions are products not of inference but of perception. From a more sensation-oriented perspective, apprehending a causal event—such as when one object collides with another, causing it to move—must be a cognitive act. One could register color, position, and motion of two objects, but their causal relation is not given in sensations. In Hume's classic analysis of causation, he claimed that recurrent experiences of succession produce causal expectations. If we have previously seen one billiard ball roll up to another and the second one move immediately afterward, we come to expect that the movement of the second ball will reliably follow the first, and we attribute a causal power to the first ball.

One of Michotte's (1963) arguments against Hume's account is that we need not experience recurrent successive events to get a causal impression; we get one on the very first exposure if certain spatial and temporal relations hold. The results of Michotte's many experiments are consistent with the idea that impressions of mechanical causality are produced by a perceptual mechanism tuned to particular spatial and temporal relationships (Scholl & Tremoulet, 2000).

Research on human infants has produced evidence of perceptual mechanisms sensitive to causality. This possibility fits with ecological views, which have hypothesized the importance of events and perceptual mechanisms attuned to them. Leslie and Keeble (1987) reported evidence of causal perception in 6½-month-olds. Infants in one group were habituated to a film showing *launching*, the term Michotte (1963) used to designate the causal impression between two objects when an initially stationary object is set into motion immediately on being contacted by a moving object. Infants in another group were habituated to a similar film that would not give adults a causal impression; it had a half-second delay between the stopping of the first object and the movement of the second. After habituation, both films were reversed. If a causal interaction was perceived in the film showing the launching event, then reversing the roles of the objects might be a more significant, attention-getting change than in the film with the delay. The results supported this hypothesis. Infants in the launching group dishabituated more to the film reversal than did infants in the delayed-reaction group. Leslie and Keeble interpreted their results as consistent with the notion that infants perceived causality and to do so they were sensitive to the spatiotemporal direction or the roles played by the two objects. Their work, however, was unable to disentangle these two possibilities.

Other research suggests that this ability is somewhat fragile and is found consistently only in relatively simple situations (Cohen & Oakes, 1993; Cohen, Rundell, Spellman, & Cashon, 1999; Oakes, 1994; Oakes & Cohen, 1990). For example, 6-month-olds have difficulty perceiving causal events when the two objects are realistic toys rather than simple geometric forms. Ten-month-olds' perception of causality is disrupted when there is a chain of events (e.g., object 1 launches object 2, which then launches object 3) and when the objects involved change from trial to trial. Six-month-olds are most successful in perceiving causality in the presence of spatial and temporal continuity cues and when the objects move along straight trajectories (Oakes, 1994; Oakes & Kannass, 1999). Moreover, 6-month-olds do not perceive *entrainment*—when one object contacts another and both continue to move in the same direction (Belanger & Desrochers, 2001).

Perception of causality in infants younger than 6 or 7 months has been difficult to document (Cohen & Amsel, 1998; Schlottman, Ray, & Surian, 2012). Rakison and Krogh (2012) note that younger infants should be aware of their own causal actions; they interact with objects and observe the consequences (e.g., dropping toys and patting compressible objects). To explore the possibility that infants' own action experiences may facilitate their perception of causality in an objective event, Rakison and Krogh provided 4½-month-old infants with experience with two balls before testing their perception of causality. Using the "sticky mitten" technique developed by Needham, Barrett, and Peterman (2002), half of the infants wore Velcro mittens and they were allowed to interact with two balls that also were covered in Velcro. The Velcro helped the infants pick up and explore the balls. The other half of the infants also wore mittens while interacting with balls, but the Velcro was absent ("nonsticky mittens"). Infants in this group were limited in the things they could do with the balls, particularly in picking them up. Following 2½ minutes of interacting with the balls, infants were habituated to a launching event (e.g., a red ball moving toward the right launches a green ball) involving two balls the same color as the ones with which they previously interacted. Following habation, they viewed the reverse of the habitation event (now the green ball moving left launches the red ball), the launching event in reverse with the same roles preserved (red ball moving left launches a green ball), and a noncausal event in which there is no contact (green ball moves left, does not touch red ball, but then the red ball starts to move). If infants perceived causality in the habituation event, the test event in which the roles are preserved should be familiar. The infants who wore sticky mittens during their interaction with the balls looked significantly less to this test event compared to the other two events. Infants who wore nonsticky mittens did not discriminate among the three test events: All garnered equal and high amounts of attention. These finding suggest that experience with the objects beforehand facilitated infants' perception of the casual relationship in the habituation event. In contrast, infants without experience may have responded to lower-level perceptual features of the events, such as continuous versus noncontinuous movement, but not the causal relationship. When the color and shape of the objects were changed between the interaction phase and the habituation/test phase, the advantage of the sticky mitten group disappeared. This is the first study to find evidence of perception of causality in infants younger than 6 months of age, and it highlights the limitations of this ability in younger infants. Only 4½-month-old infants who manually explored similar objects before being tested in a habituation paradigm provided evidence of perceiving causality. This self-produced action clearly highlighted some aspect of the objects, perhaps their solidity, that was applicable to the later viewed causal and noncausal events.

The evidence supports the idea that infants visually extract causal relationships by 6 or 7 months of age. In some contexts, infants at 4½ months also perceive causality. The dependence of infants' causal perception on particular spatial and temporal relationships is consistent with the account proposed by Michotte (1963), namely that causal impressions arise perceptually. Moreover, infants attend to the roles of agents and recipients. Whereas Michotte's (1963) hypothesis, applied to infants, remains plausible regarding the rudiments of causal knowledge, it is clear that these early appearing abilities undergo elaboration later in infancy and beyond. Still debated is whether causality is an innate ability, perhaps emerging between 4 and 6 months of age, or whether it is dependent on development of information processing skills (Cohen & Amsel, 1998; Cohen & Oakes, 1993; Leslie & Keeble, 1987; Oakes & Cohen, 1990).

Perceiving Animacy

Closely related to perception of causality is perception of *animacy*. Imagine an event similar to a launching event in which one object (A) approaches another object (B). Before contact is made, B begins to move to increase the distance from A. As A continues to approach, B continues to move away. To describe this scenario, adults might say that A wants to catch B, A likes B, B wants to get away, B is afraid of A, and the like (Scholl & Tremoulet, 2000). Implied in all of these descriptions is that A and B are alive or animate. Attributing higher-order wants and desires to geometric forms may be beyond what is specified in the visual array; however, there is clearly perceptual information indicating that these objects are animate. First, they are self-propelling: The objects initiate movement without being contacted with another object or external force. Second, the objects are able to move along an irregular trajectory; inanimate objects typically are restricted to smooth linear trajectories. Both of these variables are central to the animate–inanimate distinction (Rakison & Poulin-Dubois, 2001). Also, infants in the first year differentiate objects based on these variables.

Consider self-propulsion. Infants between 6 and 7 months differentiate self-initiated movement from externally initiated movements. For example, in a study by Markson and Spelke (2006), 7-month-olds were presented with two windup toy animals. One toy moved on its own, and the second toy was moved passively by a hand. Following habituation, infants viewed the two toys while the toys were stationary. Infants looked significantly longer to the toy that had previously been moving, suggesting that the infants expected it to continue to move. These results were not due to a confound involving one event having a hand making the movement (and potentially redirecting infants' attention away from the object) because when presented with windup vehicles, infants showed no preference for the self-starting toy compared to the passively moved toy. Whether the presence of static features of animate objects (e.g., eyes and fur) contributes to infants' perception of animacy is under debate. Markson and Spelke suggested that faces and moving jointed parts contribute to the perception of animacy; however, Pauen and Trauble

(2009) found that infants expected a moving ball to continue to move, despite it not having facial features or jointed limbs.

Few animate objects move rigidly. As discussed in Chapter 5, infants are sensitive to nonrigid motions, including biomechanical motion. In our discussion in Chapter 5, we focused on whether infants perceive biomechanical displays as people, but we can ask a more general question: Do infants perceive these displays as animate, irrespective of object identity? Schlottman and Ray (2010) addressed this question by using a "caterpillar" display developed by Michotte (1963). This geometric form appears to inch along like a caterpillar, and adults describe it as animal-like. Schlottman and Ray habituated 6-month-olds to one of two events. One event contained a rigid square (it never changed shape) that moved toward one of two circles. The second event contained the caterpillar that moved toward one of two circles. At test, the left–right position of the circles was changed, and the square or caterpillar moved toward one or the other circle on alternate trials. Infants could respond to a familiar location (but a new object) or to a familiar object (but in a new location). Infants showed increased attention to the familiar object in the new location, but only in the caterpillar condition. This finding suggests that infants attributed a goal to the animal-like moving form, namely to be near a particular circle. When tested with a nonanimate nonrigid form, infants looked equally to the test events. Thus, nonrigid changes are not sufficient for perceiving animacy; these changes must appear animal-like.

Let's return to the chasing event described previously in this section. How would infants perceive a display such as A running after B? Rochat, Morgan, and Carpenter (1997) studied the age at which infants discriminated between two displays, one showing two different colored discs moving independently and another showing two different colored discs moving in a conjoined way to suggest a chasing scenario (to adults). Infants as young as 3 months discriminated the two displays, showing early sensitivity to independent versus conjoined motion patterns—a finding that is not particularly surprising given the motion perception abilities of this age group. But did they see the discs as chasing each other? To address this question, infants were habituated to a display showing object A chasing object B (again, two different colored discs; Rochat, Striano, & Morgan, 2004). Following habituation, infants saw the same chase display seen in habation and the reverse: Now B chased A. Infants aged 8–10 months showed significant dishabituation to the reversed chase display, but younger infants did not. This finding suggests development in understanding of the relation between the two moving discs, one that may include action at a distance (object A caused object B to move without physical contact) and the attribution of goals.

The attribution of goals to others' actions is a key component to understanding others' behavior, and it is a fundamental topic in social cognition. An intriguing question is to what extent and at what age infants perceive and understand the goals and intentions, or *agency*, of others. We take up this question of agency in Chapter 10.

Whether infants younger than 6 months perceive animacy based on motion characteristics is unclear. Few studies have reported findings with younger infants, and those that have identify limitations in 4- and 5-month-olds' ability to make animate–inanimate distinctions (Cicchino & Rakison, 2008; Molina, van de Walle, Condry, & Spelke, 2004). At the same time, there is suggestive evidence that perceiving animacy from kinematic features may be an innate process in newborn chicks (Mascalzoni, Regolin, & Vallortigara, 2010). When chicks were presented with a causal launching event with two objects, chicks preferred to affiliate with the object that did the launching (or was self-propelling) over the object that moved after contact (or was externally moved). From these data, chicks clearly differentiate animate from inanimate motions. Testing this phenomenon with human newborns would be a worthy goal for future research.

Conclusion: Event Perception

Our discussion of event perception has been necessarily brief and selective; however, it should be clear that infants' event perception based on motion is robust. Two generalizations are nevertheless obvious. First, infants in the first half year of life possess startling competencies to extract and represent important functional relations from perceived events. Second, the very notion of event perception, especially in combination with its early beginnings, stretches our conceptions about the nature of perception and its relation to the rest of cognition. We return to these important matters in Chapter 11.

7 Auditory Perception

INTRODUCTION

Much of our focus in this book has been on visual perception. This emphasis is reasonable in one way and unfortunate in another. It is reasonable because vision is preeminent among perceptual systems in giving us detailed representations of spatial arrangements and events. It is unfortunate if we are misled into underestimating the richness and importance of other sources of information, such as sound. For some other species, such as bats, auditory information is primary in perceiving objects and navigating through space. We need not travel to the world of the bat, however, to uncover the informativeness of sound and perceptual systems for extracting information from it. Auditory perception provides human perceivers with a rich array of properties of objects and events. Moreover, auditory perception is crucial for perceiving speech, an ability that is of utmost importance for effective communication.

ECOLOGY OF AUDITORY PERCEPTION

You may have heard the following sounds at some point when walking down a street: screeching tires, a thud, and tinkling glass. Before you turn your head, you suspect that you will find a car has crashed into something. In this case, the news and location of the event arrived first through hearing. Unlike vision, which requires the observer to look in the right direction, auditory perception allows us to monitor our surroundings without restrictions. Vision does not go around corners, but hearing does. We do not detect events but locate them in space. Infants are born with some of these localization abilities, and we explore them in this chapter.

In an experiment, a participant is likely to hear a single sound source against an otherwise quiet background. In ordinary situations, we are exposed to a cacophony of superimposed auditory events. The sound of the car crash may have to be disentangled from vibrations arriving at the same two ears from other traffic on the street, conversation among you and your companions, and birds in the trees. We possess a remarkable ability to parse such complex inputs to the ears into separate streams that derive from separate physical events. Bregman (1990, 2005) has carried out groundbreaking work on this problem of auditory stream segregation and has identified many of the physical determinants of this ability.

Now consider material substance. When the morning newspaper flies out of a car and hits the sidewalk, it makes sounds different from those that would occur if a wooden block had been tossed and also different from those of a sheet of aluminum. It is unremarkable that the auditory signals from these events vary, but it is striking that we glean from them such clear classifications of *paper, wood*, or *metal*. There is more. We gain some information about form and size (or mass): It is a flat newspaper, not paper crumpled in a ball; it is a metal sheet, not a metal block; it is a wooden block, not a sheet. Auditory perception is a rich source of information about what things are made of and what forms they have. Perhaps most intriguing, we usually gain this information about material from events that involve contact between two objects or an object and a surface. We apprehend the substance of one or both colliding surfaces from such events. The synchronous sounds, as with the visible array, must be parsed into separate objects and their material composition.

Not only do we perceive material composition but also we can perceive actions of objects or transformations that objects undergo based solely on auditory information. The study of perceiving higher-order properties of objects and events based on sound is called *ecological acoustics*. The approach here is analogous to ecological optics, with a focus on information for perception and action. Although still a relatively underexplored area, there have been some important findings regarding adults' perception of their world based on auditory information. We highlight a few here.

An important task for any perceiving organism is locating objects in space. We discussed this ability based on visual information in detail in Chapter 3, but it is also possible to locate objects in space based on sound—a process called *auditory localization*. Localizing a sounding object requires determining its direction and distance. Information for localization derives from several sources. When a sound-producing event occurs to the hearer's left, the leading edge of the wave form produced in the air reaches the left ear sooner than the right ear. This difference in sound onset is zero for a sound directly in front of or directly behind the observer; the difference is greatest when the sound is on either the left or the right side of the head, on a line connecting the two ears. Often, we do not hear the onset of a sound. Instead we hear it as ongoing. Information similar to onset differences at the two ears is available for relatively low-frequency sounds in terms of phase differences at the two ears. (The differing time of arrival of the waveform at the two ears causes the positions in the cycle of the sound waves at the two ears to be different at any moment.) As sound frequency exceeds approximately 1,000 Hz, this information becomes less helpful because the phase differences become large relative to the period of the sound wave, making the determination of which ear is getting the earlier information impossible. At high frequencies, information is provided by intensity differences at the two ears. Sound power drops with the square of distance traveled, and the loss is greater for higher frequencies. Interaural differences in intensity are small at low frequencies because the wavelength is long in comparison to the head. The shorter wavelengths of higher frequencies can result in interaural differences as large as 20 dB (Moore, 1982). There are other sources of information that resolve ambiguities in onset, phase, and intensity differences, including head movements and interaction of high-frequency sounds with the peculiarly shaped pinna (external ear). Adult localization is very precise, and as discussed in Chapter 8, even newborn infants have a rudimentary ability to locate sounding objects in space. This system is also perhaps one of the most neurologically plastic. In both human and animal studies, adults show behavioral adaptation along with cortical plasticity to changes to the peripheral auditory system, often by use of a plug in one ear or a mold around one ear (Dahmen & King, 2007).

Perceiving the direction of a sound source does not fix its location in three-dimensional space because the cues that specify direction do not indicate distance. Auditory distance perception is based on intensity of the sound. Rising intensity signals the approach of the object, whereas decreasing intensity signals movement away. Adults are sensitive to intensity differences and can judge the direction of travel and the time to contact, similarly to perceiving a visually looming stimulus (Ashmead, Davis, & Northington, 1995; Neuhoff, 2001). However, there is an interesting asymmetry. Adults judge a sounding object to be closer than it really is, in some cases judging it to be 40–60% closer. Neuhoff suggests that this is an adaptive error. Thinking that an approaching object is closer than it really is allows for defensive action, albeit timed slightly earlier than necessary. When tested with reaching as a measure, distance perception based on sound is very accurate, and adults show anticipatory hand shapes for different-sized objects (Rosenblum, Wuestefeld, & Anderson, 1996; Sedda, Monaco, Bottini, & Goodale, 2011).

If one perceives a sounding object as approaching, an appropriate defensive act is to move out of the way. Relatedly, when walking around an environment without vision, it would be useful to perceive which direction of travel would be free of obstacles. Based on sound alone, adults are able to distinguish between apertures that are passable or not. In one study, Gordon and Rosenblum (2004) presented participants with doorways that varied in width or height. Audio speakers were located on the far side of the doorways, and participants were asked to judge which doorways were wide or high enough to pass through. A surface obstructing a sound may refract, deflect, and absorb the sound, creating an *acoustic shadow*. Participants' judgments of passage linearly increased with the size of the aperture. For example, a 2-cm opening was almost unanimously judged as impassable. In contrast, a 95-cm opening was judged as passable. Moreover, the linear functions varied by body size. Narrow-shouldered participants judged narrower apertures as passible compared to wide-shouldered participants.

In addition to locating objects in space, adult perceivers are able to determine object properties from acoustic information. Consider two events: bouncing and breaking (Figure 7.1). There are two key differences between these events. First, at the point of impact, there may not be much difference in the sound qualities of a bouncing versus a breaking object (assuming the objects are made of the same substance). Following the impact, however, the auditory stream is vastly different. When an object bounces, the subsequent sounds are of a uniform set of frequencies and the acoustic properties diminish uniformly with each subsequent contact with the surface. In contrast, when an object breaks, the individual pieces bounce along different trajectories and periodicities, resulting in varied frequencies and temporal patterns upon subsequent contact with the surface. Adults use these acoustic cues to distinguish these two events with accuracy rates greater than 98% (Warren & Verbrugge, 1984). Although participants were asked only about

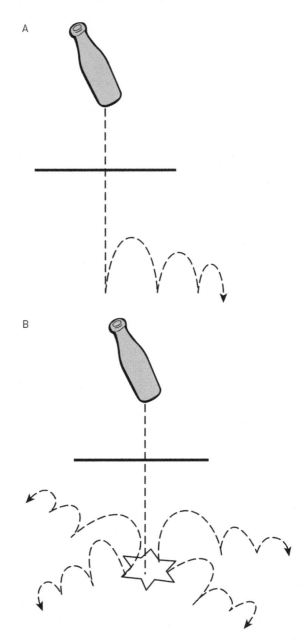

FIGURE 7.1

Schematic representation of the difference between a bouncing (A) and a breaking (B) object.
Source: Redrawn with permission of the American Psychological Association from Warren,
W. H., & Verbrugge, R. R. (1984). Auditory perception of breaking and bouncing events: A case
study in ecological acoustics. *Journal of Experimental Psychology: Human Perception and
Performance, 10,* 704–712.

whether the object bounced versus broke, information is also available, potentially,
about substance or solidity (the mere fact that one object bounces vs. breaks tells us
something about its material) and number (i.e., how many objects are bouncing or
breaking). Adults show differential sensitivity to a variety of sounds and actions,

such as paper crumpling versus tearing, a gas blowing evenly versus an explosion, and liquid trickling versus dripping (Lemaitre & Heller, 2013).

Our present task, undertaken in the first part of this chapter, is to consider what we know about auditory perception in infancy with a focus on ecological acoustics. In the second part of the chapter, we take up a specialized form of auditory perception, one with enormous implications for development of our cognitive and social natures as human beings—perception of speech.

ABILITIES AND PROCESSES OF AUDITORY PERCEPTION

Auditory Localization

In Chapter 2, we discussed the fact that newborns turn in the direction of sound. In Chapter 8, we consider whether this behavior is the result of intermodal mapping of space. Here, we consider infants' precision in locating sounding objects in space. One way to test precision of localization is to assess the *minimum audible angle* (MAA). MAA is the smallest detectable angle of movement of a sound source. To assess 7-month-old infants' MAA, Ashmead, Clifton, and Perris (1987) presented infants with sounds that shifted from a center to a side loudspeaker. If infants turned their heads in the right direction, they received visual reinforcement. Ashmead et al. (1995) found an average MAA of 19 deg, with a range of 13.6–24.4 deg for 7-month-olds. Adults tested with the same stimuli showed an MAA of 1 to 2 deg (typical for adults; Mills, 1958). Slightly better MAAs were found by Morrongiello (1988). Six-month-olds reliably detected 12-deg shifts, and this ability improved to 4 deg by 18 months.

There are several possible explanations for the large difference in localization precision between adults and young infants. One factor could be age-related changes in head size. All binaural differences in sounds are smaller for smaller heads. It is also possible that the auditory system is calibrated for adult head sizes and as a result infants' localization abilities are imprecise until head size reaches adult levels. Several lines of evidence render this explanation unlikely (Clifton, Gwiazda, Bauer, Clarkson, & Held, 1988; Held, 1955). Another possibility is that infants may be relatively insensitive to interaural time differences. When these differences are small, such as when an object is located close to midline, infants may have difficulty localizing the sound source. This possibility, although intriguing, was ruled out by Ashmead, Davis, Whalen, and Odom (1991). They showed that 16- to 28-week-old infants are sensitive to interaural time differences even though infants at this age showed poor auditory localization. In several experiments, infants wearing headphones were cued to look 30 deg to the left or right based on interaural time differences (a tone was presented in one ear before the other). Using the observer-based psychoacoustic procedure, naive observers judged whether the infant was cued to look to the left or to the right. Ashmead et al. found surprising sensitivity to interaural time differences; thresholds were on the order of 50–75 msec. A third possibility is maturation of the auditory cortex. Improvement in the ability to localize objects in space may reflect refinement of cortical mechanisms mediating auditory localization.

Indirect evidence on the role of the auditory cortex in localization derives from studies of the *precedence effect*. The precedence effect, first investigated by Wallach, Newman, and Rosenzweig (1949), describes how the auditory system copes with echoes in a reverberant environment. Sounds bouncing off surfaces create reflections that in turn enter the auditory system. Generally, we hear only one sound coming from a particular location, suggesting that some suppression or matching must occur to avoid hearing echoes as separate sound sources. The precedence effect can be produced in the laboratory by presenting two brief clicks 1–5 msec apart. The two sounds will be heard as fused into a single sound emanating from the location of the first sound (hence the *precedence* effect). The effect is clearly a binaural phenomenon: The interaural difference between the two sounds allows for the localization of the sound source. Research with cats implicates the auditory cortex in the localization of precedence effect stimuli (Whitfield, Cranford, Ravizza, & Diamond, 1972). Research with human infants found that the precedence effect, shown by directional responding to sounds emanating from a single source, was present in 3- and 5-month-olds but not in 2-month-olds (Clifton, Morrongiello, & Dowd, 1984; Muir, Clifton, & Clarkson, 1989). These results in conjunction with animal research suggest that improvements in auditory localization within the first 6 months of life may be due to maturation of the auditory cortex.

Auditory Distance Perception

Do infants pick up distance information auditorily? The question can be answered by observing infants' reaching to auditory targets. Seven-month-old infants reliably reach for a sounding object that they cannot see, even when they cannot see their own hands (Clifton, Rochat, Robin, & Berthier, 1994; Perris & Clifton, 1988). Interestingly, when allowed to look, infants will reach for a nearby glowing object in the dark, not the sound source (i.e., not the speaker placed above the object; Clifton, Rochat, Litovsky, & Perris, 1991). Capitalizing on the fact that infants will reach for sounding objects in the dark, Clifton, Perris, and Bullinger (1991) tested infants' perception of direction and distance of objects specified by auditory information by presenting them with a sounding object located either within reach or beyond reach. They found significantly more reaching to the object when it was within reach.

Infants also reach successfully for moving sounding objects. LaGasse, VanVorst, Brunner, and Zucker (1999) presented infants with objects moving in a circular arc, either in the light or in the dark. Infants aged 7½–11 months were able to localize, reach for, and contact the moving object most of the time when the object (and the infant) was in the dark. Moreover, the infants' use of a grasping hand shape indicated prediction of a solid object. In all of the studies presented thus far, infants' performance in the dark (or under glowing object conditions) was less accurate than that under lighted conditions. Thus, although infants can use auditory information to locate objects in space, visual information is most infor-mative for infants, as it is for adults.

An important developmental question is whether infants are able to locate objects based on sound as soon as they start reaching. The studies discussed thus far tested infants age 7 months or older. These infants had at least 2 months of experience with skilled reaching, resulting in ample practice for coordination between arm movements and visual/auditory information for object location. To our knowledge, only one study has examined longitudinally the onset of infant reaching based on visual and auditory information for object location. Clifton, Muir, Ashmead, and Clarkson (1993) studied the reaching of seven infants aged 6–25 weeks to objects in the light and the dark. Most interesting for our purposes is the dark conditions in which sounding objects were presented. On some trials, only a sound or only a silent glowing object was presented. On others, the sounding object also glowed, and on still others the auditory and visual information were in conflict (e.g., the sound came from the left but the glowing object was on the right). The age of onset of touching and grasping to objects varied widely (7–16 weeks for touching and 11–19 weeks for grasp-ing), but there were no differences depending on light versus dark conditions. Contacts to sounding objects alone were made, but they were fewest in num-ber: 34% of trials compared to 48% to glowing objects and 59% to sounding glowing objects. It appears that as reaching emerges and is refined, auditory information can be used to locate objects in space. The suppressed rate of reach-ing to a sounding object alone compared to the other conditions could be due to infants' lack of motivation to reach for something that cannot be seen or their inability to anticipate what type of object it might be (e.g., a clothes pin or an egg shape in this experiment). Most telling is that when sound and glowing location were in conflict, infants reached for the glowing location. The interplay between auditory and visual information is elaborated further in Chapter 8 on intermodal perception.

Object Individuation and Number

It should be clear by now that our world is made up of discrete units, and in Chapter 5 we discussed at length how we segment our world into coherent objects. Several features of these parts are boundedness, uniformity of substance, and com-mon motion. Can auditory information be used to determine objects as separate or individualized from other objects? If so, can we determine how many objects are present?

Researchers addressing this question in the visual domain show that infants at 4½ months individuate objects based on shape or size, but only later, at approxi-mately 11½ months, are they able to use color or luminance (Woods & Wilcox, 2006; see also Chapter 11). To test whether infants are able to individuate objects based on sound, Wilcox, Woods, Tuggy, and Napoli (2006) presented infants with one sound repeated twice or two different sounds. In both conditions, the sounds were separated by a gap. Following the sound presentation, infants saw a display of either one object or two objects, and their level of attention was recorded. Infants who heard two different sounds looked significantly longer to the display of one object. Infants who heard two identical sounds looked equally to the one and the two object displays. Wilcox et al. concluded that infants who heard two different sounds expected to see two objects and were surprised when there was only one. Infants who heard two identical sounds had no basis on which to determine the number of objects present: One object could have made the same sounds twice, or each of two objects could have made a sound. A similar finding of infants' perception of objects and their number was found by VanMarle and Wynn (2009). They showed that 7-month-old infants discriminated differently numbered sound sequences, as long as the ratio was 1:2 (two vs. four but not two vs. three sounds). Together, these findings suggest infants' sensitivity to sounds specifying the presence of one or more objects.

Summary: Auditory Perception

The research on auditory localization suggests that some ability to localize objects based on sound is present at birth. Newborn infants know in which direction a sounding object is located, and after a few months infants know how far away an object is located (or at least whether it is reachable or not). Moreover, infants extract some object properties, such as number, from auditory information.

The precision of infants' auditory distance perception is not well understood. One approach to testing the limits of this ability is to consider the role of auditory localization in eliciting visual attention. Just as a head-orienting response serves the purpose of placing the image of an object on the retina, it is possible that observers make anticipatory convergence adjustments related to sound. That is, after hearing a sound, observers might adjust binocular convergence so that the object will be appropriately imaged in the two eyes when it comes into view. This idea might prove useful in testing infants' auditory distance sensitivity.

ABILITIES AND PROCESSES OF SPEECH PERCEPTION

Most perceptual abilities produce knowledge about objects, events, and the layout of space. The perception of speech often leads to knowledge about the world, but in quite a different way. Apart from their meanings, which the infant perceiver ultimately learns to extract, speech signals have little significance as physical events. As the gateway to language, however, the origins and development of speech perception are crucial.

Young infants are confronted at birth with the challenge of discriminating speech sounds from other environmental sounds (e.g., garbage disposals, music, coughs, and sneezes). To succeed at this task is remarkable because the acoustic signals for speech are varied and complex. Infants are also challenged to recognize sounds across different speakers as equivalent, to parse the signal into meaningful units (i.e., phrases, words, and syllables), to recognize these units, and, if possible, to give an appropriate communicative response. How much of speech perception relies on specifically linguistic mechanisms as distinguished from generalized auditory ones is controversial. We return to this issue following our discussion of the development of speech perception.

We begin by asking about the earliest beginnings of speech perception. When are infants first exposed to speech, and what do they perceive? We will find that recognition of properties of speech signals begins surprisingly early. We then examine features of the child's linguistic environment that may assist him or her in coming to comprehend speech. How infants actually parse the speech stream is addressed next. We then examine the origins of perceptual constancy in speech perception—how the perceiver categorizes items having the same significance linguistically despite their physical variation. Finally, we conclude with the general question of whether the processes underlying speech perception are specifically linguistic or the result of general auditory capacities.

The Beginnings of Speech Perception

When do infants first attend to speech and begin to extract useful information from it? Early researchers investigating the origins of infants' preferences for their mother's voice over that of another female suspected that infants hear the voice of their mother while in utero (Mills & Melhuish, 1974). Now there is no question that infants hear voices and other environmental noises in utero and that the auditory system is functional by 28 weeks of gestation (Voegtline, Costigan, Pater, & DiPietro, 2013).

After birth, very young infants prefer their mother's voice to other females' voices (DeCasper & Fifer, 1980) and prefer female voices to male voices (Brazelton, 1978), but they do not prefer their father's voice to those of other males (DeCasper & Prescott, 1984). Not only do infants have preferences for sounds heard while in utero but also they apparently can remember things about those sounds. In a study by DeCasper and Spence (1986), pregnant women were asked to read a target story to their fetuses twice a day during the last 6 weeks of pregnancy. Three target stories were used: *The King, the Mice, and the Cheese*, the first 28 paragraphs of *The Cat in the Hat*, and the last 28 paragraphs of *The Cat in the Hat* in which salient nouns were changed to create a story titled *The Dog in the Fog*. Mothers made recordings of themselves reading each story before they began reading to their fetuses regularly. After birth, 16 infants (average age was 55.8 hours) were tested for their preferences between the target story and a novel story. DeCasper and Spence found that the pre-exposed infants showed a preference for the target story regardless of whether it was read by their mother or another female. Infants who had not been exposed to the stories did not show a preference for any particular story. DeCasper and Spence concluded that infants remembered something about the acoustic cues, such as rhythm and intonation that specified their particular target passage. A relatively recent study measuring speech perception in utero found changes in fetal heart rate in response to a recording of the mother's voice but not to a strange female's voice, further suggesting that infants hear in utero and develop preferences for familiar sounds (Kisilevsky et al., 2003, 2009).

What characteristics of sound might allow matching between sound events presented before and after birth? The frequency range for ordinary speech is 400–3,000 Hz, and its intensity is approximately 60 dB (Goldstein, 1989). In utero, sounds above 1,000 Hz are attenuated, and the level of ambient noise is estimated to be 25 dB when the mother is not in labor (Querleu, Renard, Versyp, Paris-Delrue, & Crepin, 1988). Against this background noise maternal voices are audible, but the situation approximates a low-pass filter. As would be predicted, newborn infants prefer a 500-Hz low-pass filtered sample (frequencies above 500 Hz are removed) of the maternal voice over another low-pass filtered female voice (Spence & Freeman, 1996). This suggests that infants have access to prosodic characteristics of speech (e.g., frequency contours and temporal patterning), which are available at low frequencies, but not to information conveyed by high frequencies. Early after birth, the attractiveness of these prosodic features is not specific to human speech. Newborns show no preference for human speech over rhesus monkey vocalizations, but they do prefer both over synthetic nonspeech sounds (Vouloumanos, Hauser, Werker, & Martin, 2010; see Figure 7.2A). Three-month-olds, in contrast, show evidence of discrimination of human speech from that of other species and prefer it (Figure 7.2B). This developing specialization for human speech, which matches their linguistic environment, may be the start of perceptual narrowing of speech perception, a topic addressed in more detail later.

As we are reminded when we listen to fluent speech in a language we do not understand, the tasks of speech perception are immensely complicated. Several features of the infant's linguistic environment may assist the infant in coming to parse the speech stream and to recognize particular words, relations between utterances and situations, and communicative intents. We now consider two sources of information, apart from the content of speech itself. First, we discuss auditory–visual correspondence between the sounds heard and the moving faces in the infant's environment. Second, we examine infant sensitivities to the ways adults modify their speech when addressing infants and small children.

Intermodal Perception of Speech

The perception of speech is more than what meets the ear; visual information also plays a role. It is common knowledge that adults find speech to be more easily understood when they are watching the speaker, especially in noisy environments or when the listener is hard of hearing (Sumby & Pollack, 1954). In fact, a normal-hearing observer may be strongly influenced by the articulatory movements of the speaker, resulting in an illusory percept. For example, McGurk and MacDonald (1976) presented adults with auditory information specifying the sounds /baba/ and visual information specifying /gaga/. Participants reported perceiving neither; they heard /dada/. Apparently, the discrepancy between visual and auditory information (which differed on the dimension of *place of articulation*) resulted in a resolution that resembled a compromise: The place of articulation for /dada/ lies between /baba/ and /gaga/. This auditory–visual illusion is called the *McGurk effect*.

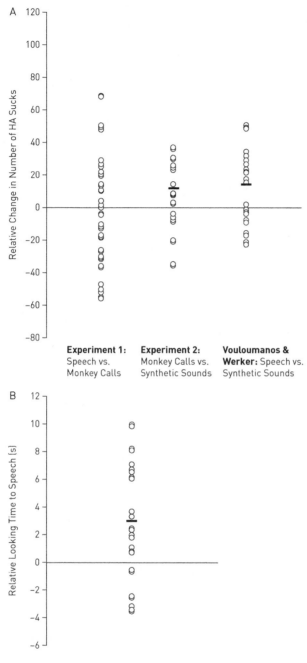

FIGURE 7.2

Scatterplots of infant preferences (each circle represents one participant; the bar is the mean).
Panel A, left side, shows no preference by newborns for speech over monkey calls. In the middle
and right of panel A, newborns show a preference for monkey calls and human speech over synthetic speech sounds. In B, 3-month-old infants show a preference for human speech over monkey calls. Source: Reprinted with permission of John Wiley and Sons, Inc. from Vouloumanos,
A., Hauser, M. D., Werker, J. F., & Martin, A. (2010). The tuning of human neonates' preference
for speech. *Child Development, 81*, 517–527; permission conveyed through Copyright Clearance
Center, Inc.

Visual information is not necessary for, but can contribute to, the perception of speech. Understanding the development of auditory–visual relations in speech perception begins with the question of whether young infants are sensitive to the visual–auditory match of speech stimuli. Chapter 8 discusses infants' intermodal perception in more detail; here, we preview one aspect of this ability. Two- and 4-month-old infants are able to identify a correspondence between lip movements and vowel sounds (Kuhl & Meltzoff, 1982, 1984; Patterson & Werker, 2003; Soto-Faraco, Calabresi, Navarra, Werker, & Lewkowicz, 2012). In one study, 4-month-old infants viewed a film of two faces, one mouthing the sound /a/ as in "pop" and one mouthing the sound /i/ as in "peep." A speaker located between the two faces presented a soundtrack of either /a/ or /i/. Infants looked significantly longer at the /a/ face than the /i/ face when the /a/ sound was played, and they looked significantly longer at the /i/ face than the /a/ face when the /i/ sound was played. Similar results were found using /i/ and /u/ (Kuhl & Meltzoff, 1988), and neurological findings suggest the audiovisual integration takes place early in processing (Hyde, Jones, Flom, & Porter, 2011). Thus, by 2 months of age, infants perceive the correspondence between lip movements and vowel sounds and have some knowledge of which movements produce which sounds.

However, there is more information besides a correspondence between lip movements and vowel sounds to which infants may have responded. The displays contained temporal patterns that may have furnished information including the contingency between the onset and offset of the sound and lip movement. Infants may have matched the visual and auditory displays based on this information rather than on the appropriate vowel sound. To investigate whether infants were responding to spectral or temporal characteristics of the auditory stimulus, Kuhl and Meltzoff (1984) presented 4-month-olds with two faces (/a/ and /i/) and a pure-tone stimulus that preserved the duration, amplitude envelope, and onset/offset characteristics of the original vowels but removed the formant frequencies (or the sound's "vowelness"). When hearing pure tones, infants did not show a preference for the matching face. Instead, infants in both /a/ and /i/ conditions preferred the /a/ face. Thus, infants did not merely respond to temporal features; instead, they represented the vowel both visually and auditorily.

Sensitivity to the audiovisual relation of speech stimuli may be present at birth. One study presented newborns with videos of two primate faces making two different types of calls, a grunt or a coo (Lewkowicz, Leo, & Simion, 2010). When the displays were presented without any auditory information, infants showed no preference for one display over the other. When a grunt or a coo sound was presented, infants looked significantly longer to the visual display that matched the sound. This finding is particularly striking because the primate calls were completely novel sounds (unlike human speech, which newborns would have heard in utero). A second experiment, in which infants heard a complex tone instead of a call, showed that the key variable was timing of the onset and offset of the sound and its match to the mouth movements. Thus, it is possible that infants' audio perception of speech begins with sensitivity to temporal synchrony, which leads to the discovery of more subtle correlations between mouth movements and particular sounds, such as those that form /a/ versus /i/.

Several studies have documented the influence of visual information on perception of phonemes, namely the McGurk effect, by infants 6 months of age or younger (Bristow et al., 2008; Burnham & Dodd, 2004; Kushnerenko, Teinonen, Volein, & Csibra, 2008; Rosenblum, Schmuckler, & Johnson, 1997). In one study, Burnham and Dodd presented 4½-month-old infants with an auditory stimulus for /ba/ and a face mouthing /ga/. After habituation, infants heard three sounds: /ba/, /da/, and /ða/ (the "th" sound in "then"). Infants dishabituated to both /ba/ and /ða/ but not /da/, suggesting that they perceived the habituation stimulus as /da/, the compromise between the visual and auditory information actually presented. Several aspects of speech fit better with the idea that amodal properties provide some support, but speech perception is primarily based on auditory properties. Visual information for speech is not as rich as the auditory information. Individuals with hearing impairments need extensive training and must rely on context in order to lipread (Massaro, Thompson, Barron, & Laren, 1986). Moreover, some aspects of speech are not available at all visually—for example, manner of articulation, such as the voice-onset time that differentiates /da/ and /ta/.

Infant-Directed Speech

Another assist infants may receive in coming to comprehend speech involves special characteristics of the acoustic signal when speech is directed to infants. Adults and older children speaking to infants modify their speech in surprisingly consistent ways. Parents across a number of different languages and cultural contexts alter their speech somewhat when speaking to infants (for review, see Soderstrom, 2007). This type of speech, initially termed *motherese*, is now referred to as *child-directed* or *infant-directed speech*. It is characterized by high pitch, exaggerated intonation contour, clearly pronounced vowels or tones, short sentences, phrases with longer pauses between them, and prosodic repetition (Wang, Seidl, & Cristia, 2015). Infant-directed speech is also accompanied by characteristic facial features, such as exaggerated lip, eye, brow, and head movements, that distinguish it from adult-directed speech (Green, Nip, Wilson, Mefferd, & Yunusova, 2010; Shepard, Spence, & Sasson, 2012). Neurologically, infants show stronger responses to infant-directed speech compared to adult-directed speech, whether spoken by a familiar or an unfamiliar person (Naoi et al., 2012). Moreover, similarly altered speech is used when talking to pets, and modifications in speech are based on perceived linguistic competence of the pet (i.e., used more with a parrot than a dog; Burnham, Kitamura, & Vollmer-Conna, 2002; Xu, Burnham, Kitamura, & Vollmer-Conna, 2013).

In addition to possibly signaling to infants that certain speech is intended for them, this type of speech may serve three related functions (Fernald, 2000; Pegg, Werker, & McLeod, 1992). First, it may be effective in eliciting and maintaining infants' attention. Adults can sustain communication with an infant for longer periods of time by modifying their speech in this way. Second, this type of speech may contribute to the positive affective interaction between parents and infants. Depending on the features of the speech, adults can communicate pleasure, ambivalence, empathy, or frustration. Finally, infant-directed speech may aid the infant in determining the linguistic units of his or her native language. These three functions are explored next.

Attentional Effects of Infant-Directed Speech

As discussed previously, infants' initial preference for their mother's voice is likely due to perception of features of this sound before birth. Yet infants' preference for infant-directed speech is not limited to the speech of their own mother. Infants from birth to at least 10 months of age prefer infant-directed speech to adult-directed speech from unfamiliar females (Cooper & Aslin, 1989; Fernald, 1984, 1985; Fernald & Kuhl, 1987), and this preference generalizes to male speakers (Pegg et al., 1992). The preference for infant-directed speech may be due to the increase in *frequency modulation* (variation in pitch) rather than an absolute elevation in pitch (Fernald & Kuhl, 1987). Infants do not show a preference for infant-directed speech over adult-directed speech when duration and amplitude characteristics of infant-directed speech are presented without frequency modulation. In other words, in the absence of pitch changes, loudness or rhythm of the speech does not affect infants' attention. Studies using eye tracking as a measure show that 3- and 5-month-old infants look longer at visual displays of a model engaging in infant-directed speech over adult-directed speech, even when there is no concurrent sound, and 5- to 8-month-old infants attend most to the eye region, compared to the nose and mouth, of faces speaking infant-directed speech (Kim & Johnson, 2014; Smith, Gibilisco, Meisinger, & Hankey, 2013). Thus, infants attend more to the auditory and visual properties of infant-directed speech.

Moreover, infant responsiveness plays a role in the interaction. When infants respond positively to infant-directed speech, the speakers increasingly use a raised pitch (Smith & Trainor, 2008). The attention-getting qualities of infant-directed speech may prolong the interaction between adult and young child, providing a rich linguistic experience.

Affect and Infant-Directed Speech

Speech directed to infants conveys more than what the words mean; it conveys affective messages, most often conveyed by prosodic features (Papoušek, Papoušek, & Symmes, 1991; Singh, Morgan, & Best, 2002; Spence & Moore, 2003; Trainor, Austin, & Desjardins, 2000). In several experiments, Fernald (1993) presented 5-month-old infants with approval ("Good!") or disapproval ("No!") speech samples. She found that 5-month-old infants raised in American English homes looked longer to neutral faces placed on speakers emitting German and Italian approvals than disapprovals. In addition, infants showed more positive affect to approvals and more negative affect to disapprovals in German, Italian, nonsense English syllables (in which the fundamental frequency was matched in range and variability), and natural English infant-directed as opposed to adult-directed speech samples. This pattern did not hold for Japanese approvals and disapprovals. (Fernald explained this finding in terms of the reduced level of emotionality in Japanese facial and vocal expressions.) These findings suggest that auditory information in the absence of facial expressions cues affect for infants 5 months of age.

Affective information conveyed by infant-directed speech may also play a role in infants' preferences for future social partners. Five-month-old infants who were familiarized to two unfamiliar adults, one speaking infant-directed speech and the other speaking adult-directed speech, later showed a stronger looking preference to the now static person who previously spoke infant-direct speech (Schachner & Hannon, 2011).

Infant-Directed Speech and Learning Language

Infant-directed speech may also help infants learn important details about the structure of their native languages and thereby facilitate language development. Many studies have documented the preference by infants for simpler exaggerated speech. From a functional standpoint, we have to ask why infants come equipped to prefer a type of speech that is atypical in the general linguistic environment. Does infant-directed speech have a functional significance in facilitating language learning?

Infant-directed speech may help the young language learner in several ways. First, the modifications found in infant-directed speech may help in parsing the unfamiliar speech stream. One difficulty in learning a new language is parsing utterances into words and phrases. Infant-directed speech may aid the parsing process because it contains longer pauses than adult-directed speech. In fact, infants prefer speech with pauses as long as they occur between clause units (Hirsh-Pasek et al., 1987; Kemler Nelson, Hirsh-Pasek, Jusczyk, & Cassidy, 1989). Hirsh-Pasek, Kemler Nelson, and their colleagues presented 7- to 10-month-old infants with two samples of infant-directed speech—one with pauses at the clause boundaries and one with pauses within clauses. Infants turned their heads and remained turned longer to the speaker who produced the sample with pauses between the clauses. No preference was found for pauses either within or between clauses in adult-directed speech. These investigators suggest that the exaggerated prosody of infant-directed speech increases the salience of acoustic cues to linguistic structure. Long pauses may help the infant parse the speech stream into meaningful and linguistically relevant units. Identifying word boundaries is more difficult because speakers do not put pauses between words as they do with phrases. As discussed later in this chapter, infants rely on statistical regularities of combinations of sounds to determine word boundaries, and infant-directed speech may facilitate this process (Thiessen, Hill, & Saffran, 2005).

There is also evidence that features of infant-directed speech put new words into focus and that this process may facilitate word learning. Fernald and Mazzie

(1991) found that mothers reading a picture book to their 14-month-old children gave exaggerated prosodic emphasis to new words. The focus words were more likely to occur at fundamental frequency peaks and at the end of the utterance. This pattern was not found when the same women were asked to teach a task that involved novel terminology to another adult. Fernald and Morikawa (1993) found cultural differences among US and Japanese mothers in terms of the objects and concepts they focused on in their speech to their 6-, 9-, and 19-month-old infants, and these differences were mirrored in the early productive vocabulary of the children. Moreover, parental tone exaggeration in Cantonese preceded 3- to 12-month-old infants' perception of tonal differences (Rattanasone, Burnham, & Reilly, 2013). Together, these findings suggest the facilitative effects of infant-directed speech for language learning.

Summary

Modified speech intended for infants appears to serve three functions: maintaining attention and extending the interaction, communicating affective information, and facilitating language learning. These findings are consistent with a conception of the infant as an active perceiver. The infant's behavior, such as paying attention, reinforces this kind of speech on the part of the speaker and increases the probability that it will continue to be used. As a result, infants are shaping the linguistic environment such that it maximizes the presences of meaningful information.

One caveat must be mentioned. Demonstration of a preference is not necessarily the demonstration of a process. Infants' preference for infant-directed speech does not by itself reveal much about how infants learn language. There is no evidence that infant-directed speech is a necessary condition for learning language. Cultures vary in the linguistic socialization techniques used with young children. For example, the Kakuli do not use child-directed speech with their children because they do not believe it is good to teach children childish forms of language (Schieffelin, 1990). These infants are exposed to speech directed toward other adults, and they learn their native language on a timetable comparable to that of infants in the United States.

In addition, identification of relationships is not necessarily demonstration of a process. Speech to children apparently does matter, but how it facilitates language learning is still not clear. For example, Weisleder and Fernald (2013) measured the amount of language spoken directly to 19-month-old infants versus overheard adult language among lower-income Latino families. They found that exposure to child-directed language predicted speed of processing efficiency of language, which in turn predicted vocabulary size. Children who received more infant-directed speech showed faster processing speeds and in turn had larger productive vocabularies at 24 months (for a similar finding with a predominantly Caucasian sample, see Ramirez-Esparza, Garcia-Sierra, & Kuhl, 2014). Identification of such relationships is a positive step toward identifying process, but there is more to learn.

An important step in learning language is breaking the continuous speech stream into meaningful units. Segmentation must occur at multiple levels. Adults parse the speech stream into sentences and more finely into phrases within sentences, words within phrases, syllables within words, and phonemes (the smallest speech units that signal differences in meaning) within syllables. Some levels of segmentation have acoustic cues to aid in the process, such as pauses between phrases, whereas other levels do not have acoustic cues but may have more subtle information, such as the combination of phonemes that cue word boundaries.

We already know that infants are sensitive to pauses delineating phrases. However, to understand speech and to learn new words, one must be able to perceive the individual words that comprise a phrase. By 7½ months, infants are able to detect familiar words in fluent speech (Jusczyk & Aslin, 1995). How do they do this?

Prosodic cues, such as pauses, often do not help with this task because pauses occur inconsistently within words and between words. An example provided by Saffran, Aslin, and Newport (1996) illustrates this point. The stream "pretty baby" has a longer pause between the phonemes /pre/ and /ty/ than between the /ty/ and /ba/. Instead, infants (and adults) must rely on more subtle cues to determine word boundaries. A powerful cue turns out to be the statistical regularity of phonemes (first identified as *clustering* by Hayes & Clark, 1970). Some phoneme combinations are highly regular and occur within words. Low-frequency phoneme combinations signal word boundaries. It appears that infants are prepared to learn high- and low-frequency phoneme combinations quite easily. Saffran et al. presented 8-month-old infants with a continuous stream of four three-syllable nonsense words repeated in random order for 2 min. Following this familiarization phase, infants were presented with two types of test stimuli. One type contained items that were presented in the familiarization phase, and the second type contained novel sequences made from the same syllables. Infants listened longer to the novel-word stimuli, suggesting that they learned the regularities that distinguished the words in the short familiarization episode.

Understanding the range and limits of segmentation based on *statistical learning* or *distributional learning* has been the focus of a tremendous amount of recent research (for reviews, see Aslin & Newport, 2009; Werker, Yeung, & Yoshida, 2012), and a full treatment of the advances and criticisms of this mechanism is beyond the scope of this chapter. This mechanism, however, is undoubtedly robust, but it is not specific to the domain of speech perception, language acquisition, or even humans. Statistical learning appears to be a general learning mechanism, demonstrated in both auditory and visual domains, beginning at birth in humans, and it is used by other species (Bulf, Johnson, & Valenza, 2011; Teinonen, Fellman, Naatanen, Alku, & Huotilainen, 2009; Werker et al., 2012).

Another cue may be stress. In English, the stress in two-syllable words is most often on the first syllable (Thiessen et al., 2005). Paying attention to stress patterns would cue word and syllable boundaries, at least for some types of words (Nazzi

Dilley, Jusczyk, Shattuck-Hufnagel, & Jusczyk, 2005). An early demonstration of such parsing based on stress patterns is provided by Karzon (1985). One- and 4-month-old infants showed evidence of discriminating /marana/ from /malana/ when the second syllable was emphasized using intonation characteristics typical of infant-directed speech (i.e., the speaker overly stressed that syllable). Infants provided no evidence of discriminating the two sequences in adult-directed speech.

Together, these findings suggest that infants are able to parse speech at multiple levels. They treat phrases as units and are further able to break language down into smaller units—namely words and syllables. The processes by which segmentation occurs may depend on the level. Two possible strategies are consistent with available data. The first strategy—bracketing—relies on prosodic information for determining the endpoints of a unit. Pauses are one such cue for the bracketing strategy because they can be used to determine the boundaries of phrases (in infant-directed speech). Stress is another cue used to parse words and syllables. The second strategy—statistical learning—relies on probabilistic dependencies between elements.

From a perceptual learning perspective, both of these explanations should not be surprising. Infants are responding to regularities in their environment—in this case, their linguistic environment. They are extracting higher-level patterns (or invariants) and using this information for perceiving and segmenting speech (Cristia, 2011). Moreover, neurological specification is likely to follow based on this perceptual experience (Karuza et al., 2013; Rivera-Gaxiola et al., 2007). This analysis can be applied to other aspects of speech perception, and we return to this point later in our discussion of infants' perception of nonnative speech contrasts.

Perceptual Constancy

Speech stimuli vary along a number of dimensions. Everyone has slight differences in the way they speak, yet listeners rarely have trouble understanding the meaning of an utterance. Some differences in speech, however, result in changes in meaning. For example, *voice-onset-time differences* distinguish /ba/ from /pa/, but whether /ba/ is spoken in a loud voice or a quiet voice or by a male or a female does not change the phoneme. These observations indicate the crucial importance of extracting relevant differences from speech signals and processing as equivalent physically varying inputs that do not differ in linguistically relevant ways. Some of these equivalence classes may derive from innate perceptual mechanisms, whereas others are learned via linguistic experience.

Categorical Perception

One example of perceptual equivalence is the phenomenon of categorical perception of phonemes. As mentioned previously, the acoustic cue underlying the phonemic distinction between /ba/ and /pa/ is voice-onset time (VOT). To produce /ba/, there is a relatively short lag between the burst (from lip opening) and the onset of laryngeal voicing. In contrast, there is a relatively long lag in voicing to produce /pa/. (You can feel the difference in VOT by holding your fingers against your neck just under your chin and saying /ba/ and /pa/ slowly.) In general, when onset of voice leads or follows the burst by less than 25 msec, adults perceive /ba/, and when voicing follows the release burst by more than 25 msec, they perceive /pa/ (Figure 7.3; Liberman, Cooper, Shankweiler, & Studdert-Kennedy, 1967). Categorical perception simplifies the listener's task by grouping similar but not identical sounds into the same phonemic category. Because of this grouping, the number of discriminable sounds is greatly reduced.

Many studies have investigated the degree to which infants' perception of speech is categorical (for reviews, see Galle & Murray, 2014; Saffran, Werker, & Werner, 2006). In an early study, Eimas, Siqueland, Jusczyk, and Vigorito (1971) investigated 1- and 4-month-old infants' perception of the voiced–voiceless distinction using the stimuli /ba/ and /pa/. Infants were familiarized to one stimulus (e.g., +20-msec VOT, perceived by adults as /ba/) and then tested for discrimination of two stimuli. Both contained a 20-msec difference; however, one was from the same phonetic category (0-msec VOT, perceived by adults as /ba/), and the other was from a different phonetic category (+40-msec VOT, perceived by adults as /pa/). Eimas et al. found that infants showed a greater increase in responding to the cross-category stimulus than to the within-category stimulus. Thus, a given amount of change in the acoustic dimension was perceived by infants as a novel stimulus only when it crossed a phonemic boundary.

The paradigm of presenting infants with stimuli varying uniformly along a particular dimension and, at times, crossing a categorical boundary has been used

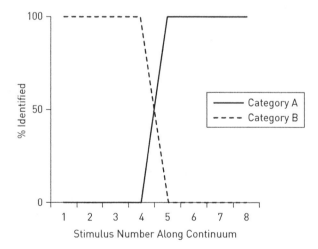

FIGURE 7.3

Schematic representation of categorical perception. Stimulus values above and below some critical value are classified as being in different categories with high probability. The *y* axis indicates percentage of sounds identified in the indicated category. Source: Redrawn with permission of the American Psychological Association from Studdert-Kennedy, M., Liberman, A. M., Harris, K. S., & Cooper, F. S. (1970). Motor theory of speech perception: A reply to Lane's review. *Psychological Review, 77,* 234–249.

to study several dimensions of speech. For example, it has been found that infants between 1 and 4 months of age categorically perceive speech sounds that are differentiated by information contained in formant transitions that signal distinctions between stop constants and semivowels such as /b-w/ along the voicing continuum (Aslin, Pisoni, Hennessy, & Perey, 1981; Eimas & Miller, 1980a). In addition, infants at 1 and 4 months differentiate manner of articulation, specifically the nasal-stop distinction in syllable initial consonants /ma-ba/ (Eimas & Miller, 1980b) and place of articulation /d/, /t/ versus /g/, /k/ versus /p/, /b/; /ma/ versus /na/ (Hillenbrand, 1983, 1984).

This apparent carving up of the continuous acoustic stream into categories has raised some concerns for the mechanism underlying infants' perception and learning of language (Galle & McMurray, 2014). Strict categorical perception would preclude infants' perception of subphoneme subtleties that might be important, particularly if infants rely on distributional patterns for word and syllable segmentation. Moreover, as discussed later, infants need to perceive subtle differences in phonemes in order to become sensitive to the phonological characteristics of the language around them. With these concerns in mind, several studies have reported within-category discrimination of phonemes (e.g., variants of /ba/) between 6 and 9 months of age, leading to the conclusion that within-category perception of phonemes is weaker, but not absent, compared to between-category phonemes (Maye, Werker, & Gerkin, 2002; McMurray & Aslin, 2005).

There may be a developmental progression in categorical perception of phonemes. Young infants aged approximately 1–4 months may take a general approach to perception of phonemes with a strong tendency toward categorical perception. This approach allows for coarse divisions of the acoustic signal into meaningful units by overlooking subtle variations. As infants gain more experience with their linguistic environment, at approximately 6–9 months they may more finely perceive aspects of the acoustic signal and make within-category discriminations. To our knowledge, between- and within-category discrimination has not been studied longitudinally, but such an investigation would enable us to more fully understand the development of categorical perception specifically and mechanisms underlying language learning more generally.

Equivalence Across Speakers

Whereas the discrimination and classification of stimuli are important for the eventual understanding of language, speech stimuli also vary on dimensions that do not influence phonemic category inclusion. For example, different speakers (male, female, adult, or child) may produce an /a/ that varies in intonation contour or pitch. Moreover, there are regional differences within countries and differences across languages in pronunciation of phonemes. For example, in the United States, a Boston native will pronounce "car" differently from a Los Angeles native; similarly, a speaker of English with a Spanish accent will pronounce /a/ differently than a speaker of English with a Midwestern or British accent. Adult listeners perceive all (or most) instances of /a/ as phonemically equivalent. Any speech recognition process must be able to extract invariance across widely differing basic parameters of the speech signal, and data suggest that this occurs within the first 6 months of life for phonemes but closer to 12 months for words.

Kuhl and colleagues conducted several studies investigating infants' ability to perceive vowel sounds (/a/ or /i/) that vary according to speaker or intonation contour as equivalent. In general, infants were either habituated to or trained to make a head-turn response to a vowel sound spoken by either a male or a female with a particular contour. As the experiment progressed, infants were tested for discrimination of the training vowel from a novel vowel as the speaker or intonation contour changed. The results suggest that infants aged 5–16 weeks can detect a vowel change within a context of random change in the pitch contour of the vowel (Kuhl & Miller, 1975). In a control condition, Kuhl and Miller determined that infants at this age can detect a change in pitch contour if the vowel is held constant. Moreover, 6-month-old infants, following training to a male speaker, recognize as similar the same vowel spoken by a female and a child (Kuhl, 1979). This work was extended to younger infants (5–16 weeks) in a study that varied pitch contours and speaker (Kuhl & Miller, 1982).

The fact that infants are able to perceive speech sounds from the same phonetic category as equivalent in the face of specific, nonlinguistically relevant transformations has implications for processes underlying learning to produce speech. Kuhl (1979) suggests that "it would be difficult, if not impossible, to learn to produce speech if the infant adopted the strategy of trying to imitate absolute formant frequencies produced by adult speakers" (p. 1677). Given the difference in size of the articulatory apparatus, it would be impossible for young infants and children to produce sounds that match exactly those sounds produced by adults. Thus, if infants can detect and represent what is similar among vowels spoken by adult and child speakers, they will be on a good footing as they begin to produce speech sounds.

Perception of words across irrelevant variations in speakers is more difficult. Using a paradigm developed by Jusczyk and Aslin (1995), several studies have found disruptive influences of affect (happy vs. neutral emotional tone), speaker (male vs. female; soft voice vs. raspy voice), and accent (foreign-accented English or dialect differences within English). The typical procedure involves a familiarization period, such as 30 sec, in which a target word is presented repeatedly. Following this phase, infants hear passages, one of which has the target word embedded and repeated several times. If infants recognize the target word in the passage, they attend to it longer than to passages not containing the target word. Infants between the ages of 7½ and 13 months are increasingly able to tolerate changes in speakers from the familiarization to the test phase. For example, change in the gender of the speaker and emotional tone disrupted 7½-month-olds' word recognition, whereas infants at 10½ months were able to tolerate such changes (Houston & Jusczyk, 2000; Singh, Morgan, & White, 2004). Changes in accent from North Midlands American English to Ontario Canadian English disrupted 9-month-olds' but not 12-month-olds' word recognition (Schmale, Cristia, Seidl, & Johnson, 2010). Similarly, 9-month-olds did not generalize word recognition across different speakers, one of whom spoke English with a Spanish accent, but 13-month-olds did (Schmale & Seidl, 2009).

Thus, a challenge for young infants is to determine what is and what is not important, and infants at different ages meet this challenge with varying degrees of success. Interestingly, categorical perception processes may help at the level of the phoneme—infants are able to recognize the same phoneme across speakers—but not at the level of the word.

Nonnative Speech Perception

Languages differ in a number of ways, such as word order, stress patterns, rhythmic structure, and phonemic contrasts. From birth, infants show a preference for the language (or languages) spoken by their mothers (Byers-Heinlein, Burns, & Werker, 2010), suggesting they enter the world recognizing some aspects of their soon-to-be native tongue. At the same time, infants arrive ready to perceive meaningful differences present in many languages, not just the one(s) spoken by the adults in their environment. For example, the difference between /l/ and /r/ is meaningful in English but not in Japanese. As a result, native English-speaking adults can discriminate these two sounds, whereas it is more difficult for native-speaking Japanese adults. Before a certain age, however, Japanese infants can also make this phonemic distinction.

Comparing infants' perception of contrasts that are and are not present in their linguistic environment is typically how researchers have studied the role of experience on speech perception. Most studies utilize the conditioned head-turn procedure in which infants are conditioned to make a head turn when a change in phoneme is heard. During conditioning, infants hear pairs of phonemes, or contrasts, that exist in their linguistic environment (adults can perceive the contrast). Following conditioning, infants are presented with contrasts that are not linguistically meaningful in their environment and that adult native speakers cannot discriminate.

Cross-language studies have shown consistently that infants approximately 6 months of age make discriminations among speech samples that older infants (~10–12 months of age) and adults cannot make (for review, see Maurer & Werker, 2014). Here, we highlight a few early examples of this large literature (Lasky, Syrdal-Lasky, & Klein, 1975; Trehub, 1976; Werker, Gilbert, Humprey, & Tees, 1981; Werker & Tees, 1983, 1984). English-learning infants discriminated contrasts from Hindi and Thomson (a language of a native Indian population spoken in central British Columbia), whereas English adults did not. English-learning infants discriminated an oral/nasal vowel distinction (/pa/ vs. /pa~/), present only in French and Polish and the feature of stridency used by Czech speakers. Spanish-learning infants detected contrasts in Thai and English resulting from VOT differences in bilabial stop consonants in Thai and English; adults did not.

The specialization of infants' speech perception occurs gradually throughout the first year of life, and it varies by type of contrast. Earliest specialization occurs for lexical tones found in Asian languages, such as Chinese (Mattock & Burnham,

2006; Yeung, Chen, & Werker, 2013). As early as 4 months, infants who are not raised in tonal linguistic environments are unable to discriminate lexical tones. Next, specialization is for vowels. At approximately 6 months, infants discriminate many (but not all) vowel contrasts in their native language but not in other languages (Kuhl, Williams, Lacerda, Stevens, & Lindblom, 1992; Polka & Werker, 1994; for review, see Tsuji & Cristia, 2014). Lastly, specialization occurs for consonants. By 10–12 months, infants discriminate contrasts in their native language but no longer those in other languages (Burns, Yoshida, Hill, & Werker, 2007; Rivera-Gaxiola, Silva-Pereyra, & Kuhl, 2005; Werker & Tees, 1984).

Moreover, specialization of speech perception extends beyond phonemes. Nine-month-old English-learning infants prefer words that have sequences of sounds that exemplify native (English) rather than nonnative sound sequences (Dutch), but 6-month-olds do not (Jusczyk, Friederici, Wessels, Svenkerud, & Jusczyk, 1993). Also, 9-month-olds prefer the stress pattern of English disyllabic words (strong–weak), whereas 6-month-olds show no preference (Jusczyk, Cutler, & Redanz, 1993). A similar pattern has been found for manual signs in American Sign Language: Four-month-old hearing infants, but not 14-month-olds, discriminate degree of hand opening (Palmer, Fais, Golinkoff, & Werker, 2012). Finally, infants' audiovisual integration of speech extends across languages early in the first year (4 and 6 months) but not later (8 months). Weikum and colleagues (2007) habituated infants with three female faces, on successive trials, speaking different sentences in English or French. Following habituation, infants saw the same females speaking new sentences either in the habituation language or in the other language. Four- and 6-month-old infants noticed when the language switched from French to English (or vice versa), whereas 8-month-olds did not, unless they were being raised in French/English bilingual homes.

Not all contrasts, however, show this pattern. For some linguistic features, the reverse pattern is found. Instead of infants showing early sensitivity that then declines, infants show improvement during the first year of life. An example is vowel length in Japanese. Four-month-old Japanese-learning infants do not discriminate subtle differences in vowel length, but 9½-month-olds do (Sato, Sogabe, & Mazuka, 2010). In cases such as these, the contrast is often subtle, and significant experience with a native language is necessary to perceive it (Narayan, Werker, & Beddor, 2010). For other lexical contrasts, such as Zulu clicks, infant discrimination does not decline with age, perhaps because these sounds are not perceived as lexical in nature and they remain discriminable based on their acoustic properties (Best, McRoberts, LaFleur, & Silver-Isenstadt, 1995; Best, McRoberts, & Sithole, 1988).

What process accounts for this shift from language-general to language-specific perception? In most perceptual domains, infants' performance improves with age. Here, we have a case in which, for the most part, infants' early competence is better than adults' competence and then declines with age. The term *perceptual narrowing* has been used to describe this phenomenon; however, Maurer and Werker (2014; see also Flom, 2014) suggest that *perceptual attunement* may be a better descriptor. Exposure to specific sounds, but not necessarily production of those sounds, maintains the discrimination capability, whereas lack of exposure leads to its loss. Perceptual attunement also allows for improvement in discrimination across the first year. As mentioned previously, for some languages, during this same time period, infants gain expertise in perceiving some contrasts, particularly those that are rare or acoustically difficult to differentiate.

There is controversy surrounding what form exposure must take. Some argue that infants may merely need auditory exposure (Aslin & Pisoni, 1980; Burnham, 1986). Thus, older infants' and adults' discrimination of nonnative contrasts declines as a result of the absence of certain sounds in the environment. An alternative account is that the changes are linguistic in nature (Eimas, 1978). With experience, infants organize sounds into phonemic contrasts relevant to their phonological system; nonnative contrasts are assimilated into existing contrasts. One argument for this viewpoint is that some speech sounds cannot be assimilated (e.g., Zulu clicks). Another argument is the fact that human interaction along with the auditory signal may be required. Kuhl, Tsao, and Liu (2003) showed that English-learning infants at 9 months could discriminate Mandarin Chinese consonant–vowel syllables after approximately 5 hours of training; however, the training had to be in an interactive context with another person. When the auditory information was presented via recording (audio and visual information was present) or only auditorily, infants did not learn the discrimination. Regardless of the type of exposure needed, it must be noted that this process depends on the infant as an active perceiver. Infants are attending to and extracting recurring patterns in speech. In other words, they are perceptually tuning into to the regularities they hear in their auditory world.

Summary: Speech Perception

Perception of speech is crucially important to our interactions with others. Infants enter the world already having heard the speech of their mother and soon develop expertise in discriminating important linguistic features of their native language. Long before infants produce speech, they are segmenting the continuous stream into phrases, words, and syllables. To do so, infants rely on prosodic cues, such as pauses and stress patterns, and on the distributional probabilities of certain sound combinations. Moreover, they are sorting out what features of speech are important linguistically (e.g., phonemes and words) and what are not (e.g., speaker differences and accents). At all times, the young infant is an active perceiver and processor of speech, setting the stage for successful language production, beginning at approximately 1 year of age, when the first real words appear.

CONCLUSION

This chapter focused on ecological acoustics and speech perception. The research on auditory perception of space and object properties in infancy is itself in its infancy. There is much to learn about how infants and adults make use of auditory information for perceiving the world around them. We know little about the development of the rich array of other spatial, object, and event properties that adults derive from sound, such as knowledge of object composition and form and the structure of events. Uncovering the informational bases for these achievements and their developmental courses remain frontiers for perception and perceptual development research.

We know considerably more about the development of infants' speech perception abilities. Long before uttering their first words, infants show preferences for certain types of speech, they perceive phonemes categorically, they match visual and auditory displays on the basis of linguistic information, and they become attuned to the phonemic contrasts of their native language. From a surprisingly early age, they parse the speech stream into smaller, meaningful units and extract statistical regularities in sequences of these units.

Whether speech perception is different from other types of perception is an interesting question. The rapid emergence of complex speech perception skills and the early presence of component abilities (e.g., categorical perception) have led many to wonder whether speech perception abilities are modular in nature and specific to the human species. There is evidence, however, against this idea. First, categorical perception is not unique to speech; it also occurs in color perception (see Chapter 2). Second, infants detect rhythmic structures in music, another complex auditory signal. Newborns have preferences at birth for music heard in utero, and older infants show culture-specific preferences for certain rhythms and musical chords, namely those present in their acoustic environment (Soley & Hannon, 2010; Virtala, Huotilainen, Partanen, Fellman, & Tervaniemi, 2013). Furthermore, we already noted that statistical learning is not limited to the auditory domain, and in Chapter 10 we discuss the fact that perceptual narrowing or attunement processes are also at work with face perception.

You may have noted that in a chapter on auditory perception, we could not constrain ourselves from presenting some work involving other perceptual systems, particularly visual. It seems odd to talk about auditory perception without also talking about visual perception. This may be due to the fact that there are limits in the range within which we hear sound, and if we are close enough to hear something, we can probably also see it (e.g., the crash of a vase hitting the floor). The reverse is not true for visual perception. We are used to seeing things at a distance in the absence of sound (e.g., seeing a bird diving into a lake without hearing the splash). Moreover, auditory and visual perception work well together. When we hear a sound, we often turn to look at its source. We take up the topic of perception from multiple sources of information and the coordinated use of that information in Chapter 8 on intermodal perception.

8 Intermodal Perception

It matters not through which sense I realize that in the dark I have blundered into a pigsty.
—von Hornbostel (1927, p. 83)

INTRODUCTION

A young child drops a vase. She both sees and hears it shatter. The sound causes her mother to turn, expecting, then seeing, the worst. Ordinary incidents such as this one illustrate the coordination of our several senses and reveal some of its most important aspects. A physical event—in this case, the transformation of a unitary object into multiple, intricately shaped pieces—comes to us through more than one sense. The event of shattering is seen and heard. The microstructures of the event as it appears in each sense coincide: At the same moment the child sees the object contact the floor, she hears the first sound of impact, and the bouncing fragments come to rest just as the last jingle subsides. The sounds alone alert the mother and also signal the nature of the event and its location; on looking, she confirms visually what she has already heard.

How do our separate senses come to furnish information about the same events and objects in the world? Why do the inputs to one sense give us expectations about what information will be available to other senses? How do our senses cooperate, and how do they diverge? How does the existence of multiple sensory channels allow us to learn about, and function with, the world? These are the questions of *intermodal* perception and its development.

ECOLOGY OF INTERMODAL PERCEPTION

No topic in perceptual development raises disagreements more fundamental than the origins of intermodal perception. To discuss the task and information of intermodal perception, we must begin with two radically different conceptions. For one view, the starting point is the following: The world available to our senses consists of various kinds of energy—electromagnetic, acoustic, mechanical, chemical, thermal, and so on. To apprehend this energy, we have separate sensory channels, each specialized to receive one kind of energy: for the eyes, light; for the ears, sound; and for different receptors in the skin, pressure and temperature. We can follow the activity in our senses from these physical inputs to their mental outputs. On receiving its special energy, each sensory system gives rise to unique sensations. Vision gives us brightness and color. Tactile senses give us sharp contact or deep pressure, warmth or cold. Our chemical senses offer up tastes and smells, and audition renders loudness and pitch. Each sense has its own unique language in which its outputs are expressed. At the crossroads of these sensory products, the mind must at first be a Tower of Babel. A sensation of bright red is not translatable into a high pitch or a feeling of sharp contact. Given these facts, the central task of development must be *integration*: We must somehow learn to coordinate and integrate our separate senses.

The other view begins with the objects and events in the world. These interact with various forms of energy. The interactions produce patterns in the energy that reach our receptor arrays. Our senses are best thought of as perceptual systems, specialized for extracting these patterns. Some of these patterns, termed *amodal*, are in fact the same in the different energy streams and can be apprehended by different senses. When one knocks on a door, the pitch and loudness of the sounds bear no sensory similarity to the colors and brightness of the hand and door. In an organism's internal framework of time, however, both of these events share the same beginning and end, and the same rhythm pattern of the knocking is both visible and audible. These temporal properties are amodal. The senses are unified in that they bring such information to us through different channels. Much of this information consists of abstract patterns available through more than one sense.

Should the newborn infant, like a newly hired worker, inquire as to her first assignment, she would, on these two perspectives of intermodal perception, be given completely different instructions. From the former perspective, the assignment would be to learn relations between the unique products of the various senses. From the latter, the assignment would be to begin to learn about the unitary world that is manifest through the several sensory channels. Let us consider each perspective and its developmental consequences in more detail, focusing on the earliest tasks and initial equipment. Subsequently, we will discuss how research has helped to decide some of the basic issues and to determine the useful contributions of both perspectives.

Integrating the Senses

What could be more obvious than the separateness of the senses? Physiologically, each sensory system has its own specialized receptors. Beyond the peripheral nervous system, our senses remain separate: We find distinct projection areas in the brain for sight, hearing, touch, and so on. Physically, each sense is specially designed to detect a particular form of energy. When acoustic wavelengths, given by a person's voice, pass through the pupil of an observer's eye and contact the retina, there is complete indifference—no response. The same fate awaits light entering the nose or ear.

Starting from the view that the senses are distinct in their inputs and products, their physiology and their selective contact with the world, the question of intermodal perception must be the following: How do we learn to relate the separate senses? The standard answer given by proponents of this perspective has been that learning occurs through the association of sensations that occur together in time or space (Titchener, 1902). Piaget's (1954) proposals modified this account somewhat, arguing that what glues together separate sensations is their connection with action. Separate streams of sensation are brought into correspondence by activity. When a child squeezes a doll, it deforms (sensed visually and tactually) and squeaks (sensed auditorily). The contingency of all of these sensory outcomes on the initial action, and their contiguity with one another, provides the basis for learning about intersensory relationships (Bushnell, 1994).

What are the requirements for associative learning? Classical views of the mind note spatial contiguity, temporal contiguity, and similarity as the bases for association (Aristotle, 1941; Hobbes, 1651/1974; Locke, 1690/1971). Regarding the inputs from separate senses, similarity would not appear to be much help, if sensory qualities are unique to each sense. This leaves contiguity in space and time. In order for activity in different senses to be related spatially or temporally, there must be a common space and time in which contiguity can be determined (Kant, 1781/1902). Even with an integration view of intersensory development (Birch & Lefford, 1967), we might expect innate sensitivity to common timing, spatial location, or both across the senses.

Perceiving the World Through Multiple Senses

Turning to the second perspective, what is the meaning of von Hornbostel's (1927) graphic example about the pigsty? In this view of intermodal perception, the emphasis is on the physical world: The objects and events in it manifest themselves to us through several sensory channels. We may smell the pigs, hear their grunts, see their bodies, and feel the squishy ground underfoot. An event or object given through several senses remains one thing, not several things. This is a nice homily, but what might it mean? How does this sentiment overcome the physiological, physical, and phenomenological walls that separate our senses, one from the other?

We touched on the answer in Chapter 1. To think of the senses as detecting energy and producing separate sensations is a seductive error. Instead, according to this alternative view, our senses detect *patterns* and produce representations of *structure* of objects and events. The most important properties perceived may be those that are not specific to one sense. Rather, they are *amodal* properties (Michotte, Thines, & Crabbe, 1964). Amodal properties invariably involve spatial, temporal, or spatiotemporal concepts. Of these, the simplest is location. An event specified visually comes from a certain direction relative to the perceiver; this same event and the same direction may be given auditorily. The events will also coincide in time. In the vase example, breaking glass gives visible and audible effects in the same location at the same time, leading to the perception of a unitary event.

Other amodal properties are given as patterns. The spatial array of spines on a porcupine may be detected visually or tactually. (Detecting visually may be wiser.) The rising and falling of a boat on rough seas is given to the passenger on deck visually and also by vestibular sensations. In these cases, the patterns in space or time do not differ across the sensory modalities; they are therefore referred to as *amodal invariants*.

The distinction between amodal properties is closely related to an older distinction, suggested by the philosopher John Locke, between *primary* and *secondary qualities*. In Locke's (1690/1971) words,

Primary qualities of things ... are discovered by our senses, and are in them even when we perceive them not: such are the bulk, figure, number, situation and motion of the parts of bodies; which are really in them, whether we take notice of them or no. Secondly, the sensible secondary qualities, which, depending on these are nothing but the powers those substances have to produce several ideas in us by our senses; which ideas are not in the things themselves otherwise than as anything is in its cause .... For to speak truly, yellowness is not actually in gold, but is a power in gold to produce that idea in us by our eyes, when placed in a due light .... Had we senses acute enough to discern the minute particles of bodies, and the real constitution on which their sensible qualities depend, I doubt not but they would produce quite different ideas in us; and that which is now the yellow colour of gold would then disappear, and instead of it we should see an admirable texture of parts, of a certain size and figure. (pp. 9–11)

Primary qualities—ideas about objects and events that correspond to real physical properties—are also amodal properties in that they are not uniquely the province of only one sensory modality, and they may be detected in multiple sensory channels. Characteristically, amodal properties involve relationships in space or time. This is why we sometimes describe them as higher-order properties. Consider that the sweetness of a sugar cube is a *modal* sensory quality in that it is given only through a single sense—taste. The *form* of a sugar cube, on the other hand, may be detected visually or haptically. The property of form has to do with the arrangement of matter in space, not what the cube is made of. If we broke the cube into fragments, the pieces would still taste sweet, but the cube shape would be lost. A final way of giving the distinction between amodal and modal properties involves mental and physical predicates. Modal properties live in the world of our conscious experience: "Sweetness" is not found in the vocabulary of physics. As Locke understood more than 300 years ago, it is an effect of physical stimulation on our sensory apparatus. Descriptions of the physical world do not invoke sweetness but do require arrangements in space and time; being cube-shaped is a meaningful idea in physics. (Explaining what physical stimuli taste sweet ultimately involves spatial arrangement as well, at very small scales.)

Amodal invariants open the door to a very different view of the task and information for intermodal perception. One task is to detect objects and events by means of amodal invariants. Another is to optimize behavior by using the differing advantages of the multiple windows onto the world afforded by separate perceptual systems.

From this perspective, what do we make of the separate physiology, physics, and phenomenology of the sense? The development of multiple sensory channels allows us to pick up patterns carried by different kinds of energy. However, the patterns may be the same. Each receptor system, and each energy type, may have its uniquely helpful properties. Because light moves in straight lines and our visual apparatus preserves directional information, we obtain exquisite spatial detail visually. Sounds, given our auditory system, are less spatially precise but may more readily tell us about an event in the next room. Answering the question of whether the physical world is unitary or multiple depends on whether we focus on the separate streams of energy or the unitary objects and events about which they carry information. Recent advances in neurophysiology show us that the separate senses are not so separate at certain levels of the nervous system. Some brain areas contain multimodal neurons—that is, single cells responsive to inputs from different modalities (Bergen & Knudsen, 2009).

So far, we have described amodal perception as underlying a single viewpoint about intermodal development. Actually, several different hypotheses have been proposed regarding the role of amodal invariants in development. One view (Bahrick, 1994; Gibson, 1969; Spelke, 1988) postulates that an innate sensitivity to amodal invariants forms the bedrock of early intermodal learning. Experience brings about finer differentiation of detail within and between modalities, but perception begins with a multichannel attunement to a common external world. A more modest version of the idea that intersensory coordination is built into the nervous system was suggested by Morrongiello (1994) regarding auditory–visual coordination. The infant begins with a mapping between modalities that controls some reflexive behavior. A sound may trigger head and eye movement to look in the sound's direction. This reflexive base promotes learning about auditory–visual relationships by getting the infant to look at what she is hearing.

Perhaps the most exotic notion of inborn sensory coordination was suggested by Bower (1974; see also Maurer, 1993). The role of amodal information might be so extreme that initially an infant has no awareness of sensory modality at all. Information about spatial location, timing, or intensity might be picked up without any awareness that it has come from vision, audition, touch, and so on. As development proceeds, the infant would gradually become aware of the separateness of the sensory channels. A more restricted version of this hypothesis is that initially infants are most sensitive to stimulus intensity, regardless of modality (Turkewitz, Lewkowicz, & Gardner, 1966). At an early stage, stimulus intensity may add or substitute across modalities to influence responding.

ABILITIES AND PROCESSES OF INTERMODAL PERCEPTION

We have described two sets of ideas that differ greatly in their implications for the development of intermodal perception. Although we have pointed out the fallacy in the idea that our senses must have only sensations as their outputs, the fallacy indicates not that the classical view is wrong but only that it cannot be established by logic. On the other side of the theoretical fence, it is clear that there is more than one specific way in which intermodal coordination might be built into the infant's nervous system or acquired by learning.

A question of high priority is whether amodal invariants support intermodal perception prior to specific experience. If they do, we might proceed to ask how. Do they act through a few early reflexes, via true intermodal knowledge, or must the separate sensory channels themselves be differentiated from an initial unity of experience?

Intermodal development also involves other questions. What about correlated properties of objects and events that are not supported by amodal invariants? One might learn, for example, that an apple is red and tastes sweet. Nothing about the common reality of space and time (or chemistry and optics, for that matter) guarantees this connection. It is imaginable that something red and apple-shaped could taste bitter. Yet learning of intersensory correlations that happen to be true in our world, such as red apples taste sweet, is an important kind of knowledge. When do infants become able to learn such correlations? Are some kinds more easily acquired than others?

Throughout the years, researchers have approached these questions in two different, but related, ways. One way is to ask about the perception of objects and events based on multisensory information. For example, how does the information simultaneously available from vision and touch inform us of object properties? This is a question about multisensory perception. An alternative approach is to ask how information from one sense articulates with or transfers to information from another sense. For example, if you only feel an object, do you know what it would look like? This is a question about cross-modal transfer of information. In practice, the same processes may underlie both questions; however, we should be aware that the task demands (e.g., attention and memory) for infants may be different.

Auditory–Visual Intermodal Perception

Links in Space and Time

In 1961, Michael Wertheimer reported that a newborn infant younger than 10 min old would turn her eyes to look in the direction of a sound. A toy "cricket" was clicked next to one ear or the other, and although the infant made an eye movement on only approximately half of the 52 trials, when eye movements occurred they were almost always directed toward the sound.

The sensitivity to sound demonstrated by this neonate should not be surprising after our discussion of auditory perception in Chapter 7. What was surprising to readers and researchers in 1961 was the mapping of sound onto space and the indication of some innate audiovisual (or audio-oculomotor) coordination. Such coordination may represent highly adaptive exploratory behavior. The central part of the visual field has greater acuity than the periphery. On hearing a sound from a particular location, newborns may turn to get a better look.

There are less expansive interpretations (e.g., Morrongiello, 1994). The infant may be born with a reflex to turn in the direction of sound. Such a reflex could be guided by a simple mechanism. A discrete sound to one side reaches one ear before the other. A continuing sound reaches the two ears with a lower intensity and a slight delay in its cycle (phase) at the far ear. These interaural differences may be wired into an eye movement reflex. The auditory information may not even have a spatial character at this stage: The direction of interaural differences might trigger visual orienting in the right direction not to any particular location. Such a reflex may require no initial intermodal knowledge at all. Instead, it might be a simple mechanism that helps the infant discover intermodal relationships.

We can separate two issues here. One is the issue of whether orienting is a reflex or an exploratory act. The other concerns the sophistication of intermodal mapping revealed by orienting. Do visual and auditory information feed into a common spatial coordinate system? Or is something much more rudimentary going on—for example, merely turning in the right direction, with no spatial metric?

Taking the second question first, there is evidence that orienting is sensitive to spatial location. Morrongiello, Fenwick, Hillier, and Chance (1994) presented newborn infants with a 20-sec recording of a rattle sound from a loudspeaker located by varying degrees to the left or right of the midline. Perfect accuracy would have produced a linear function with a slope of 1 and intercept of 0; the data show the right intercept but a slope of approximately 0.7. Although the data show imperfect accuracy, they show an orderly relationship between auditory and visual information about space.

Returning to the first issue, several observations support a reflex interpretation of visual orienting in the newborn period. Newborns orient toward sounds in the dark and even when their eyes are closed (Mendelson & Haith, 1976; Turkewitz et al., 1966). In addition, Clifton, Morrongiello, Kulig, and Dowd (1981) observed little habituation of orienting over trials when no visual target was present. In contrast, at approximately 5 months of age, rapid habituation was observed when no visual target was present. These observations support the idea that orienting is not under voluntary control initially or at least not very sensitive to the availability of visual information.

On the other hand, early auditory–visual coordination has properties that are not reflex-like. First, reflexes ordinarily involve specific, stereotypic sensorimotor combinations. Consider your own motor reflex when someone taps your leg just below your knee. The trigger is the tap, and the reflexive action is the movement of the lower part of your leg. All reflexes have one trigger and one action. Moreover, the action cannot be modified once it has begun (e.g., once your leg starts to move up, it cannot change direction to move toward the side). Wertheimer (1961) measured eye movements, but many subsequent reports have involved head-turning movements (Clifton et al., 1981; Muir & Field, 1979). Both actions are appropriate in spatial direction. If these behaviors are reflexive, there are at least two reflexes here. Second, auditory–visual orienting appears to violate the primary laws of reflex action, such as the intensity–magnitude law and the intensity–probably law (Millenson, 1967). The former law states that as intensity of the trigger increases, the magnitude of response increases. The latter states that as intensity increases, the probability of response increases. Experiments on early audiovisual orienting have shown that soft sounds elicit eye movements in the direction of sounds but that loud sounds are more likely to produce looks away from the sound source. Studies on habituation of head turning have shown that newborns are sensitive to stimulus novelty. With repeated exposure, infants will reliably begin turning away from a sound (Zelazo, Weiss, & Tarquinio, 1991). A change in the sound reinstates head turning, even if that change is less intense sound. These properties of infant orienting to sounds do not fit a reflex interpretation.

Other data indicate flexibility in ongoing responding that seems more like exploratory behavior than reflex action. In the experiments by Morrongiello et al. (1994), some trials were shift trials in which an initial sound location was used until the infant started to respond, after which the sound was shifted to a new location. Infants made compensatory responses in this situation, indicating that their monitoring of the sound's location is ongoing. Morrongiello et al. compared the situation to the updating of saccadic eye movements in adults when a target moves (Becker & Jurgens, 1979). On balance, neonate auditory–visual coordination does not appear to be a reflex. It appears to be more like rudimentary spatial exploratory behavior.

Neural Bases of Auditory–Visual Coordination

Exciting developments in neurophysiology give us important evidence from other species about the neural implementation of early auditory–visual coordination and how it changes with experience. The superior colliculus is a subcortical structure associated with attention and orienting functions (recall the discussion of this structure in Chapters 2 and 6 when discussing visual pathways). Some individual neurons in this region, at least in barn owls and cats, respond to both auditory and visual inputs. Specifically, each unit responds to sounds or visual events that come from the same spatial direction, and such units may be activated much more by simultaneous auditory–visual inputs than by either alone (Bergen & Knudsen, 2009). Sound localization in a variety of species, including humans, depends on intensity and phase differences in the sounds at two ears. An earplug placed in one ear will attenuate sound intensity and produce a small phase shift at that ear, thus remapping the intensity and phase differences for sounds originating from any direction. Knudsen (1983, 1985) raised young barn owls with one ear plugged and found that units in the superior colliculus had compensated so that they were receptive to sounds and sights from a single location. If the earplug was removed, discrepancies in the appropriate direction appeared (Figure 8.1). With experience, recalibration of receptive fields was possible as long as the owl had not reached adulthood. If the plug was removed after adulthood, the altered relations between auditory and visual locations remained permanent (Knudsen & Knudsen, 1985). Similar effects were found for visual distortion. Owls wearing prisms, which distorted the real location of objects in space, recalibrated their auditory space (DeBello & Knudsen, 2004; Knudsen, 2002).

These neuropsychological findings suggest that at least the owl brain is wired to coordinate sights and sounds and to recalibrate the relationship (up to some point in development) as necessary. The existence of some intermodal orienting in human neonates suggests that at least a coarse matching of auditory and visual maps exists from the beginning. Each map must change somewhat because of growth (e.g., changing separation between ears caused by growth alters intensity and phase differences), and the precision of the two spatial maps is not the same. The auditory map is less precise, whether in terms of neuronal receptive fields in animals or precision of localization performance (Knudsen & Knudsen, 1985;

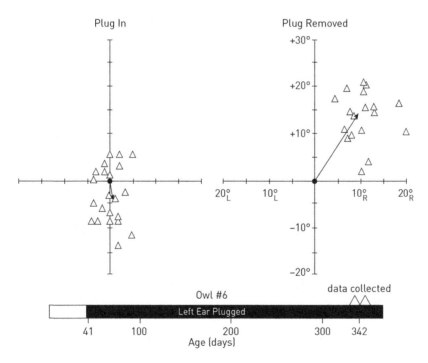

FIGURE 8.1

Shifts in the auditory spatial turning of tectal units in an owl following monaural occlusion at 41 days of age. The centers of the auditory best areas (delta) of all bimodal units located in the rostral tectum are plotted relative to the centers of their visual receptive fields. The vectors represent the median auditory visual misalignment of these samples. The auditory history of this owl and the period during which the data were collected are indicated at the bottom. Source: Reprinted with permission of the Society for Neuroscience from Knudsen, E. I. (1985). Experience alters spatial tuning of auditory units in the optic tectum during a sensitive period in the barn owl. *Journal of Neuroscience*, 5, 3094–3109.

Meredith & Stein, 1986; Morrongiello, 1994; Stein, Meredith, & Wallace, 1994). However, the amodal invariant of spatial location appears to provide in some form an innate foundation for intermodal perception. Later in this chapter, we discuss other examples of innate preparedness for intermodal perception.

Simultaneity

How far can we get in explaining intermodal perception by virtue of a common space in which sounds and sights occur? There are severe limitations. Different sounds and sights occur in a given direction at different times. Without a common *time* in which sensory experiences unfold, our cognition might remain incoherent despite a common space. Also, we may have mismatches in a given spatial direction between perceptible events. For instance, you may sit in a room and hear the sound of a car's motor outdoors. When you look in the direction of that sound, you may see only a stationary lamp and an opaque wall behind it. Intermodal development may require initial sensitivity to synchrony in time, and it may require some ability to match event structure. The car sound and the stationary lamp should not be linked in intermodal learning, despite being in the same spatial direction at the same time.

If temporal and spatial relationships figure in early intersensory perception, we might be able to discover the relevant properties by separating them. For example, detecting an event of similar temporal structure in vision and audition might lead to the expectation that the visually and auditorily given locations should match. Spelke (1976) developed a measure to test this expectation. It is based on the visual preference method and exploits infants' tendencies to look in the direction of a sound. In the task, two side-by-side visual events are displayed, and the sounds are played by a speaker centered between them. In the original experiments of this type, Spelke showed 16-week-olds two films—one showing percussion events between a baton, tambourine, and wooden block and the other showing a person playing peek-a-boo. When a soundtrack from one event was played, infants looked reliably longer to the appropriate visual event. Bahrick, Walker, and Neisser (1981) found similar results using a variety of event pairs, and Pickens (1994) showed that infants matched changes in sound with visual changes in depth, such that infants matched an increasing and decreasing sound intensity with an approaching and receding object. We also showed visual–auditory integration in speech perception by newborns in Chapter 7.

Subsequent work sought to specify the bases of intermodal perception. A large body of work confirms that temporal synchrony is the first type of information that infants use for perceiving amodal invariants; rhythm, tempo, and intensity come later (Lewkowicz, 2000). Consistently, when temporal synchrony is disrupted, young infants do not perceive the amodal invariants in events. This synchrony, however, does not need to be perfect. In an auditory–visual stimulus, the sound might precede the visual event (e.g., you hear the sound of an impact before seeing the object hit the table; this is called A-V asynchrony), or the sound may follow the visual event (e.g., you see the object hit the table and then hear the impact;

this is called V-A asynchrony). Adults tolerate small amounts of asynchrony: up to 65-msec offsets for A-V asynchrony and up to 112-msec offsets for V-A asynchrony (Lewkowicz, 1996). The *intersensory temporal synchrony window* is much larger for 2- to 8-month-old infants: A-V offsets can occur up to 350 msec before infants perceive the asynchrony, and V-A offsets are larger still at 450 msec (Lewkowicz, 1996). These estimates, both for adults and for infants, were based on events in which a circular object bounced up and down. The tolerance for asynchrony by infants is even higher with speech stimuli (Lewkowicz, 2010).

These findings suggest an interesting paradox: Temporal synchrony is a foundation for intermodal perception, but infants are forgiving in its timing. This forgiveness may be a positive design flaw. Infants' neural processing of auditory and visual events is slower than that of adults, and auditory and visual information is processed at different speeds within infants (Kopp & Dietrich, 2013). Thus, a window that is too narrow would lead the infant to misperceive truly multimodal events as two separate events, one visual and one auditory. At the same time, infants may be in the position to misperceive two separate but closely occurring events as unified.

Single Versus Multiple Objects

Another property that is perceived intermodally is number. Bahrick (1987, 1992) was the first to test infants' perception of single and multiple objects. One stimulus consisted of a large marble moving back and forth in a plastic tube (single stimulus). A second consisted of several small marbles moving in a tube (compound stimulus). The tubes' motions consisted of rotations around an axis perpendicular to the long axes of the cylinders, causing the marbles to fall downward. In a visual preference procedure, 4-month-old infants showed preferences based on the synchrony of impact sounds with visual impacts. They did not show reliable preferences based on the temporal microstructure (e.g., single impact vs. multiple) specifying single or multiple objects until 6 months of age. In a different procedure, Bahrick (1988) found evidence of learnability of sound and sight pairings by 3½-month-olds. Infants who were habituated to visual and auditory events corresponding in both global synchrony and temporal microstructure detected a change in auditory–visual relationships afterwards. Infants habituated to sound–sight pairings that did not correspond in synchrony or microstructure showed no evidence of learning.

The quantity distinction infants made in Bahrick's studies was one versus many. Infants may have more precise numerical skills, such that they can detect one versus two or one versus three objects. We explore numerosity in more detail in Chapter 11; however, it is worth noting here that infants appear to use multiple sources of information for number perception. One of the earliest studies to address this topic was conducted by Starkey, Spelke, and Gelman (1983, 1990). Infants viewed two displays, side by side, of household items (e.g., comb, memo pad, and green pepper); one display had two items, and the other display had three items. The soundtrack played either two or three drum beats. Six- to 8-month-old infants looked significantly longer to the visual display containing the number of items that matched the number of sounds. In another experiment, the researchers showed that presentation of the visual displays and the sounds does not have to be simultaneous (Starkey et al., 1990). Whether this and other experiments show that infants have an abstract concept of number is addressed later (Farzin, Charles, & Rivera, 2009). For our present purposes, this finding is consistent with the work we have already discussed about infants' auditory–visual integration. Number appears to be amodally specified, and young infants are sensitive to this information in both auditory and visually domains.

Moreover, Starkey and colleagues have shown that infants can make arbitrary sound–object pairings. Up to this point in our discussion, the sounds have been ecologically consistent with the visual events, at least for adults: We expect a bouncing object to make an impact sound, an approaching train's whistle to increase in intensity, and one marble to make a "clunk" sound in a cylinder. In the study by Starkey et al. (1983, 1990), drumbeats were paired with static images of household objects. The ability of infants to make arbitrary auditory–visual pairings may not be limited to infants 6 months of age or older. In fact, newborns may be able to do so under some conditions (Morrongiello, Fenwick, & Chance, 1998; Slater, Quinn, Brown, & Hayes, 1999). Slater and colleagues demonstrated that newborn infants who were shown a geometric shape paired with its "own" sound learned the pairing as long as the sound played when the infants fixated the visual stimulus. In other words, the visual–sound pairing was controlled by the infants' attention, thus giving them an active role in learning.

Substance

Can substance be perceived intermodally? On sensation-based accounts, notions of substance, such as solidity, rigidity, and elasticity, might be considered exclusively the province of tactile or haptic perception. On an ecological view, we might consider properties such as solidity and rigidity to be fundamentally abstract ones—that is, characteristics of physical objects that might be perceived via different perceptual systems. In Chapter 6, we previewed this question about intermodal perception. You may recall that Gibson and Walker (1984) allowed infants to mouth a rigid or elastic object and then tested to determine if the infants visually recognized it. Bahrick (1983) studied 4-month-olds' intermodal perception of substances with visible and audible events. One visual display showed two wet sponges squeezing against each other, and the other visual display showed two wooden blocks hitting each other. One soundtrack played a "squishing" sound and the other a "clacking" sound. When the corresponding audible and visible displays were in synchrony, infants visually attended to the appropriate (matching) event. When the display of wooden blocks was synchronized to the squishing sound and vice versa, however, infants did not look more to the synchronized display. The results indicate that both hearing and sight can pick up information about substances, such as their rigidity and nonrigidity, just as younger infants are able to do so from oral exploration.

Summary: Auditory–Visual Intermodal Perception

Our tour of auditory–visual intermodal perception suggests several conclusions. First, at least some of the links across these two perceptual systems are hardwired. Early visual orienting toward a sound might conceivably be reflexive, but several of its properties are more compatible with the interpretation that it is a rudimentary system for exploration in a common auditory–visual space. Neurophysiological evidence in other species supports the idea of an abstract spatial representation that can be accessed through different sensory channels. A second conclusion is that besides colocation in space, synchrony in time allows young perceivers to detect the same event through sight and sound. Other amodal invariants also support early intermodal event perception under at least some circumstances, including rate and temporal microstructure of collision events. Some of the latter variables appear to develop later than synchrony. A third conclusion is that infants may be overly generous in pairing auditory and visual information. Temporal synchrony does not have to be perfectly timed, and impact sounds occurring with a change in direction, without visible impact, are sufficient for intermodal perception. The result is infants' privileging multimodal specification of objects and events by use of overinclusive rules that may be refined as perceptual systems develop and as infants gain increasing experience with objects and events.

Visual–Haptic Intermodal Perception

Coordination between seen and felt properties of objects is such a subtle aspect of skilled perception and action that we do not often reflect on it. Perhaps this is one reason why haptic perception, compared to visual and auditory perception, has not been as extensively studied in adult perception. We might usefully distinguish between *tactile* and *haptic* perception. Tactile perception—receiving information from contact of the skin with objects—has long been acknowledged as a basic sensory mode. The implicit idea is that this mode functions by mere contact—stimulation of mechanoreceptors (or temperature receptors, etc.) in the skin. This conceptualization, however, provides only a limited view of what is possible through contact. For example, an object pressed into the hand is seldom recognizable (Gibson & Gibson, 1955). A more comprehensive concept is that of *haptic perception*. Tactile information is picked up in combination with systematic exploratory movement of the hand (or mouth), yielding much more information than passive contact.

Haptic perception furnishes information about form, substance, solidity, temperature, texture, and other object properties. Research with adults suggests that adults possess characteristic types of object exploration related to these different properties (Klatzky & Lederman, 1993). The combination of vision is especially powerful in underwriting skilled action. We see and reach toward an object, confirm our grasp by touch, maintain contact, and change the object's position (e.g., a steering wheel) while looking elsewhere to pick up information that guides an overall action (e.g., driving a car).

For adults, there are many varieties of haptic exploration (Lederman & Klatzky, 2009; see Figure 9.3). For example, an object's temperature and solidity may be detected merely by grasping it, but a coordinated set of movements along object edges combined with tactile feedback is required to detect three-dimensional form. Thus, the development of intermodal relationships between vision and touch depends not only on tactile receptivity but also on selective and coordinated motor behavior that goes with it.

Oral–Visual Coordination

What are the roots of intermodal coordination between haptic and visual perception? Skilled reaching and manipulation of objects do not emerge until 4 or 5 months of age. Accordingly, the earliest visual–tactile coordination has been sought using a part of the motor system that seems to be more advanced in the early weeks of life—the mouth. Young infants will mouth an object in an exploratory manner. Meltzoff and Borton (1979) reported evidence that 1-month-old infants relate shape and texture information obtained orally and visually. After mouthing, but not seeing, a pacifier with either a small cube with nubs on it or a smooth sphere, infants looked longer at a visual display matching the one they had mouthed. After mouthing a rigid or elastic cylinder, infants looked significantly longer to a visual display of a novel substance. As discussed in Chapter 6 and previously in this chapter, information about substance was perceived both orally and visually at approximately the same age (Gibson & Walker, 1984).

These results suggest some relating of oral and visual object properties. It is not entirely clear why these effects are sometimes manifest as familiarity preferences and sometimes as novelty preferences (as would be typical for habituation studies within a single modality). Interpreting a familiarity preference in a single experiment seems problematic. One might even be so perverse as to suggest that infants match tactual information for nonrigidity to visual information for rigidity and vice versa. Because modality change always produces substantial novel aspects in both members of a pair of test trials, cross-modal familiarity preferences may indicate the infants' recognition of commonality within a novel context. Whether novelty or familiarity preferences occur may depend on the degree of novelty of the test situation. Moreover, the extent to which infants are familiarized (given a few seconds of experience) or habituated to a criterion may also affect responding (Sann & Streri, 2007). In any case, the fact that these familiarity preferences are common in cross-modal tests but not in intramodal ones tends to argue against the idea that very young infants are aware only of amodal information (Bower, 1974; Maurer, 1993). Change of modality clearly makes a difference.

Visual–Manual Coordination

Until recently, studies of visual–manual coordination have been conducted with infants aged 6 months or older, given limitation in infants' control over manual behavior. The results of early visual–manual transfer tasks have yielded somewhat cryptic results. For example, Rose, Gottfried, and Bridger (1981a, 1981b) found evidence for visual recognition of a previously felt object by 6- and 12-month-olds but no evidence of oral–visual matching at 6 months. A later study using similar methods and stimuli found no reliable evidence of visual–tactual matching at 12 months. Other studies have found tactile to visual transfer as indicated by familiarity preferences in 6-month-olds (Ruff & Kohler, 1978), as well as nonhuman infant primates (Gundersen, 1983). As Streri (1993) suggested, many of these conflicting findings may be due to differences in stimuli, methodology, and type of task.

These discrepancies aside, older infants' perception of object properties across modalities is impressive. For example, 5-month-old infants perceive the number of objects experienced haptically and transfer this knowledge to a visual test (Feron, Gentaz, & Streri, 2006). Across habituation trials, infants were allowed to explore two or three haptically distinct objects (a solid cube, a solid sphere, and a ring with a hole in the center). Following habituation, infants viewed displays of two and three objects (but not the ones experienced in the habituation phase). Infants looked significantly longer to the display containing the novel number of objects. Jovanovic, Duemmler, and Schwarzer (2008) showed the extent to which infants perceive the correlation of object features across visual and haptic modalities. They constructed objects that varied in size (large and small), shape (cube and cone), and texture (smooth and indented). Following habituation to two of the objects, infants were presented with a familiar object, a "switched" object in which one of the properties was changed, and a completely novel object (a broad flat ring with rough texture). When tested visually in both habituation and test phases, 8-month-olds, but not 6-month-olds, detected the switch, suggesting that the older infants processed the objects configurally (or the relations among the features). The younger infants most likely processed the individual object features but not the relation among them or perhaps their colocation on the same object. In contrast, when infants were allowed to look at and manually explore the objects, providing multimodal information about the features, both 6- and 8-month-olds looked significantly longer to the switch trials. This latter finding suggests an advantage for multimodal information over unimodal information.

More recently, researchers have found clever ways to assess younger infants' perception across the visual and haptic systems despite the limitations in their manual repertoire. Newborns will grasp objects, and some object properties, such as shape and texture, can be perceived from a single grasp or multiple grasps across trials. Research with newborn infants gets to the heart of Molyneux's question presented in the Preface. As you may recall, Molyneaux asked Locke (1690/1971) whether a blind man who had the luck of restored sight would recognize objects without first touching them. Held et al. (2011) reported the answer to be "no," agreeing with Locke. In their study, Held et al. assessed visual, haptic, and cross-modal shape recognition in children (aged 8–17 years) who had correctable congenital visual impairment. Two days after surgery, the participants matched object shape within modality (visual or haptic) with close to perfect accuracy. Participants' performance did not exceed 60% correct when they were asked to match shape from touch to vision. Four days after surgery, cross-modal performance exceeded 80%. Thus, it appears that people with significant visual deprivation learn quickly to associate touched object properties with visual ones.

What about the newborn baby? Is there coordination between manual touch and vision as we have seen for 1-month-olds for oral exploration and vision? Or do they need a period of time to learn how touch and vision articulate with one another, as the newly sighted adults? In one study, Sann and Streri (2007) tested for cross-modal transfer of shape and texture information. In two experiments on shape, infants were habituated to either a cylinder or a prism. Following habituation, infants viewed both the cylinder and the prism, one of which was the shape presented during habitation and the other was a novel shape. When infants were habituated haptically (the shape was placed in their hand without them seeing it), they looked significantly longer to the novel shape during the test phase. When infants were habituated visually (they viewed one of the shapes), they held onto both shapes equally in the test phase. Cross-modal transfer of textural information did not show this asymmetry. To test newborns' perception of object texture, infants were habituated to either a smooth or a nubby cylinder; following habituation, infants were presented with both the smooth and the nubby cylinder. Regardless of whether infants first felt or looked at the cylinder during habituation, they looked at or held the novel-textured stimulus significantly longer than the familiar one during the test phase. The asymmetry in the transfer of shape information but not texture information has been found with older children and adults (Juurmaa & Lehtinen-Railo, 1988; Streri, 1987). Thus, for some object properties, newborn infants appear to perceive them amodally. Their limitations in perceiving some properties amodally may not be a reflection of the infants but of the information itself. In this case, shape provides more information about objects than does texture. Nevertheless, we see an example of young infants' responsiveness mirroring that of adults and a reliance on the most veridical information.

Haptic Perception of Unity and Boundaries

Many studies of haptic–visual coordination have primarily centered on shape information. A different, perhaps more basic, question concerns perception of unity and boundaries. Under what conditions will parts of objects, separated in space, be perceived as connected? Visually, as discussed in Chapter 5, infants in the first half year depend on common motion of visible parts, but not on surface or form similarities, to detect unity. Streri and Spelke (1988) tested whether this developmental pattern holds in haptic perception of objects. Infants aged 4 or 5 months haptically explored two rings, one in each hand, that were either rigidly connected and moved together or were independently movable. After habituation, infants were tested for looking time to two visual displays—one with two rings rigidly connected and the other with two rings separated by a gap. Relative to baseline looking performance, infants who habituated haptically to the rigidly connected display looked longer at the two disconnected movable rings; infants who habituated haptically to the independently movable rings looked longer at the rigidly connected ring display. In subsequent studies, infants' perception of unity persisted based on motion characteristics of the objects despite changes in substance, texture, or shape (Streri & Spelke, 1989) and direction of translation of the connected parts (vertically or horizontally; Streri, Spelke, & Rameix, 1993).

These findings are strikingly similar to those of Kellman, Spelke, Johnson and their colleagues (reviewed in Chapter 5): When objects undergo common motion, 2- and 4-month-old infants perceive object unity. The one exception found in the visual domain was rotary motion. Infant perception of unity of a partly occluded rotating rod did not emerge until 6 months of age (Eizenman & Bertenthal, 1998). Would the same be true of haptic exploration of a rotating display? Streri, Gentaz, Spelke, and van de Walle (2004) explored this question. In one experiment, 4½-month-old infants were haptically habituated to either two unconnected rings that moved independently or two connected rings that together rotated around a central point (Figures 8.2A and 8.2B). Following habituation, infants viewed visual displays of two connected and two unconnected rings. Infants habituated to the independent rings looked significantly longer to the connected ring test display, whereas infants habituated to the connected rings looked significantly longer to the independent ring test display. A follow-up experiment showed that rotary motion was only effective when both rings moved in the same direction (Figure 8.2C). These findings suggest earlier sensitivity to rotary motion in the haptic domain than in the visual domain, and they lend support to one explanation of why rotary motion does not specify object unity before 6 months (Eizenman & Bertenthal, 1998). In the typical visual display, the visible ends move in different directions (e.g., behind the block, the top part of the rod moves left while the lower part moves right) and parts of the rod move at different speeds, resulting in a more complex motion pattern than with translation. Moreover, this visual rotary motion was more complex than the rotary motion present in the haptic displays of Streri et al. (2004). Notably, in the study by Streri et al., infants perceived object unity only when the two objects moved in the same direction and the extent of rotary motion was constrained, moving much less than the full 360 deg used previously in unimodal tasks.

Together, these results suggest that motion relationships given haptically lead to perception of unity or separateness in much the same way as visually given motion relationships. In order to complete our understanding of haptic perception of unity and the comparative developmental story between vision and touch, data from younger infants are needed. As discussed in Chapter 5, 2-month-olds also perceived the unity from common motion, but newborns did not. Newborns' patterns of looking suggest that they perceived the visible ends of the rods as two separate pieces, a surprising example of an incorrect perceptual rule with which to start life (see Chapter 5 for alternative interpretations). It may not be possible to test object unity with newborns given their limits in manual exploration, but such a study certainly would be worth the effort.

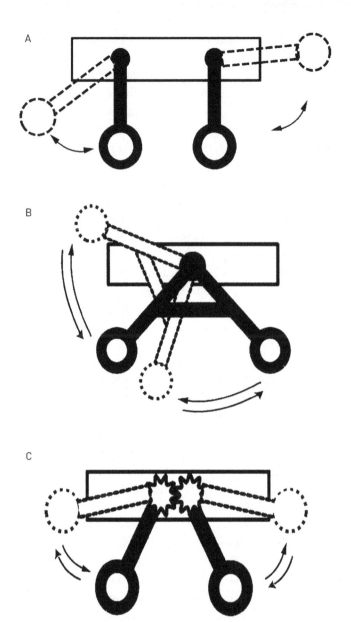

FIGURE 8.2

Stimuli used to test infants' perception of unity from haptic information. Infants were allowed to manually explore (but not look at) stimuli that rotated, either in a connected manner or independently. A allows for unconnected independent movement of the two rings. B allows for connected rigid rotational movement in the same direction, whereas C allows for connected rigid rotational movement in opposite directions. Source: From Streri, A., Gentaz, E., Spelke, E., & van de Walle, G. (2004). Infants' haptic perception of object unity in rotating displays. *The Quarterly Journal of Experimental Psychology*, 57A, 523–538; reprinted with permission by Taylor and Francis, Ltd., (http://www.tandfonline.com).

Summary: Haptic–Visual Intermodal Perception

Infants' visual–haptic coordination appears early, much like that of auditory-visual integration. Whether exploring objects by mouth or using their hands, infants gain considerable information about objects and their properties. Newborn infants have some capacity to transfer shape and texture information from touch to vision. One-month-old infants perceive object properties such as substance, and 4½-month-olds perceive object unity from visual and haptic information. Older infants benefit from multimodal experiences with objects, leading to improved object recognition across modalities and perhaps representation of abstract concepts such as number.

It is interesting to note that most of the research we discussed in this section asked questions about transfer of information across modalities. Very few studies have addressed perception of haptic and visual information simultaneously, as we did in the previous section on auditory–visual intermodal perception. This difference may have arisen due to methodological considerations or from the philosophical foundation of this line of inquiry. Indeed, Molyneux's question was about recognition of an object visually after only having haptic experience. The simultaneous coordination of visual and haptic information is common in infants' everyday lives; we would not want you to think otherwise. It increasingly occurs as infants are able to sit independently and explore objects on their own. We discuss a number of examples, and the outcomes, of this type of exploration in Chapter 9 on perception and action.

The Nature of Intermodal Perception

By this point, it should be clear that the young infant's world is experienced intermodally. From birth or soon after, infants perceive events across multiple modalities (e.g., seeing and hearing an approaching person), and they are able to transfer object and event information across modalities (e.g., the texture of an object). Two remaining questions are how this information is processed and what advantage multimodal experience provides the developing child.

First, let us consider how the information is processed. Each intermodal encounter must begin with registration of energy at the sensory receptors. At what point is the information integrated amodally such that a unified event is perceived (a bouncing puppet) rather than auditory signals and visual patterns? Figure 8.3 provides two possible accounts of intermodal matching in the context of a unit formation task. In the first account (called here "parallel processing"; Figure 8.3A), information from the different senses is processed in parallel, resulting in a combined representation (in this case, of the connectedness of the objects). Theoretically, in this account source information from both sensory systems is still available at this final stage. In the second account (called here "amodal processing"; Steri et al., 1993; Figure 8.3B), information from the different senses is combined in an amodal step before the formation of a representation. In this case, source information from the different senses may be lost; the resulting representation is of an object and it's properties irrespective of how those properties were specified.

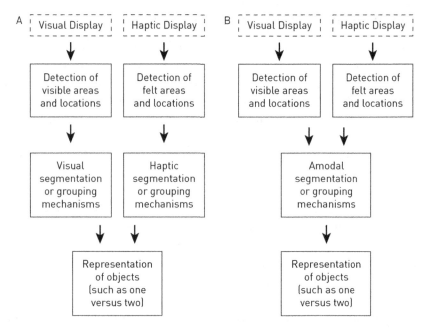

FIGURE 8.3

Two possible accounts of intermodal matching. (A) Processes in each perceptual system (e.g., vision and touch) perform segmentation and grouping and produce object representations in a common format. (B) Outputs of each perceptual system consist of unsegmented representations of surfaces and movements. An amodal mechanism parses these into units. Outputs of this amodal mechanism are connected on separate objects.

Although it is difficult to directly test these two alternatives, it might help to consider the neural architecture. In animals, multimodal neurons exist, and areas of the cortex that primarily respond to one type of sensory information, such as sound, also show responsiveness to information from other senses, such as vision (Stein & Stanford, 2008). Although these examples could merely be a sign of flexible architecture, they could also be indicative of neural support for an amodal perceptual and representational system. Behavioral data, however, suggest a parallel processing account. Adults show flexibility in which perceptual information is used in a context in which one type of information (e.g., haptic) may be more reliable or veridical than another (e.g., from vision). Ernst and Banks (2002) showed that adults based their judgments on the less noisy (more accurate) information from one system in haptic–visual tasks; this reliance is based on the quality of the information within each particular context. There is no general rule regarding one system always dominating the other. Moreover, in bimodal tasks, information from the two perceptual systems is not lost, whereas in some cases, multiple sources of information in one modality are lost (Hillis, Ernst, Banks, & Landy, 2002). Hillis et al. suggest a fusion of information occurring within modality but not across modalities. The evidence reviewed here is not wholly convincing in supporting one approach over the other, and future research that illuminates this process will be fruitful.

As should be obvious by now, intermodal perception results in a redundancy of information. Why does a young infant, even a newborn, who does not do much on his own need multiple sources of information for objects and events? Would it not be easier for the young infant to attend to and/or process information from only one modality at a time? From a traditional perspective, the answer would be "yes." From an ecological perspective, the quality of the information is what is important, not how much of it there is to process. Bahrick and Lickliter (2012) suggest that redundancy of information across modalities aids learning. Their hypothesis, *the intersensory redundancy hypothesis*, emphasizes the importance of multimodal events in capturing infant attention, which then facilitates information processing, learning, and memory. A predicted outcome is that multimodal events will have an advantage for infant attention, learning, and memory. Indeed, this advantage has been seen in infants' performance. We already noted that infants at 6 months perceive the correlation among object properties when they are able to simultaneously view and manipulate objects but not when only visually inspecting them (Jovanovic et al., 2008). Another example comes from an auditory localization task (Neil, Chee-Ruiter, Scheier, Lewkowicz, & Shimojo, 2006). Infants are faster to respond to location changes with bimodal audiovisual stimuli than with only auditory or visual stimuli alone. Allocating more attentional resources to redundant information has also been shown in event-related potentials. Five-month-olds showed greater Nc responsiveness (a measure of attention) to synchronous face–voice displays compared to asynchronous face–voice displays or a visual display of a person speaking without sound (Reynolds, Bahrick, Lickliter, & Guy, 2014). Another prediction of the intersensory redundancy hypothesis is that unimodally specified properties (e.g., orientation of a hammer) would not be as salient as multimodally specified properties (e.g., the rhythm of hammer–surface contact). In support of this prediction, 3- and 5-month-olds did not detect a change in the orientation of a hammer when the events were specified bimodally; they did so when events were unimodal (Bahrick, Lickliter, & Flom, 2006). Toward the end of the first year of life, infants show increasing ability to attend to both unimodal and bimodal object and event properties (Bahrick, Lickliter, Castellanos, &Vaillant-Molina, 2010; Flom & Bahrick, 2010). From this perspective, infants begin life attending to objects and events that are multiply specified, and they learn about salient and often important object and event features or invariants; with age, infants attend to and learn about less salient unimodal properties.

CONCLUSION

Our treatment in this chapter concentrated on auditory–visual and visual–haptic perception of events. Elsewhere are excellent reviews of intermodal perception among other senses (e.g., Bremner, Lewkowicz, & Spence, 2012). The research we have considered hardly does justice to the many creative and informative contributions of researchers in these areas. It suffices to give us some perspective, however, on the development of intermodal perception. Intermodal coordination begins at birth and rests heavily on amodal invariants, as theorized by ecological theorists of perception. There are strong reasons to believe that perceptual systems are attuned to a common physical environment and that their outputs are abstract representations of objects and events in that environment. Not all amodal information is found to be usable in the early months of life, and infants' intermodal coordination shows limitations that are not fully understood but that may rest on changing attentional dispositions as well as maturation and learning within each perceptual modality.

Associating sensory information from separate senses, predicted to be the main developmental agenda from traditional views of perception, plays a different role. Guided by amodal information that unifies our separate sensory channels, correlations among sensory attributes that are not based on amodal properties can be learned, allowing the developing child to discover and remember that apples are sweet and to anticipate the face that will appear momentarily when particular footsteps are heard.

9 Perception and Action

We must perceive in order to move, but we must also move in order to perceive.
—J. Gibson (1979, p. 223)

INTRODUCTION

Perception and action are so interdependent that it is difficult to imagine the evolution of either without the other already in place. Would some immobile, action-less organism ever have developed rudimentary perceptional ability? Doubtful. Knowledge without a capability for action seems useless. Did some ancient organism move about randomly, without information from the environment, to feed, escape, or reproduce? Perhaps.

The chicken-and-egg problems of perception and action in evolution are quite remote from us, but the same issues are close by and fascinating when considering the development of an individual. We have already encountered some of them. Young infants display little coordinated action and for a long time were considered similarly inert perceptually. Methods to study infant perception have capitalized on a few subtle actions to reveal that the young infant can perceive far better than he can act. Unlike the case of our primordial immobile organism, perception without action for a developing individual makes functional sense because the infant can learn now and act later. We have also seen the importance of action in the service of perception, as in oculomotor activity and observer motion in the perception of objects and spatial layout. In this chapter, we focus directly on the relationship between perception and action, searching for general principles and elaborating specific examples.

ECOLOGY OF PERCEPTION AND ACTION

The ecology of any organism is conditioned by its capacities for action, just as it is conditioned by the information available for perception. How perception and action develop is a controversial matter, one that goes to the heart of traditional theoretical debates. In Piaget's view, reality itself is constructed by relating action to the pickup of sensory information. Initially, behavior consists of reflex reactions to specific stimuli along with some spontaneous movements. Later, sensory consequences of random action are noted, and the actions tend to be repeated. Such sequences are referred to as *primary circular reactions* (Piaget, 1952). According to this account, neither perception nor action is well organized at first. The development of coordinated action structures and the emergence of perceived objects, instead of sensations or "interesting sights," occur together through the first 2 years of life.

The idea that perceptual reality must be constructed by action is not shared by ecological views. They assert a different, but equally close, coupling of perception and action. Human and animal behavior might in general be described in terms of *perception–action loops* (Gibson, 1966). Adjustment of active perceptual systems facilitates the extraction of information that is used in guiding action and additional seeking of information (Gibson, 1979; Mace, 1974; Turvey, Shaw, Reed, & Mace, 1981; Figure 9.1). Extreme versions of this view deny that perception leads to memory representations. In lieu of stored descriptions and thought as the architects of action, the effects of the past on the future are conceived in terms of perception extended over time (Mace, 1974).

In the case of the human infant, a new view is called for (von Hofsten, 1990, 2004). The perceptual world is not, in general, constructed through action. The infant perceives a coherent environment and many of its important properties before the beginnings of directed reaching, crawling, or walking. The ecological view of perception–action loops does not seem quite right either. It may characterize much of adult human and animal behavior, but something is missing when this view is applied to human infants. The young infant does not usually perceive in order to act and is seldom engaged in complex perception–action loops. We suggest a new, lopsided perspective: Perceptual skills develop ahead of action skills and form the foundation for their development.

On reflection, one might conclude that it almost has to be this way. Piaget's vision of action and sensation mutually constructing reality is a profound and creative hypothesis. However, it may have one too many degrees of freedom. If the infant begins by neither perceiving nor acting in an organized three-dimensional space, building reality would be a momentous task. Now add the problem of poor

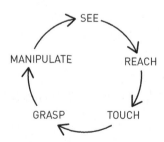

FIGURE 9.1

A schematic representation of a perception–action loop illustrating the interplay of perceptual and motor skills in manual exploration. Source: Reprinted with permission of Elsevier from Corbetta, D., & Snapp-Childs, W. (2009). Seeing and touching: The role of sensory–motor experience on the development of infant reaching. *Infant Behavior and Development, 32,* 44–58; permission conveyed through Copyright Clearance Center, Inc.

motor control; later, we discuss the fact that early in infancy, motor activity is undifferentiated and imprecise. (We cannot even consider the problem of perceptual error because perception on this account does not yet exist.) The Piagetian enterprise is to arrive at perceptual reality by attunement of action to sensation. However, this process, once begun, would be fraught with mismatches due to errors in the motor system, the perceptual system, or both. Without a firm foundation in perception or action, how would development proceed? Perhaps with appropriate constraints and a great deal of time, such a learning situation might lead to coherent perception and action. However, in Chapters 4 and 6 we discussed evidence that the infant perceives the positions, shapes, and sizes of objects in three-dimensional space *before* it has developed the ability of directed reaching. Now recall the following finding, which we considered in Chapter 6: At approximately 4½ to 5 months of age, when the infant first begins to reach for a stationary object in a directed manner, the infant can be tested with a different stimulus—an object that moves in an arc passing briefly in front of her. The infant, on seeing this object, reaches not for where it is but, rather, for its anticipated position farther along in its trajectory (von Hofsten, 1983). As discussed later, this anticipatory reaching is based on perceptual information of the object's speed, trajectory, and spatial location and on the infant's perception of the catchability of the object based on his own catching abilities (van Hof, van der Kamp, & Savelsbergh, 2008). This example illustrates the interplay of perceptual and motor competence.

We thus approach perception and action with a perspective derived from our observations of early perceptual ability. A major task during the first year of life may be the acquisition of motor skills under the guidance of maturation and information provided by perception. In turn, new action systems make available new information and refine perceptual exploration.

ABILITIES AND PROCESSES

We begin our study of perception–action relationships with a basic concern—the maintenance of posture. We highlighted the role of visual information for the control of posture in Chapter 6. In fact, information for postural stability can be provided by kinesthetic, vestibular, and visual information. Kinesthetic information involves sensing one's own movement through receptors in joints and muscles. Vestibular information comes from gravity and accelerations. Much of our orienting and acting in the environment, however, depends on information obtained through vision. Gibson (1966) drew attention to the crucial role played by vision, coining the phrase *visual kinesthesis*. A standing observer will adjust posture every second or two without conscious awareness, based primarily on visual information. The moving observer can discern important properties of her locomotion, such as heading, from optic flow or the continuous optical changes given as the observer moves through an environment. As discussed in Chapter 6, optic flow alone can induce the observer to perceive herself in motion, and this fact has been used in tests of the roles of visual and vestibular inputs in postural control with both adults and children. Maintaining control of posture allows perceivers the freedom to use their eyes, arms, and legs for action, much of which is exploratory (Bertenthal & von Hofsten, 1998).

Some of the earliest actions performed by infants involve exploratory activity. In the classic visual cliff studies by Gibson and Walk (1960), the authors discovered that infants' actions (e.g., crawling over the deep or shallow side of the cliff) were dependent on visual and haptic exploration. According to Gibson and Walk, it was not uncommon for hesitant infants to pat the glass or put their face close to the glass to look into the deep side. Infants in this situation were using the information gained from exploration to decide whether the surface was traversable.

We might think of perceptual exploration as involving complicated actions such as reaching, crawling, or walking. However, perceptual exploration can be accomplished with seemingly simple actions such as eye movements or mouthing that often go unnoticed. Most of the behavioral methods responsible for progress in infant perception research rely on infants' exploratory tendencies. These tendencies were observed in great detail by Piaget, who considered them perhaps the most crucial ingredients in the construction of reality. In light of infants' perceptual competencies that arise much earlier than Piaget anticipated, we can reinterpret infants' persistent exploratory behaviors. Rather than developing procedures to "make interesting sights last," infants are seeking information about objects and relationships in their environment.

Development of Reaching

An important milestone in perception–action coordination is the development of reaching at approximately 4½ months of age. Successfully reaching for and grasping an object requires perception of the object's location and appropriate generation of movements to that location. These movements involve the coordination of shoulder and arm muscles to move the hand toward the object and fine adjustments in hand orientation and grip shape before a successful contact can be made.

Prereaching and Visually Guided Reaching

Undoubtedly, very young infants execute arm movements, but whether these arm movements constitute reaching movements has been debated. Traditionally, arm movements of infants up to 4 months of age have been called *prereaching* (Trevarthen, 1975). Prereaching has been thought of as an early type of reaching that shares some of the characteristics of later visually guided reaching but that is qualitatively different. This conclusion follows from several pieces of evidence. First, prereaching is less accurate than visually guided reaching. Newborn infants show a hit rate—actual contact with the object—of only 9% (von Hofsten, 1982). In contrast, 17-week-olds typically show a hit rate of 93% to objects at the midline (Provine & Westerman, 1979). A second difference between visually guided reaching and prereaching is the nature of the trajectory of the reach. Prereaching has been thought to be ballistic in that once the movement begins, no corrections are made. Visually guided reaching involves a continuous feedback process with trajectory adjustments made during the reach. A third difference between visually guided reaching and prereaching involves coordination between the target and the hand. In prereaching, the coordination is between a seen target and a felt hand. In other words, the infant executes an arm movement in response to seeing an object but does not visually monitor the progress of the arm or hand as the movement continues. In visually guided reaching, the coordination is between a seen target and a seen hand. A final difference between prereaching and reaching is that prereaching is dominated by a synergy in which the fingers extend as the arm extends. As a result, in prereaching the fingers do not close around the object. With functional reaching, the reach ordinarily terminates in a grasp.

There is some question regarding the apparent differences between prereaching and visually guided reaching. Despite some differences in kinematics, neonatal reaching may be more similar to mature reaching than once thought (Berthier & Keen, 2006; Bhat, Heathcock, & Galloway, 2005). In a careful analysis of newborn reaching, von Hofsten (1982) found evidence that certain precursors of directed reaching are present in newborns' arm movements. In addition, his research suggests that this reaching behavior may be under the influence of vision. Infants ranging between 5 and 9 days of age were videotaped while a ball moved in front of them within reach. Infants' motor and visual behaviors were recorded. Von Hofsten found that infants made more forward arm extensions while they were fixating the ball than when they were not. Furthermore, on the best-aimed reaches, the infants' hands slowed down as they neared the object and exhibited some hand opening, as if anticipating a grasp.

Von Hofsten and Ronnqvist (1993) further investigated the structure of newborn infants' reaching. They found that these early arm movements are subject to several sets of organizing principles. Neonatal reaching has a distinct temporal structure in that neonates change arm direction between movement units and show straight trajectories within movement units. This pattern of movement is similar to that found in more mature reaching. Older infants and adults typically show two movement units when executing a reach: The first movement is long, whereas the second movement is shorter and allows for correction (Ashmead, McCarty, Lucas, & Belvedere, 1993). The change in direction between movement units found by von Hofsten and Ronnqvist indicates a means for correction of the trajectory of the reach in newborns. From these results, von Hofsten and Ronnqvist concluded that coordination between the eye and the hand does exist in newborns and that the precursors for mature reaching are present, even though this type of reaching is prefunctional at best (for review, see von Hofsten, 2004).

A second area of research suggests that neonatal reaching is influenced by visual information. Van der Meer, van der Weel, and Lee (1995) attached small weights to newborn infants' wrists and pulled the hands in the direction of their toes. Van der Meer et al. found that infants moved their arms to keep a seen hand in view. In a clever manipulation, infants were presented with a view of the hand that was not actually in the direction of their line of sight on a video monitor. In other words, infants looking to their left side saw their right hand on the video monitor. Even in this situation, infants moved the seen hand more than the unseen hand. When neither hand was visible, infants did not show many arm movements. Similarly, in another study, neonates moved a hand to keep it visible in a spotlight (van der Meer, 1997). Infants spent most of the 6-min trials with their visible hand in the light (the rest of the room was dark, and the infants' bodies were also in the dark). Moreover, infants' movements were controlled. As infants moved a hand to the lighted area, they slowed down the movement before the hand entered the light. Thus, vision appears to play a role in activating arm movements.

A third area of research questions the assumption that the onset of mature reaching is actually visually guided. Clifton, Muir, Ashmead, and Clarkson (1993) assessed whether sight of the hand was needed for the onset of mature reaching and grasping. In a longitudinal study, they tested seven infants' reaching and grasping between 6 and 25 weeks of age. Infants were observed under two conditions—reaching for an object in the light and reaching for a glowing object in the dark. Results showed that the ages of onset for reaching and grasping did not differ between conditions. The mean age was 12.3 weeks for reaching in the light and 11.9 weeks for reaching in the dark. For grasping objects in the light and the dark, mean age was 16.0 and 14.7 weeks (a nonsignificant difference), respectively. Because infants could not see their hands or arms in the dark, Clifton et al. concluded that infants did not use visual information to guide their reaching. This work has been replicated and extended by others, and the consistent finding is that within the first 6 months, infants reach less often in the dark, but when they do execute a reach they are equally skilled with or without sight of their hand. As infants age, the kinematics of the arm movement differs as a function of reaching under light and dark conditions, suggesting that vision of the hand plays a role in reaching after age 6 months (Babinsky, Braddick, & Atkinson, 2012; Berthier & Carrico, 2010). Vision does play a role in eliciting the arm movement but not in guiding it. Infants need to have a reason to reach (e.g., a glowing object in an otherwise dark room), and as discussed later, blind infants' delay in reaching is often attributed to infants' difficulty in making the connection between a sound and an object located in space.

Thus, the prevailing view is that early reaching is under kinesthetic or proprioceptive, not visual, control. Vision plays an important role in the improvement of reaching accuracy, but its use takes time to develop. Corbetta, Thurman, Wiener, Guan, and Williams (2014) studied the emergence of reaching in three infants across 11 weeks, starting at approximately 2 months of age. By documenting looking patterns using eye tracking and documenting reaching patterns using motion analysis, they confirmed that the earliest arm movements were not under visual guidance. Instead, infants gained spatial proprioceptive knowledge of their arm movement prior to the integration of visual information in their reaching. These observations are consistent with those of Berthier and Carrico (2010): Infants at 6 months start to use vision of the hand to guide it to the target, and it is at this time that infants begin to preshape the hand for successful contact. This integration of vision into reaching initially slows reaching down in lighted conditions compared to darkened conditions at 6 months. Nine-month-olds show equal speed in reaching in lighted conditions as in darkened conditions, and 12-month-olds show faster reaching under illumination compared to the dark.

Catching

At the same time that infants begin to show skilled reaching to a stationary target, they also are able to catch a moving target. Whether the target, usually a toy or a ball, is moving across the line of sight (e.g., from the infant's left to the right), approaches head on (e.g., toward the body), or disappears for a brief time during its trajectory, infants are surprisingly skilled at making contact (Fagard, Spelke, & von Hofsten, 2009; Hespos, Gredeback, von Hofsten, & Spelke, 2009; Robin, Berthier, & Clifton, 1996; Spelke & von Hofsten, 2001; van der Meer, van der Weel, & Lee, 1994). This ability shows sophisticated coordination of perception to determine object trajectory and action to coordinate the hand and arm for interception.

What information do infants use? One possible strategy is to begin a reach when the object is at a certain distance from the endpoint (or catch zone). This strategy works well when the object moves at a constant velocity, and infants appear to use it when objects move laterally (perpendicular to the line of sight) and when objects approach (Kayed & van der Meer, 2009; van der Meer et al., 1994; van Hof et al., 2008). Not all objects, however, move at a constant velocity. A strategy that takes rate of change of velocity into account is a timing strategy. The relative rate of change as the ball moves guides prediction of the timing of the object's arrival into the catch zone. Sometime between 6 and 8 months of age, infants switch strategies from distance to timing, a switch that also coincides with more successful contacts (van Hof et al., 2008).

Infants gain increasing skill in catching across several months, and they come to determine which targets are catchable or not given their current skills. Van Hof et al. (2008) distinguished between infants' perception boundary and catchable boundary. The perception boundary is the observer's assessment of whether a target is catchable or not. Faster-moving targets are more difficult to catch, and there is a speed—and likely a trajectory—beyond which it does not make sense to attempt a catch. Thus, the perception boundary pertains to attempts to catch a moving target regardless of success. The catchable boundary is the actual speed (and location) below which the perceiver meets with a successful catch. In a study with balls approaching at various speeds, 3- to 9-month-old infants' perceptual and catchable boundaries were determined (Figure 9.2). At 3–5 months of age, infants appeared to be unable to judge which balls were catchable or not. They were not very proficient catchers, but they also showed a high refusal rate, suggesting an inability to judge which balls were catchable or not. Slightly older infants, ages 6 or 7 months, were likely to catch a catchable ball, but their perceptual judgments were not fully accurate. Moreover, they showed a low percentage of refusals for difficult (fast-moving) balls. Van Hof et al. interpreted infants at this age as overestimating their catching abilities. Moreover, the large amount of variability at 6 and 7 months may reflect variability in infants' use of a distance versus a timing strategy to anticipate the future location of the ball. Eight- and 9-month-olds were

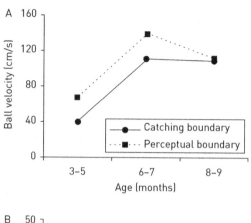

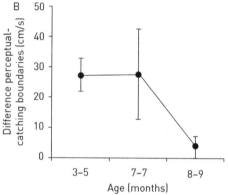

FIGURE 9.2
(A) Infants' perceptual and catching boundary speeds as a function of age. (B) The differ-
ence between these two boundaries and the considerable variability at 6 and 7 months of age
compared to the other two age groups. Source: Reprinted with permission of the American
Psychological Association from van Hof, P., van der Kamp, J., & Savelsbergh, G. J. P. (2008).
The relation between infants' perception of catchableness and the control of catching.
Developmental Psychology, 44, 182–194.

the most accurate. Their perceptual boundary was nearly identical to their catchable boundary, and they showed a high refusal rate of difficult catches.

What Accounts for the Onset of Accurate Reaching and Catching?

Several possibilities have been proposed to explain the improvement in reaching
and catching that occurs across the first year of life. Early on, attentional changes
and neurophysiological maturation were advanced as possibilities (Boudreau &
Bushnell, 2000). Bower (1974) suggested that visually guided reaching is absent
until 4 months because younger infants lack attentional capacities to attend
to both target and hand. Alternatively, maturation of the motor system may be
crucial. Kuypers' (1962, 1973) research suggests that arm and shoulder movements are governed by a proximal system (a subcortical system possibly tied to
the extrapyramidal tract), whereas fine motor movements are governed by a distal

system (a cortical system possibly tied to the pyramidal tract). In infant rhesus monkeys, the proximal system develops earlier than the distal system. Within the first 3 months of life, for example, monkeys show arm movements to the location of objects but fail to execute hand and finger movements (Lawrence & Hopkins, 1972). Improvements in human reaching may also be due to the differential rates of maturation of these two systems. This suggestion might explain a number of developmental asynchronies in infant manual behavior (Lockman & Ashmead, 1983).

Perceptual development may also facilitate the development of reaching. Stereopsis emerges at approximately 4 months of age, and improvements in reaching accuracy appear at approximately the same time as the rapid onset of sensitivity to binocular disparity. Infants may be able to make fine motor adjustments as a result of their improved spatial perception. This possibility is indirectly supported by findings of Yonas and Hartman (1993). In their study, 4- and 5-month-olds were presented with an object that was either within or just beyond their arm length. Infants who could lean forward (not all can at this age) adjusted their behavior depending on whether the object was within or beyond reach. In other words, they reached and leaned to come into contact with an out-of-reach object. Yonas and Hartman concluded that the 4- and 5-month-olds acted as if they had sensitivity to the absolute distance of an object and the length of their arm, as well as the effect that leaning forward had on their ability to make contact with a distant object. Similarly, infants at 4 or 5 months of age who were sensitive to binocular disparity reached more reliably to the closer of two objects than did infants who showed no evidence of disparity sensitivity (Granrud, 1986).

A more direct assessment of the role of spatial vision in the development of reaching was conducted by van Hof et al. (2006; see also Ekberg et al., 2013). They tested 2- to 8-month-old infants' catching skills under monocular and binocular conditions. In this task, a ball frontally approached the infant, and if the infant did not catch it, the ball moved just past the infant's right shoulder. From 3 months onward, catches were more accurate under binocular view; however, significant improvement in the timing of the reach emerged at approximately 5 or 6 months of age under binocular conditions. Thus, infants' improved ability to locate objects in space, most likely from the onset of stereopsis, contributed to increased accuracy in contacting the moving object.

Current Perspectives on Reaching

Reaching to and catching objects shows sophisticated coordination of perception and action. Early on, infants need sight of the object to begin a reach, and then they move their arm toward a location relying on proprioceptive information. Thus, by 4½ months of age, infants have a sense of their own body in space and enough information about the distance of objects to successfully execute an arm movement. This perceptual information, and its coordination with action, has been developing since birth. Young infants perceive objects around them at the same time that they are practicing moving their arms. As they gain more control over their arms, they are more successful in their contacts with objects. With increased practice with reaching and catching, infants discover which strategies lead to greater success, such as using a timing strategy rather than a distance strategy for catching an object. The interplay between perception and action described here is consistent with the ecological view and a dynamical systems approach. Both perception and action are constrained and enriched by the other; both are crucial to success in interacting with the world of objects.

Exploring Objects

Most reaches terminate once there is contact with an object or a surface. Anticipating the hand configuration necessary for contact is the next challenge for infants. This ability is refined between 5 and 7½ months of age, and it may be governed initially by tactile information (the hand shape is formed after contact) and with age by visual information (the hand is preemptively shaped before contact; Barrett, Traupman, & Needham, 2008; Witherington, 2005). Moreover, at approximately this same time, infants show evidence of sensitivity to the biomechanical properties of hand movements, including which hand configurations are possible for grasping objects and which are not (Geangu, Senna, Croci, & Turati, 2015). Once infants are able to make contact with objects, they have many new opportunities to explore. Infants who have just attained skilled reaching launch into a multimodal binge, picking up objects, manipulating them, looking at them, and mouthing them (Lobo, Kokkoni, de Campos, & Galloway, 2014; Rochat, 1989).

Oral exploration can be informative even before the advent of skilled reaching. When objects are placed in the mouth, infants are able to detect surface properties and object characteristics such as rigidity (Gibson & Walker, 1984; Meltzoff & Borton, 1979; Rochat, 1987). These explorations become increasingly refined as infants develop control over their arms and hands. Rochat (1989) documented eye–hand–mouth coordination in 2-month-olds, and this coordination becomes more sophisticated and differentiated through 12 months of age (see also Palmer, 1989; Ruff, 1984).

Others have noted that infants' rudimentary manual actions, long before skilled reaching emerges, can also provide them with information about objects. We presented several examples of manual exploration by neonates when we discussed intermodal perception in Chapter 8. Within the first few months of life, young infants perceive texture, shape, substance, and object unity based on haptic information alone (Molina & Jouen, 1998, 2004; Sann & Streri, 2008; Streri, Spelke, & Rameix, 1993; Striano & Bushnell, 2005).

There is no doubt that use of the hands for object exploration allows for the discovery of object properties. In their work with adults, Lederman and Klatzky (1987; Klatzky & Lederman, 2013) identified different exploratory procedures for the acquisition of different object features. As seen in Figure 9.3, different finger and/or hand actions provide haptic information specifying different object properties, such as size, weight, shape, texture, and temperature. Infants' exploratory actions vary from those of adults, but many of the same properties can be perceived haptically. By mouthing, banging, fingering, scratching, squeezing, two-handed

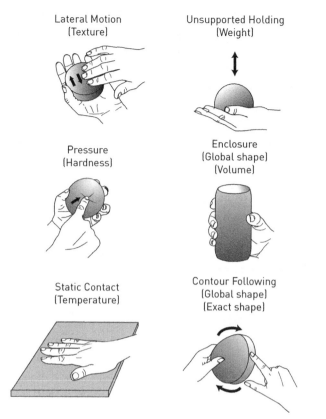

Lateral Motion
(Texture)

Unsupported Holding
(Weight)

Pressure
(Hardness)

Enclosure
(Global shape)
(Volume)

Static Contact
(Temperature)

Contour Following
(Global shape)
(Exact shape)

FIGURE 9.3

Exploratory procedures used by adults to gain haptic information for different object properties.
Source: This figure originally appeared as Figure 1 in Lederman, S. J., & Klatzky, R. L. (1987).
Hand movements: A window into haptic object recognition. *Cognitive Psychology, 19,* 342–368.
With permission of the authors, the original figure was modified and published by Oxford
University Press as Figure 5.1 in Jones, L. A., & Lederman, S. J. (2006). *Human hand function.*

grasping, and waving objects, infants perceive weight, texture, shape, volume,
temperature, and compliance. The frequency of these actions changes across age,
as does the role of vision in infants' exploration (Rochat, 1989). In a longitudinal
study across the first 2 years of life, Lobo et al. (2014) documented infants' ability
and drive to act on objects from the first month of life and the changes in their
actions. Activity with objects increased throughout the months, and infants at
each age showed adeptness in their interactions with objects. Exploration under-
went significant changes between birth and 6 months, during a time of significant
increases in manual control, postural stability, and visual development. Moreover,
infants' postural position—lying supine, prone, or sitting—also has implications
for manual activity (Lobo et al., 2014; Soska & Adolph, 2014). While lying down,
young infants are able to engage with objects, but exploration possibilities significantly increase with the onset of independent sitting.

In addition to engaging with objects, infants match their actions with objects
to the object properties. In other words, infants also adapt their exploratory

behavior to specific properties of objects. Three- and 4-month-olds exhibit flexibility in their manipulation when presented with two different objects, one mouthable and the other scratchable (Rochat, 1989). Similarly, infants between 4 and 8 months of age show different actions (mouthing or grasping) depending on object size and orientation (Whyte, McDonald, Baillargeon, & Newell, 1994) and different manual activities based on object composition (soft vs. hard; Morange-Majoux, 2011). Older infants use different repertoires of action on objects in conjunction with different surface characteristics (Bourgeois, Khawar, Neal, & Lockman, 2005; Fontenelle, Kahrs, Neal, Newton, & Lockman, 2007; Morgante & Keen, 2008; Palmer, 1989). Infants differentiate support surfaces (hard table vs. foam surface) and adjust their actions with the objects on those surfaces (e.g., banging vs. not banging and sliding vs. pressing). Thus, as early as 6 months, infants not only are sensitive to object properties and the appropriate exploratory actions but also are aware of possible object and support-surface interactions.

Clearly, infants' actions with objects and surfaces allow for the discovery of object and surface properties. But is there more to it? It is possible that these early manual activities set the stage for later tool use (Keen, 2011; Lockman; 2000). Through the use of tools, new potentials for action emerge. According to Kahrs and Lockman (2014), "Tools change the properties or affordances of the limbs. The challenge for the would-be tool user is to learn how these new affordances can be exploited for adaptive ends in the environment" (p. 89). The idea that tool use emerges from early manual activity is supported by several examples. Infants' banging actions allow for practice and coordination of using one object to hit another, a skill that translates well to use of a hammer (Kahrs, Jung, & Lockman, 2012, 2013). Across 6–14 months, banging actions become more efficient and consistent. Relatedly, infants' grasping facilitates holding objects to maximize their utility. If you want to eat food off of a spoon without making a mess, you hold the handle of the spoon and not the bowl. Infants need to learn which grip will maximize getting the food to their mouths; a radial grip, in which the thumb is toward the bowl of the spoon, is best but difficult for infants when the handle is on the side of their nondominant hand (McCarty, Clifton, & Collard, 1999). Moreover, as tool use develops into the second year, execution of actions toward the self (e.g., feeding and brushing hair) is easier than toward another person or object (McCarty, Clifton, & Collard, 2001), suggesting infants' difficulty in modifying actions as they are developing.

As infants gain control over their motor systems, perception and action become intricately tied. The newborn baby who is limited to oral and rudimentary manual exploration grows into a 12-month-old who has developed an efficient and effective coordination of multiple perceptual and motor processes that allow discovery of information about objects and surfaces. These early manual activities evolve into more sophisticated skills involving tools, which further expand the infant's (and older child's) action repertoire and potential for learning about and interacting with objects.

Surface Exploration and Locomotion

At approximately 6 months of age, infants begin to crawl, vastly expanding their possibilities for action in their environment. Although crawling is typical, some infants are quite adept at rolling or scooting in a sitting position. Later in the first year, infants begin cruising (walking upright while holding onto supports, such as a low table), and then finally sometime around their first birthday, infants begin to walk independently. The onset of locomotion elevates to central importance information specifying surface characteristics such as support. Since the classic visual cliff studies by Gibson and Walk (1960), researchers have investigated perception and action with regard to surfaces in several related paradigms.

Gibson and colleagues (Gibson et al., 1987) asked whether young locomotors are sensitive to surface characteristics specifying support and whether they adjust their actions to most effectively locomote. Crawling and walking infants were presented with walkways composed of either a rigid or a deforming surface. The rigid surface was composed of a piece of plywood covered with a textured cloth. The deforming surface was a waterbed (agitated by an experimenter) also covered with a textured cloth. Most of the infants crossed both surfaces, and all crawled rather than walked across the waterbed. The walkers showed greater latency to cross than the crawlers and engaged in considerable visual and haptic exploration. When presented with a choice of traversing either a rigid or a deforming surface (i.e., when the two surfaces were placed side by side), walkers showed a strong preference for the rigid surface. Crawlers showed no preference.

Surface properties other than rigidity have important implications for action. Surface slope, surface slipperiness, changes in height (e.g., with steps), and holes in surfaces all require changes in locomotion strategies (Adolph & Robinson, 2015). Some slopes do not allow for safe walking, but they can be crawled up or down (sliding down also works; Figure 9.4). Some steps are too high for stepping

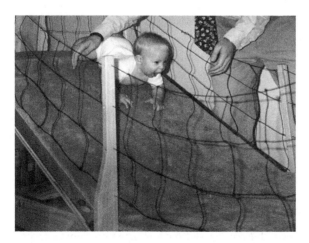

FIGURE 9.4

Apparatus used to test infants' locomotion across different surface slopes. Source: Photograph courtesy of K. Adolph.

(especially if one has short legs), but they can be more easily and more safely crawled over. Similarly, some slippery surfaces are best traversed on four limbs rather than two or avoided all together depending on the surface slope. Holes in supporting surfaces might result in falling; however, some can be avoided by changing one's direction of travel or traversed with the help of bridges or handrails (Berger, Adolph, & Kavookjian, 2010; Berger, Chan, & Adolph, 2014).

Infants' locomotor decisions arise from exploratory behaviors (Adolph, 1995; Adolph, Eppler, Marin, Weise, & Clearfield, 2000). Often, infants engage in one or more of the following behaviors: exploration from a distance, exploration from direct contact, and exploration of alternate means. Consider an infant approaching a surface sloping downward. Exploration from a distance is based on visual information acquired as infants approach the change in surface orientation. Movement of the eyes, head, and body provides information, particularly from depth cues, for the discontinuity in surface slope. Exploration from direct contact occurs once infants are within reach (or step) of the surface. Crawling infants touch and pat the surface; walking infants may touch a foot to the surface or rock over their ankles at the edge where the surface slope begins. Finally, infants may engage in exploring other means for locomotion. Walking infants may decide to crawl; crawling infants may consider turning around and going down the slope backward. Adolph et al. suggest that these exploratory procedures occur sequentially, and it is easy to understand how they also may be iterative, particularly as infants try out various alternatives for traversing the changes in surface.

Unfortunately, not all exploratory procedures result in successful decisions. Infants, and particularly toddlers, are well known for taking risks that can lead to injury. (Adolph and colleagues routinely have to rescue infants in their studies from falling over cliffs, off bridges, or tumbling down slopes; Adolph & Tamis-LeMonda, 2014.) Particularly striking is the difference in the same infants as they transition from experienced crawlers to novice walkers. Experienced crawlers make few mistakes in judging which slopes or step heights are safe, but inexperienced walkers plunge forward. In one study with 12-month-old infants, the experienced crawlers avoided the unsafe steps, whereas the inexperienced walkers stepped off (Kretch & Adolph, 2013). Thus, as infants' mode of locomotion changes, they need to learn anew how to move safely through their environment.

Transition from crawling to walking takes several months. Despite the challenges related to safety, walking provides infants with new opportunities for exploration—both of their own abilities and of their environment. Table 9.1 shows comparisons between crawling and walking in terms of both the biometrics, such as number of steps and falls, and opportunities for object interaction. Despite the dangers due to falling, walkers compared to crawlers gain speed and distance in their movements, and they enjoy increased interactions with objects. Transition to walking also provides infants with a different view of the world. Crawling infants spend a considerable amount of time looking at the floor in front of their hands, whereas walking infants are able to look around, such as ahead of them, to the side, and to farther objects, while locomoting (Kretch, Franchak, & Adolph, 2014). Finally, social interactions change: Mothers responded to walkers' object bids

Table 9.1 Differences in Activity Level for Experienced Crawlers Compared to Novice Walkers as Summarized in Adolph and Tamis-LeMonda (2014)[a]

Activity	Crawlers	Walkers
Falls	17	32
% of time in motion	20	33
Number of steps	636	1456
Distances traveled (m)	297	1000
Retrieve distant object	4	12
Carry object	6	43
Steps per object carry	10.50	13.85
Steps per second while carrying an object	1.58	2.30

[a] Values indicate activity per hour unless otherwise noted.

(a child holds up or approaches to show an object) with more action-related directives or comments than they do to crawlers' object bids (Karasik, Tamis-LeMonda, & Adolph, 2014).

Perceiving Affordances

Perception of surface support or traversability has been claimed to illustrate a particular idea about perception in general—that what is perceived are *affordances* (Gibson, 1979). Not only do we perceive an object's shape or color but also we perceive what can be done with the object. Affordances relate to the needs and capabilities of the organism, but they are properties of objects and surfaces in the environment, and they are there to be discovered by the perceiver. As Gibson (1979) stated, "An affordance is not bestowed upon an object by a need of an observer and his act of perceiving it. The object offers what it does because it is what it is" (p. 139). The sensitivity of infants' locomotor behavior to surface characteristics has often been interpreted in terms of affordances, and it may be best viewed in a probabilistic manner: Affordances represent the likelihood of successful performance (Franchak & Adolph, 2014).

The concept is by no means universally accepted as a way of describing what is perceived. We may inquire about the value of this type of description and also how it may be possible to determine infants' perception of affordances. Infant researchers observe infants' actions with objects and infer that they have perceived specific object properties. Can it also be concluded that affordances have been perceived? How does one know the difference between perceiving an object property (e.g., it is hard) and perceiving an affordance (e.g., it is good for banging on a table)? Are there specific conditions that must be met to conclude that an affordance has been perceived?

A framework for studying the perception of affordances has been offered by Adolph, Eppler, and Gibson (1993). They posit three conditions for claiming that infants (and adults) are responding to affordances. The first condition is a description of how an action is constrained by the fit between environmental properties and action capabilities. Thus, the researcher must identify the range of variation in action allowed by the affordance. As an example, they cite work on stair climbing demonstrating that successful climbing depends on a fit between properties of the actor (e.g., leg and foot length) and properties of the stairs (e.g., riser height and tread depth). The second condition is that specific information must specify the affordance. The third condition is a close correspondence between perceived and actual actor–environment fit.

These criteria may prove useful in assessing how closely perception and action are coupled in particular domains. They capture the essence of the affordance notion—that perception supports the current actions and goals of the organism. It is not clear that these criteria alone distinguish the notion that what we perceive are affordances from the notion that perception furnishes descriptions of the environment. Representations of the environment produced by perception must be able to support immediate action, but they may also be more general, flexible, and enduring than required by the organism's immediate behavioral task.

The Relation Between Perception and Action

The research presented in this chapter suggests that early in life, perception and action are closely linked. In fact, this is a point on which all theories agree. Disagreement centers on whether action precedes and serves to construct meaningful perception, whether perceptual skill precedes and guides motor development, or whether both emerge together. Research we have considered in previous chapters suggests that perception of objects, surfaces, and events does not depend on motoric experiences such as reaching or locomotion, simply because the relevant perceptual abilities can be demonstrated before directed reaching and crawling begin. Even later-appearing abilities do not show these connections. For example, Arterberry, Yonas, and Bensen (1989) found that the onset of 7-month-olds' sensitivity to pictorial depth cues—the latest-appearing class of spatial information—was not predicted by locomotor status (precrawler, belly crawler, or hands-and-knees crawler).

Perception Precedes Action

Perception does not seem to be created from action, and in many cases it is relatively advanced when action begins. A possible exception we have noted is the contribution of spatial perception—specifically the emergence of stereoscopic depth perception—to the guidance of reaching. Often, however, advances in the motor system seem to be paced on their own timetable. When they do emerge, they benefit from representations of the spatial layout given by perception. After beginning to reach, for example, an infant does not undergo protracted learning to reach for an object in motion, even though catching the object requires reaching not to where the object is seen but, rather, to where it will be when the reach is complete. This overview fits what we know of the timing of the emergence of many perceptual abilities and motor activity.

Blind children provide a natural experiment to examine some relations between perception and action. If perceptual development—and vision, in particular—guides motor development, we might expect blind children's initial attainment of basic motor milestones to be delayed. Observations by Fraiberg (1968) and Bigelow (1986, 1992) confirm such delays in blind infants' motor development. The onset of reaching occurs from 1½ to 8 months later than in sighted infants. Moreover, the onset of self-produced locomotion—crawling and walking—is also delayed compared to sighted infants. In a sample of three children studied by Bigelow (1992), the age of onset of walking was 17, 32, and 36 months, respectively—considerably later than the average age of 12 months for sighted infants. Bigelow (1986, 1992) suggests that these delays stem from deficits in perceptual knowledge. The lack of visual input would be expected to affect action on almost any account of development. The fact that certain actions, such as reaching and walking, appear much later in blind children is nevertheless revealing. It suggests that the emergence of these abilities in sighted children depends on information about the environment (and the self) already available through vision. This strong dependence appears to run counter to traditional notions, such as those of Piaget and Berkeley, that visual reality gains its meaning through action and locomotion.

Action Facilitates Perception

Of course, this generalization about perception preceding action is only part of the story. Action brings about new opportunities for perceiving and leads to perceptual refinements. Some of these must include recalibration of perceptual information due to growth. Information used in binocular vision must change as the eyes grow farther apart. Also, there must be a drastic remapping of the visual space as retinal receptors migrate to new positions during the early months of life (Aslin, 1993a). Although it is possible that some recalibration can be accomplished by comparisons among different sources of perceptual information, it is likely that perception–action loops provide much of the basis for recalibration. In fact, rapid remapping of space across senses as a result of action can be observed even in adults under conditions of changed input to one sense (Bedford, 1989; Rock & Harris, 1967).

There is evidence for improvements in perception related to developing action systems. Bertenthal and Campos (1990) reported that some perceptual and cognitive developments in the second half of the first year benefit from the experience gained from self-produced locomotion (crawling). They suggested that "locomotor experience does not directly affect the emergence of any basic processing skill, but rather demands that the infant begin either to use information that was previously neglected or to use this information in novel ways" (p. 5). This view has notable antecedents (e.g., Held & Hein, 1963). Self-produced locomotion has been implicated in the enhancement of infants' visual–vestibular control of posture; sensitivity to emotional communication from others regarding ambiguous situations (called *social referencing*; see Chapter 10); memory; sensitivity to self-propelled motion; and sensitivity to heights, as on the visual cliff (Adolph, Karasik,

& Tamis-LeMonda, 2010; Campos et al., 2000; Cicchino & Rakison, 2008; Herbert, Gross, & Hayne, 2007; Uchiyama et al, 2008). Before crawling, infants perceive depth; what may change with crawling experience is the coordination of depth and surface perception with their own motion in space. Similarly, perceptual advances may emerge once infants begin walking. Their view of the world is now changed, as discussed previously, and this new mode of locomotion opens up new possibilities for perception.

Another domain in which the development of action may enhance perception involves haptically perceived object properties (Bushnell & Boudreau, 1998). Infants gain a tremendous amount of information about objects through their explorations with the objects, and this information about objects and their properties transfers to novel objects. For example, 4- to 7-month-old infants who engage in more exploratory behavior attend more to object features (Perone, Madole, Ross-Sheehy, Carey, & Oakes, 2008; Soska, Adolph, & Johnson, 2010). Most striking are studies that provide prereaching infants with experience with objects. Needham and colleagues developed the "sticky mitten" technique described in Chapter 6 (Needham, Barrett, & Peterman, 2002). Providing mittens with Velcro allowed infants lacking manual control, typically 3-month-olds, to pick up and interact with objects in a more advanced way than they normally could. In a number of studies, Needham and colleagues showed that experience with sticky mittens resulted in more advanced perceptual abilities (Libertus & Needham, 2010, 2011; Sommerville, Woodward, & Needham, 2005). Moreover, experience with reaching for and interaction with objects may also facilitate infants' understanding of others' reaching goals (Gerson & Woodward, 2014).

An important component in the development and coordination of perception and action is *prospective control* (Bertenthal, 1996; von Hofsten, 2004). Actions must be controlled prospectively to coordinate with events because of time lags involved in initiating and carrying out body movements. Consequently, predicting what will happen next is a central problem in perceptual and cognitive guidance of behavior. To some extent, perception appears to be adapted in certain ways to provide this information, as discussed in the case of anticipatory reaching. However, prospective control in perception and action systems also improves with experience in particular perception–action relationships (Adolph et al., 2000). It involves learning to seek the information that will be needed next along with coordinating action. Obviously, this is not a unitary ability; attunement to relevant information and accurate motor anticipation may develop separately for particular skills (Bertenthal, 1996).

Dissociations Between Action and Knowledge

A number of findings in adult perception and action, neurophysiological research with nonhuman primates, and studies of patients with neurological deficits are consistent with the idea of multiple perceptual representations serving separate functions. For example, observers show drastic foreshortening in estimating distances from visual information, but when asked to walk blindfolded to targets, they show excellent accuracy (Loomis, Da Silva, Philbeck, & Fukusima, 1996). One generalization that may capture many of these facts was proposed by Goodale and Milner (1992; Milner & Goodale, 2008). As described in Chapter 6, they suggested that humans have distinct neural systems for perceptual control of action (the dorsal pathway) and for perception and recognition of objects and events (the ventral pathway; see Figure 6.1). This dichotomy may turn out to be incomplete or inaccurate, but there is little doubt that perception leads to multiple representations that may be recruited for different tasks by adults and infants (van Wermeskerken, van der Kamp, Savelsbergh, & von Hofsten, 2013).

Not much is known about the origins of multiple perceptual representations in infancy. There are some hints of dissociations, including some between action and knowledge. For example, infants by 4½ months show considerable knowledge about the existence of hidden objects, as discussed in Chapter 6, but they do not accurately search for a hidden object until approximately 8 months of age (Piaget, 1954). Moreover, this ability to search for a hidden object can be manipulated by time delays between the hiding and finding phases, but such delays do not interfere with infants' ability to remember the location of a hidden object if tested in a looking paradigm (Baillargeon, DeVos, & Graber, 1989; Diamond, 1988). Similarly, very young infants have knowledge of solidity and continuity, such that an object moving along a trajectory will stop at a barrier rather than move through it (Baillargeon, Graber, DeVos, & Black, 1990; Spelke, Breinlinger, Macomber, & Jacobson, 1992). However, when toddlers (2- and 2½-year-olds) see a ball roll down a ramp and disappear behind a panel containing four doors, they have trouble using information regarding the location of a barrier to determine which door to open in order to find the ball (Berthier, DeBlois, Poirier, Novak, & Clifton, 2000; Keen, 2003). Finally, infants, including newborns, show excellent perception of object size and shape, but older children (13- to 27-month-olds) make *scale errors*, such as trying to get into a toy car that is much too small for their body size (Rosengren, Gutierrez, Anderson, & Schein, 2009). Other examples imply competence in the action domain before competence in the cognitive domain. When infants begin reaching for static objects, they are also able to reach for moving objects. Predicting the moving object's trajectory and future location would be difficult without an implicit understanding of inertia and gravity; however, this understanding appears to be a later developing ability (Kim & Spelke, 1992; Spelke, Katz, Purcell, Ehrlich, & Breinlinger, 1994). These observations suggest that humans initially have separate representational systems for knowledge and action, and a topic for future research is how these two systems work together.

CONCLUSION

Much remains to be learned about the development of action and its relations to perception. By the same token, much has been learned in just a few decades of active experimentation on these questions. Action does not appear to be the source of early perceptual reality, as Piaget (1969) suggested. The description of behavior in terms of perception–action loops may characterize much of skilled behavior later on, but it is not adequate to characterize young perceivers, whose perceptual abilities in general emerge earlier than their action skills. A tentative generalization about perception and action in the first year of life is that a gradual maturation and attunement of action systems occurs under the guidance of perception. As action systems mature, they lead to refinements in the pickup of information that in turn support more effective action. One emerging theme in perception and action is that perception may lead to the formation of multiple representations useful for different tasks. Representations for guiding action may be special, and even among these, the refinement of perception–action connections with experience may be quite task-specific. Distinguishing and tracing the origins of separable tasks and representational systems remain high priorities for research. Such efforts will lead to a better understanding of the connections between perception and action as well as the underlying mechanisms that produce both.

10 Perceptual Foundations of Social Development

INTRODUCTION

An organism's survival and well-being depend on action guided by perception. Often, the individual acts directly on the physical world, as in reaching for an object or navigating around an obstacle. In a social species, however, direct action on the physical environment is not the sole means to survival and well-being. Much of the time, we fulfill our needs and those of others by acting in the social world; instead of foraging for food, we arrange by telephone to have pizza delivered. The balance between acting directly on the physical world and acting in the social world is even more lopsided for an infant. An infant's abilities to act usefully on the physical environment are modest, whereas abilities to influence caretakers are quite powerful from the start. Moreover, there is strong motivation to do so. Elizabeth Spelke noted (as quoted in Angier, 2012), "All this time I've been giving infants objects to hold, or spinning them around in a room to see how they navigate, when what they really wanted to do was engage with other people!" (p. D1).

ECOLOGY OF SOCIAL PERCEPTION

This capsule view of the infant's situation points to some priorities of early perceptual activity. Perhaps the most basic is to distinguish social beings from other objects. Because the social and nonsocial worlds require different kinds of behavior, acting effectively depends first of all on sorting correctly. A further priority is to learn about the workings of the social world. Through it, the infant interacts indirectly with the physical world; thus, understanding the rules of the social world takes on great significance. This learning includes representing the roles and potentials of specific individuals and forming important generalizations and classifications about social phenomena.

The process will attain astonishing sophistication in a short time. A toddler shows obvious empathy in offering a crying child his teddy bear but feels none at all for a vase that falls from a shelf and shatters. Even such ordinary incidents require complex and subtle perceptual and cognitive achievements. In this chapter, we probe some of the foundations and initial achievements of social perception.

When and how infants acquire knowledge of people and their interactions has been an intriguing question for researchers. According to Piaget (1981), the emergence of social cognition is tied to advances in other areas of cognitive development within the first 2 years. He claimed that infants begin life with instinctual behaviors and affective reactions, such as smiling or crying. These behaviors, although communicative in impact, are not intentionally directed toward people and do not reflect mature social–cognitive understanding. Between 1 and 6 months, infants begin to have feelings of pleasure, pain, and so on, which are acquired through experience. They also begin to differentiate needs and interests. Yet at this stage, feelings are still directed toward the self. According to Piaget, the child is undifferentiated in that she does not yet understand the boundaries between herself, others, and the world. As she begins to differentiate between objects and people at approximately 6–8 months, feelings and actions become directed toward other people. People begin to be appreciated as separate objects that are localizable and that are autonomous sources of causality. In addition to the appearance of true exchange relationships, imitation of others appears. Thus, from a Piagetian perspective, the foundation for social cognition, perception of other people as special objects, emerges in conjunction with differentiation of the self and advancing object knowledge in the second half of the first year of life. This understanding matures over the sensorimotor period. Stern (1985) also hypothesized a prolonged period of development in which infants come to differentiate themselves from others and acquire a sense of self.

Others have suggested that infants begin life as social beings (Trevarthen, 1979). As a result of observing face-to-face interactions between 6- and 8-week-old infants and their mothers or an object, Trevarthen concluded that infants at 8 weeks behaved very differently facing their mothers than they did facing a familiar object. Trevarthen claimed that in order to be social participants, infants must possess subjectivity and intersubjectivity. *Subjectivity* is individual consciousness and intentionality, and it involves relating objects and situations to oneself. For example, infants focus their attention on objects, they manipulate objects with an interest in consequences, and they anticipate events with intent to avoid or orient to them. *Intersubjectivity* occurs when interacting with other people. Infants mesh their behavior with that of others, and they signal anticipation or avoidance of interaction with specific behaviors, such as orienting or looking away from others. Hence, Trevarthen proposed that social participation is founded on a differentiation of self from objects, including social objects, and the ability to coordinate one's intentions with the intentions of others to regulate an exchange. Relatively recently, Trevarthen (2011) suggested that these abilities are even present in neonates.

It is difficult to imagine that infant perception research will any time soon furnish a detailed account of how and when the several and subtle dimensions of self-concepts arise. We take up a more modest task. Social development requires distinguishing social and nonsocial beings, as previously discussed. On many accounts, it also requires truly social interactions. By examining several lines of research, we can gain some idea of when social perception and interaction begin. We begin by examining newborn imitation.

Imitation

In 1977, Meltzoff and Moore published the first paper reporting imitation abilities in newborns. They claimed that infants between 12 and 21 days imitated gestures. In this study, an adult modeled a gesture (tongue protrusion, lip protrusion, mouth opening, or sequential finger movement), and observers coded the infants' responses (Figure 10.1). Infants were more likely to produce the gesture that was being modeled than any other action. Later work found similar effects in infants from 42 min to 32 hours old (Meltzoff & Moore, 1983). To rule out the possibility that infants were in some way matching the action based on a reflexive response, Meltzoff and Moore (1983) restricted the infant from responding immediately to the model's action. During the modeling phase in which an infant viewed the gesture (either tongue protrusion or mouth opening), a pacifier was placed in the infant's mouth. Following modeling, the pacifier was removed, the model assumed a passive face, and the infant's response was recorded. As in the initial study, infants imitated the two gestures.

These early findings on newborn imitation were hotly disputed, but the results have survived tests of numerous alternative explanations and at least 25 replications by 13 different laboratories (Meltzoff, 2011; Meltzoff & Moore, 1997; Ray & Heyes,

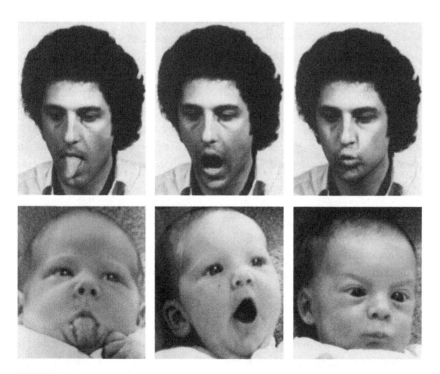

FIGURE 10.1

Examples of imitative responses by 2- and 3-week-old infants to an adult protruding his tongue, opening his mouth, and pursing his lips. Source: From Meltzoff, A. N., & Moore, M. K. (1977). Imitation of facial and manual gestures by human neonates. *Science, 198*, 75–78. Reprinted with permission from AAAS.

2011). Further work suggested that infants' imitation was not limited to the previously mentioned gestures. Newborns show differential mouth movements when viewing a smile, frown, or surprised facial expression, and they show mouth openings when they hear or see the sound /a/ and clutch their lips together when they hear and see the sound /m/ (Chen, Striano, & Rakoczy, 2004; Coulon, Hemimou, & Streri, 2013; Field, Woodson, Greenberg, & Cohen, 1982). Newborn imitation is not limited to the head region: Infants imitate one-, two-, and three-finger movements (Nagy, Pal, & Orvos, 2014). Finally, neonate imitation is seen in nonhuman primates (Paukner, Simpson, Ferrari, Mrozek, & Suomi, 2014; Simpson, Paukner, Suomi, & Ferrari, 2014).

Today and at this point in this book, you may not be surprised by these findings. We have already discussed impressive abilities by newborn infants: They remember what they heard in utero, they perceive some object properties across modalities, and they perceive size and shape constancy. We can sympathize with critics, however, because newborn imitation is nothing short of astonishing. It seems to imply sophisticated capacities not just of perception but also of representation and action, some of which have not been previously documented and some of which have been theorized to be impossible. On the face of it, to imitate a seen event, one must perceive the event as an event—not as patches of brightness and color or as a set of activations of orientation-sensitive cortical cells but as a representation of objects, surfaces, and changes occurring. Furthermore, this representation must be abstract; it does not live solely in the visual world because it must be able to connect to other representations, particularly those that produce action. The infant does not see his or her own face when imitating. To imitate tongue protrusion requires making some kind of match between a tongue that is seen and one's own tongue that is felt and moved by motor commands. Finally, it is possible that imitation involves true social awareness, as we discuss later. The infant may realize he is involved with a social being and perhaps resembles it, that this being and he both have tongues, that both are protruding their tongues, and so on. In short, through imitation, infants may discover others who are "like me" (Meltzoff, 2007, 2011).

Mechanisms of Imitation

If imitation implies all or even part of this array of abilities, it is impressive indeed. None of it is remotely possible for newborns or infants of several weeks—or months—according to Piaget's view of development or traditional constructivist accounts of perception, representation, and action. Perhaps it is no wonder that a number of possibilities have been raised to explain it, including arousal, associations among motor patterns, and reflexes (Paulus, 2014; for review, see Oostenbroek, Slaughter, Nielsen, & Suddendorf, 2013). Nagy and colleagues (2013) provide clear evidence that newborn imitation is not the by-product of arousal. In a study of more than 100 newborns, they compared imitation and arousal to baseline levels. Infants' arm and finger movements, their metric for arousal, actually declined during periods of imitation.

Despite evidence to the contrary, some have maintained that imitation is a reflex or *fixed-action pattern* (FAP; Abravenel & Sigafoos, 1984; Bjorklund, 1987). Such a hypothesis would not require any intermodal matching mechanism, any representational capacity, any capacity for voluntary action, or any social awareness. The stimulus event "releases" an innately determined action pattern because the infant's nervous system is wired this way. The explanation for such a wiring pattern, as for others studied by ethologists, might be sought in the adaptive value of such behavior. Imitation FAPs might serve to foster social interaction with conspecifics. This approach appears to be stretched in accounting for the variety of responses—mouth movements, tongue protrusion, finger movements, and head rotation—that young infants have been found to imitate.

Additional research, however, helps to clarify the ongoing controversy. Meltzoff and Moore (1994) tested several hypotheses about early imitation relevant to the FAP hypothesis and their own *active intermodal matching* (AIM) view. Six-week-old infants were tested on 3 consecutive days. Each infant was assigned to a treatment group in which the adult model produced tongue protrusion at the side of the mouth, tongue protrusion in the middle of the mouth, mouth opening, or no oral movement. Infants' responses were recorded during 90-sec test trials. During these periods, the model displayed the gesture for 15-sec periods alternating with 15-sec periods of no gesturing. After one 90-sec trial on the first day, infants were tested on a second day in a memory trial in which the adult model presented a neutral face for the entire period. This was followed by another 90-sec trial of the same sort as the day 1 imitation trial, using the same facial gesture. Day 3 testing was the same as day 2 testing.

Results showed that infants imitated the modeled gesture reliably more than the other gesture (the two types of tongue protrusions were not distinguished for this analysis). Remarkably, this was true for the memory trials as well. Infants' behavior while viewing the passive model included markedly higher frequency of the facial gesture it had seen on the previous day. This finding indicates that imitation performance at 6 weeks rests on a representational capacity that can preserve information for long periods of time and is presumably abstract enough to mediate the connections among situations, perceived events, and actions. Meltzoff and Moore (1994) also examined the detailed topography of responding over trials to the gesture of tongue protrusion to the side. They found evidence that infants made progressively better approximations to this gesture over trials. The gradual changing of the response to conform more to the model suggests a very different interpretation of what infants are doing, according to Meltzoff and Moore (1994). They stated, "The capacity to organize actions based on a stored representation of perceptually absent events is a starting point in infancy, not its culmination" (Meltzoff & Moore, 1994, p. 95). According to the AIM proposal, early imitation involves an active intention to match the model.

Some conjectures about infants' motivation for imitating are also offered by Meltzoff (2007). After a full day's delay, infants viewing the passive model may produce the gesture seen earlier as a means of identifying and querying the person, perhaps to determine whether this is the same person or whether the social encounter will work today as it did yesterday. This hypothesis is consistent with the notion that infants use their perceptual and action abilities from an early time to explore, learn about, and classify objects and events in the social world.

Should imitation be viewed as an example of social interaction? The AIM hypothesis could be consistent with infants' imitating a perceived physical event that is not social in nature. Protrusion of the model's tongue could be seen by the infant as an interesting event in which an object appears between two surfaces. Imitation may occur as a means of attempting to comprehend or motorically encode the event. It is difficult to draw firm conclusions about a social component in early imitation, but some data support the idea that imitation is truly social. First, imitation is limited to the actions of live models or human-like two-dimensional stimuli, such as a robotic face (Soussignan, Courtial, Canet, Danon-Apter, & Nadel, 2011); it does not generalize to inanimate objects simulating gestures such as tongue protrusion and mouth opening (Abravanel & DeYong, 1991; Legerstee, 1991a; but see Jacobson, 1979). When infants were shown a tube with a red cylinder appearing and disappearing from the tip, they failed to produce a tongue-protrusion action (Legerstee, 1991b). Second, imitation involves turn taking (Meltzoff & Moore, 1983). Early imitative interactions include a balance of actions and pauses that are tied to the actions and pauses of others. This coordination of the infants' actions with those of others may demonstrate a rudimentary understanding of intersubjectivity.

Imitation and Learning in Infancy

For our conceptions of perception and development, infant imitation phenomena have profound significance. For the infant, imitative abilities may be equally profound in their importance for learning. We can glimpse the possibilities in two types of imitation that emerge beyond the newborn period—vocal imitation and imitation of object manipulation. Imitation of vowel sounds has been found in 3- and 4-month-olds (Kuhl & Meltzoff, 1988; Legerstee, 1990), a finding relevant to learning about language and linguistic interactions. Imitation of object manipulation has been documented at 6 months of age for simple actions, such as waving an object to make it rattle (von Hofsten & Siddiqui, 1993). At 9 months of age, infants imitate more complex actions, such as pressing a button on a box to make a beeping sound or breaking a novel toy into two pieces (Meltzoff, 1988a). Nine-month-olds immediately imitate novel object manipulations modeled by a person and also imitate after a 24-hour delay between modeling and imitation (Meltzoff, 1988a). Fourteen-month-olds imitate a live model after a 1-week delay (Meltzoff, 1988b). Infants at this age also imitate models on television and other 14-month-old models (Hanna & Meltzoff, 1993; Meltzoff, 1988c). Imitation occurs despite changes in context (e.g., moving to a different room) and object features (e.g., changing object size or color). Imitation also is influenced by the infant's perceived trustworthiness of the model (Barnat, Klein, & Meltzoff, 1996; Poulin-Dubois, Brooker, & Polonia, 2011).

Not only do infants learn how to perform new actions by watching others in their environment but also they also learn something about intended actions. Meltzoff (1995) asked whether 18-month-olds would produce an action that the model intended but did not perform. In one study, for example, infants viewed an adult attempting to pull apart a toy that looked like a dumbbell. On three attempts, the adult's hand slipped off one of the ends so the infants never saw the toy in two pieces. When infants were given the toy, they produced the intended action: They grasped the two ends of the dumbbell and pulled it apart. A second study suggested that infants were in fact responding based on a psychological understanding of the actor's intentions. When infants were presented with a mechanical device that slipped off the ends of the dumbbell, failing to pull it apart, infants did not imitate the "intended action." Hamlin, Hallinan, and Woodward (2008) extended this work to 7-month-old infants. In their study, infants viewed two reaching events—one goal-directed (the experimenter grasped a toy) and one ambiguous regarding the goal (the experimenter placed the back of her hand against a toy). Following viewing these actions, the two toys were presented to the infants and they were allowed to reach for them. Infants reached significantly more to the toy that the experimenter had grasped compared to the one she had contacted with the back of her hand. Thus, infants' imitation may involve considerable social understanding (Meltzoff, 2011).

Human infants' imitative abilities beginning at birth are striking. The unlearned connections between event perception and action evident in newborn imitation are among the most compelling phenomena for revamping our notions of early perception and representation. It is difficult to account for the data without a view of perception as producing meaningful representations suitable for supporting action. Some nuances also suggest that infant imitation is truly social and that infants are predisposed to engage in social interaction. The consequences for development are enormous. Given their generality and flexibility, infant imitative abilities appear to compromise a key foundation, specially adapted to a social species, for learning about the physical and social worlds.

People Versus Other Objects

People behave differently from other objects, and the way we act with people is different from our actions with objects. Not only do people react to us and our actions in ways that objects cannot but also people's actions are guided by nonobservable properties, such as beliefs, intentions, and desires. In other words, people have *agency*. Thus, to be a true social partner, infants need to distinguish people from objects, and their interactions with people will be facilitated if infants have an understanding of what guides behavior.

In Chapter 6, we touched on one important variable that will help infants make the distinction between people and objects. Infants by at least 6 months of age distinguish animate and inanimate objects based on their motion. Animate objects are self-propelled, can travel along a nonlinear trajectory, and play a role in causing events. People, however, may be a special case of animate objects.

Distinguishing People

Previously, we described the ability to discriminate people from objects as the beginning of social cognition. Piaget's (1981) observations of his own children led him to conclude that not until 8 months do they recognize people as different from objects. A number of other observations fit this developmental timetable. Infants in the second half of the first year point at both objects and people but seem to expect a response only from people, such as a comment about the object, action on the object, or a change in direction of gaze of another person to look at the object (Harding & Golinkoff, 1979; Sugarman, 1978). Observers of spontaneous infant behaviors can judge when 10-month-old infants are interacting with their mothers as opposed to objects but cannot do so with 3-month-olds (Frye, Rawling, Moore, & Myers, 1983). In another study, 9- and 12-month-olds reacted negatively when a robot responded to their mothers' verbal commands (Poulin-Dubois, LePage, & Ferland, 1996). These examples are a few of many that support Piaget's contention that the distinction between people and objects emerges at approximately 8 months of age.

Our discussion of infant imitation may already lead us to suspect, however, that the distinction between people and objects arises earlier. Recall that imitation seems specific to human models and tends not to occur for mechanical events. Other research converges on this point. For example, Legerstee (1991b) conducted several studies in which she compared infants' interactions with people and inanimate objects. In a longitudinal study beginning at 3–5 weeks of age, infants were observed while viewing their mother, an unfamiliar female, or a doll. Each object was either active (interacting with the infant in the case of the people or moving in the case of the doll) or passive. By 9 weeks of age, infants showed evidence of distinguishing the people from the doll. For example, infants produced melodic speech-like vocalizations more frequently to the active mother and active stranger than to the doll. Even at 7 weeks, infants vocalized positively (laughed and cooed) and smiled more in the presence of a person than a doll, and their arm and hand movements differed depending on whether a person or a doll was present (Legerstee, Corter, & Kienapple,1990; Legerstee, Pomerleau, Malcuit, & Feider, 1987). These findings suggest that infants can distinguish between people and objects earlier than 8 months of age. In fact, this ability may emerge by 8 weeks of age. Infants respond to people using a constellation of distinctive behaviors, including vocalizations, facial expressions, and arm movements. Spelke and Kinzler (2007) suggest that this propensity to be social—attend to social beings and selectively engage with certain people—is one area of core knowledge with which infants are endowed.

On what basis do infants make the distinction between social and nonsocial objects? One possibility, already mentioned, is that animate objects initiate their own movements, and their movements are sometimes contingent on the infant's behavior. For example, when an infant points and gazes toward an object, an adult will often turn to look at the object and possibly will name the object. Perhaps infants are sensitive to such contingencies. Legerstee (1991b) studied this possibility by linking a doll's movement to an infant's action and comparing the infant's reactions to the doll, to his or her mother, or to a female stranger. When the infant fixated the doll, it moved and jingled. In this study, 7-week-old infants still produced more speech-like vocalizations and more emotional sounds facing their mother and facing a stranger than facing a doll, and Legerstee found no difference between responses to an active and a passive doll. Thus, rudimentary contingency of movement is not enough for distinguishing between people and objects.

Infants' distinction may be finer than just distinguishing between people and objects. They may make more subtle distinctions among people—namely people who are like them and people who are not like them. Infants at 3 months of age show a preference for same-race faces, and by 5 months infants show preferences for people speaking in their native-accented language (Kelly et al., 2005; Kinzler, Dupoux, & Spelke, 2007). Moreover, infants in the second half of the first year of life appear to have expectations for the way members of a group should behave (Powell & Spelke, 2013). These early preferences may suggest the early beginnings of *in-group biases* (Tajfel, 1981); later in this chapter, we discuss a potential role for familiarity effects based on infants' experiences with people.

Thus, by 2 months of age, infants exhibit different behaviors toward people and objects. The informational bases lie in perception—motion characteristics, auditory patterns, and the like. Moreover, infants may make finer distinctions among different people, showing a preference for people who have characteristics similar to themselves and to those around them. The emergence of infants' distinguishing between people and objects is consistent with Trevarthen's observations that infants at 2 months behave very differently with people than they do with objects. Less clear from this work is when infants truly possess intersubjectivity. Intersubjectivity entails more than distinguishing people and objects; it requires sensitivity to the intentions of others. We take up this important component of social knowledge next.

Agency

Previously, we highlighted the difference between animate and inanimate objects. Animate objects are capable of self-propulsion and can take the role of a causal agent from a distance—that is, without physical contact. Some animate objects also have agency, in that they have goals, attentional states, and are capable of mental states such as beliefs and desires. An amoeba has agency. In its own way, it can move and act on other objects. But does it have desires? Does it move to achieve particular goals? It is difficult to know. Humans, however, certainly do have agency, and understanding others' goals and intentions facilitates social interaction.

Do infants understand intentions of actions? If so, does this understanding reflect an understanding of others' mental states? In our discussion of imitation, we already have seen two hints for an affirmative answer to the first question. Infants at 18 months imitated intended actions, even though they did not see the results of the action, and 7-month-olds imitated actions with clear goals rather than actions with ambiguous goals (Hamlin et al., 2008; Meltzoff, 1995). Gergely and Csibra (2003) provide a framework for thinking about goal-directed actions. From their perspective, an observed event has three components: the physical context, a behavior, and an end state. The interpretation of this event includes perceived constraints, the means of the action, and the goal (Figure 10.2). They suggest that infants are sensitive to the three components (means, constraints, and goals), and if given two, they can infer the third.

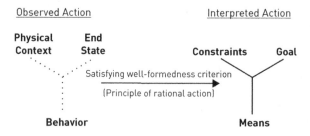

FIGURE 10.2

Schematic representation of the observed and interpreted components of an event.
Source: Reprinted with permission of Elsevier from Csibra, G., Biro, S., Koos, O., & Gergely, G. (2003). One-year-old infants use teleological representations of actions productively. *Cognitive Science, 27*, 111–133; permission conveyed through Copyright Clearance Center, Inc.

In several experiments, Gergely, Csibra, and colleagues tested infants' under-standing of these three components (Csibra, Gergely, Biro, Koos, & Brockbank, 1999; Gergely, Nadasdy, Csibra, & Biro, 1995). Using the violation of expectation paradigm, infants were habituated to events in which geometric forms, typically circles, engaged in an event. In one event, the circle moved across the screen to join another circle. In between the two circles was a barrier, so the circle jumped over

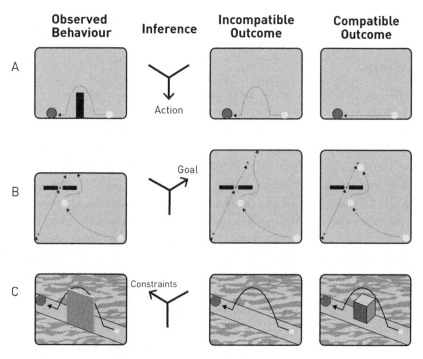

FIGURE 10.3

Schematic representation of events to test infants' understanding of means of action (A), the goal (B), or constraints (C) in events across three different experiments. The left panel shows the habituation displays, and the right panels show the two test events. Source: Reprinted with per-mission of Elsevier from Gergley, G., & Csibra, G. (2003). Teleological reasoning in infancy: The naive theory of rational action. *Trends in Cognitive Sciences, 7*, 287–292.

it (Figure 10.3A). Following habituation, the barrier was removed, and the circle either continued to jump along its path to the other circle (an old action, but not necessary) or moved straight across to the other circle (a new action, but a more efficient route to the goal). Twelve-month-old and 9-month-old, but not 6-month-old, infants looked significantly longer to the jump test display, despite is familiar motion trajectory. Gergely et al. concluded that infants were sensitive to which path of movement (i.e., means) was most efficient for accomplishing the goal.

To explore infants' responsiveness to goals, infants again viewed an event involving two circles (Csibra, Biro, Koos, & Gergely, 2003). One small circle moved from the bottom of the screen to the top (and off the screen) by moving through a small slit in a barrier. The second, larger circle trailed the smaller circle as it also moved toward the top of the screen, but due to its size it had to go around the barrier rather than through the slit. Adults interpreted this event as the larger circle chasing the smaller circle. The test events presented (1) the larger circle bypassing the smaller circle and continuing off the screen or (2) the larger circle catching up to the smaller circle and stopping (Figure 10.3B). Twelve-month-old, but not 9-month-old, infants looked significantly longer to the catching test event, suggesting that they inferred the unseen goal in the habituation event.

Finally, infants also at 12 months, but not 9 months, are able to infer hidden constraints. To test this understanding, infants viewed an event in which one circle moved toward another circle (Figure 10.3C). The central region of the display was occluded from the infant. As the circle moved toward the other circle, it jumped (what it jumped over was hidden by the occluder). Following habituation, the occluder was removed, and infants saw one event in which the circle jumped over nothing and a second event in which the circle jumped over an obstacle. Infants looked significantly longer to the event in which the circle jumped when there was no obstacle present. This finding suggests that the infants inferred that there was an obstacle behind the occluder and that there was a need to jump over it.

Together, these experiments suggest sophisticated understanding of actions, goals, and constraints by the end of the first year of life. One concern is the use of nonhuman objects to represent the actors in these events. Despite the fact that the displays contained characteristics of animate objects (e.g., self-produced motion and nonlinear trajectories), they still were geometric forms moving on a computer screen. Would we find earlier sensitivity to goals and intentions of actual humans? This seems to be the case. Woodward and colleagues have shown that infants are sensitive to a variety of goals and intentions based on human action (Woodward, 2009). For example, when a person reached repeatedly for an object, 6-month-old infants looked longer if the person reached for a new object in the old location compared to the old object in a new location (Luo & Johnson, 2009; Woodward, 1998). The same pattern of results was not found when a clawlike tool did the reaching. Moreover, infants at 5 and 9 months distinguished between goal-directed reaches and arm movements that unintentionally came into contact with an object (Woodward, 1999). Similarly, infants' attribution of gaze shifts, as discussed later, suggests that at least by 10 months infants may perceive attention as goal-directed (Johnson, Ok, & Luo, 2007).

Thus, in the second half of the first year of life, infants perceive agency: They perceive events in terms of actors' goals, situational constraints, and means. Does this mean infants attribute mental states to actors? In other words, do infants have a theory of mind? *Theory of mind* is our understanding that others have minds, and the contents of the mind, such as beliefs, desires, and intentions, determine behavior (Premack & Woodruff, 1978). Whether infants have an understanding of theory of mind is a contentious question and one that is difficult to answer (Baillargeon, Scott, & He, 2010; Csibra & Gergely, 2007; Mandler, 2012; Woodward, 2009). It is also beyond the scope of this chapter. In brief, some believe that these early infant skills represent a theory of mind; others believe that infants appreciate goals, intentions, and situational constraints based on interpretation of behavior or the associations between people and objects but not on an understanding of others' mental states.

Regardless of how we view infants' capabilities in this area, it is clear that infants are equipped to be competent social partners in the first year of life. They distinguish between people and other objects, they distinguish among people who are and are not like them, and they interpret events involving animate beings in terms of goals and efficiency of actions. They accomplish all of this from a firm perceptual foundation.

Perceiving Faces

It is likely that no other topic in infant perception has attracted as much attention as the development of face perception. This topic was among the earliest investigated with newly developed methods. In Chapter 4, it was shown that it is possible to demonstrate a preference for faces over other stimuli in newborns. The tendency is modest at first but robust by 2 months. This change in sensitivity, like others in the early weeks of life involving basic visual variables, has been attributed to cortical maturation, including a probable subcortical to cortical shift in the control of attention (Bronson, 1974; Morton & Johnson, 1991). Here, we take a more socially inspired look at face perception abilities.

Newborn Face Perception

In Chapter 4, it was shown that newborn face preferences are for the most part driven by stimulus variables (e.g., amplitude and top-heaviness), but there is some responsiveness to how a face looks (phase). Here, we consider several examples of newborn face preferences that suggest infants are responding to considerably more than just energy patterns and/or a general configuration of features.

First, newborns prefer attractive over unattractive faces. Infants only hours old (mean age, 68 hours) look preferentially to an attractive face compared to an unattractive face, as judged by adults (Slater, Bremner, et al., 2000; Slater, Quinn, Hayes, & Brown, 2000). When the faces are viewed upside down, infants do not show this preference. (Inversion of a face disrupts processing that relies on the relations among the features (configural processing) rather than each feature individually (featural processing); Valentine, 1988; see also Leo & Simion, 2009.) Moreover, there is evidence that infants are basing their judgments on the internal features of the face rather than on the external features (Slater, Bremner, et al., 2000). Slightly older infants, 3- and 4-month-olds, also show a preference for attractive cat (domestic and wild tiger) faces over unattractive ones, suggesting that this preference extends beyond human faces (Quinn, Kelly, Lee, Pascalis, & Slater, 2008). Sensitivity to and preference for attractive faces in older children and adults have been attributed to a responsiveness to a prototype (Langlois & Roggman, 1990). Slater and colleagues ascribe to a prototype explanation and suggest that if not innate, it certainly is an early developing process.

Second, newborns prefer to look at faces with eyes open compared to eyes closed, and they prefer faces with direct gaze, or looking straight ahead, versus averted gaze, or looking to one side (Batki, Baron-Cohen, Wheelwright, Connellan, & Ahluwalia, 2000; Farroni, Csibra, Simion, & Johnson, 2002). As with attractive faces, this preference disappears when faces are inverted (Farroni, Menon, & Johnson, 2006). Moreover, the preference disappears when the faces are presented at a 45-deg angle (Farroni et al., 2006). In other words, when the head is turned slightly to the side but eye gaze is still directed at the viewer, newborn infants do not show a preference for this face compared to one in which the eyes are pointed to the side (in the direction that the head is pointed). Direct eye gaze also facilitates face recognition, certainly by 4 months and possibly in newborns, and infants show differential neural responding to faces with direct versus averted gaze early in infancy (Farroni, Johnson, & Csibra, 2007; Farroni, Massaccesi, Menon, & Johnson, 2007; Rigatto, Menon, Johnson, & Farroni, 2011). Two suggestions for an underlying mechanism have been put forth. One relies on an innate eye direction detector mechanism (Baron-Cohen, 1995), whereas another suggests that infants respond to face stimuli based on a subcortical innate facelike template (Morton & Johnson, 1991). Both accounts, however, have difficulty explaining why an averted eye may be more difficult to detect than a direct eye, especially in an upright display. We consider a third explanation after discussing one more newborn preference.

Now consider this: Newborn infants show a preference for their mother's face over the face of another female (Bushnell, Sai, & Mullin, 1989; Sai, 2005). This preference suggests recognition of a specific face. We have moved well beyond perceiving general facial features or configurations or subcortical responsiveness to facelike stimuli. How do they do this? Bushnell and colleagues considered the role of olfactory discrimination, given that within days after birth infants come to recognize their own mother's smell. In their study, mothers stood behind a screen with two windows, allowing for live presentation of the mother's and a stranger's face and head region though a small window. The screen was saturated with air freshener to remove any olfactory cues, and the two women were matched in terms of hair color and complexion. Infants, an average of 48 hours old, showed a 62% preference for their mother over the stranger. This preference disappeared (47%) when they could not see the women but only smell them (in this case, no air freshener was used and the women stood behind a screen without windows). If infants were not responding to olfactory information, then they must have known what their mother looked like. Specifically, they recognized the external features of her face: When only the internal features are shown, the visual preference for their mother's face disappears (Pascalis, de Schonen, Morton, Deruelle, & Fabre-Grenet, 1995).

Key to understanding this phenomenon is that the infants were 48 hours old. In this brief time after birth, infants may have learned what their mother looked like, and it is suggested that infants may match their mother's voice, which would have been heard in utero, to her face in the first few hours after birth. To address this possibility, Sai (2005) tested two groups of infants who were 2–12 hours old. Half of the mothers were asked to not speak to their infants before testing; the other half were not given any specific instructions regarding interacting with their infants. Later when tested, infants who heard their mother's voice and saw her face showed a preference for her, whereas infants who did not hear their mother's voice along with seeing her face did not. These findings suggest that infants quickly learned what their mother looked like by matching the familiar sound of her voice to her face. This fast learning explanation is supported by other findings that newborns can quickly learn arbitrary sight–sound pairings and that they recognize initially unfamiliar faces after a period of time of seeing and hearing them speak (Coulon, Guellai, & Streri, 2011; Slater, Quinn, Brown, & Hayes, 1999).

Thus, newborns arrive into the world with several face preferences: They prefer attractive faces, faces with direct eye contact, and their mother's face. These preferences suggest that newborn infants are not as limited perceptually as one might predict given their visual competencies, as outlined in Chapter 2, nor are they functioning solely at a subcortical level (von Hofsten et al., 2014). We have also discussed different explanations for the mechanism underlying each preference (e.g., prototype sensitivity, innate eye detector, subcortical template for face-like stimuli, and rapid learning). Multiple innate or early developing mechanisms for different types of face processing are not a very good design. Is it possible to explain these preferences with one, perhaps, general face processing mechanism? Maybe. The rapid learning account underlying preference for mother's face proposed by Sai (2005) could be applied to direct eye gaze preference. The infants' early social interactions are likely to be with adults looking directly into their eyes at a close distance. Through these interactions, infants may come to expect faces to have direct eye gaze, and thus they show a familiarity preference for faces showing this type of gaze. Therefore, there is no need to appeal to specialized innate processes. Instead, infants may have an innate predisposition to socially interact (e.g., imitation), and through this early interaction with people they come to learn about faces, namely which face is that of their mother, eye gaze, and the overall configuration of features. A rapid learning account is less easily applied to infants' preferences for attractive faces. Mothers generally do not look their best following the birth of a baby, medical personnel may have parts of their faces covered when interacting with a newborn (e.g., wearing a mask), and infants may not see sufficient range of attractive and unattractive faces from which to develop a prototype. However, some have suggested that prototype learning could be very quick, even for newborn infants (Slater et al., 2010).

Other-Race Effect

During the course of the first year of life, infants' face processing becomes tuned to faces of their own race. This phenomenon provides a good example of the role experience can play in shaping perceptual processes.

We previously discussed that as early as 3 months, infants show a preference for faces of their own race (Kelly et al., 2005; Liu et al., 2015). This preference develops into more adept processing of faces of one's own race than of another race, called the *other-race effect* (for review, see Anzures, Quinn, Pascalis, Slater, & Lee, 2013). One study illustrating the developmental progression compared Caucasian infants' recognition of faces, either of their own race or of another race (Kelly et al., 2007). Three-, 6-, and 9-month-olds were habituated to one face (Caucasian, African, Chinese, or Middle Eastern). Following habituation, infants viewed two faces side by side. One face was the same face from the habituation phase, and the other face was a novel face of the same race as the face seen in habituation. Between habituation and test, the pose of the faces was changed to ensure infants were recognizing the face rather than responding to low-level pattern variables. Thus, some infants were habituated to a frontal view of the same person and tested with profile views of the same and a different person, and other infants were habituated to a profile view of the same person and tested with frontal views of the same person and a new person. The results are shown in Figure 10.4. Three-month-olds showed a significant novelty preference to all the faces regardless of race. This finding indicates that they recognized the face from habituation in the test phase and spent more time attending to the novel face. Six-month-olds showed a significant novelty

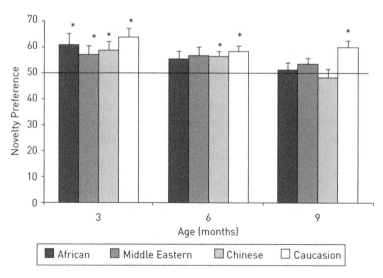

FIGURE 10.4

Infants' recognition of own (Caucasian) and other-race faces as a function of age. *Significant recognition ($p < 0.05$). A decline in recognition abilities for other-race faces occurs across 3 to 9 months. Source: Graphic representation created with permission of SAGE Publications from data reported in Kelly, D. J., Quinn, P. C., Slater, A. M., Lee, K., Ge, L., & Pascalis, O. (2007). The other-race effect develops during infancy. *Psychological Science, 18*, 1084–1089.

preference only to Caucasian and Chinese faces, whereas 9-month-olds showed a significant novelty preference only for Caucasian faces. Thus, with age, infants showed a decrease in their ability to recognize faces from other races. A similar pattern was found for Chinese infants: Three-month-olds recognized the faces across African, Caucasian, and Chinese groups, whereas 6- and 9-month-olds were limited to Chinese faces only (Kelly et al., 2009). Moreover, the same pattern of results was found when comparing infants' perception of human versus monkey faces (Pascalis, de Haan, & Nelson, 2002). These findings suggest that with age, infants' face processing becomes more attuned to the faces they encounter in their everyday environment.

The other-race effect is not restricted to recognition of specific faces. Infants' categorization of faces also becomes more specific for own-race but not for other-race faces with age (Quinn, Lee, Pascalis, & Tanaka, 2015). Caucasian 6-month-old infants who were familiarized to different Black or Asian faces looked longer to a face of a novel race at test, but 9-month-old infants did not. Instead, 9-month-olds familiarized to non-White faces formed a broad category that included other non-White faces, with Black and Asian faces being members of the same category. Infants' scanning of faces also changes across this time period. Between 3 and 9 months, infants' attention to different regions of the face becomes increasingly differentiated depending on whether they are viewing own- and other-race faces (Gaither, Pauker, & Johnson, 2012; Liu et al., 2015; Wheeler et al, 2011).

Exposure to different races affects infants' preferences for own- and other-race faces. Bar-Haim, Ziv, Lamy, and Hodes (2006) tested 3-month-old infants' preferences for Caucasian and African faces. The infants came from one of three groups living in Israel or Africa (Ethiopia). One group was Caucasian Israeli infants living in a predominantly Caucasian community. Another group was African infants living in Ethiopia in a predominantly African community. The third group was African Ethiopians (African-Israeli) recently arrived in Israel and living in an immigration center composed of both African and Caucasian residents. All infants were tested for their preference between a Caucasian and an African face. The Caucasian and African infants living in homogeneous racial communities preferred their own race. The African-Israeli infants did not show a preference for one race over another. Thus, the experience of seeing other-race faces on a daily basis reduced the own-race preference in 3-month-olds.

A preference for one race over another may be a precursor to the other-race effect, but such a preference does not indicate limitations in face processing. Thus, we need to ask whether experience impacts face recognition. The answer appears to be "yes." Training studies with both monkey and Chinese faces presented in picture books reduced the other-race effect in 9-month-old Caucasian infants (Heron-Delaney et al., 2011; Pascalis et al, 2005; Scott & Monesson, 2010). By seeing photos of another race (or species) regularly between 6 and 9 months, infants retained their ability to perceive and recognize individual faces. Another study addressed whether experience with other-race faces can impact face recognition after the onset of the other-race effect. To this end, infants between ages 8 and 10 months were shown video recordings of either same- or other-race females across 3 weeks (Anzures et al., 2012). Initially, all infants showed poor face recognition of other-race faces. After 3 weeks of exposure to the video, Caucasian infants who saw other-race faces discriminated other-race faces in the laboratory. Caucasian infants who saw same-race faces, in contrast, continued to have difficulty with other-race face recognition.

Thus, it is commonly accepted that the other-race effect is due to experience: Infants develop perceptual expertise for the faces they see around them. This explanation should be reminiscent of the explanation for infants' loss of the ability to perceive nonnative speech contrasts (see Chapter 7). Young infants perceive speech contrasts not present in their native language, whereas older infants and adults cannot. This perceptual narrowing or attunement in speech perception occurs between 6 and 12 months of age, and it is attributed to a tuning of infants' auditory perception to the sounds present in their linguistic environment. It appears that a same, or related, process may be at work in face perception (Nelson, 2001). Infants appear to begin life as equal-opportunity face perceivers. Their face preferences are soon narrowed to faces of their own race by 3 months of age. These preferences may guide infants' attention to own-race faces, leading them to become expert processors of own-race faces, a skill that servers them well in face recognition and categorization tasks. However, the system is flexible; own-race biases are reduced when infants are provided with relevant, and apparently brief amounts of, experience. It is on this point that face perception may differ from perception of nonnative speech contrasts. It is very difficult to maintain nonnative speech contrasts, and it has been shown to be successful only in interactive communicative contexts, whereas for face perception, regularly viewing a few images in a picture book or in a video may suffice to maintain perceptual flexibility.

Obtaining Information from Faces

In addition to being interesting and complex stimuli that signal the presence of a person, faces also signal emotional states. As we watch someone eat a novel food, we monitor the person's expression to see if he likes the food or not. By watching facial expressions, infants have the opportunity to learn about the feelings of others, and through this knowledge they may also come to know much about nonsocial objects and events. When do infants become able to extract the information in facial expressions and use it to guide their behavior?

Sensitivity to Emotional Expressions At approximately 1½ to 2 months of age, infants consistently discriminate among different facial expressions of emotion; at 3 months, they generalize emotional expressions among familiar faces (namely their parents); and by 5 months, they distinguish the intensity of some emotional expressions (Walker-Andrews, Krogh-Jespersen, Mayhew, & Coffield, 2011). Moreover, infants' scanning of threat-related facial expressions, such as fear and anger, develops during this time period, with increased avoidance of the eye region (Hunnius, de Wit, Vrins, & von Hofsten, 2011). Perception of more subtle displays of emotion emerges by approximately 6 or 7 months (Ichikawa, Kanazawa, & Yamaguchi, 2014; Ichikawa & Yamaguchi, 2014). This staggered emergence of perception of facial expressions suggests a role for experience.

Some argue that interactions with others shape perception, and perhaps the communicative intent, of facial expressions (Wörmann, Holodynski, Kärtner, & Keller, 2012). Research with infants of depressed mothers provides additional support for a role for experience (Bornstein, Arterberry, Mash, & Manian, 2011). For example, infants of depressed mothers did not show discrimination between a smiling and a neutral expression. This pattern of results was found despite the fact that both groups (infants of depressed and infants of non-depressed mothers) habituated similarly to the repeated presentation of the expression, suggesting that results were not due to some general difference in information processing. Thus, the experience of having a depressed mother may affect infants' perceptual development and subsequent responsiveness to facial expressions.

An important task for infants is to perceive the expressions of the same category as the same despite variation in people showing the expression and the intensity of the expression. Consider smiling: This expression varies in intensity. Whether only the lips are slightly turned up or the lips form a broad grin showing teeth, we describe this expression as a smile, and adults know that it corresponds to the emotion of happiness. Infants, at least by 5 months, are able to categorize the variation exhibited in different intensities of smiling and discriminate a smile from a different emotion. Moreover, infants can do so across different people. In one study, Bornstein and Arterberry (2003) habituated infants to four smile intensities, modeled by four different females (Figure 10.5). Following habituation, infants viewed a fifth smile, the midrange of the smiles seen during habituation, modeled by a new female and a fearful expression, modeled by yet another new female. Infants showed significant looking to the fearful expression compared to the new intensity of smiling, suggesting that they perceived the different intensities as the same expression and fear as something different.

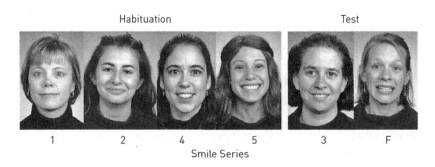

FIGURE 10.5

Facial expressions presented to infants during habituation (1, 2, 4, 5) and test (3, F). 1-5 represent the intensity of the smiling facial expression and F indicates a fearful expression.
Source: Reprinted with permission of John Wiley and Sons, Inc. from Bornstein, M. H., & Arterberry, M. E. (2003). Recognition, categorization, and apperception of the facial expression of smiling by 5-month-old infants. *Developmental Science, 6,* 585–599.

When do infants know that a smile means positive affect, a frown means negative affect, or a fearful expression means potential danger? Infants may respond differently to different facial configurations (e.g., eyebrow position or mouth open or closed) without assigning specific emotional meanings to them. Information about affect in a facial expression is often accompanied by auditory information (a laugh, a sob, or a gasp). Infants between ages 3 and 5 months discriminate vocal expressions of happy and sad and match visual and auditory information for affect in adult and other infant faces (Vaillant-Molina, Bahrick, & Flom, 2013; Walker-Andrews, 1997; Witherington, Campos, Harriger, Bryan, & Margett, 2010). However, matching stimuli such as a smiling face with a happy vocalization does not mean that infants necessarily apprehend positive affect.

Research to date does not allow firm conclusions about when infants know that facial expressions are correlated with specific emotional states. It is interesting to ask how such knowledge may be acquired. One intriguing observation is that several basic facial expressions appear to be universal across cultures (Darwin, 1896; Eibl-Eibesfelt, 1989). The connection between felt emotion and facial expression may originate in innate links between the infants' own feelings and expressions. Being able to match one's own facial gestures with seen expressions is an additional step—one that may be facilitated by early imitation abilities.

Social Referencing Emotional expressions provide the viewer with information regarding the internal feelings of a person. However, these emotional states are often triggered by external events. For example, most people smile when they receive a gift and show fear, or at least surprise, when someone unexpectedly jumps out of a closet. Infants have the potential to learn about events in their world by monitoring the emotional reactions shown by adults. They may be able to use others' reactions to interpret novel situations and possibly guide action.

The monitoring of others' emotions is called *social referencing*. It has been defined as a process of emotional communication in which one's perception of another person's interpretation of events is used to form one's own understanding of that event (Feinman, 1982). In a typical study on social referencing, the infant and an adult are placed in an ambiguous situation (e.g., on a visual cliff or in a room in which a novel toy appears; Kim & Kwak, 2011). The adult is instructed to give a particular emotional expression (e.g., happiness and fear), and the infants' behavior is measured. Generally, it is found that infants approximately 12 months of age tailor their behavior to the emotional expression of an adult, typically the mother (Saarni, Campos, Camras, & Witherington, 2006), but infants will also reference their fathers and friendly strangers (Barrett, Campos, & Emde, 1996; Moller, Majdandzic, & Bogels, 2014; Sternberg, 2013). For example, infants will be less likely to cross the visual cliff if their mothers give a fear expression; however, they will do so if their mothers smile. Similarly, infants will approach a novel toy if their mothers smile but not if their mothers frown. Infants at 12 months of age also reference emotional information presented by televised models (Mumme & Fernald, 2003), and they also retain information across delays (Hertenstein &

Campos, 2004). Peers are also recognized as sources of information, but not until approximately 24 months of age (Nichols, Svetlova, & Brownell, 2010).

Recall that infants between 4 and 10 months of age discriminate and categorize facial expressions. Social referencing, however, does not appear until several months later. Three possible explanations for this delay appear plausible. First, the phenomenon of social referencing may indicate the onset of children's understanding of emotional expressions. It may be the case that infants do not learn the meaning of facial expressions until several months after they successfully discriminate the expressions.

Alternatively, infants may understand the meaning of facial expressions earlier than 12 months of age but come to comprehend that the expression of another person has meaning for their own behavior or well-being. For example, infants might have to learn that on witnessing their mothers' fear, they should behave cautiously. Relatedly, infants may need to learn which adults are trustworthy. Experience with their parents may provide infants with a sense of whether the emotional displays are reliable indicators. Moreover, depending on the context, an unfamiliar adult may have more knowledge about the situation than a parent, and it may take infants time to evaluate the relative expertise of the adults in their environment (Schmitow & Sternberg, 2013; Sternberg, 2013).

Shared Attention

Facial expressions, as discussed previously, provide information about another person's internal state, and, at times, knowledge of this internal state can help evaluate ambiguous situations. If a mother shows a fearful expression, her 12-month-old is less likely to approach a strange object. Infants can obtain more subtle information about objects by attending to what others find attention deserving. By monitoring another's line of sight, infants can learn about objects and can engage in a shared interaction with the other person.

During most interactions, adults monitor where infants are looking (for review, see Schaffer, 1984). In order to be effective social partners, infants too must learn to monitor and influence the attention of others, and indeed very young infants make social bids to the adults around them by attempting to get the attention of conversing adults (Tremblay & Rovira, 2007). There are two ways for social partners to engage in *joint attention*. The easiest way, and the way that first emerges in infancy, is to follow someone else's bid for joint attention. *Gaze following* is one example of a successful response to such a bid, and one that infants can accomplish in the first few days of life (Farroni, Massaccesi, Pividori, & Johnson, 2004). Infants merely need to follow the gaze of another person and fixate. Initially, gaze following can be accomplished only with near objects, but with age infants show more mature responses to others' gaze, including following the gaze of a social robot by 18 months (Meltzoff, Brooks, Shon, & Rao, 2010). Ten months appears to be an important transition point. For example, Brooks and Meltzoff (2005) showed that infants at this age, but not younger, follow head turns but only when adults' eyes are open. At approximately 10 months, infants also understand gaze in third-party interactions (Beier & Spelke, 2012). Infants expect social partners to look at each other when conversing. Thus, at 10 months, infants appear to understand the role that vision plays in joint attention and the way that joint attention is used in communication.

Infants' first overt initiations of joint attention involve pointing. Pointing is an effective gesture for capturing a person's attention to an object or an event, and pointing begins in an apparently communicative manner in the latter half of the first year of life (Butterworth, 2003). Early in the second year of life, infants point and look at the face of social partners as though checking to be sure that they are looking at the designated targets. Such checking suggests that the infant is pointing to communicate and influence the other person's attention (Tomasello, Carpenter, & Liszkowski, 2007). During the course of the second year, infants point in increasingly sophisticated ways, with older children pointing more when the other person did not appear to have seen or looked at the interesting target (Moore & D'Entremont, 2001).

CONCLUSION

Perceptual abilities are prerequisite for a human infant to begin social interaction and development. Conversely, by examining social contexts, we have discussed some of the most stunning examples of the sophistication of infant perception, as well as representation and action. We underscore just two of these. Newborn imitation demonstrates a complex constellation of abilities that come prepackaged, including the ability to perceive and represent functionally important events in an abstract format, suitable for guiding actions. Face recognition by infants from birth is equally startling. These observations serve two purposes in the current context. First, they confirm and extend the picture of sophisticated perceptual abilities producing useful representations in the human infant. Second, they indicate that the infant begins life on firm footing in her explorations of the social world. She arrives prepared to be engaged with others, and through this engagement she learns more about those around her—their emotions, intentions, and limitations. These learning endeavors will make her a fully functioning member of the human community.

11 Perceptual Foundations of Cognitive Development

INTRODUCTION

The origins of knowledge through perception have concerned philosophers and scientists for centuries. Systematic scientific research on human infant perception has been with us for only decades. Preceding it and continuing until very recently was a dominant view of how reality emerges—that it is constructed by associating raw sensory impressions with each other and with action. According to this view, no external world, no three-dimensional space, and no people, objects, or events can be known until such constructions have been achieved. Gradually, meaning emerges as current impressions activate stored sensory and motor patterns, a process that extends well into the second year of life (Piaget, 1954).

This view must be discarded, for the evidence we have considered requires a radically different view of the origins of perception. It is more consistent with a view grounded in evolution, as are contemporary ecological and computational views of perception. Infants perceive an external world, its objects and events, from the beginning of life. This is made possible by perceptual mechanisms that respond to patterns in stimulation and produce abstract representations, rather than memory traces of sensory activations. These transformations from input patterns to abstract representations are made possible by constraints embodied in perceptual machinery. Perception improves with maturation; some abilities do not arise until later, and some may be learned. A rich endowment of perceptual competence, however, derives not from learning by the individual but, rather, from earlier evolution of the species.

We have discussed numerous examples. Newborns respond to the real sizes of objects, taking into account their positions in three-dimensional space. Pattern information characteristic of the human face attracts infant attention from the start, and the ability to encode and later recognize specific faces may also begin at birth. Abstract temporal and spatial patterns are matched across different senses in the early months of life; some specify particular events in the world, such as collision, substance, and numerosity. Amazingly, newborn infants imitate several facial gestures made by adults, an ability that requires abstract encoding and matching of perceived events in a form that traverses perceptual and action systems. From an early age, objects are perceived visually and haptically from information given over time, despite spatial gaps in the input. Infants detect objects using mechanisms that follow the laws of projective geometry to recover three-dimensional structure from transforming two-dimensional projections. Moving infants perceive which parts of the world move and which remain at rest during their own movements. As soon as they become able to reach in a controlled manner, they anticipate in their reaches the future position of a moving object.

In this chapter, we consider the consequences of this relatively new picture of perception for views of cognitive development. We also draw out some implications about the nature of perception that are suggested by our knowledge of perception in infancy.

COGNITIVE DEVELOPMENT ON A NEW FOUNDATION

In Piaget's classic view of cognitive development, the first tasks are protracted ones. In a sensorimotor period, which itself encompasses six stages over 2 years, actions, beginning with reflexes, become encoded along with their sensory consequences as *sensorimotor schemata*. The gradual accumulation and coordination of schemata ultimately gives way to true internal representations of external reality during the preoperational period. Perception, action, and knowledge representation are inseparable in Piaget's sensorimotor stage.

But what if there is no sensorimotor stage? To most developmental psychologists, the suggestion sounds heretical. If the view of perception we have described is correct, however, the designation of initial development as *sensorimotor* is a mistake that must be corrected. This is hardly to suggest that Piaget, a remarkably keen observer, did not pinpoint important aspects of early development. Rather, his observations must be seen in a different theoretical light.

What we have seen is that the characterization of early infancy as sensorimotor will not do for perception. It is not possible, however, simply to add meaningful perceptual reality to the sensorimotor perspective and leave its views of knowledge and action otherwise untouched. We discussed some implications for action in Chapter 9; here, we focus on implications for knowledge and cognitive development.

What does perception give us? A straightforward answer is that it gives knowledge about the environment (and about ourselves). In computational views of perception, this knowledge takes the form of descriptions—that is, mental representations. These are the sorts of things that can be remembered, thought about, and so on. Some ecological theorists (E. Gibson, 1984; J. Gibson, 1979; Mace, 1974) prefer to think about the results of perception in a less representational way: What is perceived are affordances—that is, the functional possibilities an environment offers. Rather than producing representations, perception guides ongoing action, which in turn produces new requirements and opportunities for perceiving. As discussed in Chapter 9, these cyclic events are described as perception–action loops.

Some of perception surely works this way, but we prefer to think of perception as producing descriptions of the environment. These descriptions can support ongoing action, but they also can be stored and recruited for later thought and action. The rest of cognition—such as memory, categorization, thinking, and problem-solving—requires representations obtained from perceiving.

We have seen that very young infants perceive objects, people, spatial relations, and events. In many studies, infants' perception was assessed by methods requiring encoding and comparison of stimuli over time. Some striking recent work suggests that representations of individuals, such as the infant's mother, form very early. Other studies point toward the abstractness of representations formed from perception, even at the beginning. Cognitive development begins with meaningful descriptions of external reality delivered by perceptual mechanisms.

THE SCOPE OF PERCEPTION

How far does perception go? When perception was thought to consist of the adding up of sensations, its ultimate products could not stray too far from concrete elements of sensation, involving brightness, color, pitch, loudness, and so on. With the Gestalt psychologists arose the realization that perceptual processes utilize abstract relationships as inputs and produce abstract outputs, such as perceived form, that are not explicable as sums of sensory qualities. This realization was developed further by Gibson, who argued that perceptual systems respond to higher-order relationships in stimulation, especially patterns given over time. It was also developed by others, such as Michotte (1963), who emphasized that perception has an amodal and functional character:

> Its biological role is to initiate and direct behavior of men and animals. It not only provides material for their contemplation, but invites them to action, and allows them to adjust this action to the world in which they live. The phenomenal world does not consist of a simple juxtaposition of "detached pieces," but of a group of things which act upon each other and in relation to each other. Thus the regulation of conduct requires a knowledge of what things do or can do and what living creatures (and ourselves in particular) can do with them. (p. 3)

This view of perception raises anew the question of how much of human knowledge might be perceptual. As discussed in Chapter 6, event perception research suggests that some forms of knowledge that are abstract or that intuitively seem to involve inference and belief systems might actually be products of perception. Causality, object solidarity, weight, biological motion, and even social intention may be perceived. It seems likely that the outputs of perception produce representations consisting of *basic physical descriptions*—static structure in the three-dimensional spatial environment and physical mechanics of moving things. Such descriptions of objects and surfaces and their relations in space and time are not the province of a single sense but, rather, abstract representations to which various sensory channels contribute.

Perceptual Descriptions as Knowledge

The understanding of perception as producing representations of the physical environment and ecologically important events is controversial. Many recent discussions of cognitive development acknowledge empirical findings about early perception but reject the idea that perception goes this far (Leslie, 1995; Mandler, 1988, 1992; 2007, 2012). Some, in fact, deny that perception produces true knowledge of any sort.

There are several issues to consider. One issue regarding perception and knowledge concerns not the process but the outputs of perception. Ordinarily, these are conscious for adults. We can find no reason to suspect that infants do not have conscious experiences from perceptions. None of the methods used in infant perception is capable of directly assessing consciousness, but the same is true, of course, about the methods we use in studying adults. In any case, a criterion based on consciousness does not seem to be very useful in making claims about infant knowledge.

A second issue concerns the abstractness of knowledge and recall abilities. These would seem to be reasonable criteria for assessing the nature of representations. If the outputs of perception were always closely tied to particular actions or were never encoded in a long-term store, they would be qualitatively different from many adults' perceptual representations. The evidence suggests, however, that much of infant perception produces representations that are abstract, as previously discussed. To imitate viewed facial or manual gestures using one's own facial or manual movements, perception must produce abstract representations capable of supporting action. Imitation experiments, and others, also address the issue of recall. Meltzoff and Moore (1994) found evidence of imitation in newborns 24 hours after their exposure to modeled facial expressions. Moreover, information experienced before birth (e.g., mother's voice) is recalled after birth (see Chapter 7).

In this book, we have discussed numerous examples of the abstractness of perceptual representations. In addition, we have mentioned that animals that locomote from birth demonstrate abstract perceptual knowledge, such as knowledge about the tangible physical world obtained by seeing. Based on seeing, a newborn goat will step onto a solid surface that offers support, but it will not step off a precipice. A newborn chick will locate and peck at a kernel of corn but not at a random location on the ground. The idea that visual information does not specify solidity—that vision gives some intangible representations that achieve tangibility only when worked on by cognitive theories of mechanics—seems specious in the case of the goat. The idea that the environment is carved into bits of corn by domain-specific cognitive theories seems overly glamorous for the chick. Why must we assume such processes for chicks, goats, or human infants?

Perceptual Versus Cognitive Processes

The previous examples of the goat and the chick might be used to insist that vision informs viewers about the physical world and not merely about a visual world.

However, if we accept that perception can yield abstract knowledge, we still do not know its limits. Where do percepts stop and concepts begin? It is doubtful that we are going to get the concept of prime number out of perceptual mechanisms.

Of immediate concern are the claims about events and functional relations so basic to ecological views of perception. Are notions such as causality and animacy really perceived? Perhaps perception stops with some representation of moving things, and concepts handle these more advanced notions (Gelman, Durgin, & Kaufman, 1995). How can we tell?

There do not appear to be compelling logical grounds that indicate where the boundary between perception and cognition should be placed. (For a useful discussion, see Fodor, 1983, pp. 86–88.) The matter seems to be an empirical one. Fodor sets forth some useful criteria for distinguishing perceptual mechanisms (*input modules*, in his terminology) from more central cognitive mechanisms. Among the criteria are the following:
Input models

- are domain specific (we might expect, for instance, separate ones for visual perception of form and auditory localization of sound);
- operate quickly and their operation is often mandatory (you need not make an effort to hear from which direction a sound comes);
- appear to be associated with particular neural architectures;
- may exhibit specific breakdown patterns; and
- depend primarily on innate or maturationally given mechanisms.

One of the most important criteria suggested by Fodor, and one of the most useful for perception researchers, is the notion that input modules are *informally encapsulated*, meaning that their processing depends on certain characteristic sources of information and is not influenced by general knowledge, beliefs, and so on. A similar criterion has a long history in perception studies. A classic case was Wertheimer's (1912) argument (see Chapter 6) about the dependence of apparent motion on tightly constrained spatial and temporal relations.

Many examples we have labeled as *event perception* meet these criteria. We considered the idea that an object's persistence is specified visually as it passes behind an occluder. In this case, there are specific sources of information—namely characteristic projective changes and deletion of texture—that control perceptual responses in both adults and infants (Michotte, Thines, & Crabbe, 1964). Many relevant experiments have been carried out on computer monitors. Information encapsulation is suggested by the fact that accretion and deletion of texture readily creates illusions of depth order and object persistence for adults whose general knowledge tells them that there is no depth order and no hidden object in the monitor. What about causality or animacy? We do not yet know of specialized neural architecture subserving causal or animate perception. Regarding the specificity of information, Michotte's research suggested that causality depends on highly constrained spatial and temporal relations and not on prior experience. Johansson (1975) showed that a compelling impression of animacy (and of a particular action, such as a person walking) was obtained from films of moving light points in as few as two motion picture frames. Evidence that infants in the early months of life are also sensitive to such relations strengthens the case that animacy and causal descriptions could be the results of perceptual mechanisms (Bertenthal, 1993; Leslie, 1988; Simion, Regolin, & Bulf, 2008).

A problem in distinguishing perceptual and cognitive explanations for infant performance is that cognitive mechanisms may also be endogenously determined (Baillargeon, 2008; Mandler, 1992; Spelke, 1988; Spelke & Kinzler, 2007). If cognitive mechanisms were hypothesized to arise later than and less stereotypically than perceptual ones, the empirical task of distinguishing them would be simpler. If a mechanism is nonperceptual, perhaps its processing should be susceptible to influences from general knowledge and reasoning—that is, it may not be informationally encapsulated. Perhaps experiments could be designed around this issue. Spelke (1988) notes, however, that some clearly cognitive processes appear somewhat encapsulated and gives examples.

We cannot now draw a definitive line between perception and cognition, but we can embrace two important conclusions. First, no argument or evidence of which we are aware rules out the possibility that perception produces abstract representations, such as seeing a physical object as solid, or "complex" classifications, such as seeing an entity as animate or an event as causal. Second, what we know about infant perception and perception in general is consistent with this possibility. Perception need not stop short of events; on the contrary, it may be fundamentally about events (Gibson, 1966, 1979; Johansson, 1970; Michotte, 1963; Shepard, 1984). Those who have suggested that perceptual descriptions fall short of "deeper" conceptual structures may have taken too narrow of a view of perception. As Jones and Smith (1993) state, "The perceptual properties that matter are ones that are highly relevant to causal beliefs about objects and their origins" (p. 122).

INTERACTING PERCEPTUAL AND COGNITIVE FOUNDATIONS

The discovery that coherent perceptual reality arrives without a protracted sensorimotor construction of reality reverberates throughout developmental theory. Other cognitive capacities might use the products of perception and might begin their ascent much earlier than previously believed. We turn now to some of these cognitive domains that benefit from perception and furnish other kinds of knowledge. Our goal is to highlight both the perceptual contributions to these cognitive developments and their own unique foundations. We examine domains of number, categorization, and physical laws of objects.

Number

Our understanding of number may have its roots in infant perceptual and cognitive abilities. Consider two tasks that appear to rely on some type of sensitivity to number. In one task, infants first hear a sequences of sounds (e.g., "ra" repeated 4 or 12 times within 1 minute), and then they see displays with geometric forms (4 or 12 items) that either match (consistent) or mismatch (inconsistent) the number of sounds (Figure 11.1). Infants' looking to the visual displays is measured, and significant looking to the consistent display, a familiarity preference, is taken as evidence of perception of number. In a second task, infants see a central occluding panel. From behind this panel to the left, a yellow rubber duck emerges and then hides again. Next, from the right side of the panel, a white foam ball emerges and then hides again. This sequence is repeated a number of times (e.g., four emergences for each object). Next, the occluding panel is lowered, and either one or two objects are present (Figure 11.2). Infants' greater attention to the one object display is taken as perception of the two objects as discrete individual objects. The following are two questions we can ask: Which task is easier for infants? Does the same type of perceptual information underlie success in these two numerical tasks?

Newborns succeed in the first task but only with comparisons that exceed a 1:3 ratio. For example, Coubart, Izard, Spelke, Marie, and Streri (2014) found successful matching of sound and visual displays with sets of 4 versus 12 and 3 versus 9, but not 2 versus 3. Older infants can make finer discriminations. Infants at 6 months discriminate sets with a 1:2 ratio, and infants at 9 months discriminate sets with a 1:1.5 ratio (Lipton & Spelke, 2004). At all ages, however, infants' performance was better with larger (4 items or more) compared to smaller sets. For example, 9-month-olds discriminated sets of 4 versus 6 sounds but not 2 versus 3. The evidence that infants are more successful with larger sets than smaller sets would predict later success on the second task described previously (with 1 or 2 objects peeking out behind the occluder). And apparently it does. Initial investigations showed that infants at 12 months, but not 10 months, are able to determine whether 1 or 2 objects are present behind the occluder (Xu & Carey, 1996).

Familiarization (1 minute)   Test (4 trials)

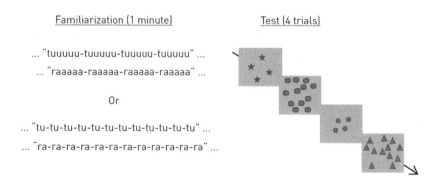

... "tuuuuu-tuuuuu-tuuuuu-tuuuuu" ...
... "raaaaa-raaaaa-raaaaa-raaaaa" ...

Or

... "tu-tu-tu-tu-tu-tu-tu-tu-tu-tu-tu-tu" ...
... "ra-ra-ra-ra-ra-ra-ra-ra-ra-ra-ra-ra" ...

FIGURE 11.1

Auditory and visual stimuli to test newborn infants' discrimination of 4 versus 12 items.
Source: Redrawn with permission of John Wiley and Sons, Inc. from Coubart, A., Izard, V., Spelke, E. S., Marie, J., & Streri, A. (2014). Dissociation between large and small numerosities in newborn infants. *Developmental Science, 17,* 11–22; permission conveyed through Copyright Clearance Center, Inc.

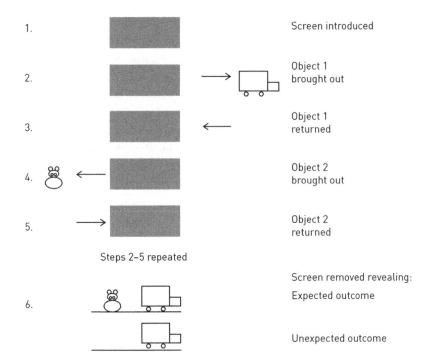

1. Screen introduced

2. Object 1 brought out

3. Object 1 returned

4. Object 2 brought out

5. Object 2 returned

Steps 2–5 repeated

Screen removed revealing:

6. Expected outcome

Unexpected outcome

FIGURE 11.2

Schematic representation of familiarization and test events used to test infants' object individuation. Across trials, two very distinct objects emerged from behind a central occluder. Test events showed either one or two objects present. Source: Redrawn with permission of the American Psychological Association from Xu, F., & Carey, S. (1996). Infants' metaphysics: The case of numerical identity. *Cognitive Psychology, 30,* 111–153.

Two Number Systems

The suggestion that infants perceive and/or have a concept of number long before counting and symbolic arithmetic emerges is controversial. Early studies claiming numerical competence in young infants (Antell & Keating, 1983; Starkey & Cooper, 1980; Strauss & Curtis, 1981) have since been questioned based on the possibility that infants could have been responding to low-level perceptual variables, such as duration, density, pattern complexity, and/or spatial arrangement (Davis, Albert, & Barron, 1985; Feigenson, Carey, & Spelke, 2002; for review, see Feron, Gentaz, & Streri, 2006).

If infants are not merely recognizing differences among patterns, then what is the best way to characterize this early numerical competence? There are several processes by which one can apprehend the numerosity of a set of items (Davis & Perusse, 1988). Counting is the process that comes to mind, but there are ways to make numerosity judgments that are less sophisticated than counting. One such process is relative numerousness judgments. When infants discriminate 2- and 3-item displays, they might be noting the inequality between the displays rather than the absolute number of the set. Adults and nonhuman primates are very good at making these relative judgments; however, their success is limited by the ratio of elements between sets (Barth, Kanwisher, & Spelke, 2003; Jordan & Brannon,

2006). Referred to as an *approximate number system* (Coubart et al., 2014), this process is governed by Weber's law. Newborns need a ratio of 1:3, 6-month-olds need a ratio of 1:2, and 9-month-olds need a ratio of 2:3. Moreover, the sets need to be composed of 4 items or more. For example, Coubart et al. showed that newborns looked at the numerically consistent display when 4 versus 12 items were presented but not when 2 versus 6 items were presented, despite both tests involved a comparison differing by a factor of 3.

A second, more precise numerical system is apparently used for processing sets containing a small number of elements. Although not explicitly counting, infants may individuate the objects and create separate *object files* for them (this approach is also called the *object tracking system*; Mou & vanMarle, 2014). The object file contains important information about the objects, such as color, shape, texture, kind, and location. Discrete object files can be accounted for and used to determine set number and changes in set number (e.g., addition or subtraction). Key to this process, then, is determining when one is seeing a new object or the same object twice.

Keeping track of individual objects is at the crux of Xu and Carey's (1996; see also Xu, 1999) work, and their initial reports suggested that perceptual information was not very helpful for individuating objects. In the task illustrated in Figure 11.2, there is a wealth of information that two different objects are present: A yellow duck and a white foam ball differ in shape, texture, and color, and each appeared in a different spatial location. Moreover, the information for occlusion, successively going out of sight and successively reappearing, specifies the continued existence of the objects, as discussed in Chapter 6. However, it was not until 12 months that infants responded to a one-object display following familiarization to two objects emerging from behind the occluder. Even when two trials were presented in which both objects were visible at the same time beside the occluder, infants showed no evidence of perceiving two objects. A difficulty here may be the integration of information over space and time, a surprising limitation given young infants' sensitivity to motion-carried information but one that has been confirmed by others (Arterberry, 1993, 1995, 1997a, 1997b).

Individuation abilities are documented earlier when information processing demands are minimized(van de Walle, Carey, & Prevor, 2000; Xu & Baker, 2005). One modification made by McCurry, Wilcox, and Woods (2009) involved presenting infants with a screen through which they could reach. Infants saw two types of events. In one, an object fully visible to the left moved behind the screen and then emerged to the right of the screen. The object that emerged was either the same object (e.g., a red box) or a different object (e.g., a green ball). Then the apparatus was moved within reach of the child, and the researchers noted where the infant reached. Infants who saw the same object on either side of the occluder were predicted to reach to the object, which was still next to the occluder. Infants who saw a different object were predicted to reach toward the screen, presumably to find the missing, second, object. In this task, 5-month-olds reached 85% of trials to the screen in the two-object condition and 70% of trials to the object in the one-object condition.

Evidence of younger infant's ability to keep track of individual objects is consistent with earlier evidence of addition and subtraction at 5 months (Wynn, 1992). In Wynn's experiment, infants viewed events in which the number of objects either increased from one to two or decreased from two to one. For example, in one event, infants viewed an object placed in a display case. Then a screen hid the object, and infants watched as a second object was added behind the screen. The screen was then removed, and infants viewed either two objects (a likely, or possible, outcome) or one object (an unlikely, or impossible, outcome). Infants looked significantly longer at the impossible events, suggesting that they knew the number of objects was incorrect. In a second experiment, infants were presented with test events that contained two (possible) or three (impossible) objects. Infants showed a significant increase in looking to the three-object event. Wynn concluded that infants possess true numerical concepts: "They have access to the ordering of and numerical relationships between small numbers, and can manipulate these concepts in numerically meaningful ways" (p. 750).

One might attempt to explain these effects without explicit use of numerosity information. Simon, Hespos, and Rochat (1998) replicated Wynn's (1992) findings, showing 5-month-olds looking longer to the numerically impossible events even when the identity of the objects involved changed. They suggested that infants' numerical competence is tied to physical knowledge of objects, particularly as it pertains to understanding physical existence. Understanding the persistence of hidden objects might allow infants to encode each object as it goes into the display case and expect to see it again when the barrier is removed. With age, infants can keep track of increasingly more objects: Nine-month-olds respond to changes in the number of larger sets (e.g., 5 + 5 or 10 − 5; McCrink & Wynn, 2004). Thus, these early abilities to track individual objects may likely serve as the first step on a long trajectory of developing mathematical skills.

Clearly, preverbal infants are not counting in the way that older children and adults do, namely by assigning linguistic labels to individuated items. However, they are able to discriminate and, more importantly, individuate the items in the array based on perceptual features. Not all perceptual features, however, are useful. As Xu and Carey (1996) demonstrated, despite a number of perceptual differences between the duck and the ball, infants were unable to individuate the two objects until 12 months. Others have also found limitations in infants' use of color and pattern differences (Wilcox, Smith, & Woods, 2011; Wilcox, Woods, & Chapa, 2008). In contrast, unique sounds and motion patterns do facilitate object individuation (Brower & Wilcox, 2012; Wilcox & Schweinle, 2003), again suggesting an important role for perception and one that relies on highly veridical information.

Summary: Number

We presented evidence supporting the existence of two processes underlying infants' numerosity perception. One, an estimation process, serves infants well with large sets as long as the ratio of elements between the two sets is sufficiently great. A second process, perhaps a process akin to creating object files, allows for individuation and tracking of smaller numbers of items. Perception plays an important role in both of these processes.

Categorization

Categorization involves creating representations that group together objects or events. Despite being discriminably different, the members are treated in some way as being the same. For certain purposes, the differences among members are much less important than what they have in common and how they differ from things outside the category.

Categorization produces cognitive economy. If you are told that lurking outside the door is a strange animal, a vorp, you can infer much about it despite never having encountered one before. Knowing the vorp is an animal, you have no doubt that it has a circulatory system and eats food, for example. The ecological trick in categorization is grouping and separating based on object properties so as to produce the greatest efficiencies in thought and behavior.

Some categorizations appear to be built into sensory mechanisms. Two examples are categorical perception of color (see Chapter 2) and phonemes (see Chapter 7). Although the stimuli may vary continuously along a physical dimension (e.g., wavelength or voice-onset time), infants perceive them categorically. There are a number of similarities between these categorizations given by sensory mechanisms and categories of generic knowledge (Medin & Barsalou, 1987).

Studies investigating young infants' categorization abilities have typically used versions of the habituation paradigm. Across habituation trials, infants are presented with different exemplars from the same category (e.g., different animals). Following habituation, infants view a new exemplar from the same category (a new animal) and an object from a different category (e.g., a vehicle). One piece of evidence of categorization is whether or not infants get bored during the habituation phase. Despite viewing different exemplars on each trial, infants should become bored if they recognize the commonality among the objects across the trials. A more robust piece of evidence for categorization derives from comparison of looking on the test trials. Infants demonstrating categorization look significantly longer at the object from the new category than at the new exemplar from the habituation category, even though the new exemplar from the habituation category is discriminably different from the exemplars presented during the habituation phase.

Categorization has been tested with a wide variety of stimuli, and we know that infants within the first 6 months of life are accomplished categorizers. For example, they categorize abstract geometric relations, such as static dot patterns and spatial relations (Bomba & Siqueland, 1983; Cohen & Younger, 1984; Quinn, 1994; Younger & Gotlieb, 1988). They categorize objects globally, including animals, vehicles, and furniture (Arterberry & Bornstein, 2001; Behl-Chadha, 1996), and they also categorize with surprising specificity, such as dogs, horses, cats, facial expressions, and motion patterns of animals and vehicles (Arterberry & Bornstein,

2001; Bornstein & Arterberry, 2003; Eimas & Quinn, 1994). Seven-month-old infants categorize different breeds of cats (Quinn, 2004; Quinn, Doran, Reiss, & Hoffman, 2010), and later still, at approximately 9 or 10 months, infants categorize more abstract relations such as between (Quinn, Adams, Kennedy, Shettler, & Wasnik, 2003).

Perceptual Versus Conceptual Processes

Perhaps the central issue in interpreting early categorization abilities involves the relative contribution of perceptual and conceptual processes (for reviews, see Mandler, 2000, 2007; Quinn, 2011; Quinn & Eimas, 1996). The issue relates directly to the question we considered previously about what kinds of outputs perception produces. Can abstract, functional properties of objects be extracted by perceptual mechanisms? Do perceptual processes produce outputs consisting of descriptions in some amodal vocabulary, such as physical structures and the mechanics of their interactions? Some have argued that the original bases of categorization are perceptual processes that pick out ecologically important properties of objects (Jones & Smith, 1993). Others claim that the outputs of perception must be redescribed or processed further in some manner for conceptual categories to be derived (Leslie, 1995; Mandler, 1988, 1992, 2000, 2007). The claim appears to rest on a theoretical assumption and related empirical observations. Infants categorize using information apart from surface similarity of the objects presented. For example, Mandler and McDonough (1993) emphasized that 7- to 11-month-olds who distinguished animals from vehicles did so despite the fact that some objects from different categories were similar, such as birds with outstretched wings and airplanes. The theoretical assumption is that perceptual categories must be sensitive to this sort of similarity, whereas use of more abstract criteria must implicate nonperceptual inputs, such as cognitive theories of natural kinds.

We have already considered and rejected this assumption about the limits of perception. It is based on a cherished but flawed view of perception as being primarily or exclusively about sensory similarities. Perception is about exactly what Mandler (2000) says of a concept: "It answers the question: What kind of thing is it?" Crucial to this view of perception is information given by events. If infants sort animals and vehicles, it may be because they have perceived that animals are self-moving and vehicles are not; that animals display jointed or elastic motions and vehicles do not; or that animals seek food, whereas vehicles do not. Not only are all of these properties perceivable but also they are the sorts of properties perceptual systems probably evolved to pick up.

Ultimately, humans surely develop concepts that are more remote from ecological perceptual encodings of reality. The notion of an even number is one example. Closer to our discussion, theories distinguishing animals from other vehicles based on more subtle properties (e.g., animals have DNA) seem unlikely to be given by early perception. By the same token, we would assume these properties are not what young infants' categories are about.

Is there any evidence that points to the relative roles of perceptual versus conceptual processes in categorization? One approach to tease apart this issue is to use a transfer-across-cues paradigm. Building on the finding that 3- and 6-month-olds categorize still images of animals and vehicles and the motion patterns of animals and vehicles (Arterberry & Bornstein, 2001), Arterberry and Bornstein (2002) asked whether infants' categorization would transcend specific stimulus information. To address this question, infants were habituated to a set of within-category exemplars (e.g., animals) specified by one type of information (e.g., static) and then tested for within-category recognition (e.g., animal) and novel-category (e.g., vehicle) novelty preference with exemplars specified by a different type of information (e.g., dynamic). In one condition, infants were habituated to up to eight exemplars of one category (animals or vehicles) specified by the information available in color static images and tested with a novel familiar-category exemplar and novel category exemplar specified by point-light displays (Figure 11.3A). Another group of infants experienced the reverse. They were habituated to up to eight point-light displays of either animals or vehicles and then tested with static images of a novel familiar-category exemplar and novel category exemplar (Figure 11.3B). Six-month-olds showed no evidence of category transfer from one source of information to another; 9-month-olds recognized the familiar category exemplar and looked significantly longer to the novel category exemplar when habituated to dynamic displays and tested with static displays.[1]

Successful transfer across cues suggests that infants formed a representation of the category that was independent of the specific perceptual information—in other words, an amodal representation. This finding supports a perceptual interpretation, one that fits with other examples of amodal perception (see Chapter 8 and the discussion on imitation in Chapter 10). What differs from the previous examples is the relatively late development of this ability—9 months when within-cue categorization is present as early as 3 months. Newborns imitate and 1-month-olds perceive the equivalency of object properties across modalities, but infants younger than 9 months did not categorize animals and vehicles across static and dynamic information. The asymmetry—transfer from dynamic to static but not the other way—is also puzzling from a perceptual perspective. Indeed, dynamic information is more informative to infant and adult perceivers than static information; however, the static images were perceptually rich, and 3-month-old infants show within-cue categorization using these same images (Arterberry & Bornstein, 2001). These findings suggest a role for later-developing conceptual knowledge. This knowledge may be as rudimentary as animals typically have legs and vehicles typically have wheels, and perception plays a role in identifying these features.

What other knowledge might facilitate categorization? Some categories of objects are found in predicable locations. For example, animals (with the exception of pets) are typically found in nature scenes, whereas vehicles (with the exception of advertisements) are typically found on streets or driveways. Previous studies have found that 10- to 12-month-old infants are sensitive to the correlation among attributes of objects (e.g., neck length and ear shape; Younger & Cohen, 1986; Younger & Fearing, 1998), and 14-month-olds can make use of location information in their

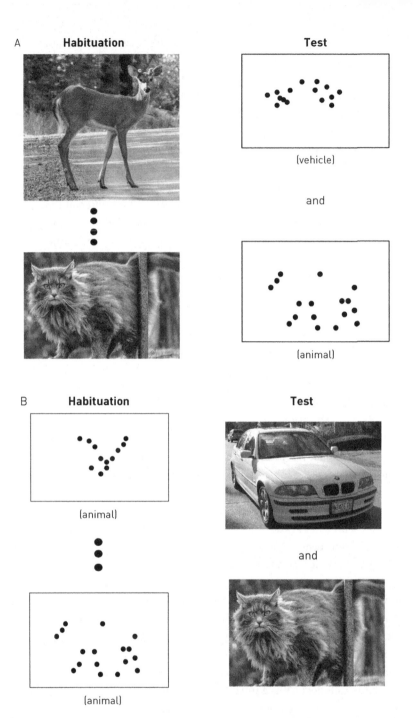

FIGURE 11.3

Example habituation and test images used by Arterberry and Bornstein (2002a) to test infants'
categorization of animals and vehicles across cues. (A) Infants were habituated to up to eight
exemplars of static color images of either animals or vehicles and then tested with dynamic
point-light displays. (B) Infants were habituated to up to eight dynamic point-light displays of
either animals or vehicles and then tested with static color images. Source: Created by M. E.
Arterberry; animal images courtesy of J. J. Richards,

classification of objects (e.g., bathroom items vs. kitchen items; Mandler, Fivush, & Resnick, 1987). Whereas past work has been about correlations among attributes of the object that are fixed, the correlation between an object and its context is probabilitistic. Animals and vehicles move such that animals can be found on streets (pets certainly are) and vehicles can be found in nature scenes (especially in Jeep commercials).

To address whether object–context congruency affects categorization, Bornstein, Arterberry, and Mash (2010) manipulated the context in which animal and vehicle stimuli were presented. In one condition, animals were presented in nature scenes and vehicles were presented on streets (congruent context). A second condition was also congruent except that the original images were excised from their original context and placed in another congruent context (manipulated congruent context, Figure 11.4A). In a third condition, the animals were shown on streets and the vehicles were shown in nature scenes (incongruent context; Figure 11.4B). A final condition showed the animals and vehicles against a white homogeneous context. Infants at 6 months who were tested for categorization using the congruent-context images showed a significant novelty preference of 69%. In contrast, infants in the other three conditions showed a novelty preference barely above chance: In all three of the manipulated conditions (congruent, incongruent, and homogeneous), the novelty preference was 55% or 56%. Clearly, the disruption of the object from its natural (and photographed) context disrupted categorization.

To explore more directly infants' perception of object and context congruency, Bornstein and colleagues measured 4-month-old infants' fixation to the focal object or background regions of the displays (Bornstein, Mash, & Arterberry, 2011a, 2011b). The most interesting result is the comparison between the manipulated congruent context condition and the incongruent context condition because these two involve photographically manipulated images, but they contrast the likely location of the two categories of stimuli. Different fixation patterns were found for animals and vehicles, suggesting different attentional strategies for animate compared to inanimate objects. Also, for both animals and vehicles, fixations were drawn away from the object when the context was incongruent. Adults tested in a similar manner showed the same fixation pattern, and this held even when the background was homogeneous. In other words, despite there being nothing to look at, the background garnered more attention than a congruent context. These findings, in conjunction with the findings from the categorization task described previously, suggest that infants are sensitive to object category context. This sensitivity may likely come from experience of perceiving certain objects in certain contexts such that infants can rely on this information for grouping objects.

Is this a truly perceptual process? Separating objects from their background and perceiving objects in specific environments is certainly the purview of perception. Detecting the regularity of these object–context pairings may be an invariant that infants pick up via perceptual processes. Remembering which objects go with which contexts, however, may be a cognitive process. Because the eye-tracking

FIGURE 11.4
One example of animal stimuli presented in a congruent, A, and an incongruent context, B. The small dots are fixation locations. Source: Reprinted with permission of the American Psychological Association from Bornstein, M. H., Mash, C., & Arterberry, M. E. (2011). Perception of object-context relations: Eye-movement analysis in infants and adults. *Developmental Psychology, 47*, 364–375.

study did not have a habituation phase, infants most likely relied on memory for object–context pairings and this memory guided their fixation patterns.

Development of Categorization

The development of categorization abilities may be an excellent example of perceptual learning. Infants begin life attending to object properties and attending to those properties that are most salient (e.g., motion characteristics or key parts). Objects can be grouped together based on these similar properties; these properties can be remembered and recognized in new exemplars of objects. As infants gain more experience with objects, they may come to discover less salient properties and/or be able to group objects based on functional rather than observable similarities (Trauble & Pauen, 2007). Moreover, experience appears to interact with infants' attentional strategies as early as 4 months of age, which may impact categorization (Kovack-Lesh, Horst, & Oakes, 2008; Quinn & Tanaka, 2007).

What facilitates development of categorization? There is evidence for the role of experience. Four-month-old infants who have pets at home are more skilled categorizers of cats and dogs (Kovack-Lesh, Oakes, & McMurray, 2012), and 3- and 4-month-old infants' categorization and recognition of faces is affected by whether they have more or less experience with female versus male caregivers (Quinn, Yahr, Kuhn, Slater, & Pascalis, 2002). Five-month-old infants who were allowed to play with a set of novel objects at home for 2 months before being tested in the lab showed recognition of the objects in the lab and superior categorization of the objects compared to infants who did not have prior experience with the objects (Bornstein & Mash, 2010). We also noted in Chapter 10 that by age 6 months, infants' categorization of faces is affected by their experience with different races (Quinn, Lee, Pascalis, & Tanaka, 2015).

There is also a role for language. Early on, others may provide infants with linguistic cues for certain objects or their properties. Ferry, Hespos, and Waxman (2013) found that infants' categorization was facilitated by linguistic sounds but not tones. For 3- and 4-month-olds, human speech or lemur calls were sufficient; but by 6 months only human speech facilitated categorization. Nouns are excellent category labels, and infants at least by 6 months perceive nouns as referring to categories of objects, such as hands and feet (Tincoff & Jusczyk, 2012). At the same time, giving the same objects, such as strollers, unique names (e.g., gonib, cuggle, and wuggum for three different strollers) instead of just calling all exemplars "strollers" disrupts categorization (Scott, 2011). Older infants show greater flexibility in categorization, such as switching from shape to material substance as the basis for categorization, and receptive language skills predict this flexibility (Ellis & Oakes, 2006). Infants' propensity to organize the world into categories may serve as a helpful precursor to learning language; at the same time, acquiring linguistic labels may highlight concepts, such as DNA, that are not immediately observable but are shared by members of a category (Graham, Keates, Vukatana, & Khu, 2013). Fundamental to this learning is attention and differentiation based on perceptual information.

Summary: Categorization

It seems likely to us that many of infants' categorization abilities in the first year of life, including those that use abstract, functional criteria, are based on properties encoded and made salient by perceptual mechanisms. We can articulate some of what that information is and how it leads to more abstract ideas. Motion clearly is an important source of information. Other regularities, whether correlations among object attributes or where objects are likely to be found, are also readily available and attended to by infants. Infants play an active role in grouping objects and events. They attend to salient object properties; they perceive commonalities among variability; and they rely on other information, such as object labels, to accomplish and refine categorization.

Physical Laws of Objects

Some research suggests that infants may be born with cognitive abilities that organize the growth of knowledge about physical interactions with objects. Consider the following event used by Spelke, Breinlinger, Macomber, and Jacobson (1992; Figure 11.5). A ball was dropped behind an occluding surface. The occluder was removed, and the ball was seen resting on the floor. After habituation, a shelf was

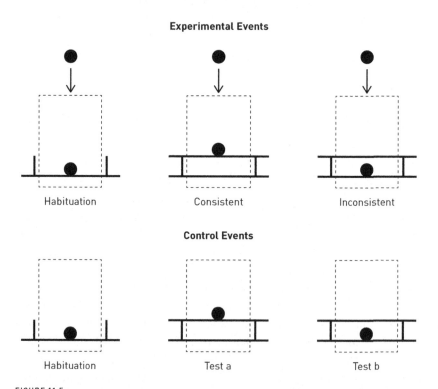

Experimental Events

Habituation   Consistent   Inconsistent

Control Events

Habituation   Test a   Test b

FIGURE 11.5

Displays used to test infants' sensitivity to the constraints of continuity and solidity.
Source: Redrawn with permission of the American Psychological Association from Spelke,
E. S., Breinlinger, K., Macomber, J., & Jacobson, K. (1992). Origins of knowledge. *Psychological Review, 99,* 605–632; permission conveyed through Copyright Clearance Center, Inc.

inserted above the floor while the infant watched. Then the occluder was reintroduced, and the ball was again dropped. Infants were tested for their looking times to two events. In one, the occluder was removed, and the ball was shown resting on the upper shelf (a novel location but one that was physically possible). In the other, the ball was shown resting on the floor (a familiar location from the habituation phase but one that is now physically impossible). If infants, like adults, perceive objects as moving continuously and not passing through solid surfaces, then the familiar location (ball on the floor) should attract more attention than the novel location (ball on the shelf). Spelke et al. found that 3- and 4-month-olds dishabituated more to the event with the ball on the floor. In another experiment in which the ball moved horizontally and appeared on one or the other side of a barrier, 2-month-olds also attended more to the novel physically impossible ball location. These findings suggest that infants as young as 2 months are sensitive to constraints of continuity and solidity.

Sensitivity to constraints such as continuity and solidity represents innate *core knowledge*, according to Spelke (2000; Spelke & Kinzler, 2007). According to the core knowledge hypothesis, infants have a small number of separate systems that enable them to reason about objects or events. The systems pertain to knowledge of objects, number, agency, space, and possibly persons. Each system has a set of principles that serve to individuate entities in its domain and to allow for inferences about the entities' behavior. Moreover, these principles serve a foundation from which infants interpret their world and continue to learn more about objects and their properties. Core knowledge of objects includes the principles of *cohesion* (objects move as connected and bounded wholes), *continuity* (objects move on connected unobstructed paths), and *contact* (objects do no interact at a distance).

Perceptual and Cognitive Contributions

What aspects of infants' performance might be understood in terms of early perceptual processes, and what might lead us to suspect additional cognitive contributions? Let's return to the example illustrated in Figure 11.5. Perception contributes in several ways. Segmentation of the scene into objects, the spatial arrangement of the display, the solidity of the ball and shelf, and the trajectory of the object are all likely products of perception. At first glance, the experiment seems to provide evidence that infants' expectations are guided by some knowledge apart from what is perceived. Specifically, a belief that objects must move along continuous space–time paths could explain the data. When the path of the ball was hidden, there was no information about whether the ball did or did not follow a continuous space–time path. One could take a contrary view, however. The initial and final positions of the ball might engage perceptual mechanisms signaling path continuity, as in Michotte's tunneling effect. More generally, perceptual systems may incorporate the assumption of spatiotemporal continuity as a constraint on perceptual processing (Marr, 1982). Phenomena of stroboscopic motion, in which continuous motion is perceived between discrete flashes of light, suggest some such constraint is indeed incorporated in perceptual processing. It appears to be very difficult to separate the knowledge obtained in two possible ways—by perceptual mechanisms that incorporate constraints about the way the world works and by cognitive theories about mechanics. Given that both could arise from innate foundations, as Spelke (1988) suggests, deciding between them empirically is difficult at best.

The results of Spelke et al. (1992) and others (for review, see Hespos & van Marle, 2012) nevertheless can be claimed to have a clear cognitive component, apart from how the constraint about spatiotemporal continuity is implemented. Perception might produce representations of the solid objects in the displays and might produce a representation of the path followed by the ball when it was occluded. Detecting a conflict between these representations seems to involve a process of comparison (the ball's path through space and the structure of objects in that space). Of course, comparisons are implicit in any habituation and recovery study, but ordinarily the change that produces novelty responding is a change in a particular object or event. In the case we are considering, something more synthetic is occurring: Novelty responding is based on a contradiction between two representations given by perception. Infants' performance may plausibly be interpreted as involving rudimentary reasoning processes in this example.

The study described previously suggests that some reasoning about physical objects and events appears quite early. In fact, there are numerous examples of young infants' physical reasoning. Two-month-olds perceive contact between objects and obstructions; in other words, they know that a ball should stop when it comes to a solid wall (Spelke et al., 1992). In Chapter 6, we noted that infants' perception of occlusion facilitates their understanding of object permanence (Baillargeon, 1987; Baillargeon, Spelke, & Wasserman, 1985). However, there is more. Two- and 3½-month-old infants perceive relations between objects and their containers; for example, they know that a container needs to have an open top (Hespos & Baillargeon, 2001a, 2006). Between 5 and 7 months of age, infants come to understand the constraints regarding object size and container size (Hespos & Baillargeon, 2001b; Hespos & Spelke, 2004). Moreover, infants understand support relations: Infants who are 5½ months old perceive an object resting on a surface as a separate entity (one that could be moved or obtained) compared to an object floating above a surface, and 6½-month-olds perceive an object with 100% support as a separate entity compared to one with only 15% support (Hespos & Baillargeon, 2008; Needham & Baillargeon, 1993). This latter finding suggests an understanding of the role of gravity on object relations, which may also develop between 5 and 7 months of age (Kim & Spelke, 1992; Sitskoorn & Smitsman, 1995). With development, infants also come to understand the differences between objects and substances (e.g., sand) and also the respective principles of these two entities (Hespos & van Marle, 2012). Together, these findings suggest an early competency in physical reasoning that rests on important foundational knowledge of objects—cohesion, continuity, and contact. With age, this knowledge is refined and extended under both perceptual and cognitive processes that are likely innately endowed and guided by experience.

Summary: Physical Laws of Objects

Studies of physical principles in early infant cognition have produced startling results. Whether principles influence behavior because they are built-in constraints on the formation of perceptual representations or whether they are embodied as principles in intrinsic cognitive theories is an issue that cannot currently be resolved. What is clear is that comprehension of the physical world begins very early and that infants' behavior suggests early reasoning processes that compare representations obtained from perception.

CONCLUSION

Research on the development of perception places early cognitive development on a new foundation. There is no sensorimotor stage in which meaningful reality must be constructed from sensations and action. Perception delivers ecologically meaningful representations of objects, arrangements, and events to the new perceiver, coarsely at first and with greater precision later. These new foundations have many implications. That perception depends on relationships and produces abstract descriptions of reality opens the possibility that important aspects of knowledge traditionally considered conceptual may be obtained directly through perception. Notions such as solidity, animacy, and mechanical causality may be primitives in the vocabulary in which the outputs of perception are expressed. That meaningful perception begins early and need not be laboriously constructed implies that learning about the physical world can get underway much earlier than previously believed. These learning endeavors may be guided not only by ecologically meaningful perceptual descriptions but also by distinctly cognitive contributions, in domains such as number categorization and physical knowledge, that also appear in infancy.

NOTE

1. Infants' apparent failure in transferring category information from static to dynamic might be due to the fact that dynamic point-light displays captured the infants' attention regardless of category membership, after viewing six or more trials of static color images. In a follow-up experiment in which 9-month-olds viewed "moving" static images (the picture moved around the screen), infants during the test phase still did not show a significant novelty preference for the novel category exemplar specified by point-light displays (novelty preference was 49%).

12 Trends and Themes in Perceptual Development

INTRODUCTION

Research on the origins of perception has changed forever our conceptions of how human mental life begins. A harsh inheritance—the "blooming, buzzing confusion" envisioned by William James and generations of philosophers and psychologists—has given way to a coherent, meaningful reality furnished by perceptual mechanisms. Descriptions produced by perception make explicit abstract physical properties of objects and events, as well as functionally important relations. This birthright gives human infants a strong foothold for learning and developing their physical and social environments. In this final chapter, we distill some general ideas that have emerged from our explorations into the development of perception. Moreover, we discuss what happens when perceptual development follows an atypical path, in terms of both what we can learn about perception from studying atypical development and when and how interventions might be effective.

COMPETENCE AND LIMITS IN INFANT PERCEPTION

Our celebration of infants' competence should not obscure the limitations of early perception and the importance of developmental changes. It is difficult to name more than one or two abilities of infants in the first half year of life for which the precision or speed is on a par with those of adults. Although we have stressed the attunement of infants' visual perception to events, even the most optimistic estimates of infants' visual velocity thresholds are an order magnitude higher than those of adults. Equally important, human infants' contact with reality, as we have discussed, occurs through a subset of the perceptual abilities available later on. Recall, for example, that adults perceive three-dimensional form using either kinematic or static information but that infants appear to require kinematic information to perceive form until sometime late in the first year. Pictorial depth information and the edge-sensitive process in perceiving objects under occlusion are other examples. In short, our portrait of infant perception is a distinctive one and not merely a faint copy of the adults' profile.

The Risk-Averse Perceiver

We can say more about the portrait. The strengths and weaknesses in early perception may conform to an intelligible pattern. Consider first that the omissions, numerous as they are, always involve information sources and not tasks. In surveying the gamut of infant perception, we did not find a single important perceptual task—such as object, depth, motion, or intermodal perception—for which the infant was not prepared in some manner. It never turned out that infants could perceive patterns but not depth or depth but not motion or that no links initially connected sounds and sights, and so forth. We have found no major aspect of the infant's environment marked "access denied."

What we do find is that in many domains, adults utilize a variety of information sources, whereas infants have a more limited arsenal. In many domains, we observed the precocity of abilities based on kinematic information and the delay of abilities based on static spatial relationships. Much of object and space perception fits this description. We could encompass these observations with the generalization that motion-processing mechanisms are prewired, whereas others require maturation or learning.

A different generalization may be more apt, however (Kellman, 1993). Development may be described as risk averse in that early appearing perceptual skills are those using information of highest ecological validity—that is, those virtually guaranteed to produce accurate perception. Many examples of perception based on kinematic relationships fit this category of high validity (Gibson, 1966; Johansson, 1970; Shepard, 1984), but they do not exhaust it. Relationships in static arrays that are high in ecological validity, such as size–distance invariance, also appear early in development. Recall Gottlieb's (1971) pronouncement that "evolution is a consequence of nature's more successful experiments in ontogeny" (p. 106). The key to this experiment may be the importance of accurate perception in the infancy period. As has been argued at several junctures in this book, the infant's motor capabilities do not support escaping from predators, foraging for food, or weaving among obstacles at high speed. Accordingly, the infant's priorities, unlike those of the adult, do not require perceptual mechanisms that can deliver rapid descriptions of reality under the widest possible range of circumstances. For the infant, the priority may be on accurate rather than comprehensive perception. Indeterminacy or ambiguity of some aspects of the environment is less of a problem for an infant, who cannot do much, than for an adult, who can. Conversely, errors of perception may have far greater repercussions in infant development than later on. An adult may misperceive, out of the corner of an eye, a distant aircraft as a nearby insect. Turning to look directly, the mistake is realized at once. An infant possesses fewer capacities for error correction. Lower sensory resolution and less mobility may preclude further investigation. Worse, the infant may not know whether insects ever turn into airplanes. Instead of realizing perceptual errors, the infant may simply arrive at faulty beliefs.

We arrive at two conjectures, which we might call *access* and *risk aversion*. The infant is born with perceptual abilities giving access to most, if not all, major features of his or her environment (i.e., objects, events, and spatial arrangements), albeit with less precision than will come later. Within each perceptual domain, however, access is based on a subset of adult abilities, and that subset tends to include those information sources of highest ecological validity. These are broad characterizations and are not subject to a single definitive test. Like many evolutionary arguments, they are perhaps unsatisfyingly post hoc. However, we would be remiss not to point out how neatly these conjectures apply. Perhaps due to imperatives of successful development, infants' perception is broad in its access to aspects of the environment and narrow in its selective reliance on information sources of the highest ecological validity.

We need to be mindful, however, of the fact that most studies of perceptual development attempt to minimize attentional and memory limitations, distractions, task complexity, and other variables in testing particular abilities. Clearly, this strategy is most appropriate for making inferences about competence apart from potentially interfering performance variables. It has served us well in allowing inferences about the origins and processes of perception. We should not be misled, however, into thinking that infants' abilities as seen under optimal conditions function consistently under ordinary conditions. The study of performance limitations—attention, memory, situational complexity, and other variables—on infant perception and cognition in natural environments has hardly begun. Research in sterile settings has given us the broad outlines of perceptual competence, but we know relatively little of the microstructure of perceiving and thinking in development.

DESCRIPTION AND EXPLANATION IN PERCEPTION

From the beginning of the modern-era infant research to the present, the focus has been on discovering what infants perceive and when various perceptual abilities come to operate. These questions are obvious starting points for understanding perceptual development, and they have been pursued with notable success. Experimental findings have in many cases answered centuries-old questions and corrected enduring misconceptions about the origins of human knowledge.

Beyond discovering that infants can perceive a certain aspect of their environment at a certain age, much research has sought to specify the information that engages particular perceptual abilities. Understanding what information is used in a perceptual task is a key priority at the ecological level of analysis and one that opens the door to meaningful inquiry about the process and biological mechanisms of perception.

A much smaller subset of research, however, has revealed in detail the computational processes or neurophysiological mechanisms of early perceptual abilities. Clearly, advancing our understanding of computational and neural mechanisms is a major challenge for the future of perception research at all ages. The tasks may appear formidable (recall those 10^{14} neural connections!); however, advances in neuroimaging technologies and more user- and participant-friendly equipment for electroencephalography (EEG) recording have already begun to help us understand the neural underpinnings of perception (Stiles, Brown, Haist, & Jernigan, 2015). Moreover, the research we have seen to date in infant perception may have surmounted less difficult tasks than those remaining. This perspective is to some degree the result of the success that infant perception research has enjoyed in actually answering many of its key questions at the level of competence and information. To have in hand a reasonably clear description of perceptual development, like we do now, is remarkable. Such a description was certainly out of reach for hundreds of years, despite intense interest in the topic.

Perceptual Mechanisms

There is more to be done, however, to achieve complete explanations of how perception works. Some of it may call for new methods and new creativity. We have seen already examples of research that illuminates not only the ecological level of task and information but also process and mechanism. For example, findings that vision and hearing provide human infants with information for a common external space converge with neurophysiological findings in other species of neurons whose receptive fields cover a region of space, whether the input from that region is auditory or visual. These converging lines of research do not yet pinpoint specific neural mechanisms in humans, but we are dealing with data and hypotheses remarkably advanced from when infant perception research begin in earnest in the 1960s. Research relating changes in a variety of visual abilities to maturation of the visual cortex at approximately 6–8 weeks, or the separate maturation of stereoscopic depth perception at approximately 16 weeks, provides other examples. Such connections are based on convergent behavioral and electrophysiological methods. Ideal observer analyses have located limitations of early infant vision at particular levels of the nervous system; these efforts bring together computational, psychophysical, anatomical, and physiological data.

Perceptual Processes and Representations

Research in infant perception has also begun to shed light on the processes that extract information from the environment and produce perceptual descriptions. In fact, they allow us to comment on issues of process that have divided ecological and computational views of perception. For Gibson, Johansson, and other theorists of direct perception, an important theoretical tenet (and break with prior inferential theories) is that perception is a response to higher-order relations and not merely to first-order sensory dimensions. Computational theorists (e.g., Marr, 1982) also embrace the use of higher-order relationships but argue that perceptual computations are algorithmic, consisting of operations on intermediate levels of representation and involving constraints or assumptions that allow perceptual processes to reach determinate (and sensible) results.

From what we have seen, the answer is "yes" to both views. Infant perception has yielded many examples of perception as a response to complex spatial and temporal relationships, consistent with specialized neural mechanisms. Perceptual mechanisms in a number of domains appear to be attuned to extract relationships far more complex than anticipated prior to the emergence of ecological views. At the same time, some of the evidence clearly points to computational schemes involving intermediate representations (what might be called *interresponse* or *dependent variable coupling*; Epstein, 1982; Hochberg, 1974). Three examples are perceiving planar shape at a slant, the dependence of object unity on perceived motion, and the detection of object motion during observer motion.

The directness of perception is an empirical issue that may have differing answers in different perceptual domains. Researchers in infant perception have already met with some success in understanding perceptual processes, but much remains to be done. As Benjamin Franklin remarked, "The reward for good work is more work."

MECHANISMS OF CHANGE

Another area in which rewards await is in revealing the mechanisms of perceptual change. We have identified classes of information that do not influence perception in early infancy, and in some cases we know when they become effective. Less is known, however, about the causes of change. We have noted instances in which evidence indicates a linkage of neural maturation to certain sensory developments in the early months. What about other mechanisms of change? E. Gibson (1969, 1984; Gibson & Pick, 2000) championed the idea of continuity in perceptual learning throughout the life span. Perceptual learning—improvements in processes of information pickup with practice in a given domain—certainly appears to underlie much of adult expertise (Goldstone, 1994; Kellman & Kaiser, 1994; Kellman & Massey, 2013). A number of studies of infants have been described in terms of differentiation of types of motion or of surface invariants and so on. These studies show sensitivity to certain kinds of information. Fewer studies demonstrate a differentiation learning process in infant perception. One notable line of work is the research on perceptual narrowing, or attunement, seen in infant face and speech perception (Flom, 2014). Early in life, infants' face recognition and non-native speech discrimination abilities are flexible and impressively applied to a wide variety of stimuli. As infants gain experience with specific types of faces (typically of their own race) and sounds from their own language, infants come to differentiate only those they experience with high frequency. Thus, perception is tuned to the information in their environment. Attunement, however, is not fixed. Reintroducing infants to faces of other races or adopted children to their native language years after they stopped using it results in a re-emergence of earlier competencies, reinforcing the notion that perceptual learning (or re-learning) is a lifelong and context-dependent process (Anzures et al., 2012; Heron-Delaney et al., 2011; Oh, Jun, Knightly, & Au, 2003; Pascalis et al., 2005).

Improved precision of perceptual skills during the first year of life is likely due to both neural maturation and perceptual learning. What about the kind of learning that we called *enrichment*—the attachment of meaning to stimulus variables with experience? Not many aspects of infant perception appear to fit this conception, which is surprising in that associative learning has long occupied the preeminent place in conjectures about perceptual development. Such conjectures persist. Nakayama and Shimojo (1992), for example, suggested that experience with the probability structure of object views from different vantage points (generic view theory) might lead to certain tendencies in image interpretation. It is possible that the "sticky mitten" work of Needham, Barrett, and Peterman (2002), in which young infants' object exploration is facilitated by wearing mittens with Velcro, illustrates enrichment learning; however, the results could just as easily be explained by infants discovering new object properties, or differentiating them, during their exploration rather than attaching meaning to previously uninterpretable stimulus information. One example that does implicate a role for learned information in perception is the depth cue of familiar size (see Chapter 3). Infants by age 7 months use remembered information about object size along with its projective size to compute its distance, at least when binocular information is excluded.

It thus remains possible that enrichment learning plays a role in other aspects of perceptual development; perhaps the kinds of experiments that would clearly demonstrate such learning in other perceptual domains have simply not been done. Not only do efforts to formulate and test detailed hypotheses about mechanisms of change need to identify what abilities are governed by maturation and/or experience but also hypotheses need to be specific enough to delineate what type of perceptual learning—differentiation or enrichment—explain change.

ATYPICAL DEVELOPMENT

Throughout the years, research on the development of perception has helped to clarify a number of philosophical and theoretical positions regarding the nature of perception and its development. In addition, we know a tremendous amount about the course of typical development with which we can evaluate atypical development. Our findings can be used as benchmarks to evaluate when things appear to be going wrong. Moreover, the way that things go wrong might also provide us with additional insight into the mechanism underlying perceptual development. Much has been learned about perception and atypical development from studying different groups, such as children with Down's syndrome, Williams syndrome, and those with hearing loss (Bavelier, Dye, & Houser, 2006; Braddick & Atkinson, 2011). Here, we consider two examples: congenital cataracts and autism spectrum disorder.

Congenital Cataracts

Some infants are born with *cataracts*. A cataract is a clouding of the lens; overall presence of light can be perceived, but fine patterned stimuli cannot. Treatment for congenital cataracts involves removing the lens and fitting the child with a compensatory contact lens. Some infants are treated for cataracts within 10 days of life. For others, the treatment may come later but typically within the first year of life. Infants born with monocular or binocular cataracts provide natural experiments to explore questions of plasticity of the visual system and the extent to which certain perceptual abilities rely on early visual input. There are several interesting outcomes.

The immediate effects of restored sight are striking (Maurer, Lewis, Brent, & Levin, 1999). Tests of visual acuity that were administered within 10 min of initial insertion of the new lenses revealed newborn-like acuity among all infants regardless of age. Remarkably, follow-up tests revealed modest but very reliable improvement in visual acuity after just 1 hour of focused visual input, and for those receiving the surgery late in the first year of life, the pace of acuity improvement was faster than the pace for normally sighted infants. In another study, infants were tested for face preference (Mondloch, Segalowitz, Lewis, Dywan, Le Grand, & Maurer, 2013). One hour after surgery, infant patients, who were between 5 and 12 weeks of age, showed a newborn-like preference for a schematic face or a face with the internal features inverted (see Figure 4.7, left panel), even though this preference disappears by 5 weeks in infants with typical visual experience. Infant patients who were older than age 12 weeks at the time of surgery did not show a preference for positive contrast faces like their same-age peers who do not experience visual deprivation. Thus, development of acuity and face preferences relies on patterned stimulation after birth; patterned stimulation is necessary to start development, but the subsequent timing of development may be speeded up.

Years after surgical correction, however, there are several lasting impairments. One example is limitations in spatial and temporal resolution. Specifically, low spatial frequencies approach normal levels, but there are large deficits in middle and high spatial frequencies for those who experienced binocular deprivation (Maurer, Ellemberg, & Lewis, 2006). Temporal sensitivity fairs better than spatial sensitivity, although there is also loss in temporal sensitivity, particularly for those who experienced binocular deprivation (Ellemberg, Lewis, Maurer, & Brent, 2000; Ellemberg, Lewis, Maurer, Brar, & Brent, 2002; Ellemberg, Lewis, Maurer, Lui, & Brent, 1999). Thus, for some foundational visual processes, reduced visual input in the first year of life has long-lasting effects, particularly if the deprivation is experienced by both eyes. This finding suggests that early wiring of the visual cortex depends on visual input, and even input from only one eye is better than none. Moreover, for some deficits, a "last to develop, most damaged" rule appears to apply (Maurer, Lewis, & Mondloch, 2005).

Face perception is also affected, but selectively. Adults and older children who experienced visual deprivation early in life perform equally well as those who did not experience deprivation in distinguishing faces from other objects, determining direction of eye gaze, discriminating facial expressions, and interpreting visually a mouth making a sound (for review, see de Heering & Maurer, 2014). Moreover, they are able to match individual faces based on internal or external features (Mondloch, Lewis, & Maurer, 2013; Mondloch, Robbins, & Maurer, 2010). However, participants who experienced early visual deprivation have difficulty recognizing faces across different viewpoints and recognizing famous and newly learned faces (de Heering & Maurer, 2014). This effect is seen years after corrective surgery: In de Heering and Maurer's (2014) study, the participants were 16–30 years old and bilateral cataracts caused visual deprivation in the first 9–238 days of life. The difficulty with face recognition may be due to less sensitivity to the spacing among the internal features of a face; spacing of internal features—information that is useful for recognizing different faces and for recognizing the same face across changes in viewpoint, such as frontal view to three-fourths view (Robbins, Mishimura, Mondloch, Lewis, & Maurer, 2010). The lack of sensitivity to spacing of internal features is specific to human faces. The same participants differentiate changes in internal features in monkey faces and in images of houses. Even in contexts in which behavioral data suggest no difference in performance between adults with a visual deprivation in infancy and those without, event-related potential responses differ between these two groups (Mondloch et al., 2013). The N170, a response to facelike stimuli, has a higher amplitude and longer latency in adults who had cataracts as infants. Participants with longer deprivation showed the largest deviations from the norm. This profile suggests difficulty in neural face processing compared to controls, and it provides further evidence that early deprivation affects the wiring of the visual cortex.

The natural experiment of congenital cataracts has provided us with an excellent example of experience-expectant development. The visual system is prepared to receive visual input, and the input tunes the neural connections. Robbins et al. (2010) suggest that the nature of the visual input is patterned stimulation more generally rather than any specific type of stimulus (e.g., faces). This conclusion is based on work with monkeys that received patterned stimulation but not exposure to faces; the monkeys showed no impairment in face recognition based on the spacing of features. Robbins et al. concluded that "pattern input sets up or preserves neural architecture that will be tuned later by experience for holistic processing of faces of one's own race or species" (p. 780). In the case of infants born with cataracts, the initial deprivation of patterned input results in a visual system that is then unable to take advantage of the experience provided by seeing, and recognizing, the faces in their environment. More generally, the fact that some abilities are spared and others affected suggests that there are specific brain regions underlying these areas and that there is plasticity in some parts but not others.

Autism Spectrum Disorder

One in every 68 children in the United States is estimated to have autism spectrum disorder (ASD). ASD can be diagnosed as early as age 2 years; however, it is typically diagnosed at a somewhat later age, often between 3 and 6 years (Lord et al., 2006). Children with ASD present a variety of perceptual, motor, cognitive, linguistic, and social deficits, resulting in profound challenges, particularly in their interactions with the social world.

For many children, there may have been signs of ASD in the year(s) prior to diagnosis, despite a common belief that the children were normal in the first year of life and then started to regress developmentally. By examining home movies made during infancy of children later diagnosed with ASD, Maestro and colleagues (2005, 2006) found signs of ASD in 85% of cases. These signs in early infancy, compared to typically developing children, include less eye contact, less social smiling, and less responding when the child's name is called. See Figure 12.1 for a summary of the age of onset of signs of ASD across domains in the first 2 years of life.

Of interest to us is the extent to which the challenges faced by children (and adults) with ASD is due to perceptual limitations. It is difficult to provide a clear picture of the perceptual abilities of children with ASD. The presentation of the disorder is variable (hence the term "spectrum"); children vary to the extent to which they can communicate, which has implications for behavioral assessments; and different researchers have used different stimuli to test the same questions (e.g., motion coherence; Kaiser & Shiffrar, 2009; Simmons et al., 2009). Nevertheless, there are some generalizations that can be made regarding how perception differs for those with ASD compared to those without. First, children with ASD differ in their attention to local versus global properties (Simmons et al., 2009). This difference is seen in attention to facial features (mouths vs. eyes and individual features vs. configuration of features), poor use of Gestalt cues for grouping elements, and superior performance on embedded figure tasks (e.g., find a triangle in a drawing of an object, such as a stroller). Second, some aspects of motion perception differ. Although the evidence is mixed, children with ASD may have elevated thresholds for motion coherence, suggesting slower

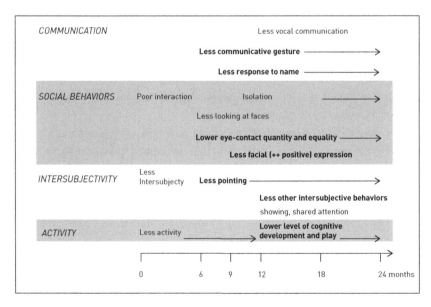

FIGURE 12.1
The onset of signs of autism spectrum disorder as a function of age and domain.
Source: Redrawn with permission of Elsevier from St. Georges, C., Cassel, R. S., Cohen, D., Chetouani, M., Laznik, M., . . . Muratori, F. (2010). What studies of family movies can teach us about autistic infants: A literature review. *Research in Autism Spectrum Disorders, 4,* 355–366; permission conveyed through Copyright Clearance Center, Inc.

processing of moving stimuli (Jones, Gliga, Bedford, Charman, & Johnson, 2014). Also, there are differences in perception of point-light displays depicting animate (e.g., human) versus inanimate (e.g., tractor) objects; typically developing children show faster processing of animate point-light displays, whereas children with ASD process the two types of displays equally fast (Kaiser & Shiffrar, 2009). Children with ASD are as skilled as typically developing children in identifying actions in point-light displays (e.g., walking vs. running), but they have difficulty perceiving emotional states (e.g., happy vs. sad). Third, perception–action coupling appears to be compromised because of difficulties in the spatial–temporal control of movement (Whyatt & Craig, 2013). Gross motor development is delayed, and infants at 12 months show abnormalities in spontaneous motor movements (Landa, Gross, Stuart, & Bauman, 2012). Moreover, children with ASD also show challenges with postural control, starting as early as 4 months, which may be due to motoric limitations and/or less sensitivity to optic flow (Flannagan, Landa, Bhat, & Bauman, 2012; Gepner, Mestre, Masson, & de Schonen, 1995). Finally, neurophysiological studies show that children with ASD process perceptual information differently—different time course, different levels of activation, and/or different areas involved—compared to typically developing children (Simmons et al., 2009). In addition, children with ASD have less cortical connectivity (Just, Cherkassky, Keller, Kana, & Minshew, 2007).

Much of the research on perceptual functioning has been conducted with children after diagnosis, limiting our ability to speculate about cause–effect relations regarding these perceptual and motor limitations. A more promising approach to trying to understand the origins of the perceptual differences in children with and without ASD is to compare perceptual development in infants who are high and low risk for developing ASD (for review, see Jones et al., 2014). Having a sibling with ASD increases the risk of developing ASD; thus, these high-risk infants (H-ASD) can be studied early in life and then evaluated for ASD after age 2 years. This line of work draws heavily on what we already know about typical perceptual, cognitive, and social development in infancy.

Perhaps most striking are differences in attention. H-ASD infants' attention to the eyes in faces declines between 2 and 6 months of age, beginning a lasting preference for the mouth region (Jones & Klin, 2013). H-ASD infants who later are diagnosed with ASD show overattention to faces, even in contexts in which the social interaction is disrupted (namely the still-face paradigm; Lambert-Brown et al., 2014). Despite this overattention to faces, H-ASD infants at age 9 months do not appear to notice manipulations of internal facial features, even in the region where they attend to most (the mouth, as opposed to the eye, region; Key & Stone, 2012). H-ASD 14-month-old, but not 7-month-old, infants are less distracted by a peripheral stimulus when focusing on a "boring" central stimulus, reflecting an overall inability to disengage their attention (Elsabbagh et al., 2013). H-ASD infants at 6 months respond to joint attention bids by others but do not initiate joint attention (Bhat, Galloway, & Landa, 2010; Gangi, Ibanez, & Messinger, 2014). Similarly, H-ASD infants at 12 months are less likely to use gestures, such as pointing or showing, to engage the attention of others (Rozga et al., 2011), but they show high amounts of visual attention to objects, including unusual visual exploration (Ozonoff et al., 2008).

It is tempting to appeal to a domain-general explanation for ASD based on early differences in attention. Attentional biases may direct infants toward certain types of stimuli and not others, resulting in differential experiences that in turn impact neural specialization during the first years of life. A similar suggestion was made by Jones et al. (2014): "Early emerging behavioral symptoms alter the child's self-directed patterns of attention, changing their experiences of the environment, and further restricting social learning opportunities" (p. 2). Attention, however, does not explain everything. For example, why are H-ASD infants less "cuddly" at 14 months than at 7 months (Clifford et al., 2013)? Why do H-ASD infants show a decline in responding to their own name between 9 and 12 months after an initial overresponsiveness at 4 months (Nadig et al., 2007; Yirmiya et al., 2006)?

Clearly, there is still more to learn about the relation between perception and ASD. The comparison of high-risk and low-risk infants is a good start to understanding the origins of this disorder; however, studies with younger infants need to be conducted. In this book, we have discussed a host of examples of newborn competencies that have important implications for later social and cognitive functioning—for example, imitation, preference for mother's face, preference for native language, and responsiveness to biological motion. Understanding potential differences between high- and low-risk infants at the very beginning of life is central for a complete understanding of the emergence and underlying causes of this disorder. This understanding is of theoretical and practical importance, particularly for designing interventions as early as possible (Schreibman et al., 2015).

Summary

In both of our examples of atypical development, we see the effects of early experience, or deprivation, impacting the course of development of later perception and social cognition. In the case of congenital cataracts, the deprivation is often short and appears to have long-term effects on a few perceptual tasks. In the case of ASD, the resulting effects are vast and far-reaching. In both cases, differential perceptual experiences are implicated in a rewiring of the visual pathways, leading to differences in how perceptual information is processed.

CONCLUSION

Systematic research on perception in the human infant is a relatively new venture, begun in the latter half of the 20th century. From modest beginnings, this research has proceeded a great distance toward answering classic questions about human nature and producing a coherent picture of the origins of perceptual knowledge. This picture mandates a new account of the origins of the mind and human development, one in which a human being interacts from the start with a meaningful and coherent reality. It changes permanently our views of how perception works and how much of human knowledge derives from it. We have tried in this book to convey the nature and implications of these advances. We hope that what has been learned will provide a foundation for investigations leading to even deeper insights into the nature of perception and its development.

References

Abravanel, E., & DeYong, N. G. (1991). Does object modeling elicit imitative-like gestures from young infants? *Journal of Experimental Child Psychology, 52*, 22–40.

Abravanel, E., & Sigafoos, A. D. (1984). Exploring the presence of imitation during early infancy. *Child Development, 55*, 381–392.

Adams, O. S., Fitts, P. M., Rappaport, M., & Weinstein, M. (1954). Relations among some measures of pattern discriminability. *Journal of Experimental Psychology, 48*, 81–88.

Adams, R. J., & Courage, M. L. (2002). A psychophysical test of the early maturation of infants' mid- and long-wavelength retinal cones. *Infant Behavior and Development, 25*, 247–254.

Adler, S. A., & Gallego, P. (2014). Search asymmetry and eye movements in infants and adults. *Attention, Perception, and Psychophysics, 76*, 1590–1608.

Adolph, K. E. (1995). Psychophysical assessment of toddlers' ability to cope with slopes. *Journal of Experimental Psychology: Human Perception and Performance, 21*, 734–750.

Adolph, K. E., Eppler, M. A., & Gibson, E. J. (1993). Development of perception of affordances. In C. Rovee-Collier & L. P. Lipsitt (Eds.), *Advances in infancy research* (Vol. 8, pp. 51–98). Norwood, NJ: Ablex.

Adolph, K. E., Eppler, M. A., Marin, L., Weise, I. B., & Clearfield, M. W. (2000). Exploration in the service of prospective control. *Infant Behavior and Development, 23*, 441–460.

Adolph, K. E., Karasik, L. B., & Tamis-LeMonda, C. S. (2010). Using social information to guide action: Infants' locomotion over slippery slopes. *Neural Networks, 23*, 1033–1042.

Adoph, K. E., & Robinson, S. E. (2015). Motor development. In L. S. Liben & U. Muller (Eds.), *Handbook of child psychology and developmental science* (Vol. 2, pp. 113–157). New York, NY: Wiley.

Adolph, K. E., & Tamis-LeMonda, C. S. (2014). The costs and benefits of development: Transition from crawling to walking. *Child Development Perspectives, 8*, 187–192.

Allam, M. D., Marlier, L., & Schaal, B. (2006). Learning at the breast: Preference formation for an artificial scent and its attraction against the odor of maternal milk. *Infant Behavior and Development, 29*, 308–321.

Allen, D., Tyler, C. W., & Norcia, A. M. (1996). Development of grating acuity and contrast sensitivity in the central and peripheral visual field of the human infant. *Vision Research, 36*, 1945–1953.

Allman, J., Miezin, F., & McGuinness, E. (1985). Direction and velocity specific responses from beyond the classical receptive field in the middle temporal visual area. *Perception, 14,* 105–126.

Ames, A. (1951). Visual perception and the rotating trapezoidal window. *Psychological Monographs,* Series No. 324.

Amso, D., & Johnson, S. P. (2006). Learning by selection: Visual search and object perception in young infants. *Developmental Psychology, 42,* 1236–1245.

Anand, K. J. S., & McGrath, P. J. (Eds.). (1993). *Neonatal pain and distress.* Amsterdam, The Netherlands: Elsevier.

Andersen, G. J., & Cortese, J. M. (1989). 2-D contour perception resulting from kinetic occlusion. *Perception & Psychophysics, 46,* 49–55.

Angier, N. (2012, May 1). From the minds of babies. *The New York Times,* p. D1.

Antell, S. E., & Keating, D. P. (1983). Perception of numerical invariance in neonates. *Child Development, 54,* 695–701.

Anzures, G., Quinn, P. C., Pascalis, O., Slater, A. M., & Lee, K. (2013). Development of own-race biases. *Visual Cognition, 21,* 1165–1182.

Anzures, G., Wheeler, A., Quinn, P. C., Pascalis, O., Slater, A. M., Heron-Delaney, M., . . . Lee, K. (2012). Brief daily exposures to Asian females reverses perceptual narrowing for Asian faces in Caucasian infants. *Journal of Experimental Child Psychology, 112,* 484–495.

Aristotle. (1941). *Basic works* (R. McKeon, Trans.). New York, NY: Random House.

Armstrong, V., Maurer, D., Ellemberg, D., & Lewis, T. L. (2011). Sensitivity to first- and second-order drifting gratings in 3-month-old infants. *i-Perception, 2,* 440–457.

Arterberry, M. E. (1993). Development of spatiotemporal integration in infancy. *Infant Behavior* and *Development, 16,* 343–363.

Arterberry, M. E. (1995). Perception of object number through an aperture by human infants. *Infant Behavior and Development, 18,* 359–362.

Arterberry, M. E. (1997a). Development of sensitivity to spatial and temporal information. In P. v. d. Broek, P. Bauer, & T. Bourg (Eds.), *Developmental spans in event comprehension and representation: Bridging fictional and actual events* (pp. 51–78). Hillsdale, NJ: Erlbaum.

Arterberry, M. E. (1997b). Spatiotemporal integration in infancy. In C. Rovee-Collier & L. Lipsitt (Eds.), *Advances in infancy research* (Vol. 11, pp. 219–268). Norwood, NJ: Ablex.

Arterberry, M. E. (2001). Perceptual unit formation in infancy. In T. F. Shipley & P. J. Kellman (Eds.), *From fragments to objects: Segmentation and grouping in vision* (pp. 37–69). Amsterdam, The Netherlands: Elsevier.

Arterberry, M. E. (2008). Infants' sensitivity to the depth cue of height-in-the-picture-plane. *Infancy, 13,* 544–555.

Arterberry, M. E., Bensen, A. S., & Yonas, A. (1991). Infants' responsiveness to static monocular depth information: A recovery from habituation approach. *Infant Behavior and Development, 14,* 241–251.

Arterberry, M. E., & Bornstein, M. H. (2001). Three-month-old infants' categorization of animals and vehicles based on static and dynamic attributes. *Journal of Experimental Child Psychology, 80,* 333–346.

Arterberry, M. E., & Bornstein, M. H. (2002). Infant perceptual and conceptual categorization: The roles of static and dynamic attributes. *Cognition, 86,* 1–24.

Arterberry, M. E., & Yonas, A. (1988). Infants' sensitivity to kinetic information for three-dimensional object shape. *Perception & Psychophysics, 44,* 1–6.

Arterberry, M. E., & Yonas, A. (2000). Perception of structure from motion by 8-week-old infants. *Perception and Psychophysics, 62,* 550–556.

Arterberry, M. E., Yonas, A., & Bensen, A. S. (1989). Self-produced locomotion and the development of responsiveness to linear perspective and texture gradients. *Developmental Psychology, 25,* 976–982.

Ashmead, D. H., Clifton, R. K., & Perris, E. E. (1987). Precision of auditory localization in human infants. *Developmental Psychology, 23,* 641–647.

Ashmead, D. H., Davis, D. L., & Northington, A. (1995). Contribution of listeners' approaching motion to auditory distance perception. *Journal of Experimental Psychology: Human Perception & Performance, 21,* 239–256.

Ashmead, D. H., Davis, D. L., Whalen, T., & Odom, R. D. (1991). Sound localization and sensitivity to interaural time differences in human infants. *Child Development, 62,* 1211–1226.

Ashmead, D. H., McCarty, M. E., Lucas, L. S., & Belvedere, M. C. (1993). Visual guidance in infants' reaching toward suddenly displaced targets. *Child Development, 64,* 1111–1127.

Aslin, R. N. (1977). Development of binocular fixation in human infants. *Journal of Experimental Child Psychology, 23,* 133–150.

Aslin, R. N. (1981). Development of smooth pursuit in human infants. In D. F. Fisher, R. A. Monty, & J. W. Senders (Eds.), *Eye movements: Cognition and visual perception* (pp. 31–51). Hillsdale, NJ: Erlbaum.

Aslin, R. N. (1993a). Infant accommodation and convergence. In K. Simons (Ed.), *Early visual development: Normal and abnormal* (pp. 30–38). New York, NY: Oxford University Press.

Aslin, R. N. (1993b). Perception of visual direction in human infants. In C. Granrud (Ed.), *Visual perception and cognition in infancy* (pp. 91–119). Hillsdale, NJ: Erlbaum.

Aslin, R. N., & Newport, E. L. (2009). What statistical learning can and can't tell us about language acquisition. In J. Colombo, P. McCardle, & L. Freund (Eds.), *Infant pathways to language* (pp. 15–29). New York: NY: Psychology Press.

Aslin, R. N., & Shea, S. L. (1990). Velocity thresholds in human infants: Implications for the perception of motion. *Developmental Psychology, 26,* 589–598.

Aslin, R, N., & Pisoni, D. B. (1980). Some developmental processes in speech perception. In G. H. Yeni-Komshian, J. F. Kavanagh, & C. A. Ferguson (Eds.), *Child phonology: Vol. 2. Perception* (pp. 67–96). New York, NY: Academic Press.

Aslin, R. N., Pisoni, D. B., Hennessy, B. L., & Perey, A. J. (1981). Discrimination of voice onset time by human infants: New findings and implications for the effects of early experience. *Child Development, 52,* 1135–1145.

Aslin, R. N., & Salapatek, P. (1975). Saccadic localization of visual targets by the very young human infant. *Perception & Psychophysics, 17,* 293–302.

Aspell, J. E., Wattam-Bell, J., Atkinson, J., & Braddick, O. J. (2010). Differential human brain activation by vertical and horizontal global textures. *Experimental Brain Research, 202,* 669–679.

Atkinson, J. (1984). Human visual development over the first 6 months of life: A review and a hypothesis. *Human Neurobiology, 3,* 61–74.

Atkinson, J. (2000). *The developing visual brain.* Oxford, UK: Oxford.

Atkinson, J., & Braddick, O. (1981). Development of optokinetic nystagmus in infants: An indicator of cortical binocularity. In D. F. Fisher, R. A. Mondy, & J. W. Senders (Eds.), *Eye movements: Cognition and visual perception* (pp. 53–64). Hillsdale, NJ: Erlbaum.

Atkinson, J., Braddick, O., & Moar, K. (1977a). Contrast sensitivity of the human infant for moving and static patterns. *Vision Research, 17,* 1045–1047.

Atkinson, J., Braddick, O., & Moar, K. (1977b). Development of contrast sensitivity over the first three months of life in the human infant. *Vision Research, 17,* 1037–1044.

Atkinson, J., Hood, B., Wattam-Bell, J., Anker, S., & Tricklebank, J. (1988). Development of orientation discrimination in infancy. *Perception, 17,* 587–595.

Babinsky, E., Braddick, O., & Atkinson, J. (2012). Infants and adults reaching in the dark. *Experimental Brain Research, 217,* 237–249.

Bahrick, L. E. (1983). Infants' perception of substance and temporal synchrony in multimodal events. *Infant Behavior and Development, 6,* 429–451.

Bahrick, L. E. (1987). Infants' intermodal perception of two levels of temporal structure in natural events. *Infant Behavior and Development, 10,* 387–416.

Bahrick, L. E. (1988). Intermodal learning in infancy: Learning on the basis of two kinds of invariant relations in audible and visible events. *Child Development, 59,* 197–209.

Bahrick, L. E. (1992). Infants' perceptual differentiation of amodal and modality-specific audio-visual relations. *Journal of Experimental Child Psychology, 53,* 180–199.

Bahrick, L. E. (1994). The development of infants' sensitivity to arbitrary intermodal relations. *Ecological Psychology, 6,* 111–123.

Bahrick, L. E., & Lickliter, R. (2012). The role of intersensory redundancy in early perceptual, cognitive and social development. In A. J. Bremner, D. J. Lewkowicz, & C. Spence (Eds.), *Multisensory development* (pp. 183–206). New York, NY: Oxford University Press.

Bahrick, L. E., Lickliter, R, Castellanos, I., & Vaillant-Molina, M. (2010). Increasing task difficulty enhances effects of intersensory redundancy: Testing a new prediction of the intersensory redundancy hypothesis. *Developmental Science, 13,* 731–737.

Bahrick, L. E., Lickliter, R., & Flom, R. (2006). Up versus down: The role of intersensory redundancy in the development of infants' sensitivity to the orientation of moving objects. *Infancy, 9,* 73–96.

Bahrick, L. E., Walker, A. S., & Neisser, U. (1981). Selective looking by infants. *Cognitive Psychology, 13,* 377–390.

Bailey, C. H., & Kandel, E. R. (2009). Synaptic and cellular basis of learning. In G. G. Berntson & J. T. Cacioppo (Eds.), *Handbook of neuroscience for the behavioral sciences* (Vol. 1, pp. 528–551). Hoboken, NJ: Wiley.

Baillargeon, R. (1987). Object permanence in 3.5- and 4.5-month-old infants. *Developmental Psychology, 23*(5), 655–664.

Baillargeon, R. (2008). Innate ideas revisited: For a principle of persistence in infants' physical reasoning. *Perspectives on Psychological Science, 3,* 2–13.

Baillargeon, R., DeVos, J., & Graber, M. (1989). Location memory in 8-month-old infants in a non-search AB task: Further evidence. *Cognitive Development, 4,* 345–367.

Baillargeon, R., Graber, M., DeVos, J., & Black, J. (1990). Why do young infants fail to search for hidden objects? *Cognition, 36,* 255–284.

Baillargeon, R., Scott, R. M., & He, Z. (2010). False belief understanding in infants. *Trends in Cognitive Sciences, 14,* 110–118.

Baillargeon, R., Spelke, E. S., & Wasserman, S. (1985). Object permanence in 5-month-old infants. *Cognition, 20,* 191–208.

Baker, T. J., Norcia, A. M., & Candy, T. R. (2011). Orientation tuning in the visual cortex of 3-month-old human infants. *Vision Research, 51,* 470–478.

Banks, M. S. (1980). The development of visual accommodation during early infancy. *Child Development, 51,* 646–666.

Banks, M. S., Aslin, R. N., & Letsin, R. D. (1975). Critical period for the development of human binocular vision. *Science, 190*, 675–677.

Banks, M. S., & Bennett, P. J. (1988). Optical and photoreceptor immaturities limit the spatial and chromatic vision of human neonates. *Journal of the Optical Society of America A, 5*, 2059–2079.

Banks, M. S., & Dannemiller, J. L. (1987). Infant visual psychophysics. In P. Salapatek & L. Cohen (Eds.), *Handbook of infant perception: Vol. 1. From sensation to perception* (pp. 115–184). Orlando, FL: Academic Press.

Banks, M. S., Geisler, W. S., & Bennett, P. J. (1987). The physical limits of grating visibility. *Vision Research, 27*, 1915–1924.

Banks, M. S., & Ginsburg, A. P. (1985). Early visual preferences: A review and a new theoretical treatment. In H. W. Reese (Ed.), *Advances in child development and behavior* (pp. 207–246). New York, NY: Academic Press.

Banks, M. S., & Salapatek, P. (1978). Acuity and contrast sensitivity in 1-, 2-, and 3-month-old human infants. *Investigative Ophthalmology and Visual Science, 77*, 361–365.

Banks, M. S., & Salapatek, P. (1981). Infant pattern vision: A new approach based on the contrast sensitivity function. *Journal of Experimental Child Psychology, 31*, 1–45.

Banks, M. S., & Shannon, E. (1993). Spatial and chromatic visual efficiency in human neonates. In C. Granrud (Ed.), *Visual perception and cognition in infancy: Carnegie Mellon symposia on cognition* (pp. 1–46). Hillsdale, NJ: Erlbaum.

Banton, T., & Bertenthal, B. I. (1996). Infants' sensitivity to uniform motion. *Vision Research, 36*, 1633–1640.

Banton, T., Dobkins, K., & Bertenthal, B. I. (2001). Infant direction discrimination thresholds. *Vision Research, 41*, 1049–1056.

Barbu-Roth, M., Anderson, D. I., Despres, A., Provasi, J., Cabrol, D., & Campos, J. J. (2009). Neonatal stepping in relation to terrestrial optic flow. *Child Development, 80*, 8–14.

Barbu-Roth, M., Anderson, D. I., Despres, A., Streeter, R. J., Cabrol, D., Trujillo, M., . . . Provasi, J. (2014). Air stepping in response to optic flows that move toward and away from the neonate. *Developmental Psychobiology, 56*, 1142–1149.

Bardi, L., Regolin, L., & Simion, F. (2011). Biological motion preference in humans at birth: Role of dynamic and configural properties. *Developmental Science, 14*, 353–359.

Bardi, L., Regolin, L., & Simion, F. (2014). The first time ever I saw your feet: Inversion effect in newborns' sensitivity to biological motion. *Developmental Psychology, 50*, 986–993.

Bargones, J. Y., & Werner, L. A. (1994). Adults listen selectively; Infants do not. *Psychological Science, 5*, 170–174.

Bar-Haim, Y., Ziv, T., Lamy, D., & Hodes, R. M. (2006). Nature and nurture in own-race face processing. *Psychological Science, 17*, 159–163.

Barlow, H. B., & Reeves, B. C. (1979). The versatility and absolute efficiency of detecting mirror symmetry in random dot displays. *Vision Research, 19*, 783–793.

Barnat, S. B., Klein, P. J., & Meltzoff, A. N. (1996). Deferred imitation across changes in context and object: Memory and generalization in 14-month-old infants. *Infant Behavior and Development, 19*, 241–251.

Baroncelli, L., Sale, A., Maya Vetencourt, J. F., DePasquale, R., Baldini, S., & Maffei, L. (2010). Experience-dependent reactivation of ocular dominance plasticity in the adult visual cortex. *Experimental Neurology, 226*, 100–109.

Baron-Cohen, S. (1995). *Mindblindness: An essay on autism and theory of mind.* Boston, MA: MIT Press.

Barrett, K. C., Campos, J., & Emde, R. N. (1996). Infants' use of conflicting emotion signals. *Cognition and Emotion, 70*, 113–135.

Barrett, T. M., Traupman, E., & Needham, A. (2008). Infants' visual anticipation of object structure in grasp planning. *Infant Behavior and Development, 31*, 1–9.

Barth, H., Kanwisher, N., & Spelke, E. S. (2003). The construction of large number representations in adults. *Cognition, 86*, 201–221.

Batki, A., Baron-Cohen, S., Wheelwright, S., Connellan, J., & Ahluwalia, J. (2000). Is there an innate module? Evidence from human neonates. *Infant Behavior and Development, 23*, 223–229.

Bavelier, D., Dye, M. W. G., & Hauser, P. C. (2006). Do deaf individuals see better? *Trends in Cognitive Sciences, 10*, 512–518.

Bayley, N. (1969). *Bayley scales of infant development.* New York, NY: Psychological Corporation.

Beauchamp, G. K., Cowart, B. J., Mennella, J. A., & Marsh, R. R. (1994). Infant salt taste: Developmental, methodological, and contextual factors. *Developmental Psychobiology, 27*, 353–365.

Becker, W., & Jurgens, R. (1979). An analysis of the saccadic system by means of double step stimuli. *Vision Research, 19*, 967–983.

Bedford, F. L. (1989). Constraints on learning new mappings between perceptual dimensions. *Journal of Experimental Psychology: Human Perception & Performance, 15*, 232–248.

Behl-Chadha, G. (1996). Basic-level and superordinate-like categorical representations in early infancy. *Cognition, 60*, 105–141.

Beier, J. S., & Spelke, E. S. (2012). Infants' developing understanding of social gaze. *Child Development, 83*, 486–496.

Belanger, N. D., & Desrochers, S. (2001). Can 6-month-old infants process causality in different types of causal events? *British Journal of Developmental Psychology, 19*, 11–21.

Bergen, J. F., & Knudsen, E. I. (2009). Visual modulation of auditory responses in the owl inferior colliculus. *Journal of Neurophysiology, 101*, 2924–2933.

Berger, S. E., Adolph, K. E., & Kavookjian, A. E. (2010). Bridging the gap: Solving spatial means-ends relations in a locomotor task. *Child Development, 81*, 1367–1375.

Berger, S. E., Chan, G. L. Y., & Adolph, K. E. (2014). What cruising infants understand about support for locomotion. *Infancy, 19*, 117–137.

Berkeley, G. (1910). *Essay towards a new theory of vision.* London, England: Dutton. (Original work published 1709)

Bertenthal, B. I. (1993). Infants' perception of biomechanical motions: Intrinsic image and knowledge-based constraints. In C. Granrud (Ed.), *Visual perception and cognition in infancy: Carnegie Mellon symposia on cognition* (pp. 175–214). Hillsdale, NJ: Erlbaum.

Bertenthal, B. I. (1996). Origins and early development of perception, action, and representation. *Annual Review of Psychology, 47*, 431–459.

Bertenthal, B. I., & Bai, D. L. (1989). Infants' sensitivity to optical flow for controlling posture. *Developmental Psychology, 25*, 936–945.

Bertenthal, B. I., & Bradbury, A. (1992). Infants' detection of shearing motion in random-dot displays. *Developmental Psychology, 28*, 1056–1066.

Bertenthal, B. I., & Campos, J. J. (1990). A systems approach to the organizing effects of self-produced locomotion during infancy. In C. K. Rovee-Collier & L. P. Lipsitt (Eds.), *Advances in infancy research* (Vol. 6, pp. 1–60). Norwood, NJ: Ablex.

Bertenthal, B. I., Campos, J. J., & Haith, M. M. (1980). Development of visual organization: The perception of subjective contours. *Child Development, 51*, 1072–1080.

Bertenthal, B. I., Longo, M. R., & Kenny, S. (2007). Phenomenal permanence and the development of predictive tracking in infancy. *Child Development, 78*, 350–363.

Bertenthal, B. I., Proffitt, D. R., & Cutting, J. E. (1984). Infant sensitivity to figural coherence in biomechanical motions. *Journal of Experimental Child Psychology, 37*, 213–230.

Bertenthal, B. I., Proffitt, D. R., & Kramer, S. J. (1987). Perception of biomechanical motions by infants: Implementation of various processing constraints [Special issue]. *Journal of Experimental Psychology: Human Perception and Performance, 13*(4), 577–585.

Bertenthal, B. I., Proffitt, D. R., Kramer, S. J., & Spetner, N. B. (1987). Infants' encoding of kinetic displays varying in relative coherence. *Developmental Psychology, 23*, 171–178.

Bertenthal, B. I., Proffitt, D. R., Spetner, N. B., & Thomas, M. A. (1985). The development of infant sensitivity to biomechanical motions. *Child Development, 56*, 531–543.

Bertenthal, B. I., & von Hofsten, C. (1998). Eye, head and trunk control: The foundation for manual development. *Neuroscience and Biobehavioral Reviews, 22*, 515–520.

Berthier, N. E., & Carrico, R. L. (2010). Visual information and object size in infant reaching. *Infant Behavior and Development, 33*, 555–566.

Berthier, N. E., DeBlois, S., Poirier, C. R., Novak, M. A., & Clifton, R. K. (2000). Where's the ball? Two and three-year-olds reason about unseen events. *Developmental Psychology, 36*, 394–401.

Berthier, N. E., & Keen, R. L. (2006). Development of reaching in infancy. *Experimental Brain Research, 169*, 507–518.

Bertin, E., & Bhatt, R. S. (2006). Three-month-olds' sensitivity to orientation cues in the three-dimensional depth plane. *Journal of Experimental Child Psychology, 93*, 45–62.

Best, C. T., McRoberts, G. W., LaFleur, R., & Silver-Isenstadt, J. (1995). Divergent developmental patterns for infants' perception of two normative consonant contrasts. *Infant Behavior and Development, 18*, 339–350.

Best, C. T., McRoberts, G. W., & Sithole, N. M. (1988). Examination of perceptual reorganization for normative speech contrasts: Zulu click discrimination by English-speaking adults and infants. *Journal of Experimental Psychology: Human Perception and Performance, 14*, 345–360.

Bhat, A., Heathcock, J., & Galloway, J. C. (2005). Toy-oriented changes in hand and joint kinematics during the emergence of purposeful reaching. *Infant Behavior and Development, 28*, 445–465.

Bhat, A. N., Galloway, J. C., & Landa, R. J. (2010). Social and non-social visual attention patterns associative learning in infants at risk for autism. *Journal of Child Psychology and Psychiatry, 51*, 989–997.

Bhatt, R. S., & Waters, S. E. (1998). Perception of three-dimensional cues in early infancy. *Journal of Experimental Child Psychology, 70*, 207–224.

Bidet-Iidei, C., Kitromilides, E., Orliaguet, J., & Gentz, E. (2014). Preference for point-light human biological motion in newborns: Contribution of translational displacement. *Developmental Psychology, 50*, 113–120.

Biederman, I. (2013). The psychophysical and neural correlates of the phenomenology of shape. In L. Albertazzi (Ed.), *Handbook of experimental phenomenology: Visual perception of shape, space, and appearance* (pp. 417–436). Boston, MA: Wiley-Blackwell.

Bigelow, A. E. (1986). The development of reaching in blind children. *British Journal of Developmental Psychology, 4*, 355–366.

Bigelow, A. E. (1992). Locomotion and search behavior in blind infants. *Infant Behavior and Development, 15*, 179–189.

Birch, E. E., Gwiazda, J., & Held, R. (1982). Stereoacuity development for crossed and uncrossed disparities in human infants. *Vision Research, 22,* 507–513.

Birch, H. G., & Lefford, A. (1967). Visual differentiation, intersensory integration, and voluntary motor control. *Monographs of the Society for Research in Child Development, 32,* 1–87.

Birtles, D. B., Braddick, O. J., Wattam-Bell, J., Wilkinson, A. R., & Atkinson, J. (2007). Orientation and motion-specific visual cortex responses in infants born preterm. *Neuroreport, 18,* 1975–1979.

Bjorklund, D. F. (1987). A note on neonatal imitation. *Developmental Review, 7,* 86–92.

Blumenthal, E. J., Bosworth, R. G., & Dobkins, K. R. (2013). Fast development of global motion processing in human infants. *Journal of Vision, 13,* 1–13.

Bobier, W. R., Guinta, A., Kurtz, S., & Howland, H. C. (2000). Prism induced accommodation in infants 3 and 6 months of age. *Vision Research, 40,* 529–537.

Bomba, P. C., & Siqueland, E. R. (1983). The nature and structure of infant form categories. *Journal of Experimental Child Psychology, 35,* 294–328.

Booth, A. E., Pinto, L., & Bertenthal, B. I. (2002). Perception of the symmetrical patterning of human gait by infants. *Developmental Psychology, 38,* 554–563.

Bornstein, M. H. (1975). Qualities of color vision in infancy. *Journal of Experimental Child Psychology, 19,* 401–419.

Bornstein, M. H. (2006). Hue categorization and color naming. I: From physics to sensation to perception. In C. P. Biggam & N. Pitchford (Eds.), *Progress in colour studies: Psychological aspects* (pp. 1–34). Philadelphia, PA: Benjamins.

Bornstein, M. H., & Arterberry, M. E. (2003). Recognition, categorization, and apperception of the facial expression of smiling by 5-month-old infants. *Developmental Science, 6,* 585–599.

Bornstein, M. H., Arterberry, M. E., & Mash, C. (2010). Infant object categorization transcends diverse object–context relations. *Infant Behavior and Development, 33,* 7–15.

Bornstein, M. H., Arterberry, M. E., Mash, C., & Manian, N. (2011). Discrimination of facial expression by 5-month-old infants of nondepressed and clinically depressed mothers. *Infant Behavior and Development, 34,* 100–106.

Bornstein, M. H., Ferdinandsen, K., & Gross, C. G. (1981). Perception of symmetry in infancy. *Developmental Psychology, 17,* 82–86.

Bornstein, M. H., Kessen, W., & Weiskopf, S. (1976). Color vision and hue categorization in young human infants. *Journal of Experimental Psychology: Human Perception & Performance, 2,* 115–129.

Bornstein, M. H., & Krinsky, S. J. (1985). Perception of symmetry in infancy: The salience of vertical symmetry and the perception of pattern wholes. *Journal of Experimental Child Psychology, 39,* 82–86.

Bornstein, M. H., Krinsky, S. J., & Benasich, A. A. (1986). Orientation discrimination and shape constancy in young infants. *Journal of Experimental Child Psychology, 41,* 49–60.

Bornstein, M. H., & Mash, C. (2010). Experience-based and on-line categorization of objects in early infancy. *Child Development, 81,* 884–897.

Bornstein, M. H., Mash, C., & Arterberry, M. E. (2011a). Perception of object–context relations: Eye-movement analysis in infants and adults. *Developmental Psychology, 47,* 364–375

Bornstein, M. H., Mash, C., & Arterberry, M. E. (2011b). Infant object perception: Eye-movement analyses of "natural" scenes and "experimental" scenes. *Infant Behavior and Development, 34,* 206–210.

Bornstein, M. H., & Stiles-Davis, J. (1984). Discrimination and memory for symmetry in young children. *Developmental Psychology, 20*, 637–649.

Boudreau, J. P., & Bushnell, E. W. (2000). Spilling thoughts: Configuring attentional resources in infants' goal-directed actions. *Infant Behavior and Development, 23*, 543–566.

Bourgeois, K. S., Khawar, A. W., Neal, S. A., & Lockman, J. J. (2005). Infant manual exploration of objects, surfaces, and their interrelations. *Infancy, 8*, 233–252.

Bower, T. G. R. (1974). *Development in infancy.* San Francisco, CA: Freeman.

Braddick, O. (1993). Segmentation versus integration in visual motion processing. *Trends in Neurosciences, 16*, 263–268.

Braddick, O., & Atkinson, J. (2011). Development of human visual function. *Vision Research, 51*, 1588–1609.

Braddick, O., Atkinson, J., & Wattam-Bell, J. R. (1986). Development of the discrimination of spatial phase in infancy. *Vision Research, 26*, 1223–1239.

Braddick, O., Birtles, D., Wattam-Bell, J., & Atkinson, J. (2005). Motion- and orientation-specific cortical responses in infancy. *Vision Research, 45*, 3169–3179.

Brainard, D. H., Wandell, B. A., & Chichilnisky, E. J. (1993). Color constancy: From physics to appearance. *Current Directions in Psychological Science, 2*, 165–170.

Brandt, T., Dichgans, J., & Koenig, E. (1973). Differential effects of central versus peripheral vision on egocentric and exocentric motion perception. *Experimental Brain Research, 16*, 476–491.

Braunstein, M. (1976). *Depth perception through motion.* New York, NY: Academic Press.

Brazelton, T. B. (1978). The remarkable talents of the newborn. *Birth and the Family Journal, 5*, 187–191.

Bredberg, G. (1968). Cellular pattern and nerve supply of the human organ of Corti. *Acta Otolaryngologica, 236*(Suppl.).

Bregman, A. S. (1990). *Auditory scene analysis: The perceptual organization of sound.* Cambridge, MA: MIT Press.

Bregman, A. S. (2005). Auditory scene analysis and the role of phenomenology in experimental psychology. *Canadian Psychology/Psychologie canadienne, 46*, 32–40.

Bremner, A. J., & Bryant, P. (2001). The effect of spatial cues on infants' responses in the AB task, with and without a hidden object. *Developmental Science, 4*, 408–415.

Bremner, A. J., Lewkowicz, D. J., & Spence, C. (2012). *Multisensory development.* New York, NY: Oxford University Press.

Bremner, J. G., Slater, A. M., Johnson, S. P., Mason, U. C., & Spring, J. (2012). Illusory contour figures are perceived as occluding contours by 4-month-old infants. *Developmental Psychology, 48*, 398–405.

Bremner, J. G., Slater, A. M., Mason, U. C., Spring, J., & Johnson, S. P. (2013). Trajectory perception and object continuity: Effects of shape and color change in 4-month-olds' perception of object identity. *Developmental Psychology, 49*, 1021–1026.

Bristow, D., Deheane-Lambertz, G., Mattout, J., Soares, C., Gliga, T., . . . Mangin, J. (2008). Hearing faces: How the infant brain matches the face it sees with the speech it hears. *Journal of Cognitive Neuroscience, 21*, 905–921.

Bronson, G. (1974). The postnatal growth of visual capacity. *Child Development, 45*, 873–890.

Bronson, G. W. (1990). Changes in infants' visual scanning across the 2- to 14-week age period. *Journal of Experimental Child Psychology, 49*, 101–125.

Brooks, R., & Meltzoff, A. N. (2005). The development of gaze following and its relation to language. *Developmental Science, 8*, 535–543.

Brower, T., & Wilcox, T. (2012). Shaking things up: Young infants' use of sound information for object individuation. *Infant Behavior and Development, 35*, 323–327.

Brown, A. M., Adusumilli, V., & Lindsey, D. T. (2005). Detection of Vernier and contrast-modulated stimuli with equal Fourier energy spectra by infants and adults. *Journal of Vision, 5*, 230–243.

Brown, A. M., Lindsey, D. T., Satgunam, P., & Miracle, J. A. (2007). Critical immaturities limiting infant binocular stereopsis. *Investigative Ophthalmology & Visual Science, 48*, 1424–1424.

Brunswik, E. (1956). *Perception and the representative design of psychological experiments*. Berkeley, CA: University of California Press.

Buffart, H., & Leeuwenberg, E. (1981). Coding theory of visual pattern completion. *Journal of Experimental Psychology: Human Perception & Performance, 7*, 241–274.

Bulf, H., Johnson, S. P., & Valenza, E. (2011). Visual statistical learning in the newborn infant. *Cognition, 121*, 127–132.

Bulf, H., Valenza, E., & Simion, F. (2009). The visual search of an illusory figure: A comparison between 6-month-old infants and adults. *Perception, 38*, 1313–1327.

Bull, D., Schneider, B. A., & Trehub, S. E. (1981). The masking of octave-band noise by broad-spectrum noise: A comparison of infant and adult thresholds. *Perception & Psychophysics, 30*, 101–106.

Burnham, D., & Dodd, B. (2004). Auditory–visual speech integration by prelinguistic infants: Perception of an emergent consonant in the McGurk effect. *Developmental Psychobiology, 45*, 204–220.

Burnham, D., Kitamura, C., & Vollmer-Conna, U. (2002). What's new, pussycat? On talking to babies and animals. *Science, 296*, 1453.

Burnham, D. K. (1986). Developmental loss of speech perception: Exposure to and experience with a first language [Special issue]. *Applied Psycholinguistics, 7*, 207–239.

Burns, T. C., Yoshida, K. A., Hill, K., & Werker, J. F. (2007). The development of phonetic representation in bilingual and monolingual infants. *Applied Psycholinguistics, 28*, 455–474.

Bushnell, E. W. (1994). A dual-processing approach to cross-modal matching: Implications for development. In D. J. Lewkowicz & R. Lickliter (Eds.), *The development of inter-sensory perception: Comparative perspectives* (pp. 19–38). Hillsdale, NJ: Erlbaum.

Bushnell, E. W., & Boudreau, J. P. (1998). Exploring and exploiting objects with the hands during infancy. In K. J. Connolly (Ed.), *The psychobiology of the hand* (pp. 144–161). London, England: Mac Keith Press.

Bushnell, I. W. (1979). Modification of the externality effect in young infants. *Journal of Experimental Child Psychology, 28*, 211–229.

Bushnell, I. W. R., Sai, F., & Mullin, J. T. (1989). Neonatal recognition of the mother's face. *British Journal of Developmental Psychology, 7*, 3–15.

Butterworth, G. (2003). *Pointing: Where language, culture, and cognition meet*. Mahwah, NJ: Erlbaum.

Butterworth, G., & Hicks, L. (1977). Visual proprioception and postural stability in infancy: A developmental study. *Perception, 6*, 255–262.

Byers-Heinlein, K., Burns, T. C., & Werker, J. F. (2010). The roots of bilingualism in newborns. *Psychological Science, 21*, 343–348.

Campos, J. J., Anderson, D. I., Barbu-Roth, M. A., Hubbard, E. M., Hertenstein, M. J., & Witherington, D. (2000). Travel broadens the mind. *Infancy, 1*, 149–219.

Caron, A. J., Caron, R. F., & Carlson, V. R. (1979). Infant perception of the invariant shape of objects varying in slant. *Child Development, 50*, 716–721.

Casaer, P, (1993). Old and new facts about perinatal brain development. *Journal of Child Psychology & Psychiatry & Allied Disciplines, 34*, 101–109.

Cassia, V. M., Simion, F., Milani, I., & Umilta, C. (2002). Dominance of global visual properties at birth. *Journal of Experimental Psychology: General, 131*, 398–411.

Chabris, C. F., & Simons, D. J. (2010). *The invisible gorilla: And other ways our intuitions deceive us.* New York: NY: Crown/Random House.

Charles, E. P., & Rivera, S. M. (2009). Object permanence and method of disappearance: Looking measures further contradict reaching measures. *Developmental Science, 12*, 991–1006.

Chen, X., Striano, T., & Rakoczy, H. (2004). Auditory–oral matching behavior in newborns. *Developmental Sciences, 7*, 442–447.

Chomsky, N. (1980). *Rules and representations.* New York, NY: Columbia University Press.

Cicchino, J. B., & Rakison, D. H. (2008). Producing and processing self-propelled motion in infancy. *Developmental Psychology, 44*, 1232–1241.

Clifford, A., Franklin, A., Davies, I. R. L., & Holmes, A. (2009). Electrophysiological markers of categorical perception of color in 7-month-old infants. *Brain and Cognition, 71*, 165–172.

Clifford, A., Franklin, A., Holmes, A., Drivonikou, V. G., Ozgen, E., & Davies, I. R. L. (2012). Neural correlates of acquired color category effects. *Brain and Cognition, 80*, 126–143.

Clifford, S. M., Hudry, K., Elsabbagh, M., Charman, T., Johnson, M. H., & the BASIS Team. (2013). Temperament in the first two years of life in infants at high-risk for autism spectrum disorders. *Journal of Autism and Developmental Disorders, 43*, 673–686.

Clifton, R. K., Gwiazda, J., Bauer, J. A., Clarkson, M. G., & Held, R. (1988). Growth in head size during infancy: Implications for sound localization. *Developmental Psychology, 24*, 477–483.

Clifton, R. K., Morrongiello, B. A., & Dowd, J. M. (1984). A developmental look at an auditory illusion: The precedence effect. *Developmental Psychobiology, 17*, 519–536.

Clifton, R. K., Morrongiello, B. A., Kulig, J. W., & Dowd, J. M. (1981). Newborns' orientation toward sound: Possible implications for cortical development. *Child Development, 52*, 833–838.

Clifton, R. K., Muir, D., Ashmead, D. H., & Clarkson, M. G. (1993). Is visually guided reaching in early infancy a myth? *Child Development, 64*, 1099–1110.

Clifton, R. K., Perris, E. E., & Bullinger, A. (1991). Infants' perception of auditory space. *Developmental Psychology, 27*, 187–197.

Clifton, R. K., Rochat, P., Litovsky, R. Y., & Ferris, E. E. (1991). Object representation guides infants' reaching in the dark. *Journal of Experimental Psychology: Human Perception & Performance, 17*, 323–329.

Clifton, R. K., Rochat, P., Robin, D. J., & Berthier, N. E. (1994). Multimodal perception in the control of infant reaching. *Journal of Experimental Psychology: Human Perception and Performance, 20*, 876–886.

Cohen, L. B., & Amsel, G. (1998). Precursors to infants' perception of the causality of a simple event. *Infant Behavior and Development, 21*, 713–732.

Cohen, L. B., & Oakes, L. M. (1993). How infants perceive a simple causal event. *Developmental Psychology, 29*, 421–433.

Cohen, L. B., Rundell, L. J., Spellman, B. A., & Cashon, C. H. (1999). Infants' perception of causal chains. *Psychological Science, 10*, 412–418.

Cohen, L. B., & Younger, B. A. (1984). Infant perception of angular relations. *Infant Behavior and Development, 7*, 37–47.

Colombo, J., Freeseman, L. J., Coldren, J. T., & Frick, J. E. (1995). Individual differences in infant fixation duration: Dominance of global versus local stimulus properties. *Cognitive Development, 10,* 271–285.

Condry, K., & Yonas, A. (2013). Six-month-old infants use motion parallax to direct reaching in depth. *Infant Behavior and Development, 36,* 238–244.

Conel, J. L. (1939–1963). *The postnatal development of the human cerebral cortex.* (Vols. 1–7). Cambridge, MA: Harvard University Press.

Cooper, R. P., & Aslin, R. N. (1989). The language environment of the young infant: Implications for early perceptual development [Special Issue]. *Canadian Journal of Psychology, 43,* 247–265.

Corbetta, D., & Snapp-Childs, W. (2009). Seeing and touching: The role of sensory-motor experience on the development of infant reaching. *Infant Behavior and Development, 32,* 44–58.

Corbetta, D., Thurman, S. L., Wiener, R., Guan, Y., & Williams, J. L. (2014). Mapping the feel of the arm with the sight of the object: On the embodied origins of infant reaching. *Frontiers in Psychology, 5,* ArtID 576.

Cornman, J. W. (1975). *Perception, common sense, and science.* New Haven, CT: Yale University Press.

Corrow, S., Granrud, C. E., Mathison, J., & Yonas, A. (2011). Six-month-old infants perceive the hollow-face illusion. *Perception, 40,* 1376–1383.

Corrow, S., Granrud, C. E., Mathison, J., & Yonas, A. (2012). Infants and adults use line junction information to perceive 3D shape. *Journal of Vision, 12,* 1–7.

Coubart, A., Izard, V., Spelke, E. S., Marie, J., & Streri, A. (2014). Dissociation between large and small numerosities in newborn infants. *Developmental Science, 17,* 11–22.

Coulon, M., Guellai, B., & Streri, A. (2011). Recognition of unfamiliar talking faces at birth. *International Journal of Behavioral Development, 35,* 229–241.

Coulon, M., Hemimou, C., & Streri, A. (2013). Effects of seeing and hearing vowels on neonatal facial imitation. *Infancy, 18,* 782–796.

Craig, K. D., Whitfield, M. F., Grunau, R. V., Linton, J., & Hadjistavropoulos, H. D. (1993). Pain in the preterm neonate: Behavioural and physiological indices. *Pain, 52,* 287–299.

Craton, L. G. (1996). The development of perceptual completion abilities: Infants' perception of stationary, partially occluded objects. *Child Development, 67,* 890–904.

Craton, L. G., & Yonas, A. (1988). Infants' sensitivity to boundary flow information for depth at an edge. *Child Development, 59,* 1522–1529.

Craton, L. G., & Yonas, A. (1990). Kinetic occlusion: Further studies of the boundary-flow cue. *Perception & Psychophysics, 47,* 169–179.

Cristia, A. (2011). Fine-grained variation in caregivers' /s/ predicts their infants' /s/ category. *Journal of Acoustical Society of America, 129,* 3271–3280.

Crowell, J. A., & Banks, M. S. (1993). Perceiving heading with different retinal regions and types of optic flow. *Perception & Psychophysics, 53,* 325–337.

Csibra, G. (2001). Illusory contour figures are perceived as occluding surfaces by 8-month-old infants. *Developmental Science, 4,* F7–F11.

Csibra, G., Biro, S., Koos, O., & Gergely, G. (2003). One-year-old infants use teleological representations of actions productively. *Cognitive Science, 27,* 111–133.

Csibra, G., Davis, G., Spratling, M. W., & Johnson, M. H. (2000). Gamma oscillations and object processing in the infant brain. *Science, 290,* 1582–1585.

Csibra, G., & Gergely, G. (2007). Obsessed with goals: Functions and mechanisms of teleological interpretation of actions in humans. *Acta Psychologica, 124,* 60–78.

Csibra, G., Gergely, G., Biro, S., Koos, O., & Brockbank, M. (1999). Goal attribution without agency cues: The perception of "pure reason" in infancy. *Cognition, 72,* 237–267.

Curran, W., Braddick, O. J., Atkinson, J., Wattam-Bell, J., & Andrew, R. (1999). Development of illusory-contour perception in infants. *Perception, 28,* 527–538.

Cutting, J. E. (1981). Coding theory adapted to gait perception. *Journal of Experimental Psychology: Human Perception & Performance, 7,* 71–87.

Dahmen, J. C., & King, A. J. (2007). Learning to hear: Plasticity of auditory cortical processing. *Current Opinion in Neurobiology, 17,* 456–464.

Dannemiller, J. L. (1989). A test of color constancy in 9- and 20-week-old human infants following simulated illuminant changes. *Developmental Psychology, 25,* 171–184.

Dannemiller, J. L., & Freedland, R. L. (1989). The detection of slow stimulus movement in 2- to 5-month-olds. *Journal of Experimental Child Psychology, 47,* 337–355.

Dannemiller, J. L., & Freedland, R. L. (1991). Detection of relative motion by human infants. *Developmental Psychology, 27,* 67–78.

Dannemiller, I. L., & Hanko, S. A. (1987). A test of color constancy in 4-month-old human infants. *Journal of Experimental Child Psychology, 44,* 255–267.

Dannemiller, J. L., & Stephens, B. R. (1988). A critical test of infant pattern preference models. *Child Development, 59,* 210–216.

Darwin, C. (1896). *The expression of the emotions in man and animals.* New York, NY: Appleton-Century-Crofts.

Davis, H., Albert, M., & Barron, R. W. (1985). Detection of number or numerousness by human infants. *Science, 228,* 1222.

Davis, H., & Perusse, R. (1988). Numerical competence in animals: Definitional issues, current evidence, and a new research agenda. *Behavioral and Brain Sciences, 11,* 561–615.

Daw, N. W. (2013). *Visual development.* New York, NY: Springer.

Day, R. H., & McKenzie, B. E. (1973). Perceptual shape constancy in early infancy. *Perception, 2,* 315–320.

Day, R. H., & McKenzie, B. E. (1981). Infant perception of the invariant size of approaching and receding objects. *Developmental Psychology, 17,* 670–677.

de Heering A., & Maurer, D. (2014). Face memory deficits in patients deprived of early visual input by bilateral congenital cataracts. *Developmental Psychobiology, 56,* 96–108.

DeBello, W. M., & Knudsen, E. I. (2004). Multiple sites of adaptive plasticity in the owl's auditory localization pathway. *Journal of Neuroscience, 24,* 6853–6861.

DeCasper, A. J., & Fifer, W. P. (1980). Of human bonding: Newborns prefer their mothers' voices. *Science, 208,* 1174–1176.

DeCasper, A. J., & Prescott, P. A. (1984). Human newborns' perception of male voices: Preference, discrimination, and reinforcing value. *Developmental Psychobiology, 17,* 481–491.

DeCasper, A. J., & Spence, M. J. (1986). Prenatal maternal speech influences newborns' perception of speech sounds. *Infant Behavior and Development, 9,* 133–150.

DeValois, R., & DeValois, K. (1988). *Spatial vision.* New York, NY: Oxford University Press.

Diamond, A. (1988). Differences between adult and infant cognition: Is the crucial variable presence or absence of language? In L. Weiskrantz (Ed.), *Thought without language* (pp. 337–370). Oxford, England: Clarendon.

Diamond, A., & Goldman-Rakic, P. S. (1983). Comparison of performance on a Piagetian object permanence task in human infants and rhesus monkeys: Evidence for involvement of prefrontal cortex. *Neuroscience Abstracts, 9,* 641.

Dodwell, P. C. (1983). Spatial sense of the human infant. In A. Hein & M. Jeannerod (Eds.), *Spatially oriented behavior* (pp. 197–213). New York, NY: Springer-Verlag.

Dubois, J., Dehaene-Lambertz, G., Soares, C., Cointepas, Y., Le Bihan, D., & Hertz-Pannier, L. (2008). Microstructural correlates of infant functional development: Example of the visual pathways. *Journal of Neuroscience, 28*, 1943–1948.

Duncker, D. K. (1929). *Llber inditzierfe Bewegung (Ein Beitrag zur Theorie optisch wahrgenommener Bewegung)*. London, England: Kegan Paul Trench Trubner.

Eibl-Eibesfelt, I. (1989). *Human ethology*. New York, NY: Adline.

Eimas, P. D. (1978). Developmental aspects of speech perception. In R. Held, H. W. Leibowitz, & H. L. Teuber (Eds.), *Handbook of sensory physiology: Vol. 8. Perception* (pp. 357–374). Berlin, Germany: Springer-Verlag.

Eimas, P. D., & Miller, J. L. (1980a). Contextual effects in infant speech perception. *Science, 209*, 1140–1141.

Eimas, P. D., & Miller, J. L, (1980b). Discrimination of information for manner of articulation. *Infant Behavior and Development, 3*, 367–375.

Eimas, P. D., & Quinn, P. (1994). Studies on the formation of perceptually based basic-level categories in young infants. *Child Development, 65*, 903–917.

Eimas, P. D., Siqueland, E. R., Jusczyk, P., & Vigorito, J. (1971). Speech perception in infants. *Science, 171*, 303–306.

Eisele, W. A., Berry, R. C., & Shriner, T. H. (1975). Infant sucking response to patterns as a conjugate function of changes in the sound pressure level of auditory stimuli. *Journal of Speech and Hearing Research, 18*, 296–307.

Eizenman, D. R., & Bertenthal, B. I. (1998). Infants' perception of object unity in translating and rotating displays. *Developmental Psychology, 34*, 426–434.

Ekberg, T. L., Rosander, K., von Hofsten, C., Olsson, U., Soska, K. C., & Adolph, K. E. (2013). Dynamic reaching in infants during binocular and monocular viewing. *Experimental Brain Research, 229*, 1–12.

Ellemberg, D., Lewis, T. L., Maurer, D., & Brent, H. P. (2000). Influence of monocular deprivation during infancy on the later development of spatial and temporal vision. *Vision Research, 40*, 3283–3295.

Ellemberg, D., Lewis, T. L., Maurer, D., Brar, S., & Brent, H. P. (2002). Better perception of global motion after monocular than after binocular deprivation. *Vision Research, 42*, 169–179.

Ellemberg, D., Lewis, T. L., Maurer, D., Lui, C. H., & Brent, H. P. (1999). Spatial and temporal vision in patients treated for bilateral congenital cataracts. *Vision Research, 39*, 3480–3489.

Elliott, L. L., & Katz, D. R. (1980). Children's pure-tone detection. *Journal of the Acoustical Society of America, 67*, 343–344.

Ellis, A. E., & Oakes, L. M. (2006). Infants flexibly use different dimensions to categorize objects. *Developmental Psychology, 42*, 1000–1011.

Elsabbagh, M., Fernandes, J., Webb, S. J., Dawson, G., Charman, T., Johnson, M. H., & the BASIS Team. (2013). Disengagement of visual attention in infancy is associated with emerging autism in toddlerhood. *Biological Psychiatry, 74*, 189–194.

Engen, T., & Lipsitt, L. (1965). Decrement and recovery of responses to olfactory stimuli in the human neonate. *Journal of Comparative and Physiological Psychology, 59*, 312–316.

Epstein, W. (1982). Percept–percept couplings. *Perception, 11*, 75–83.

Epstein, W. (1966). Perceived depth as a function of relative height under three background conditions. *Journal of Experimental Psychology, 72*, 335–338.

Ernst, M. O., & Banks, M. S. (2002). Humans integrate visual and haptic information in a statistically optimal fashion. *Nature, 415*, 429–433.

Exner, S. (1875). Uber das sehen von bewegungen and dies theories des zusammengesetzen auges. *S. B. Akad. Wiss. (Wien), 72*, 156–190.

Fagard, J., Spelke, E., & von Hofsten, C. (2009). Reaching and grasping a moving object in 6-, 8-, and 10-month-old infants: Laterality and performance. *Infant Behavior and Development, 32*, 137–146.

Fantz, R. L. (1958). Pattern vision in young infants. *Psychological Record, 8*, 43–47.

Fantz, R. L. (1961). The origin of form perception. *Scientific American, 204*, 66–72.

Fantz, R. L., Fagan, J. F., III, & Miranda, S. B. (1975). Early visual selectivity as a function of pattern variables, previous exposure, age from birth and conception, and expected cognitive deficit. In L. B. Cohen & P. Salapatek (Eds.), *Infant perception: From sensation to cognition: Vol. I. Basic visual processes* (pp. 249–345). New York, NY: Academic Press.

Fantz, R. L., & Miranda, S. B. (1975). Newborn infant attention to form of contour. *Child Development, 46*, 224–228.

Farroni, T., Csibra, G., Simion, F., & Johnson, M. H. (2002). Eye contact detection in humans from birth. *Proceedings of the National Academy of Sciences of the USA, 90*, 9602–9605.

Farroni, T., Johnson, M. H., & Csibra, G. (2007). Mechanisms of eye gaze perception during infancy. *Journal of Cognitive Neuroscience, 16*, 1320–1326.

Farroni, T., Massaccesi, S., Menon, E., & Johnson, M. H. (2007). Direct gaze modulates face recognition in young infants. *Cognition, 102*, 396–404.

Farroni, T., Massaccesi, S., Pividori, D., & Johnson, M. H. (2004). Gaze following in newborns. *Infancy, 5*, 39–60.

Farroni, T., Menon, E., & Johnson, M. H. (2006). Factors influencing newborns' preference for faces with eye contact. *Journal of Experimental Child Psychology, 95*, 298–308.

Farzin, F., Charles, E. P., & Rivera, S. M. (2009). Development of multimodal processing in infancy. *Infancy, 14*, 563–578.

Feigenson, L., Carey, S., & Spelke, E. S. (2002). Infants' discrimination of number vs. continuous extent. *Cognitive Psychology, 44*, 33–66.

Feinman. S. (1982). Social referencing in infancy. *Merrill Palmer Quarterly, 28*, 445–470.

Feldman, R., Singer, M., & Zagoory, O. (2010). Touch attenuates infants' physiological reactivity to stress. *Developmental Science, 13*, 271–278.

Fernald, A. (1984). The perceptual and affective salience of mother's speech to infants. In L. Feagans, C. Garvey, & R. Golinkoff (Eds.), *The origins and growth of communication* (pp. 5–29). Norwood, NJ: Ablex.

Fernald, A. (1985). Four-month-old infants prefer to listen to motherese. *Infant Behavior and Development, 8*, 181–195.

Fernald, A. (1993). Approval and disapproval: Infant responsiveness to vocal affect in familiar and unfamiliar languages. *Child Development, 64*, 657–674.

Fernald, A. (2000). Speech to infants as hyperspeech: Knowledge-driven processes in early word recognition. *Phonetica, 57*, 242–254.

Fernald, A., & Kuhl, P. K. (1987). Acoustic determinants of infant preference for motherese speech. *Infant Behavior and Development, 10*, 279–293.

Fernald, A., & Mazzie, C. (1991). Prosody and focus in speech to infants and adults. *Developmental Psychology, 27*, 209–221.

Fernald, A., & Morikawa, H. (1993). Common themes and cultural variations in Japanese and American mothers' speech to infants. *Child Development, 64*, 637–656.

Feron, J., Gentaz, E., & Streri, A. (2006). Evidence of amodal representation of small numbers across visuo-tactile modalities in 5-month-old infants. *Cognitive Development, 21*, 81–92.

Ferry, A. L., Hespos, S. J., & Waxman, S. R. (2013). Nonhuman primate vocalizations support categorization in very young human infants. *Proceedings of the National Academy of Sciences of the USA, 110,* 15231–15235.

Field, D. J., Hayes, A., & Hess, R. F. (1993). Contour integration by the human visual system: Evidence for a local "association field." *Vision Research, 33,* 173–193.

Field, T. M., Woodson, R., Greenberg, R., & Cohen, D. (1982). Discrimination and imitation of facial expressions by neonates. *Science, 218,* 179–181.

Flannagan. J. E., Landa, R., Bhat, A., & Bauman, M. (2012). Head lag in infants at risk for autism: A preliminary study. *American Journal of Occupational Therapy, 66,* 577–585.

Flom, R. (2014). Perceptual narrowing: Retrospect and prospect. *Developmental Psychobiology, 56,* 1442–1453.

Flom, R., & Bahrick, L. E. (2010). The effects of intersensory redundancy on attention and memory: Infants' long-term memory for orientation in audiovisual events. *Developmental Psychology, 46,* 428–436.

Fodor, J. A. (1983). *The modularity of mind: An essay on faculty psychology.* Cambridge, MA: MIT Press.

Fodor, J. A., & Pylyshyn, Z. W. (1981). How direct is visual perception? Some reflections on Gibson's "ecological approach." *Cognition, 9,* 139–196.

Fontenelle, S. A., Kahrs, B. A., Neal, S. A., Newton, A. T., & Lockman, J. J. (2007). Infant manual exploration of composite substrates. *Journal of Experimental Child Psychology, 98,* 153–167.

Fraiberg, S. (1968). Parallel and divergent patterns in blind and sighted infants. *Psychoanalytic Study of the Child, 23,* 264–300.

Franchak, J., & Adolph, K. (2014). Affordances as probabilistic functions: Implications for development, perception, and decisions for action. *Ecological Psychology, 26,* 109–124.

Franklin, A., Bevis, L., Ling, Y., & Hurlbert, A. (2010). Biological components of colour preference in infancy. *Developmental Science, 13,* 346–354.

Franklin, A., & Davies, I. R. L. (2004). New evidence for infant colour categories. *British Journal of Developmental Psychology, 22,* 349–377.

Freedland, R. L., & Dannemiller, J. L. (1987). Detection of stimulus motion in 5-month-old infants [Special issue]. *Journal of Experimental Psychology: Human Perception & Performance, 13,* 566–576.

Frisby, J. P., & Stone, J. V. (2010). *Seeing.* Cambridge, MA: MIT Press.

Frisen, L., & Glansholm, A. (1975). Optical and neural resolution in peripheral vision. *Journal of Investigative Ophthalmology, 14,* 528–536.

Frye, D., Rawling, P., Moore, C., & Myers, I. (1983). Object–person discrimination and communication at 3 and 10 months. *Developmental Psychology, 19,* 303–309.

Gaither, S. E., Pauker, K., & Johnson, S. P. (2012). Biracial and monoracial infant own-race face perception: An eye tracking study. *Developmental Science, 15,* 775–782.

Galle, M. E., & McMurray, B. (2014). The development of voicing categories: A quantitative review of over 40 years of infant speech perception research. *Psychological Bulletin and Review, 21,* 884–906.

Gangi, D. N., Ibanez, L. V., & Messinger, D. S. (2014). Joint attention initiation with and without positive affect: Risk group differences and associations with ASD symptoms. *Journal of Autism and Developmental Disorders, 44,* 141–1424.

Ganon, E. C., & Schwartz, K. B. (1980). Perception of internal elements of compound figures by one-month-old infants. *Journal of Experimental Child Psychology, 30,* 159–170.

Gantaz, E., & Streri, A. (2004). Infants' haptic discrimination of spatial orientations. *Current Psychology Letters, 9*, 61–71.

Geangu, E., Senna, I., Croci, E., & Turati, C. (2015). The effect of biomechanical properties of motion on infants' perception of goal-directed grasping. *Journal of Experimental Child Psychology, 129*, 55–67.

Geisler, W. S. (1984). Physical limits of acuity and hyperacuity. *Journal of the Optical Society of America, 1*, 775–782.

Geisler, W. S. (2011). Contributions of the ideal observer analysis theory to vision research. *Vision Research, 51*, 771–781.

Gelman, R., Durgin, F., & Kaufman, L. (1995). Distinguishing between animates and inanimates: Not by motion alone. In D. Sperber, D. Premack, & A. J. Premack (Eds.), *Causal cognition: A multidisciplinary debate. Symposia of the Fyssen Foundation* (pp. 150–184). New York, NY: Clarendon Press/Oxford University Press.

Gepner, B., Mestre, D. R., Masson, G., & de Schonen, S. (1995). Postural effects of motion vision in young autistic children. *Neuroreport, 6*, 1211–1214.

Gergley, G., & Csibra, G. (2003). Teleological reasoning in infancy: The naïve theory of rational action. *Trends in Cognitive Sciences, 7*, 287–292.

Gergely, G., Nadasdy, Z., Csibra, G., & Biro, S. (1995). Taking the intentional stance at 12 months of age. *Cognition, 56*, 165–193.

Gerson, S. A., & Woodward, A. L. (2014). The joint role of trained, untrained, and observed actions at the origins of goal recognition. *Infant Behavior and Development, 37*, 94–104.

Ghim, H. R. (1990). Evidence for perceptual organization in infants: Perception of subjective contours by young infants. *Infant Behavior and Development, 73*(2), 221–248.

Ghim, H. R., & Eimas, P. D. (1988). Global and local processing by 3- and 4-month-old infants. *Perception & Psychophysics, 43*, 165–171.

Gibson, E. J. (1969). *Principles of perceptual learning and development*. New York, NY: Appleton-Century-Crofts.

Gibson, E. J. (1984). Perceptual development from an ecological approach. In M. Lamb, A. Brown, & B. Rogoff (Eds.), *Advances in developmental psychology* (Vol. 3, pp. 243–285). Hillsdale, NJ: Erlbaum.

Gibson, E. J., Riccio, G., Schmuckler, M. A., Stoffregen, T. A., Rosenberg, D., & Taormina, J. (1987). Detection of the traversability of surfaces by crawling and walking infants. Special Issue: The ontogenesis of perception. *Journal of Experimental Psychology: Human Perception & Performance, 13*, 533–544.

Gibson, E. J., & Pick, A. D. (2000). *An ecological approach to perceptual learning and development*. New York, NY: Oxford University Press.

Gibson, E. J., & Walk, R. D. (1960). The visual cliff. *Scientific American, 202*, 64–71.

Gibson, E. J., & Walker, A. S. (1984). Development of knowledge of visual–tactual affordances of substance. *Child Development, 55*, 453–460.

Gibson, J. J. (1950). *The perception of the visual world*. New York, NY: Appleton-Century-Crofts.

Gibson, J. J. (1966). *The senses considered as perceptual systems*. Boston, MA: Houghton Mifflin.

Gibson, J. J. (1979). *The ecological approach to visual perception*. Boston, MA: Houghton Mifflin.

Gibson, J. J., & Gibson, E. J. (1955). Perceptual learning: Differentiation or enrichment? *Psychological Review, 62*, 32–41.

Gibson, J. J., & Gibson, E. J. (1957). Continuous perspective transformations and the perception of rigid motion. *Journal of Experimental Psychology, 54*, 129–138.

Gibson, J. J., Kaplan, G. A., Reynolds, H. N., Jr., & Wheeler, K. (1969). The change from visible to invisible: A study of optical transitions. *Perception & Psychophysics, 5,* 113–116.

Gilchrist, A. L., Delman, S., & Jacobsen, A. (1983). The classification and integration of edges as critical to the perception of reflectance and illumination. *Perception & Psychophysics, 33,* 425–436.

Gilmore, R. O., Baker, T. J., & Grobman, K. H. (2004). Stability in young infants' discrimination of optic flow. *Developmental Psychology, 40,* 259–270.

Gilmore, R. O., Hou, C., Pettit, M. W., & Norcia, A. M. (2007). Development of cortical responses to optic flow. *Visual Neuroscience, 24,* 845–856.

Ginsburg, A. P. (1978). *Visual information processing based on spatial filters constrained by biological data.* Doctoral dissertation, University of Cambridge, Cambridge, England.

Glover, S. G. (2004). Separate visual representations in the planning and control of action. *Behavioral and Brain Sciences, 27,* 3–78.

Gogel, W. C. (1982). Analysis of the perception of motion concomitant with a lateral motion of the head. *Perception & Psychophysics, 32,* 241–250.

Goldstein, B. E. (1989). *Sensation and perception.* Belmont, CA: Wadsworth.

Goldstone, R. L. (1994). Influences of categorization on perceptual discrimination. *Journal of Experimental Psychology: General, 123,* 178–200.

Goldstone, R. L. (2003). Learning to perceive while perceiving to learn. In R. Kimchi, M. Behrmann, & C. R. Olson (Eds.), *Perceptual organization in vision: Behavioral and neural perspectives* (pp. 233–380). Mahwah, NJ: Erlbaum.

Goodale, M. A., & Milner, A. D. (1992). Separate visual pathways for perception and action. *Trends in Neuroscience, 15,* 20–25.

Goodman, N. (1951). *The structure of appearance.* Cambridge, MA: Harvard University Press.

Gordon, M. S., & Rosenblum, L. D. (2004). Perception of sound-obstructing surfaces using body-scaled judgments. *Ecological Psychology, 16,* 87–113.

Goren, C. C., Sarty, M., & Wu, P. Y. K. (1975). Visual following and pattern discrimination of face-like stimuli by newborn infants. *Pediatrics, 56,* 544–549.

Gottlieb, G. (1971). Ontogenesis of sensory function in birds and mammals. In E. Tobach, L. Aronson, & E. Shaw (Eds.). *The biopsychology of development* (pp. 67–128). New York, NY: Academic Press.

Graham, S. A., Keates, J., Vukatana, E., & Khu, M. (2013). Distinct labels attenuate 15-month-olds' attention in an inductive inference task. *Frontiers in Psychology, 3,* ArtID 586.

Granrud, C. E. (1986). Binocular vision and spatial perception in 4- and 5-month-old infants. *Journal of Experimental Psychology: Human Perception & Performance, 12,* 36–49.

Granrud, C. E. (1987). Size constancy in newborn human infants. *Investigative Ophthalmology and Visual Science, 28*(Suppl.), 5.

Granrud, C. E. (2006). Size constancy in infants: 4-Month-olds' responses to physical versus retinal image size. *Journal of Experimental Psychology: Human Perception and Performance, 32,* 1398–1404.

Granrud, C. E., Haake, R. J., & Yonas, A. (1985). Infants' sensitivity to familiar size: The effect of memory on spatial perception. *Perception & Psychophysics, 37,* 459–466.

Granrud, C. E., & Yonas, A. (1984). Infants' perception of pictorially specified interposition. *Journal of Experimental Child Psychology, 37,* 500–511.

Granrud, C. E., Yonas, A., & Opland, E. A. (1985). Infants' sensitivity to the depth cue of shading. *Perception & Psychophysics, 37,* 415–419.

Granrud, C. E., Yonas, A., & Pettersen, L. (1984). A comparison of monocular and binocular depth perception in 5- and 7-month-old infants. *Journal of Experimental Child Psychology, 38,* 19–32.

Granrud, C. E., Yonas, A., Smith, I. M., Arterberry, M. E, Glicksman, M. L., & Sorknes, A. C. (1984). Infants' sensitivity to accretion and deletion of texture as information for depth at an edge. *Child Development, 55,* 1630–1636.

Gredeback, G., von Hofsten, C., & Boudreau, J. P. (2002). Infants' visual tracking of continuous circular motion under conditions of occlusion and non-occlusion. *Infant Behavior and Development, 25,* 161–182.

Gredeback, G., von Hofsten, C., Karlsson, J., & Aus, K. (2005). The development of two-dimensional tracking: A longitudinal study of circular pursuit. *Experimental Brain Research, 163,* 204–213.

Green, J. R., Nip, I. S. B.,Wilson, E. M., Mefferd, A. S., & Yunusova, Y. (2010). Lip movement exaggerations during infant-directed speech. *Journal of Speech, Language, and Hearing Research, 53,* 1529–1542.

Greenough, W. T., Black, J. E., & Wallace, C. S. (1987). Experience and brain development. *Child Development, 58,* 539–559.

Greenough, W. T., Volkmar, F. R., & Juraska, J. M. (1973). Effects of rearing complexity on dendritic branching in frontolateral and temporal cortex of the rat. *Experimental Neurology, 41,* 371–378.

Gregory, R. L. (1972). *Eye and brain: The psychology of seeing* (2nd ed.). London, England: Weidenfeld & Nicolson.

Gronqvist, H., Gredeback, G., & von Hofsten, C. (2006). Developmental asymmetries between horizontal and vertical tracking. *Vision Research, 46,* 1754–1761.

Grossberg, S. (1994). 3-D vision and figure-ground separation by visual cortex. *Perception & Psychophysics, 55,* 48–120.

Grunau, R. V., Johnston, C. C., & Craig, K. D. (1990). Neonatal facial and cry responses to invasive and non-invasive procedures. *Pain, 42,* 295–305.

Gunderson, V. M. (1983). Development of cross-modal recognition in infant pigtail monkeys (Macaca nemestrina). *Developmental Psychology, 19,* 398–404.

Gunter, J. B. (2002). Benefit and risks of local anesthetics in infants and children. *Paediatric Drugs, 4,* 649–672.

Hainline, L., Riddell, P., Grose-Fifer, J., & Abramov, I. (1992). Development of accommodation and convergence in infancy. Special Issue: Normal and abnormal visual development in infants and children. *Behavioural Brain Research, 49,* 33–50.

Haith, M. M. (1978), Visual competence in early infancy. In R. Held, H. Leibowitz, & H.-L. Teuber (Eds.), *Handbook of sensory physiology: Vol. 8. Perception* (pp. 311–356). Berlin, Germany: Springer-Verlag.

Haith, M. M. (1980). *Rules that babies look by: The organization of newborn visual activity.* Hillsdale, NJ: Erlbaum.

Haith, M. M., Bergman, T., & Moore, M. J. (1977). Eye contact and face scanning in early infancy. *Science, 198,* 853–855.

Hamlin, J. K., Hallinan, E. V., & Woodward, A. L. (2008). Do as I do: 7-month-old infants selectively reproduce other's goals. *Developmental Science, 11,* 487–494.

Hanna, E., & Meltzoff, A. N. (1993). Peer imitation by toddlers in laboratory, home, and daycare contexts: Implications for social learning and memory. *Developmental Psychology, 29,* 701–710.

Harding, C. G., & Golinkoff, R. M. (1979). The origins of intentional vocalizations in prelinguistic infants. *Child Development, 50,* 33–40.

Harris, P. (1983). Infant cognition. In M. M. Haith & J. J. Campos (Eds.), *Cognitive development* (pp. 689–782). New York, NY: Wiley.

Hayes, J. R., & Clark, H. H. (1970). Experiments on the segmentation of an artificial speech analogue. In J. R. Hayes (Ed.), *Cognition and the development of language* (pp. 221–234). New York, NY: Wiley.

Haynes, H., White, B. L., & Held, R. (1965). Visual accommodation in human infants. *Science, 148,* 528–530.

Hebb, D. O. (1949). *The organization of behavior.* New York, NY: Wiley.

Hecht, H., & Savelsbergh, G. J. P. (2004). Theories of time-to-contact judgment. *Advances in Psychology, 135,* 1–11.

Heinemann, E. G., Tulving, E., & Nachmias, J. (1959). The effect of oculomotor adjustments on apparent size. *American Journal of Psychology, 72,* 32–45.

Held, R. (1955). Shifts in binaural localization after prolonged exposures to atypical combinations of stimuli. *American Journal of Psychology, 68,* 526–548.

Held, R., Birch, E., & Gwiazda, J. (1980). Stereoacuity in human infants. *Proceedings of the National Academy of Sciences, USA, 77,* 5572–5574.

Held, R., Dichgans, J., & Bauer, J. (1975). Characteristics of moving visual scenes influencing spatial orientation. *Vision Research, 15,* 357–365.

Held, R., & Hein, A. (1963). Movement produced stimulation in the development of visually guided behavior. *Journal of Comparative and Physiological Psychology, 56,* 872–876.

Held, R., Ostrovsky, Y., de Gelder, B., Gandhi, T., Ganesh, S., Mathur, U., & Sinha, P. (2011). The newly sighted fail to match seen with felt. *Nature neuroscience, 14,* 551–553.

Helmholtz, H. v. (1965). Handbook of physiological optics. In R. Herrnstein & E. G. Boring (Eds.), *A sourcebook in the history of psychology* (Vol. 3, pp. 151–163). Cambridge, MA: Harvard University Press. (Original work published 1885)

Hemker, L., Granrud, C. E., Yonas, A., & Kavšek, M. (2010). Infant perception of surface texture and relative height as distance information: A preferential-reaching study. *Infancy, 15,* 6–27.

Herbert, J., Gross, J., & Hayne, H. (2007). Crawling is associated with more flexible memory retrieval by 9-month-old infants. *Developmental Science, 10,* 183–189.

Hering, E. (1861–1864). *Beitrage zur physiologic.* Leipzig, Germany: Engelmann.

Heron-Delaney, M., Anzures, G., Herbert, J. S., Quinn, P. C., Slater, A. M., Tanaka, J. W., . . . Pascalis, O. (2011). Perceptual training prevents the emergence of the other race effect during infancy. *PLos One, 6,* e19858.

Hershberger, W. (1970). Attached shadow orientation perceived as depth by chickens reared in an environment illuminated from below. *Journal of Comparative and Physiological Psychology, 73,* 407–411.

Hertenstein, M. J., & Campos, J. J. (2004). The retention effects of an adults' emotional displays on infant behavior. *Child Development, 75,* 595–613.

Hespos, S., Gredeback, G., von Hofsten, C., & Spelke, E. S. (2009). Occlusion is hard: Comparing predictive reading for visible and hidden objects in infants and adults. *Cognitive Science, 33,* 1483–1502.

Hespos, S. J., & Baillargeon, R. (2001a). Reasoning about containment events in very young infants. *Cognition, 78,* 207–245.

Hespos, S. J., & Baillargeon, R. (2001b). Infants' knowledge about occlusion and containment events: A surprising discrepancy. *Psychological Science, 12,* 141–147.

Hespos, S. J., & Baillargeon, R. (2006). Decalage in infants' knowledge about occlusion and containment events: Converging evidence from action tasks. *Cognition, 99*, B31–B41.

Hespos, S. J., & Baillargeon, R. (2008). Young infants' actions reveal their developing knowledge of support variables: Converging evidence for violation-of-expectation findings. *Cognition, 107*, 304–316.

Hespos, S. J., Dora, B., Rips, L. J., & Christie, S. (2012). Infants make quantity discriminations for substances. *Child Development, 83*, 554–567.

Hespos, S. J., Ferry, A. L., & Rips, L. J. (2009). Five-month-old infants have different expectations for solids and liquids. *Psychological Science, 20*, 603–611.

Hespos, S. J., & Spelke, E. S. (2004). Conceptual precursors to language. *Nature, 430*, 453–456.

Hespos, S. J., & van Marle, K. (2012). Physics for infants: Characterizing the origins of knowledge about objects, substances and number. *WIREs Cognitive Science, 3*, 19–27.

Hess, E. H. (1956). Space perception in the chick. *Scientific American, 195*, 71–80.

Hickey, T. L., & Peduzzi, J. D. (1987). Structure and development of the visual system. In P. Salapatek & L. B. Cohen (Eds.), *Handbook of infant perception: From sensation to perception* (pp. 1–42). New York, NY: Academic Press.

Hillenbrand, J. (1983). Perceptual organization of speech sounds by infants. *Journal of Speech and Hearing Research, 26*, 268–282.

Hillenbrand, J. (1984). Speech perception by infants: Categorization based on nasal consonant place of articulation. *Journal of the Acoustical Society of America, 75*, 1613–1622.

Hillis, J. M., Ernst, M. O., Banks, M. S., & Landy, M. S. (2002). Combining sensory information: Mandatory fusion within but not between senses. *Science, 298*, 1627–1630.

Hirrlinger, J., & Nave, K. A. (2014). Adapting brain metabolism to myelination and long-range signal transduction. *Glia, 62*, 1749–1761.

Hirshkowitz, A., & Wilcox, T. (2013). Infants' ability to extract three-dimensional shape from coherent motion. *Infant Behavior and Development, 36*, 863–872.

Hirsh-Pasek, K., Kemler Nelson, D. G., Jusczyk, P. W., Cassidy, K. W., Druss, B., & Kennedy, L. (1987). Clauses are perceptual units for young infants. *Cognition, 26*(3), 269–286.

Hobbes. T. (1974). *Leviathan.* Baltimore, MD: Penguin. (Original work published 1651)

Hochberg, C. B., & Hochberg, J. E. (1953). Familiar size and subception in perceived depth. *Journal of Psychology, 36*, 341–345.

Hochberg, J. (1968). In the mind's eye. In R. N. Haber (Ed.), *Contemporary theory and research in visual perception* (pp. 309–331). New York, NY: Holt, Rinehart & Winston.

Hochberg, J. (1971). Perception II: Space and movement. In J. W. Kling & L. A. Riggs (Eds.), *Woodworth and Schlosberg's experimental psychology* (pp. 475–550). New York, NY: Holt, Rinehart & Winston.

Hochberg, J. (1974). Higher-order stimuli and inter-response coupling in the perception of the visual world. In R. B. McLeod & H. L. Pick (Eds.), *Perception: Essays in honor of J. J. Gibson* (pp. 17–39). Ithaca, NY: Cornell University Press.

Hochberg, J. (1978). *Perception* (2nd ed.). Englewood Cliffs, NJ: Prentice-Hall.

Hochberg, J. (1981). On cognition in perception: Perceptual coupling and unconscious inference. *Cognition, 10*, 127–134.

Hoffman, D. D., & Flinchbaugh, B. E. (1982). The interpretation of biological motion. *Biological Cybernetics, 42*, 195–204.

Holloway, R. L., Jr. (1966). Dendritic branching: Some preliminary results of training and complexity in rat visual cortex. *Brain Research, 2,* 393–396.

Holtmaat, A., Wilbrecht, L., Knott, G. W., Welker, E., & Svoboda, K. (2006). Experience-dependent and cell-type-specific spine growth in the neocortex. *Nature, 441,* 979–983.

Holway, A. H., & Boring, E. G. (1941). Determinants of apparent visual size with distance variant. *American Journal of Psychology, 54,* 21–37.

Horwood, A. M., & Riddell, P. M. (2013). Developmental changes in the balance of disparity, blur, and looming/proximity cues to drive ocular alignment and focus. *Perception, 42,* 693–715.

Houston, D. M., & Jusczyk, P. W. (2000). The role of talker-specific information in word segmentation by infants. *Journal of Experimental Psychology: Human Perception and Performance, 26,* 1570–1582.

Howland, H. C., Dobson, V., & Sayles, N. (1987). Accommodation in infants as measured by photorefraction. *Vision Research, 27,* 2141–2152.

Hubel, D. H., & Wiesel, T. N. (1963). Receptive fields, binocular interaction and functional architecture in the cat's visual cortex. *Journal of Physiology, 160,* 106–154.

Hubel, D. H., & Wiesel, T. N. (1965). Receptive fields and functional architecture in two non-striate visual areas (18 and 19) of the cat. *Journal of Neurophysiology, 28,* 229–289.

Hubel, D. H., & Wiesel, T. N. (1970). Stereoscopic vision in macaque monkey: Cells sensitive to binocular depth in area 18 of the macaque monkey cortex. *Nature, 225,* 41–42.

Humphrey, G. K., & Humphrey, D. E. (1989). The role of structure in infant visual pattern perception. *Canadian Journal of Psychology, 43,* 165–182.

Hunnius, S., de Wit, T. C. J., Vrins, S., & von Hofsten, C. (2011). Facing threat: Infants' and adults' visual scanning of faces with neutral, happy, sad, angry, and fearful emotional expressions. *Cognition and Emotion, 25,* 193–205.

Hussin, H. M. (2009). Long-term visual function outcomes of congenital cataract surgery with intraocular lens implantation in children under 5 years of age. *European Journal of Ophthalmology, 19,* 754–761.

Huttenlocher, P. R. (1990). Morphometric study of human cerebral cortex development. *Neuropsychologia, 28,* 517–527.

Huttenlocher, P. R. (1994). Synaptogenesis in human cerebral cortex. In G. Dawson & K. W. Fischer (Eds.), *Human behavior and the developing brain* (pp. 137–152). New York, NY: Oxford University Press.

Hyde, D. C., Jones, B. L., Flom, R., & Porter, C L. (2011). Neural signatures of face–voice synchrony in 5-month-old human infants. *Developmental Psychobiology, 53,* 359–370.

Ichikawa, H., Kanazawa, S., & Yamaguchi, M. K. (2014). Infants recognize the subtle happiness expression. *Perception, 43,* 235–248.

Ichikawa, H., & Yamaguchi, M. K. (2014). Infants' recognition of subtle anger facial expression. *Japanese Psychological Research, 56,* 15–23.

Ittelson, W. H. (1953). A note on "Familiar size and the perception of depth." *Journal of Psychology, 35,* 235–240.

Jacobson, M. (1991). *Developmental neurobiology* (3rd ed.). New York, NY: Plenum.

Jacobson, S. W. (1979), Matching behavior in the young infant. *Child Development, 50,* 425–430.

James, W. (1890). *The principles of psychology* (Vol. 2). New York, NY: Holt.

Jando, G., Miko-Barath, E., Marko, K., Hollody, K., Torok, B., & Kovacs, I. (2013). Early-onset binocularity in preterm infants reveals experience-dependent visual development in humans. *Proceedings of the National Academy of Sciences, 109,* 11049–11052.

Jean, A. D. L., & Stack, D. M. (2012). Full-term and very-low-birth-weight preterm infants' self-regulating behaviors during a still-face interaction: Influences of maternal touch. *Infant Behavior and Development, 35,* 779–791.

Johansson, G. (1950). *Configurations in event perception.* Uppsala, Sweden: Almkvist & Wiksell.

Johansson, G. (1970). On theories for visual space perception: A letter to Gibson. *Scandinavian Journal of Psychology, 77,* 67–74.

Johansson, G. (1973). Visual perception of biological motion and a model for its analysis. *Perception and Psychophysics, 14,* 201–211.

Johansson, G. (1975). Visual motion perception. *Scientific American, 232,* 76–88.

Johansson, G. (1977). Studies on visual perception of locomotion. *Perception, 6,* 365–376.

Johansson, G., von Hofsten, C., & Jansson, G. (1980). Event perception. *Annual Review of Psychology, 31,* 27–63.

Johnson, M. H. (1990). Cortical maturation and the development of visual attention in early infancy. *Journal of Cognitive Neuroscience, 2,* 81–95.

Johnson, M. H. (2005). Subcortical face processing. *Nature Reviews Neuroscience, 6,* 1–9.

Johnson, M. H., Dziurawiec, S., Ellis, H., & Morton, J. (1991). Newborns' preferential tracking of face-like stimuli and its subsequent decline. *Cognition, 40,* 1–19.

Johnson, S. C., Ok, S.-J., & Luo, Y. (2007). The attribution of attention: 9-month-olds' interpretation of gaze as a goal-directed action. *Developmental Science, 10,* 530–537.

Johnson, S. P., & Aslin, R. N. (1995). Perception of object unity in 2-month-old infants. *Developmental Psychology, 31,* 739–745.

Johnson, S. P., & Nanez, J. E. (1995). Young infants' perception of object unity in two-dimensional displays. *Infant Behavior and Development, 18,* 133–143.

Johnson, S. P., Bremner, J. G., Slater, A. M., Mason, U. C., & Foster, K. (2002). Young infants' perception of unity and form in occlusion displays. *Journal of Experimental Child Psychology, 81,* 358–374.

Johnson, S. P., Cohen, L. B., Marks, K. H., & Johnson, K. L. (2003). Young infants' perception of object unity in rotation displays. *Infancy, 4,* 285–295.

Johnson, S. P., Davidow, J., Hall-Hao, C., & Frank, M. C. (2008). Development of perceptual completion originates in information acquisition. *Developmental Psychology, 44,* 1214–1224.

Johnson, S. P., & Mason, U. (2002). Perception of kinetic illusory contours by two-month-old infants. *Child Development, 73,* 22–34.

Johnson, S. P., Slemmer, J. A., & Amso, D. (2004). Where infants look determines how they see: Eye movements and object perception performance in 3-month-olds. *Infancy, 6,* 185–201.

Jokisch, D., Daum, I., Suchan, B., & Troje, N. F. (2005). Structural encoding and recognition of biological motion: Evidence from event-related potentials and source analysis. *Behavioral Brain Research, 157,* 195–204.

Jones, E. J. H., Gliga, T., Bedford, R., Charman, T., & Johnson, M. H. (2014). Developmental pathways to autism: A review of prospective studies of infants at risk. *Neuroscience and Biobehavioral Reviews, 39,* 1–33.

Jones, L. A., & Lederman, S. J. (2006). *Human hand function.* New York, NY: Oxford University Press.

Jones, S. S., & Smith. L. B. (1993). The place of perception in children's concepts. *Cognitive Development, 8*, 113–139.

Jones, W., & Klin, A. (2013). Attention to eyes is present but in decline in 2-6-month-old infants later diagnosed with autism. *Nature, 504*, 427–431.

Jordan, K. E., & Brannon, E. M. (2006). A common representational system governed by Weber's law: Nonverbal numerical similarity judgments in 6-year-olds and rhesus macaques. *Journal of Experimental Child Psychology, 95*, 215–229.

Jouen, F., Lepecq, J., Gapenne, O., & Bertenthal, B. I. (2000). Optic flow sensitivity in neonates. *Infant Behavior and Development, 23*, 271–284.

Jovanovic, B., Duemmler, T., & Schwarzer, G. (2008). Infant development of configural object processing in visual and visual–haptic contexts. *Acta Psychologica, 129*, 376–386.

Julesz, B. (1971). *Foundations of cyclopean perception*. Chicago, IL: University of Chicago Press.

Jusczyk, P. W., & Aslin, R, A. (1995). Infants' detection of the sound patterns of words in fluent speech. *Cognitive Development, 29*, 1–23.

Jusczyk, P. W., Cutler, A., & Redanz, N. J. (1993). Infants' preference for the predominant stress patterns of English words. *Child Development, 64*, 675–687.

Jusczyk, P. W., Friederici, A. D., Wessels, J. M., Svenkerud, V. Y., & Jusczyk, A. M. (1993). Infants' sensitivity to the sound patterns of native language words. *Journal of Memory and Language, 32*, 402–420.

Just, M. A., Cherkassky, V. L, Keller, T. A., Kana, R. K., & Minshew, N. J. (2007). Functional and cortical underconnectivity in autism: Evidence from an fMRI study of an exective function task and corpus callosum morphometry. *Cerebral Cortex, 17*, 951–961.

Juurmaa, J., & Lehtinen-Railo, S. (1988). Cross-modal transfer of forms between vision and touch. *Scandinavian Journal of Psychology, 29*, 95–110.

Kaga, K., & Tanaka, Y. (1980). Auditory brainstem response and behavioral audiometry: Developmental correlates. *Archives of Otolaryngology, 106*, 564–566.

Kahrs, B. A., Jung, W. P., & Lockman, J. J. (2012). What is the role of infant banging in the development of tool use? *Experimental Brain Research, 218*, 315–320.

Kahrs, B. A., Jung, W. P., & Lockman, J. J. (2013). Motor origins of tool use. *Child Development, 84*, 810–816.

Kahrs, B. A., & Lockman, J. J. (2014). Building tool use from object manipulation: A perception–action perspective. *Ecological Psychology, 26*, 88–97.

Kaiser, M. D., & Shiffrar, M. (2009). The visual perception of motion by observers with autism spectrum disorders: A review and synthesis. *Psychonomic Bulletin & Review, 16*, 761–777.

Kajiura, H., Cowart, B. J., & Beauchamp, G. K. (1992). Early developmental change in bitter taste responses in human infants. *Developmental Psychobiology, 25*, 375–386.

Kalar, D. J., Garrigan, P., Wickens, T. D., Hilger, J. D., & Kellman, P. J. (2010). A unified model of illusory and occluded contour interpolation. *Vision Research, 50*, 284–299.

Kane, D., Guan, P., & Banks, M. S. (2014). The limits of human stereopsis in space and time. *Journal of Neuroscience, 34*, 1397–1408.

Kanizsa, G. (1979). *Organization in vision*. New York, NY: Praeger.

Kant, I. (1902). *Critique of pure reason* (F. Max Muller, Trans.; 2nd ed.). New York, NY: Macmillan. (Original work published 1781)

Kaplan, G. (1969). Kinetic disruption of optical texture: The perception of depth at an edge. *Perception & Psychophysics, 6*, 193–198.

Karasik, L. B., Tamis-LeMonda, C. S., & Adolph, K. E. (2014). Crawling and walking infants elicit different verbal responses from mothers. *Developmental Science, 17,* 388–395.

Karmel, B. Z. (1974). Contour effects and pattern preferences in infants: A reply to Greenberg and O'Donnell (1972). *Child Development, 45,* 196–199.

Karuza, E. A., Newport, E. L., Aslin, R. N., Sarling, S. J., Tivarus, M. E., & Bavelier, D. (2013). The neural correlates of statistical learning in a word segmentation task: An fMRI study. *Brain and Language, 127,* 46–54.

Karzon, R. G. (1985). Discrimination of polysyllabic sequences by one- to four-month-old infants. *Journal of Experimental Child Psychology, 39,* 326–342.

Kaufman, L. (1974). *Sight and mind.* New York, NY: Oxford University Press.

Kaufmann, F., Stucki, M., & Kaufmann-Hayoz, R. (1985). Development of infants' sensitivity for slow and rapid motions. *Infant Behavior and Development, 8,* 89–98.

Kaufmann-Hayoz, R., Kaufmann, F., & Stucki, M. (1986). Kinetic contours in infants' visual perception. *Child Development, 57,* 292–299.

Kavšek, M. J. (1999). Infants' responsiveness to line junctions in curved objects. *Journal of Experimental Child Psychology, 72,* 177–192.

Kavšek, M. J. (2002). The perception of static subjective contours in infancy. *Child Development, 73,* 331–344.

Kavšek, M. (2009). Infant perception of static two-dimensional transparency information. *European Journal of Developmental Psychology, 6,* 281–293.

Kavšek, M. J. (2013). Infants' responsiveness to rivalrous gratings. *Vision Research, 76,* 50–59.

Kavšek, M. J., & Granrud, C. E. (2013). The ground is dominant in infants' perception of relative distance. *Attention, Perception, and Psychophysics, 75,* 341–348.

Kavšek, M. J., Granrud, C. E., & Yonas, A. (2009). Infants' responsiveness to pictorial depth cues in preferential-reaching studies: A meta-analysis. *Infant Behavior and Development, 32,* 245–253.

Kavšek, M., & Yonas, A. (2006). The perception of moving subjective contours by 4-month-old infants. *Perception, 35,* 215–227.

Kavšek, M. J., Yonas, A., & Granrud, C. E. (2012). Infants' sensitivity to pictorial depth cues: A review and meta-analysis of looking studies. *Infant Behavior and Development, 35,* 109–128.

Kayed, N. S., Farstad, H., & van der Meer, A. L. H. (2008). Preterm infants' timing strategies to optical collisions. *Early Human Development, 84,* 381–388.

Kayed, N. S., & van der Meer, A. (2000). Time strategies used in defensive blinking to optical collisions in 5- to 7-month-old infants. *Infant Behavior and Development, 23,* 253–270.

Kayed, N. S., & van der Meer, A. L. H. (2007). Infants' timing strategies to optical collisions: A longitudinal study. *Infant Behavior and Development, 30,* 50–59.

Kayed, N. S., & van der Meer, A. L. H. (2009). A longitudinal study of prospective control in catching by full-term and preterm infants. *Experimental Brain Research, 194,* 245–258.

Keen, R. (2003). Representation of objects and events: Why do infants look so smart and toddlers look so dumb? *Current Directions in Psychological Science, 12,* 79–83.

Keen, R. (2011). The development of problem solving in young children: A critical cognitive skill. *Annual Review of Psychology, 62,* 1–21.

Kellman, P. J. (1984). Perception of three-dimensional form by human infants. *Perception & Psychophysics, 36,* 353–358.

Kellman, P. J. (1993). Kinematic foundations of infant visual perception. In C. Granrud (Ed.), *Visual perception and cognition* in *infancy. Carnegie Mellon symposia on cognition* (pp. 121–173). Hillsdale, NJ: Erlbaum.

Kellman, P. J. (1995). Ontogenesis of space and motion perception. In W. Epstein & S. Rogers (Eds.), *Handbook of perception and cognition* (Vol. 5, pp. 327–364). New York, NY: Academic Press.

Kellman, P. J. (1996). The origins of object perception. In R. Gelman & T. K. Au (Eds.), *Perceptual and cognitive development: Handbook of perception and cognition* (2nd ed.-). San Diego, CA: Academic Press.

Kellman, P. J., & Arterberry, M. E. (1998). *The cradle of knowledge: Development of perception in infancy.* Boston, MA: MIT Press.

Kellman, P. J., & Arterberry, M. E. (2006). Perceptual development. In W. Damon, D. Kuhn, & R. Siegler (Eds.), *The handbook of child psychology: Cognition, perception, and language* (6th ed., pp. 109–160). Hoboken, NJ: Wiley.

Kellman, P. J., Garrigan, P., & Shipley, T. F. (2005). Object interpolation in three dimensions. *Psychological Review, 112,* 586–609.

Kellman, P. J., Gleitman, H., & Spelke, E. S. (1987). Object and observer motion in the perception of objects by infants [Special issue]. *Journal of Experimental Psychology: Human Perception & Performance, 13,* 586–593.

Kellman, P. J., & Kaiser, M. K. (1994). Perceptual learning modules in flight training. *Proceedings of the 38th Annual Meeting of the Human Factors and Ergonomics Society, 38,* 1183–1187.

Kellman, P. J., & Massey, C. M. (2013). Perceptual learning, cognition, and expertise. In B. H. Ross (Ed.), *The psychology of learning and motivation* (Vol. 58, pp. 117–165). Amsterdam, The Netherlands: Elsevier.

Kellman, P. J., & Shipley, T. F. (1991). A theory of visual interpolation in object perception. *Cognitive Psychology, 23,* 141–221.

Kellman, P. J., & Shipley, T. F. (1992). Perceiving objects across gaps in space and time. *Current Directions in Psychological Science, 1,* 193–199.

Kellman, P. J., & Short, K. R. (1987). Development of three-dimensional form perception [Special issue]. *Journal of Experimental Psychology: Human Perception & Performance, 13,* 545–557.

Kellman, P. J., & Spelke, E. S. (1983). Perception of partly occluded object in infancy. *Cognitive Psychology, 15,* 483–524.

Kellman, P. J., Spelke, E. S., & Short, K. R. (1986). Infant perception of object unity from translatory motion in depth and vertical translation. *Child Development, 57,* 72–86.

Kellman, P. J., & von Hofsten, C. (1992). The world of the moving infant: Perception of motion, stability, and space. *Advances in Infancy Research, 7,* 147–184.

Kellman, P. J., Yin, C., & Shipley, T. F. (1998). A common mechanism for illusory and occluded object completion. *Journal of Experimental Psychology: Human Perception & Performance. 24,* 859–869.

Kelly, D. J., Liu, S., Lee, K., Quinn, P. C., Pascalis, O., Slater, A. M., & Ge, L. (2009). Development of other-race effect during infancy: Evidence toward universality? *Journal of Experimental Child Psychology, 104,* 105–114.

Kelly, D. J., Quinn, P. C., Slater, A. M., Lee, K., Ge, L., & Pascalis, O. (2007). The other-race effect develops during infancy. *Psychological Science, 18,* 1084–1089.

Kelly, D. J., Quinn, P. C., Slater, A. M., Lee, K., Gibson, A., Smith, M., . . . Pascalis, O. (2005). Three-month-olds, but not newborns, prefer own-race faces. *Developmental Science, 8,* 31–36.

Kemler Nelson, D. G., Hirsh-Pasek, K., Jusczyk, P. W., & Cassidy, K. W. (1989). How the prosodic cues in motherese might assist language learning. *Journal of Child Language, 16*, 55–68.

Kestenbaum, R., Termine, N., & Spelke, E. S. (1987). Perception of objects and object boundaries by 3-month-old infants. *British Journal of Developmental Psychology, 5*, 367–383.

Key, A. P. F., & Stone, W. L. (2012). Same but different: 9-month-old infants at average and high risk for autism look at the same facial features but process them using different brain mechanisms. *Autism Research, 5*, 253–266.

Kim, H. I., & Johnson, S. P. (2014). Detecting 'infant-directedness' in face and voice. *Developmental Science, 17*, 621–627.

Kim, G., & Kwak, K. (2011). Uncertainty matters: Impact of stimulus ambiguity on infant social referencing. *Infant and Child Development, 20*, 449–462.

Kim, I. K., & Spelke, E. S. (1992). Infants' sensitivity to effects of gravity on visible object motion. *Journal of Experimental Psychology: Human Perception & Performance, 18*, 385–393.

Kinzler, K D., Dupoux, E., & Spelke, E. S. (2007). The native language of social cognition. *Proceedings of the National Academy of Sciences of the USA, 104*, 12577–12580.

Kiorpes, L., Price, T., Hall-Haro, C., & Movshon, J. A. (2012). Development of sensitivity to global form and motion in macaque monkeys (*Macaca nemestrina*). *Vision Research, 63*, 34–42.

Kiorpes, L., Tang, C., Hawken, M. J., & Movshon, J. A. (2003). Ideal observer analysis of the development of spatial contrast sensitivity in macaque monkeys. *Journal of Vision, 3*, 630–641.

Kisilevsky, B. S., Hains, S. M. J., Brown, C. T. L., Cowperthwaite, B., Stutzman, S. S., & Wang, Z. (2009). Fetal sensitivity to properties of maternal speech and language. *Infant Behavior and Development, 32*, 59–71.

Kisilevsky, B. S., Hains, S. M. J., Lee, K., Xie, X., Huang, H., Ye, H. H., . . . Wang, Z. (2003). Effects of experience on fetal voice recognition. *Psychological Science, 14*, 220–224.

Kisilevsky, B. S., Stach, D. M., & Muir, D. W. (1991). Fetal and infant response to tactile stimulation. In M. J. S. Weiss & P. R. Zelazo (Eds.), *Newborn attention: Biological constrains and the influence of experience* (pp. 63–98). Norwood, NJ: Ablex.

Klatzky, R. L., & Lederman, S. J. (1993). Spatial and nonspatial avenues to object recognition by the human haptic system. In N. Elan, R. A. McCarthy, & B. Brewer (Eds.), *Spatial representation: Problems in philosophy and psychology* (pp. 191–205). Oxford, England: Blackwell.

Klatzky, R. L., & Lederman, S. J. (2013). Touch. In I. B. Weiner (Ed.), *Handbook of psychology* (Vol. 4, pp. 152–178). New York, NY: Wiley.

Klein, A. J. (1984). Frequency and age-dependent auditory evoked potential thresholds in infants. *Hearing Research, 16*, 291–297.

Kleiner, K. A. (1987). Amplitude and phase spectra as indices of infants' pattern preferences. *Infant Behavior and Development, 10*, 49–59.

Kleiner, K. A., & Banks, M. S. (1987). Stimulus energy does not account for 2-month-olds' face preferences. *Journal of Experimental Psychology: Human Perception & Performance, 13*, 594–600.

Knudsen, E. I. (1983). Early auditory experience aligns the auditory map of space in the optic tectum of the barn owl. *Science, 222*, 939–942.

Knudsen, E. I. (1985). Experience alters spatial tuning of auditory units in the optic tectum during a sensitive period in the barn owl. *Journal of Neuroscience, 5*, 3094–3109.

Knudsen, E. I. (2002). Instructed learning in the auditory localization of pathway of the barn owl. *Nature, 417,* 322–328.

Knudsen, E. I., & Knudsen, P. F. (1985). Vision guides the adjustment of auditory localization in young barn owls. *Science, 230,* 545–548.

Koffka, K. (1935). *Principles of Gestalt psychology.* New York, NY: Harcourt, Brace & World.

Kopp, F., & Dietrich, C. (2013). Neural dynamics of audiovisual synchrony and asynchrony perception in 6-month-old infants. *Frontiers in Psychology, 4,* ArtID 2.

Kostovic, I., & Goldman-Rakic, P. S. (1983). Transient cholinesterase staining in the mediadorsal nucleus of the thalamus and its connections in the developing human and monkey brain. *Journal of Comparative Neurology, 219,* 431–447.

Kovack-Lesh, K. A., Horst, J. S., & Oakes, L. M. (2008). The cat is out of the bag: The joint influence of previous experience and looking behavior on infant categorization. *Infancy, 13,* 285–307.

Kovack-Lesh, K. A., Oakes, L. M., & McMurray, B. (2012). Contributions of attentional style and previous experience to 4-month-old infants' categorization. *Infancy, 17,* 324–338.

Kraebel, K. S., & Gerhardstein, P. C. (2006). Three-month-old infatns' object recognition across changes in viewpoint using an operant learning procedure. *Infant Behavior and Development, 29,* 11–23.

Kretch, K. S., & Adolph, K. E. (2013). Cliff or step? Posture-specific learning at the edge of a drop-off. *Child Development, 84,* 226–240.

Kretch, K. S., Franchak, J. M., & Adolph, K. E. (2014). Crawling and walking infants see the world differently. *Child Development, 85,* 1503–1518.

Kuhl, P. K. (1979). Speech perception in early infancy: Perceptual constancy for spectrally dissimilar vowel categories. *Journal of the Acoustical Society of America, 66,* 1668–1679.

Kuhl, P. K., & Meltzoff, A. N. (1982). The bimodal perception of speech in infancy. *Science, 218,* 1138–1141.

Kuhl, P. K., & Meltzoff, A. N. (1984). The intermodal representation of speech in infants. *Infant Behavior and Development, 7,* 361–381.

Kuhl, P. K., & Meltzoff, A. N. (1988). Speech as an intermodal object of perception. In A. Yonas (Ed.), *Perceptual development* in *infancy. The Minnesota symposia on child psychology* (Vol. 20, pp. 235–266). Hillsdale, NJ: Erlbaum.

Kuhl, P. K., & Miller, J. D. (1975). Speech perception by the chinchilla: Voiced–voiceless distinction in alveolar plosive consonants. *Science, 190,* 69–72.

Kuhl, P. K., & Miller, J. D. (1982). Discrimination of auditory target dimensions in the presence or absence of variation in a second dimension by infants. *Perception & Psychophysics, 31,* 279–292.

Kuhl, P. K., Tsao, F.-M., & Liu, H.-M. (2003). Foreign-language experience in infancy: Effects of short-term exposure and social interaction on phonetic learning. *Proceedings of the National Academy of Sciences of the USA, 100,* 9096–9101.

Kuhl, P. K., Williams, K. A., Lacerda, F., Stevens, K. N., & Lindblom, B. (1992). Linguistic experience alters phonetic perception in infants by 6 months of age. *Science, 255,* 606–608.

Kushnerenko, E., Teinonen, T., Volein, A., & Csibra, G. (2008). Electrophysiological evidence of illusory audiovisual speech percept in human infants. *Proceedings of the National Academy of Sciences of the USA, 105,* 11442–11445.

Kuypers, H. G. J. M. (1962). Corticospinal connections: Postnatal development in rhesus monkey. *Science, 138,* 678–680.

Kuypers, H. G. J. M. (1973). The anatomical organization of the descending pathways and their contributions to motor control especially in primates. In J. E. Desmedt (Ed.), *New developments in electromyography and clinical neuropsychology* (Vol. 3, pp. 38–68). Basel, Switzerland: Karger.

LaGasse, L. L., VanVorst, R. F., Brunner, S. M., & Zucker, M. S. (1999). Infants' understanding of auditory events. *Infant and Child Development, 8*, 85–100.

Lago, P., Garetti, E., Merazzi, D., Pieragostini, L., Ancora, G., Pirelli, A., & Bellieni, C. V. (2009). Guidelines for procedural pain in the newborn. *Acta Paediatrica, 98*, 932–939.

Lambert-Brown, B. L., McDonald, N. M., Mattson, W. I., Martin, K. B., Ibanez, L. V., & Stone, W. L. (2014). Positive emotional engagement and autism risk. *Developmental Psychology, 51*, 848–855.

Landa, R. J., Gross, A. L., Stuart, E. A., & Bauman, M. (2012). Latent class analysis of early developmental trajectory in baby siblings of children with autism. *Journal of Child Psychology and Psychiatry, 53*, 986–996.

Langlois, J. H., & Roggman, L. A. (1990). Attractive faces are only average. *Psychological Science, 1*, 115–121.

Lasky, R. E., Syrdal-Lasky, A., & Klein, R. E. (1975). VOT discrimination by four- to six-and-a-half-month-old infants from Spanish environments. *Journal of Experimental Child Psychology, 20*, 215–225.

Lawrence, D. G., & Hopkins, D. A. (1972). Developmental aspects of pyramidal motor control in the rhesus monkey. *Brain Research, 40*, 117–118.

Lederman, S. J., & Klatzky, R. L. (1987). Hand movements: A window into haptic object recognition. *Cognitive Psychology, 19*, 342–368.

Lederman, S. J., & Klatzky, R. L. (1990). Haptic classification of common objects: Knowledge-driven exploration. *Cognitive Psychology, 22*, 421–459.

Lederman, S. J., & Klatsky, R. L. (2009). Haptic perception: A tutorial. *Attention, Perception, & Psychophysics, 71*, 1439–1459.

Lee, D. N. (1974). Visual information during locomotion. In R. B. MacLeod & H. Pick (Eds.), *Perception: Essays in honor of J. J. Gibson* (pp. 250–267). Ithaca, NY: Cornell University Press.

Lee, D. N. (1976). A theory of visual control of braking based on information about time-to-collision. *Perception, 5*, 437–459.

Lee, D. N., & Aronson. E. (1974). Visual proprioceptive control of standing in human infants. *Perception & Psychophysics, 15*, 529–532.

Lee, D. N., & Lishman, J. R. (1975). Visual proprioceptive control of stance. *Journal of Human Movement Studies, 1*, 87–95,

Lee, D. N., & Reddish, P. E. (1981). Plummeting gannets: A paradigm of ecological optics. *Nature, 293*, 293–294.

Lee, J., Birtles, D. B., Wattam-Bell, J., Atkinson, J., & Braddick, O. J. (2012). Orientation-reversal VEP: Comparison of phase and peak latencies in adults and infants. *Vision Research, 63*, 50–57.

Legerstee, M. (1990). Infants use multimodal information to imitate speech sounds. *Infant Behavior and Development, 13*, 343–354.

Legerstee, M. (1991a). The role of person and object in eliciting early imitation. *Journal of Experimental Child Psychology, 51*, 423–433.

Legerstee, M. (1991b). Changes in the quality of infant sounds as a function of social and nonsocial stimulation. *First Language, 11*, 327–343.

Legerstee, M., Corter, C., & Kienapple, K. (1990). Hand, arm and facial actions of young infants to a social and nonsocial stimulus. *Child Development, 61*, 774–784.

Legerstee, M., Pomerleau, A., Malcuit, G., & Feider, H. (1987). The development of infants' response to people and a doll: Implications for research in communication. *Infant Behavior and Development, 10,* 81–95.

Lemaitre, G., & Heller, L. M. (2013). Evidence for a basic level in a taxonomy of everyday action sounds. *Experimental Brain Research, 226,* 253–264.

Leo, I., & Simion, F. (2009). Face processing at birth: A Thatcher illusion study. *Developmental Science, 12,* 492–498.

Lesher, C. W., & Mingolla, E. (1993). The role of edges and line-ends in illusory contour formation. *Vision Research, 33,* 2253–2270.

Leslie, A. M. (1988). The necessity of illusion: Perception and thought in infancy. In L. Weiskrantz (Ed.), *Thought without language* (pp. 185–210). New York, NY: Oxford University Press.

Leslie, A. M. (1995). A theory of agency. In D. Sperber, D. Premack, & A. J. Premack (Eds.), *Causal cognition: A multidisciplinary debate. Symposia of the Fyssen Foundation* (pp. 121–149). New York, NY: Clarendon Press/Oxford University Press.

Leslie, A. M., & Keeble, S. (1987). Do six-month-old infants perceive causality? *Cognition, 25,* 265–288.

LeVay, S., Wiesel, T. N., & Hubel, D. H. (1980). The development of ocular dominance columns in normal and visually deprived monkeys. *Journal of Comparative Neurology, 191,* 1–51.

Lewkowicz, D. J. (1996). Perception of auditory–visual temporal synchrony in human infants. *Journal of Experimental Psychology: Human Perception and Performance, 22,* 1094–1106.

Lewkowicz, D. J. (2000). The development of intersensory temporal perception: An epigenetic systems/limitations view. *Psychological Bulletin, 126,* 281–308.

Lewkowicz, D. J. (2010). Infant perception of audio–visual speech synchrony. *Developmental Psychology, 46,* 66–77.

Lewkowicz, D. J., Leo, I., & Simion, F. (2010). Intersensory perception at birth: Newborns match nonhuman primate faces and voices. *Infancy, 15,* 46–60.

Liberman, A. M., Cooper, F. S., Shankweiler, D. P., & Studdert-Kennedy, M. (1967). Perception of the speech code. *Psychological Review, 74,* 431–461.

Libertus, K., & Needham, A. (2010). Teach to reach: The effects of active vs. passive reaching experiences on action and perception. *Vision Research, 50,* 2750–2757.

Libertus, K., & Needham, A. (2011). Reaching experience increases face preference in 3-month-old infants. *Developmental Science, 14,* 1355–1364.

Lipsitt, L., Engen, T., & Kaye, H. (1963). Developmental changes in the olfactory threshold of the neonate. *Child Development, 34,* 371–374.

Lipton, J. S., & Spelke, E. S. (2004). Discrimination of large and small numerosities by human infants. *Infancy, 5,* 271–290.

Liu, S., Xiao, W. S., Xiao, N., Quinn, P. C., Zhang, Y., Chen, H., . . . Lee, K. (2015). Development of visual preference for own- versus other-race faces in infancy. *Developmental Psychology, 51,* 500–511.

Lobo, M. A., Kokkoni, E., de Campos, A. C., & Galloway, J. C. (2014). Not just playing around: Infants' behaviors with objects reflect ability, constraints, and object properties. *Infant Behavior and Development, 37,* 334–351.

Locke, J. (1971). *Essay concerning the human understanding.* New York, NY: World Publishing. (Original work published 1690)

Lockman, J. J. (2000). A perception–action perspective on tool use development. *Child Development, 71,* 137–144.

Lockman, J. J., & Ashmead, D, H. (1983). Asynchronies in the development of manual behavior. *Advances in Infancy Research, 2,* 113–136.

Loomis, J. M., Da Silva, J. A., Philbeck, J. W., & Fukusima, S. S. (1996). Visual perception of location and distance. *Current Directions in Psychological Science, 5,* 72–77.

Lord, C., Risi, S., DiLavore, P. S., Shulman, C., Thurm, A., & Pickles, A. (2006). Autism from 2 to 9 years of age. *Archives of General Psychiatry, 63,* 694–701.

Lou, Y., Wu, X., Lui, S., & Li, K. (2011). Reactivation of visual cortical plasticity by NEP1-40 from early monocular deprivation in adult rats. *Neuroscience Letters, 494,* 196–201.

Luo, Y., & Johnson, S. C. (2009). Recognizing the role of perception in action at 6 months. *Developmental Science, 12,* 142–149.

Mace, W. M. (1974). Ecologically stimulating cognitive psychology: Gibsonian perspectives. In W. B. Weimer & D. S. Palermo (Eds.), *Cognition and the symbolic process* (pp. 137–164). Hillsdale, NJ: Erlbaum.

Macfarlane, A. (1975). Olfaction in the development of social preferences in the human neonate. *Ciba Foundation Symposium, 33,* 103–113.

Mach, E. (1959). *The analysis of sensations, and the relation of the physical to the psychical* (translated from the 1st German ed. by C. M. Williams; revised and supplemented from the 5th German ed. by S. Waterlow). New York, NY: Dover. (Original work published 1885)

Maestro, S., Muratori, F., Cavallaro, M. C., Pecini, C., Cesari, A., Paziente, A., . . . Palacio-Espasa, F. (2005). How young children treat objects and people: An empirical study of the first year of life in autism. *Child Psychiatry and Human Development, 35,* 383–396.

Maestro, S., Muratori, F., Cesari, A., Pecini, C., Apicella, F., & Stern, D. (2006). A view to regressive autism through home movies: Is early development really normal? *Acta Psychiatrica Scandinavica, 113,* 68–72.

Mandler, J. M. (1988). How to build a baby: On the development of an accessible representational system. *Cognitive Development, 3,* 113–136.

Mandler, J. M. (1992). How to build a baby: II. Conceptual primitives. *Psychological Review, 99,* 587–604.

Mandler, J. M. (2000). Perceptual and conceptual processes in infancy. *Journal of Cognition and Development, 1,* 3–36.

Mandler, J. M. (2007). On the origins of the conceptual system. *American Psychologist, 62,* 741–751.

Mandler, J. M. (2012). On the spatial foundations of the conceptual system and its enrichment. *Cognitive Science, 36,* 421–451.

Mandler, J. M., Fivush, R., & Reznick, J. S. (1987). The development of contextual categories. *Cognitive Development, 2,* 339–354.

Mandler, J. M., & McDonough, L. (1993). Concept formation in infancy. *Cognitive Development, 8,* 291–318,

Markson, L., & Spelke, E. S. (2006). Infants' rapid learning about self-propelled objects. *Infancy, 9,* 45–71.

Marr, D. (1982). *Vision.* San Francisco, CA: Freeman.

Marr, D., & Hildreth, E. (1980). Theory of edge detection. *Proceedings of the Royal Society of London, 201B,* 187–217.

Mascalzoni, E., Regolin, L., & Vallortigara, G. (2010). Innate sensitivity for self-propelled causal agency in newly hatched chicks. *Proceedings of the National Academy of Sciences of the USA, 107,* 4483–4485.

Mash, C., Arterberry, M. E., & Bornstein, M. H. (2007). Mechanisms of object recognition in 5-month-old infants. *Infancy, 12*, 31–43.

Mason, A. J. S., Braddick, O. J., & Wattam-Bell, J. (2003). Motion coherence thresholds in infants: Different tasks identify at least two distinct motion systems. *Vision Research, 43*, 1149–1157.

Massaro, D. W., Thompson, L. A., Barron, B., & Laren, E. (1986). Developmental changes in visual and auditory contributions to speech perception. *Journal of Experimental Child Psychology, 41*, 93–113.

Mattock, K., & Burnham, D. (2006). Chinese and English infants' tone perception: Evidence for perceptual reorganization. *Infancy, 10*, 241–265.

Maurer, D. (1975). Infant visual perception: Methods of study. In L. B. Cohen & P. Salapatek (Eds.), *Infant perception: From sensation to cognition—Basic visual processes* (Vol. 1, pp. 1–76). New York, NY: Academic Press.

Maurer, D. (1985). Infants' perception of facedness. In T. M. Field & N. A. Fox (Eds.), *Social perception in infants* (pp. 73–100). Norwood, NJ: Ablex.

Maurer, D. (1993). Neonatal synesthesia: Implications for the processing of speech and faces. In B. de Boysson-Bardies, S. de Schonen, P. W. Jusczyk, P. McNeilage, & J. Morton (Eds.), *Developmental neurocognition: Speech and face processing in the first year of life* (pp. 109–124). Dordrecht, The Netherlands: Kluwer.

Maurer, D., Ellemberg, D., & Lewis, T. L. (2006). Repeated measurements of contrast sensitivity reveal limits to visual plasticity after early binocular deprivation in humans. *Neuropsychologia, 44*, 2104–2112.

Maurer, D., & Lewis, T. L. (1993). Visual outcomes after infantile cataract. In K. Simons (Ed.), *Early visual development: Normal and abnormal* (pp. 454–484). New York, NY: Oxford.

Maurer, D., Lewis, T. L., Brent, H. P., & Levin, A. V. (1999). Rapid improvement in the acuity of infants after visual input. *Science, 286*, 108–110.

Maurer, D., Lewis, T. L., & Mondloch, C. J. (2005). Missing sights: Consequences for visual cognitive development. *Trends in Cognitive Sciences, 9*, 144–151.

Maurer, D., & Salapatek, P. (1976). Developmental changes in the scanning of faces. *Child Development, 47*, 523–527.

Maurer, D., & Werker, J. F. (2014). Perceptual narrowing during infancy: A comparison of language and faces. *Developmental Psychobiology, 56*, 154–178.

Maye, J., Werker, J. F., & Gerkin, L. A. (2002). Infant sensitivity to distributional information can affect phonetic discrimination. *Cognition, 82*, B101–B111.

McCarty, M. E., Clifton, R. K., & Collard, R. R. (1999). Problem solving in infancy: The emergence of an action plan. *Developmental Psychology, 35*, 1091–1101.

McCarty, M. E., Clifton, R. K., & Collard, R. R. (2001). The beginnings of tool use by infants and toddlers. *Infancy, 2*, 233–256.

McCrink, K., & Wynn, K. (2004). Large-number addition and subtraction by 9-month-old infants. *Psychological Science, 15*, 776–781.

McCurry, S., Wilcox, T., & Woods, R. (2009). Beyond the search barrier: A new task for assessing object individuation in young infants. *Infant Behavior and Development, 32*, 429–436.

McGurk, H., & MacDonald, J. (1976). Hearing lips and seeing voices. *Nature, 264*, 746–748.

McMurray, B., & Aslin, R. N. (2005). Infants are sensitive to within-category variation in speech perception. *Cognition, 95*, B15–B26.

Medin, D., & Barsalou, L, W. (1987). Categorization processes and categorical perception. In S. Harnad (Ed.), *Categorical perception: The groundwork of cognition* (pp. 455–490). New York, NY: Cambridge University Press.

Meltzoff, A. N. (1988a). Infant imitation and memory: Nine-month-olds in immediate and deferred tests. *Child Development, 56*, 62–72.

Meltzoff, A. N. (1988b). Infant imitation after a 1-week delay: Long-term memory for novel acts and multiple stimuli. *Developmental Psychology, 24*, 470–476.

Meltzoff, A. N. (1988c). Imitation of televised models by infants. *Child Development, 59*, 1221–1229.

Meltzoff, A. N. (1995). Understanding the intentions of others: Reenactment of intended acts by 18-month-old children. *Developmental Psychology, 31*, 838–850.

Meltzoff, A. N. (2007). The "like me" framework for recognizing and becoming an intentional agent. *Acta Psychologica, 124*, 26–43.

Meltzoff, A. N. (2011). Social cognition and the origins of imitation, empathy, and theory of mind. In U. Goswami (Ed.), *The Wiley-Blackwell handbook of childhood cognitive development* (2nd ed., pp. 49–75). New York, NY: Wiley-Blackwell.

Meltzoff, A. N., & Borton, R. W. (1979). Intermodal matching by human neonates. *Nature, 282*, 403–404.

Meltzoff, A. N., Brooks, R., Shon, A. P., & Rao, R. P. N. (2010). "Social" robots are psychological agents for infants: A test of gaze following. *Neural Networks, 23*, 966–972.

Meltzoff, A. N., & Moore, M. K. (1977). Imitation of facial and manual gestures by human neonates. *Science, 198*, 75–78.

Meltzoff, A. N., & Moore, M. K. (1983). Newborn infants imitate adult facial gestures. *Child Development, 54*, 702–709.

Meltzoff, A. N., & Moore, M. K. (1994). Imitation, memory, and the representation of persons. *Infant Behavior and Development, 17*, 83–89.

Meltzoff, A. N., & Moore, K. (1997). Explaining facial imitation: A theoretical model. *Early Development and Parenting, 6*, 179–192.

Mendelson, M. J., & Haith, M. M. (1976). The relation between audition and vision in the human newborn. *Monographs of the Society for Research in Child Development, 47*, 72.

Meredith, M. A., & Stein, B. E. (1986). Visual, auditory, and somatosensory convergence on cells in superior colliculus results in multisensory integration. *Journal of Neurophysiology, 56*, 640–662.

Michotte, A. (1963). *The perception of causality.* New York, NY: Basic Books.

Michotte, A., Thines, G., & Crabbe, G. (1964). *Les complements amodaux des structures perceptives: Studia psycologica.* Louvain: Publications Universitataires de Louvain.

Mikami, A., Newsome, W. T., & Wurtz, R. H. (1986). Motion selectivity in macaque visual cortex: II. Spatiotemporal range of directional interactions in MT and V1. *Journal of Neurophysiology, 55*, 1328–1339.

Milewski, A. E. (1976). Infants' discrimination of internal and external pattern elements. *Journal of Experimental Child Psychology, 22*, 229–246.

Milewski, A. E. (1978). Young infants' visual processing of internal and adjacent shapes. *Infant Behavior and Development, 1*, 359–371.

Mill, J. S. (1965). Examination of Sir William Hamilton's philosophy. In R. Herrnstein & E. G. Boring (Eds.), *A source book in the history of psychology* (pp. 182–188). Cambridge, MA: Harvard University Press. (Original work published 1865)

Millenson, J. R. (1967). *Principles of behavioral analysis.* New York, NY: Macmillan.

Mills, A. (1958). On the minimum audible angle. *Journal of the Acoustical Society of America, 30*, 103–108.

Mills, M., & Melhuish, E. (1974). Recognition of mother's voice in early infancy. *Nature, 252*, 123–124.

Milner, A. D., & Goodale, M. A. (2008). Two visual systems re-viewed. *Neuropsychologia, 46*, 774–785.

Molina, M., & Jouen, F. (1998). Modulation of the palmar grasp behavior in neonates according to texture property. *Infant Behavior and Development, 21,* 659–667.

Molina, M., & Jouen, F. (2004). Manual cyclical activity as an exploratory tool in neonates. *Infant Behavior and Development, 27,* 42–53.

Molina, M., van de Walle, G. A., Condry, K., & Spelke, E. S. (2004). The animate–inanimate distinction in infancy: Developing sensitivity to constraints on human actions. *Journal of Cognition and Development, 5,* 399–426.

Møller, A. R. (2012). *Sensory systems: Anatomy and physiology.* Createspace Independent Publishing Platform.

Möller, E. L., Majdandzic, M., & Bogels, S. M. (2014). Fathers' versus mothers' social referencing signals in relation to infant anxiety and avoidance: A visual cliff experiment. *Developmental Science, 17,* 1012–1028.

Mondloch, C. J., Lewis, T. L., Budreau, D. R., Maurer, D., Dannemiller, J. L., Stephens, B. R., & Kleiner-Gathercoal, K. A. (1999). Face perception during early infancy. *Psychological Science, 10,* 419–422.

Mondloch, C. J., Lewis, T. L., & Maurer, D. (2013). Infant face preferences after binocular visual deprivation. *International Journal of Behavioral Development, 37,* 148–153.

Mondloch, C. J., Robbins, R., & Maurer, D. (2010). Discrimination of facial features by adults, 10-year-olds, and cataract-reversal patients. *Perception, 39,* 184–194.

Mondloch, C. J., Segalowitz, S. J., Lewis, T. L., Dywan, J., Le Grand, R., & Maurer, D. (2013). The effect of early visual deprivation on the development of face detection. *Developmental Science, 16,* 728–742.

Moore, B. C. J. (1982). *An introduction to the psychology of hearing.* London, England: Academic Press.

Moore, C., & D'Entremont, B. (2001). Developmental changes in pointing as a function of attentional focus. *Journal of Cognition and Development, 2,* 109–129.

Moore, D. G., Goodwin, J. E., George, R., Axelsson, E. L., & Braddick, F. M. B. (2007). Infants perceive human point-light displays as solid forms. *Cognition, 104,* 377–396.

Morange-Majoux, F. (2011). Manual exploration of consistency (soft vs. hard) and handedness in infants from 4 to 6 months old. *Laterality: Asymmetries of Body, Brain and Cognition, 16,* 292–312.

Morgante, J. D., & Keen, R. (2008). Vision and action: The effect of visual feedback on infants' exploratory behaviors. *Infant Behavior and Development, 31,* 729–733.

Morrongiello, B. A. (1988). Infant's localization of sounds along the horizontal axis: Estimates of minimum audible angle. *Developmental Psychology, 24,* 8–13.

Morrongiello, B. A. (1994). Effects of colocation on auditory–visual interactions and cross-modal perception in infants. In D. J. Lewkowicz & R. Lickliter (Eds.), *The development of intersensory perception: Comparative perspectives* (pp. 235–263). Hillsdale, NJ: Erlbaum.

Morrongiello, B. A., Fenwick, K. D., & Chance, G. (1998). Crossmodal learning in newborn infants: Inferences about properties of auditory–visual events. *Infant Behavior and Development, 21,* 543–554.

Morrongiello, B. A., Fenwick, K. D., Hillier, L., & Chance, G. (1994). Sound localization in newborn human infants. *Developmental Psychobiology, 27,* 519–538.

Morrongiello, B. A., & Trehub, S. E. (1987). Age-related changes in auditory temporal perception. *Journal of Experimental Child Psychology, 44,* 413–426.

Morton, J., & Johnson, M. H. (1991). CONSPEC and CONLERN: A two-process theory of infant face recognition. *Psychological Review, 98,* 164–181.

Mou, Y., & vanMarle, K. (2014). Two core systems of numerical representation in infants. *Developmental Review, 34,* 1–25.

Muir, D., & Field, J. (1979). Newborn infants orient to sounds. *Child Development, 50,* 431–436.

Muir, D. W., Clifton, R. K., & Clarkson, M. G. (1989). The development of a human auditory localization response: A U-shaped function [Special issue]. *Canadian Journal of Psychology, 43,* 199–216.

Müller, J. (1965). *Handbuch der Physiologie des Menschen,* bk. V, Coblenz. Translated by William Baly as *Elements of Physiology,* Vol. 2 (London, 1842). In R. Herrnstein & E. G. Boring (Eds.), *A sourcebook in the history of psychology* (pp. 26–33). Cambridge, MA: Harvard University Press. (Original work published 1838)

Mumme, D. L., & Fernald, A. (2003). The infant as onlooker: Learning from emotional reactions observed in a televised scenario. *Child Development, 74,* 221–237.

Munakata, Y., & Stedron, J. M. (2002). Memory for hidden objects in early infancy: Behavior, theory, and neural network simulation. In J. W. Fagen & H. Hayne (Eds.), *Progress in infancy research* (Vol. 2, pp. 25–69). Mahwah, NJ: Erlbaum.

Nadig, A. S., Ozonoff, S., Young, G. S., Rozga, A., Sigman, M., & Rogers, S. J. (2007). A prospective study of response to name in infants at risk for autism. *Archives of Pediatric and Adolescent Medicine, 161,* 378–383.

Nagy, E., Pal, A., & Orvos, H. (2014). Learning to imitate individual finger movements by the human neonate. *Developmental Science, 17,* 841–857.

Nagy, E., Pilling, K., Orvos, H., & Molnar, P. (2013). Imitation of tongue protrusion in human neonates: Specificity of the response in a large sample. *Developmental Psychology, 49,* 1628–1638.

Nakayama, K., & Shimojo, S. (1992). Experiencing and perceiving visual surfaces. *Science, 257,* 1357–1363.

Nanez, J., & Yonas, A. (1994). Effects of luminance and texture motion on infant defensive reactions to optical collision. *Infant Behavior and Development, 17,* 165–174.

Naoi, N., Minagawa-Kawai, Y., Kobayashi, A., Takeuchi, K., Nakamura, K., Yamamato, J., & Kojima, S. (2012). Cerebral responses to infant-directed speech and the effect of talker familiarity. *Neuroimage, 59,* 1735–1744.

Narayan, C. R., Werker, J. F., & Beddor, S. (2010). The interaction between acoustic salience and language experience in developmental speech perception: Evidence from nasal place discrimination. *Developmental Science, 13,* 407–420.

Nawrot, E., Mayo, S. L., & Nawrot, M. (2009). The development of depth perception from motion parallax in infancy. *Attention, Perception, & Psychophysics, 71,* 194–199.

Nawrot, E., & Nawrot, M. (2013). The role of eye movements in depth from motion parallax during infancy. *Journal of Vision, 13,* 1–13.

Nazzi, T., Dilley, L. C., Jusczyk, A. M., Shattuck-Hufnagel, S., & Jusczyk, P. W. (2005). English-learning infants' segmentation of verbs from fluent speech. *Language and Speech, 28,* 279–298.

Needham, A. (1999). The role of shape in 4-month-old infants' object segregation. *Infant Behavior and Development, 22,* 161–178.

Needham, A., & Baillargeon, R. (1993). Intuitions about support in four-and-a-half-month-old infants. *Cognition, 47,* 121–148.

Needham, A., Barrett, T., & Peterman, K. (2002). A pick-me up for infants' exploratory skills: Early simulated experiences reaching for objects using "sticky mittens" enhances young infants' exploration skills. *Infant Behavior and Development, 25,* 279–295.

Neil, P. A., Chee-Ruiter, C., Scheier, C., Lewkowicz, D. J., & Shimojo, S. (2006). Development of multisensory spatial integration and perception in humans. *Developmental Science, 9,* 454–464.

Neisser, U. (1964). Visual search. *Scientific American, 210*, 94–102.

Neisser, U., & Becklen, R. (1975). Selective looking: Attending to visually specified events. *Cognitive Psychology, 7*, 480–494.

Nelson, C. A. (2001). The development and neural bases of face recognition. *Infant and Child Development, 10*, 3–18.

Neuhoff, J. G. (2001). An adaptive bias in the perception of looming auditory motion. *Ecological Psychology, 13*, 87–110.

Nichols, S. R., Svetlova, M., & Brownell, C. A. (2010). Toddlers' understanding of peers' emotions. *Journal of Genetic Psychology: Research and Theory on Human Development, 171*, 35–53.

Norcia, A. M., & Tyler, C. W. (1985). Spatial frequency sweep VEP: Visual acuity during the first year of life. *Vision Research, 30*, 1475–1486.

Nystrom, M., Hansson, M. B., & Marklund, K. (1975). Infant preference for intermittent light. *Psychological Research Bulletin, 15*, 1–11.

Oakes, L. M. (1994). Development of infants' use of continuity cues in their perception of causality. *Developmental Psychology, 30*, 869–879.

Oakes, L. M., & Cohen, L. B. (1990). Infant perception of a causal event. *Cognitive Development, 5*, 193–207.

Oakes, L. M., & Kannass, L. M. (1999). That's the way the ball bounces: Infants' and adults' perception of spatial and temporal contiguity in collisions involving bouncing balls. *Developmental Science, 2*, 86–101.

Oh, J. S., Jun, S. A., Knightly, L. M., & Au, T. K. (2003). Holding on to childhood language memory. *Cognition, 86*, B53–B64.

Okado, N., (1981). Onset of synapse formation in the human spinal cord. *Journal of Comparative Neurology, 201*, 211–219.

Olsho, L. W., Koch, E. G., Halpin, C. F., & Carter, E. A. (1987). An observer-based psychoacoustic procedure for use with young infants. *Developmental Psychology, 23*, 627–640.

Olsho, L. W., Schoon, C., Sakai, R., Turpin, R., & Sperduto, V. (1982a). Auditory frequency discrimination in infancy. *Developmental Psychology, 18*, 721–726.

Olsho, L. W., Schoon, C., Sakai, R., Turpin, R., & Sperduto, V. (1982b). Preliminary data on frequency discrimination in infancy. *Journal of the Acoustical Society of America, 72*, 1788–1803.

Olson, G. M., & Sherman, T. (1983). Attention, learning, and memory in infants. In M. M. Haith & J. J. Campos (Eds.), *Handbook of child psychology* (Vol. 2, pp. 1001–1080). New York, NY: Wiley.

Olzak, L. A., & Thomas, J. P. (1991). When orthogonal orientations are not processed independently. *Vision Research, 31*, 51–57.

Oostenbroek, J., Slaughter, V., Nielsen, M., & Suddendorf, T. (2013). Why the confusion around neonatal imitation? A review. *Journal of Reproductive and Infant Psychology, 31*, 328–341.

Oster, H. (2005). The repertoire of infant facial expressions: An ontogenetic perspective. In J. Nadel & D. Muir (Eds.), *Emotional development: Recent research advances* (pp. 261–292). New York, NY: Oxford University Press.

Otsuka, Y., Kanazawa, S., & Yamaguchi, M. (2004). The effect of support ratio on infants' perception of illusory contours. *Perception, 33*, 807–816.

Otsuka, Y., & Yamaguchi, M. K. (2003). Infants' perception of illusory contours in static and moving figures. *Journal of Experimental Child Psychology, 86*, 244–251.

Owsley, C. (1983). The role of motion in infants' perception of solid shape. *Perception, 12*, 707–717.

Ozonoff, S., Macari, S., Young, G. S., Goldring, S., Thompson, M., & Rogers, S. J. (2008). Atypical object exploration at 12 months of age is associated with autism in a prospective sample. *Autism, 12,* 457–472.

Ozturk, O., Shayan, S., Liszkowski, U., & Majid, A. (2013). Language is not necessary for color categories. *Developmental Science, 16,* 111–115.

Palmer, C. F. (1989). The discriminating nature of infants' exploratory actions. *Developmental Psychology, 25,* 885–893.

Palmer, S. B., Fais, L., Golinkoff, R. M., & Werker, J. F. (2012). Perceptual narrowing of linguistic sign occurs in the 1st year of life. *Child Development, 83,* 543–553.

Papoušek, M., Papoušek, H., & Symmes, D. (1991). The meanings of melodies in motherese in tone and stress languages. *Infant Behavior and Development, 14,* 415–440.

Pascalis, O., de Haan, M., & Nelson, C. A. (2002). Is face processing species-specific during the first year of life? *Science, 296,* 1321–1323.

Pascalis, O., de Schonen, S., Morton, J., Deruelle, C., & Fabre-Grenet, M. (1995). Mother's face recognition by neonates: A replication and an extension. *Infant Behavior and Development, 18,* 79–85.

Pascalis, O., Scott, L. S., Kelly, D. J., Shannon, R. W., Nicholson, E., Coleman, M., & Nelson, C. A. (2005). Plasticity of face processing in infancy. *Proceedings of the National Academy of Sciences of the USA, 102,* 5297–5300.

Patterson, M. L., & Werker, J. F. (2003). Matching phonetic information in lips and voice is robust in 4.5-month-old infants. *Infant Behavior and Development, 22,* 237–247.

Pauen, S., & Trauble, B. (2009). How 7-month-olds interpret ambiguous motion events: Category-based reasoning in infancy. *Cognitive Psychology, 59,* 275–295.

Paukner, A., Simpson, E., Ferrari, P. F., Mrozek, T., & Suomi, S. (2014). Neonatal imitation predicts how infants engage with faces. *Developmental Science, 17,* 833–840.

Paulus, M. (2014). How and why do infants imitate? An ideomotor approach to social and imitative learning in infancy (and beyond). *Psychonomics Bulletin and Review, 21,* 1139–1156.

Peeples, D. R., & Teller, D. Y. (1975). Color vision and brightness discrimination in two-month-old human infants. *Science, 189,* 1102–1103.

Pegg, J. E., Werker, J. F., & McLeod, P. J. (1992). Preference for infant-directed over adult-directed speech: Evidence from 7-week-old infants. *Infant Behavior and Development, 15,* 325–345.

Pei, F., Pettet, M. W., & Norcia, A. M., (2007). Sensitivity and configuration-specificity of orientation-defined processing in infants and adults. *Vision Research, 47,* 338–348.

Perone, S., Madole, K. L., Ross-Sheehy, S., Carey, M., & Oakes, L. M. (2008). The relation between infants' activity with objects and attention to object appearance. *Developmental Psychology, 44,* 1242–1248.

Perris, E. E., & Clifton, R. K. (1988). Reaching in the dark toward sound as a measure of auditory localization in infants. *Infant Behavior and Development, 11,* 473–491.

Piaget, J. (1952). *The origins of intelligence in children.* New York, NY: International Universities Press.

Piaget, J. (1954). *The construction of reality in the child.* New York, NY: Basic Books.

Piaget, J. (1969). *Perceptual activities and secondary illusions: The mechanisms of perception.* New York, NY: Basic Books.

Piaget, J. (1976). *The psychology of intelligence* (M. Piercy & D. E. Berlynel, Trans.). Totowa, NJ: Littlefield, Adams.

Piaget, J. (1981). *Intelligence and affectivity: Their relationship during child development.* Palo Alto, CA: Annual Reviews.

Gibson, E. J., & Pick, A. D. (2000). *An ecological approach to perceptual learning and development*. New York, NY: Oxford University Press.

Pickens, J. (1994). Perception of auditory–visual distance relations by 5-month-old infants. *Developmental Psychology, 30*, 537–544.

Pirchio, M., Spinelli, D., Fiorentini, A., & Maffei, L. (1987). Infant contrast sensitivity evaluated by evoked potentials. *Brain Research, 141*, 179–184.

Polat, U., & Sagi, D. (1993). Lateral interactions between spatial channels: Suppression and facilitation revealed by lateral masking experiments. *Vision Research, 33*, 993–999.

Polka, L., & Werker, J. F. (1994). Developmental changes in perception of nonnative vowel contrasts. *Journal of Experimental Psychology: Human Perception & Performance, 20*, 421–435.

Porter, R. H., Makin, M. W., Davis, L. B., & Christensen, K. M. (1991). An assessment of the salient olfactory environment of formula-fed infants. *Physiology and Behavior, 50*, 907–911.

Porter, R. H., & Winberg, J. (1999). Unique salience of maternal breast odors for newborn infants. *Neuroscience and Biobehavioral Reviews, 23*, 439–449.

Poulin-Dubois, D., Brooker, I., & Polonia, A. (2011). Infants prefer to imitate a reliable person. *Infant Behavior and Development, 34*, 303–309.

Poulin-Dubois, D., LePage, A., & Ferland, D. (1996). Infants' concept of animacy. *Cognitive Development, 11*, 19–36.

Powell, L. J., & Spelke, E. S. (2013). Preverbal infants expect members of social groups to act alike. *Proceedings of the National Academy of Sciences of the USA, 110*, E3965–E3972.

Predebon, J., & Woolley, J. S. (1994). The familiar-size cue to depth under reduced-cue viewing conditions. *Perception, 23*, 1301–1312.

Premack, D., & Woodruff, G. (1978). Does the chimpanzee have a theory of mind? *Behavioral and Brain Sciences, 1*, 515–526.

Provine, R. R., & Westerman, J. A. (1979). Crossing the midline: Limits of early eye–hand behavior. *Child Development, 50*, 437–441.

Purpura, D. P. (1975). Dendritic differentiation in human cerebral cortex: Normal and aberrant developmental patterns. *Advances in Neurology, 12*, 91–116.

Putnam, H. (1975). *Mind, language, and reality: Philosophical papers* (Vol. 2). London, England: Cambridge University Press.

Pylyshyn, Z. (1973). What the mind's eye tells the mind's brain: A critique of mental imagery. *Psychological Bulletin, 80*, 1–24.

Querleu, D., Renard, X., Versyp, F., Paris-Delrue, L., & Crepin, G. (1988). Fetal hearing. *European Journal of Obstetrics, Gynecology, and Reproductive Biology, 28*, 191–212.

Quinn, P. C. (1994). The categorization of above and below spatial relations by young infants. *Child Development, 65*, 58–69.

Quinn, P. C. (2004). Development of subordinate-level categorization in 3- to 7-month-old infants. *Child Development, 75*, 886–899.

Quinn, P. C. (2011). Born to categorize. In U. Goswami (Ed.), *The Wiley-Blackwell handbook of childhood cognitive development* (2nd ed., pp. 129–152). Malden, MA: Wiley-Blackwell.

Quinn, P. C., Adams, A., Kennedy, E., Shettler, L., & Wasnik, A. (2003). Development of an abstract category representation for the spatial relation between in 6- to 10-month-old infants. *Developmental Psychology, 39*, 151–163.

Quinn, P. C., Doran, M. M., Reiss, J., & Hoffman, J. E. (2010). Neural markers of subordinate-level categorization in 6- to 7-month-old infants. *Developmental Science, 13*, 499–507.

Quinn, P. C., & Eimas, P. D. (1996). Perceptual organization and categorization in young infants. *Advances in Infancy Research, 10,* 1–36.

Quinn, P. C., Kelly, D. J., Lee, K., Pascalis, O., & Slater, A. M. (2008). Preference for attractive faces in human infants extends beyond conspecifics. *Developmental Science, 11,* 76–83.

Quinn, P. C., Lee, K., Pascalis, O., & Tanaka, J. W. (2015). Narrowing in categorical responding to other-race face classes by infants. *Developmental Science.*

Quinn, P. C., & Tanaka, J. W. (2007). Early development of perceptual expertise: Within-basic-level categorization facilitates the formation of subordinate-level category representations in 6- to 7-month-old infants. *Memory & Cognition, 35,* 1422–1431.

Quinn, P. C., Yahr, J., Kuhn, A., Slater, A. M., & Pascalis, O. (2002). Representation of the gender of human faces by infants: A preference for female. *Perception, 31,* 1109–1121.

Rakison, D. H., & Krogh, L. (2012). Does causal action facilitate causal perception in infants younger than 6 months of age? *Developmental Science, 15,* 43–53.

Rakison, D. H., & Poulin-Dubois, D. (2001). Developmental origin of the animate–inanimate distinction. *Psychological Bulletin, 127,* 209–228.

Ramachandran, V. S., Clarke, P. G., & Whitteridge, D. (1977). Cells selective to binocular disparity in the cortex of newborn lambs. *Nature, 268,* 333–335.

Ramirez-Esparza, N., Garcia-Sierra, A., & Kuhl, P. K. (2014). Looks who's talking: Speech style and social context in language input to infants are linked to concurrent and future speech development. *Developmental Science, 17,* 880–891.

Rasengane, T. A., Allen, D., & Manny, R. E. (1997). Development of temporal contrast sensitivity in human infants. *Vision Research, 37,* 1747–1754.

Ratoosh, P. (1949). On interposition as a cue for the perception of distance. *Proceedings of the National Academy of Sciences of the USA, 35,* 257–259.

Rattanasone, N. X., Burnham, D., & Reilly, R. G. (2013). Tone and vowel enhancement in Cantonese infant-directed speech at 3, 6, 9, and 12 months of age. *Journal of Phonetics, 41,* 332–343.

Ray, E., & Heyes, C. (2011). Imitation in infancy: The wealth of the stimulus. *Developmental Science, 14,* 92–105.

Regal, D. M. (1981). Development of critical flicker frequency in human infants. *Vision Research, 21,* 549–555.

Regolin, L., & Vallortigara, G. (1995). Perception of partly occluded objects by young chicks. *Perception & Psychophysics, 57,* 971–976.

Reid, T. (1969). *Essays on the intellectual powers of man.* Cambridge, MA: MIT Press. (Original work published 1785)

Reynolds, G., Bahrick, L. E., Lickliter, R., & Guy, M. W. (2014). Neural correlates of intersensory processing in 5-month-old infants. *Developmental Psychobiology, 56,* 355–372.

Riesen, A. H. (1947). The development of visual perception in man and chimpanzee. *Science, 106,* 107–108.

Rigatto, S., Menon, E., Johnson, M. H., & Farroni, T. (2011). Direct gaze may modulate face recognition in newborns. *Infant and Child Development, 20,* 20–34.

Ringach, D. L., & Shapley, R. (1996). Spatial and temporal properties of illusory contours and amodal boundary completion. *Vision Research, 36,* 3037–3050.

Rivera-Gaxiola. M., Silva-Pereya, J., Klarman, L., Garcia-Sierra, A., Lara-Ayala, L., Cardena-Salazar, C., & Kuhl, P. (2007). Principle component analysis and scalp distribution of the auditory P150–250 and N250–550 to speech contrasts in Mexican and American Infants. *Developmental Neuropsychology, 31,* 363–378.

Rivera-Gaxiola, M., Silva-Pereyra, J., & Kuhl, P. (2005). Brain potentials to native and non-native speech contrasts in 7- and 11-month-old American infants. *Developmental Science, 8,* 162–172.

Robbins, R. A., Mishimura, M., Mondloch, C. J., Lewis, T. L., & Maurer, D. (2010). Deficits in sensitivity to spacing after early visual deprivation in humans: A comparison of human faces, monkey faces, and houses. *Developmental Psychobiology, 52,* 775–781.

Robin, D. J., Berthier, N. E., & Clifton, R. K. (1996). Infants' predictive reaching for moving objects in the dark. *Developmental Psychology, 22,* 824–835.

Rochat, P. (1987). Mouthing and grasping in neonates: Evidence for the early detection of what hard or soft substances afford for action. *Infant Behavior and Development, 25,* 871–884.

Rochat, P. (1989). Object manipulation and exploration in 2- to 5-month-old infants. *Developmental Psychology, 25,* 871–884.

Rochat, P., Morgan, R., & Carpenter, M. (1997). Young infants' sensitivity to movement information specifying social causality. *Cognitive Development, 12,* 537–561.

Rochat, P., Striano, T., & Morgan, R. (2004). Who is doing what to whom? Young infants' developing sense of social causality in animated displays. *Perception, 33,* 355–369.

Rock, I. (1983). *The logic of perception.* Cambridge, MA: MIT Press.

Rock, I., & Anson, R. (1979). Illusory contours as the solution to a problem. *Perception, 8,* 665–681.

Rock, I., & Harris, C. S. (1967). Vision and touch. *Scientific American, 216,* 96–104.

Rogers, B., & Graham, M. (1979). Motion parallax as an independent cue for depth perception. *Perception, 8,* 125–134.

Rosander, K., Nystrom, P., Gredeback, G., & von Hofsten, C. (2007). Cortical processing of visual motion in young infants. *Vision Research, 47,* 1614–1623.

Rose, S. A., Gottfried, A. W., & Bridger, W. H. (1981a). Cross-modal transfer and information processing by the sense of touch in infancy. *Developmental Psychology, 17,* 90–98.

Rose, S. A., Gottfried, A. W., & Bridger, W. H. (1981b). Cross-modal transfer and six-month-old infants. *Developmental Psychology, 17,* 661–669.

Rosenblum, L. D., Schmuckler, M. A., & Johnson, J. A. (1997). The McGurk effect in infants. *Perception & Psychophysics, 59,* 347–357.

Rosenblum, L. D., Wuestefeld, A. P., & Anderson, K. L. (1996). Auditory reachability: An affordance approach to the perception of sound source distance. *Ecological Psychology, 8,* 1–24.

Rosengren, K. S., Gutierrez, I. T., Anderson, K. N., & Schein, S. S. (2009). Children's scale errors in everyday life. *Child Development, 80,* 1586–1591.

Rosenstein, D., & Oster, H. (1988). Differential facial responses to four basic tastes in newborns. *Child Development, 59,* 1136–1143.

Rossi-Arnaud, C., Pieroni, L., Spataro, P., & Baddeley, A. (2012). Working memory and individual differences in the encoding of vertical, horizontal, and diagonal symmetry. *Acta Psychologica, 141,* 122–132.

Royden, C. S., Crowell, J. A., & Banks, M. S. (1994). Estimating heading during eye movements. *Vision Research, 34,* 3197–3214.

Royer, F. L. (1981). Detection of symmetry. *Journal of Experimental Psychology: Human Perception & Performance, 7,* 1186–1210.

Rozga, A., Hutman, T., Young, G. S., Rogers, S. J., Ozonoff, S., Dapretto, M., & Sigman, M. (2011). Behavioral profiles of affected and unaffected siblings of children with autism: Contribution of measures of mother–infant interaction and nonverbal communication. *Journal of Autism and Developmental Disorders, 41*, 287–301.

Rubin, E. (1915). *Synoplevede Figurer.* Copenhagen, Denmark: Gyldendalske.

Ruff, H. A. (1978). Infant recognition of the invariant form of objects. *Child Development, 49*, 293–306.

Ruff, H. A. (1984). Infants' manipulative exploration of objects: Effects of age and object characteristics. *Developmental Psychology, 20*, 9–20.

Ruff, H. A., & Kohler, C. J. (1978). Tactual-visual transfer in six-month-old infants. *Infant Behavior and Development, 1*, 259–264.

Runeson, S. (1977). On the possibility of "smart" perceptual mechanisms. *Scandinavian Journal of Psychology, 18*, 172–179.

Runeson, S., & Frykholm, G. (1981). Visual perception of lifted weight. *Journal of Experimental Psychology: Human Perception & Performance, 7*, 733–740.

Runeson, S., & Frykholm, G. (1983). Kinematic specification of dynamics as an information basis for person-and-action perception: Expectation, gender recognition, and deception intention. *Journal of Experimental Psychology: General, 112*, 585–615.

Saarni, C., Campos, J. J., Camras, L. A., & Witherington, D. (2006). Emotional development: Action, communication, and understanding. In N. Eisenberg (Ed.), *Handbook of child psychology: Social, emotional, and personality development* (6th ed., Vol. 3, pp. 226–299). New York, NY: Wiley.

Saffran, J. R., Aslin, R. N., & Newport, E. L. (1996). Statistical learning by 8-month-old infants. *Science, 274*, 1926–1928.

Saffran, J. R., Werker, J. F., & Werner, L. A. (2006). The infant's auditory world: Hearing, speech, and the beginnings of language. In D. Kuhn & R. S. Siegler (Eds.), W. Damon (Series Ed.), *Handbook of child psychology: Vol. 2. Cognition, perception, and language* (6th ed., pp. 58–108). Hoboken, NJ: Wiley.

Sai, F. Z. (2005). The role of the mother's voice in developing mother's face preference: Evidence for intermodal perception at birth. *Infant and Child Development, 14*, 29–50.

Salapatek, P. (1975). Pattern perception in early infancy. In L. B. Cohen & P. Salapatek (Eds.), *Infant perception: From sensation to cognition: Vol. 7. Basic visual processes* (pp. 133–248). New York, NY: Academic Press.

Salapatek, P., & Kessen, W. (1966). Visual scanning of triangles by the human newborn. *Journal of Experimental Child Psychology, 3*, 155–167.

Salapatek, P., & Kessen, W. (1973). Prolonged investigation of a plane geometric triangle by the human newborn. *Journal of Experimental Child Psychology, 15*, 22–29.

Sann, C., & Streri, A. (2007). Perception of object shape and texture in human newborns: Evidence from cross-modal transfer tasks. *Developmental Science, 10*, 399–410.

Sann, C., & Streri, A. (2008). Inter-manual transfer of object texture and shape in human neonates. *Neuropsychologia, 46*, 698–703.

Sato, K., Masda, T., Wada, Y., Shirai N., Kanazawa, S., & Yamaguchi, M. K. (2013). Infants' perception of curved illusory contour with motion. *Infant Behavior and Development, 36*, 557–563.

Sato, K., Sogabe, Y., & Mazuka, R. (2010). Discrimination of phonetic vowel length by Japanese infants. *Developmental Psychology, 46*, 106–119.

Schachner, A., & Hannon, E. E. (2011). Infant-directed speech drives social preferences in 5-month-old infants. *Developmental Psychology, 47*, 19–25.

Schaffer, R. (1984). *The child's entry into a social world.* New York, NY: Academic Press.

Schieffelin, B. B. (1990). *The give and take of everyday life: Language socialization of Kaluli children.* New York, NY: Cambridge University Press.

Schiff, W. (1965). Perception of impending collision: A study of visually directed avoidant behavior. *Psychological Monographs, 79*(Whole No. 604).

Schiff, W., & Oldak. R. (1990). Accuracy of judging time to arrival: Effects of modality, trajectory, and gender. *Journal of Experimental Psychology: Human Perception & Performance, 16,* 303–316.

Schlottman, A., & Ray, E. (2010). Goal attribution to schematic animals: Do 6-month-olds perceive biological motion as animate? *Developmental Science, 13,* 1–10.

Schlottman, A., Ray, E. D., & Surian, L. (2012). Emerging perception of causality in action-and-reaction sequences from 4 to 6 months of age: Is it domain-specific? *Journal of Experimental Child Psychology, 112,* 208–230.

Schmale, R., Cristia, A., Seidl, A., & Johnson, E. K. (2010). Developmental changes in infants' ability to cope with dialect variation in word recognition. *Infancy, 15,* 650–662.

Schmale, R., & Seidl, A. (2009). Accommodating variability in voice and foreign accent: Flexibility in early word representations. *Developmental Science, 12,* 583–601.

Schmitow, C., & Sternberg, G. (2013). Social referencing in 10-month-old infants. *European Journal of Developmental Psychology, 10,* 533–545.

Schmuckler, M. A., & Gibson, E. J. (1989). The effect of imposed optical flow on guided locomotion in young walkers. *British Journal of Developmental Psychology, 7,* 193–206.

Schmuckler, M. A., & Li, N. S. (1998). Looming responses to obstacles and apertures. *Psychological Science, 9,* 49–52.

Schneider, B. A., Morrongiello, B. A., & Trehub, S. E. (1990). Size of critical band in infants, children, and adults. *Journal of Experimental Psychology: Human Perception & Performance, 76,* 642–52.

Scholl, B. J., & Tremoulet, P. D. (2000). Perceptual causality and animacy. *Trends in Cognitive Neurosciences, 4,* 299–309.

Schwartz, M., & Day, R. H. (1979). Visual shape perception in early infancy. *Monographs of the Society for Research in Child Development, 44,* 63.

Scott, L. S. (2011). Mechanisms underlying the emergence of object representations during infancy. *Journal of Cognitive Neuroscience, 23,* 2935–2944.

Scott, L. S., & Monesson, A. (2010). Experience-dependent neural specialization during infancy. *Neuropsychologia, 48,* 1857–1861.

Sedda, A., Monaco, S., Bottini, G., & Goodale, M. A. (2011). Integration of visual and auditory information for hand actions: Preliminary evidence for the contribution of natural sounds to grasping. *Experimental Brain Research, 209,* 365–374.

Sedgwick, H. A. (1986). Space perception. In K. R. Boff, L. Kaufman, & J. P. Thomas (Eds.), *Handbook of perception and human performance: Vol. 1. Sensory processes* (pp. 23.21–23.44). New York, NY: Wiley.

Shapley, R., & Gordon, J. (1987). The existence of interpolated illusory contours depends on contrast and spatial separation. In S. Petry & G. E. Meyer (Eds.), *Perception of illusory contours* (pp. 109–116). New York, NY: Springer-Verlag.

Shaw, L., Roder, B., & Bushnell, E. W. (1986). Infants' identification of three-dimensional from transformations of linear perspective. *Perception & Psychophysics, 40,* 301–310.

Shea, S. L., & Aslin, R. N. (1990). Oculomotor responses to step-ramp targets by young human infants. *Vision Research, 30,* 1077–1092.

Shepard, K. G., Spence, M. J., & Sasson, N. J. (2012). Distinct facial characteristics differentiate communicative intent of infant-directed speech. *Infant and Child Development, 21,* 555–578.

Shepard, R. N. (1984). Ecological constraints on internal representation: Resonant kinematics of perceiving, imagining, thinking, and dreaming. *Psychological Review, 91,* 417–447.

Shinskey, J. L., & Munakata, Y. (2003). Are infants in the dark about hidden objects? *Developmental Science, 6,* 273–282.

Shipley, T. F., & Kellman, P. J. (1990). The role of discontinuities in the perception of subjective figures. *Perception & Psychophysics, 48,* 259–270.

Shipley, T. F., & Kellman, P. J. (1992). Perception of partly occluded objects and illusory figures: Evidence for an identity hypothesis. *Journal of Experimental Psychology: Human Perception & Performance, 18,* 106–120.

Shipley, T. F., & Kellman, P. J. (1994). Spatiotemporal boundary formation: Boundary, form, and motion perception from transformations of surface elements. *Journal of Experimental Psychology: General, 123,* 3–20.

Shirai, N., Kanazawa, S., & Yamaguchi, M. K. (2005). Young infants' sensitivity to shading stimuli with radial motion. *Japanese Psychological Research, 47,* 286–291.

Shirai, N., Kanazawa, S., & Yamaguchi, M. K. (2008). Early development of sensitivity to radial motion at different speeds. *Experimental Brain Research, 185,* 461–467.

Schreibman, L., Dawson, G., Stahmer, A. C., Landa, R., Rogers, S. J., McGee, G. G., . . .Halladay, A. (2015). Naturalistic developmental behavioral interventions: Empirically validated treatments for Autism Spectrum Disorder. *Journal of Autism Developmental Disorder, 45,* 2411–2428.

Shuwairi, S. M., & Johnson, S. P. (2013). Oculomotor exploration of impossible figures in infancy. *Infancy, 18,* 221–232.

Simion, F., Di Giorgio, E., Leo, I., & Bardi, L. (2011). The processing of social stimuli in early infancy: From faces to biological motion perception. *Progress in Brain Research, 189,* 173–194.

Simion, F., Regolin, L., & Bulf, H. (2008). A predisposition for biological motion in the newborn baby. *Proceedings of the National Academy of Sciences of the USA, 105,* 808–813.

Simmons, D. R., Robertson, A. E., McKay, L. S., Toal, E., McAleer, P., & Pollick, F. E. (2009). Vision in autism spectrum disorders. *Vision Research, 49,* 2705–2739.

Simon, T. J., Hespos, S. J., & Rochat, P. (1998). Do infants understand simple arithmetic? A replication of Wynn (1992). *Cognitive Development, 10,* 253–269.

Simons, D. J., & Chabris, C. F. (1999). Gorillas in our midst: Sustained inattentional blindness for dynamic events. *Perception, 28,* 1059–1074.

Simpson, E. A., Paukner, A., Suomi, S. J., & Ferrari, P. F. (2014). Visual attention during neonatal imitation in newborn macaque monkeys. *Developmental Psychobiology, 56,* 864–870.

Singh, L., Morgan, J. L., & Best, C. T. (2002). Infants' listening preferences: Baby talk or happy talk? *Infancy, 3,* 365–394.

Singh, L., Morgan, J. L., & White, K. S. (2004). Preference and processing: The role of speech affect in early spoken word recognition. *Journal of Memory and Language, 51,* 173–189.

Sinnott, I. M., & Aslin, R. N. (1985). Frequency and intensity discrimination in human infants and adults. *Journal of the Acoustical Society of America, 78,* 1986–1992.

Sireteanu, R., Kellerer, R., & Boergen, K. P. (1984). The development of peripheral visual acuity in human infants: A preliminary study. *Human Neurobiology, 3,* 81–85.

Sitskoorn, M. M., & Smitsman, A. W. (1995). Infants' perception of dynamic relations between objects: Passing through or support? *Developmental Psychology, 31,* 437–447.

Skoczenski, A. M. (2002). Limitations on visual sensitivity during infancy: Contrast sensitivity, vernier acuity, and orientation processing. *Progress in infancy research, 2,* 169–214.

Slater, A., Bremner, G., Johnson, S. P., Sherwood, P., Hayes, R., & Brown, E. (2000). Newborn infants' preference for attractive faces: The role of internal and external facial features. *Infancy, 1,* 265–274.

Slater, A., & Findlay, J. M. (1975). Binocular fixation in the newborn baby. *Journal of Experimental Child Psychology, 20,* 248–273.

Slater, A., Johnson, S. P., Kellman, P. J., & Spelke, E. S. (1994). The role of three-dimensional depth cues in infants' perception of partly occluded objects. *Early Development and Parenting, 3,* 187–191.

Slater, A., Johnson, S. P., Brown, E., & Badenoch, M. (1996). Newborn infant's perception of partly occluded objects. *Infant Behavior and Development, 19,* 145–148.

Slater, A., Mattock, A., & Brown, E. (1990). Size constancy at birth: Newborn infants' responses to retinal and real size. *Journal of Experimental Child Psychology, 49,* 314–322.

Slater, A., Mattock, A., Brown, E., & Bremner, J. G. (1991). Form perception at birth: Cohen and Younger (1984) revisited. *Journal of Experimental Child Psychology, 51,* 395–406.

Slater, A., & Morison, V. (1985). Shape constancy and slant perception at birth. *Perception, 14,* 337–344.

Slater, A., Morison, V., & Rose, D. (1983). Locus of habituation in the human newborn. *Perception, 12,* 593–598.

Slater, A., Morison, V., & Somers, M. (1988). Orientation discrimination and cortical function in the human newborn. *Perception, 17,* 597–602.

Slater, A., Morison, V., Somers, M., Mattock, A., Brown, E., & Taylor, D. (1990). Newborn and older infants' perception of partly occluded objects. *Infant Behavior and Development, 13,* 33–49.

Slater, A., Quinn, P. C., Brown, E., & Hayes, R. (1999). Intermodal perception at birth: Intersensory redundancy guides newborn infants' learning of arbitrary auditory–visual pairings. *Developmental Science, 2,* 333–338.

Slater, A., Quinn, P. C., Hayes, R., & Brown, E. (2000). The role of facial orientation in newborn infants' preference for attractive faces. *Developmental Science, 3,* 181–185.

Slater, A., Quinn, P. C., Kelly, D. J., Lee, K., Longmore, C. A., McDonald, P. R., & Pascalis, O. (2010). Shaping the face space in early infancy: Becoming a native face processor. *Child Development Perspectives, 4,* 205–211.

Smith, N. A., Gibilisco, C., Meisinger, R. E., & Hankey, M. (2013). Asymmetry in infants' selective attention to facial features during visual processing of infant-directed speech. *Frontiers in Psychology, 4,* Article 601.

Smith, N. A., & Trainor, L. J. (2008). Infant-directed speech is modulated by infant feedback. *Infancy, 13,* 410–420.

Smith, N. A., Trainor, L. J., & Shore, D. I. (2006). The development of temporal resolution: Between-channel gap detection in infants and adults. *Journal of Speech, Language, and Hearing Research, 49,* 1104–1113.Soderstrom, M. (2007). Beyond babytalk: Re-evaluating the nature and content of speech input to preverbal infants. *Developmental Review, 27,* 501–532.

Soley, G., & Hannon, E. E. (2010). Infants prefer the musical meter of their own culture: A cross-cultural comparison. *Developmental Psychology, 46,* 286–292.

Sommerville, J. A., Woodward, A. L., & Needham, A. (2005). Action experience alters 3-month-old infants' perception of others' actions. *Cognition, 96,* B1–B11.

Soska, K. C., & Adolph, K. E. (2014). Postural position constrains multimodal object exploration in infants. *Infancy, 19,* 138–161.

Soska, K. C., Adolph, K. E., & Johnson, S. P. (2010). Systems in development: Motor skill acquisition facilitates three-dimensional object completion. *Developmental Psychology, 46,* 129–138.

Soska, K. C., & Johnson, S. P. (2008). Development of three-dimensional object completion in infancy. *Child Development, 79,* 1230–1236.

Soska, K. C., & Johnson, S. P. (2013). Development of three-dimensional completion of complex objects. *Infancy, 18,* 325–344.

Soto-Faraco, S., Calabresi, M., Navarra, J., Werker, J. F., & Lewkowicz, D. J. (2012). The development of audiovisual speech perception. In A. J. Bremner, D. J. Lewkowicz, & C. Spence (Eds.), *Multisensory development* (pp. 207–228). New York, NY: Oxford University Press.

Soussignan, R., Courtial, A., Canet, P., Danon-Apter, G., & Nadel, J. (2011). Human newborns match tongue protrusion of disembodied human and robotic mouths. *Developmental Science, 14,* 385–394.

Spears, W. C. (1964). Assessment of visual preference and discrimination in the four-month-old infant. *Journal of Comparative and Physiological Psychology, 57,* 381–385.

Spelke, E. S. (1976). Infants' intermodal perception of events. *Cognitive Psychology, 8,* 553–560.

Spelke, E. S. (1988). Where perceiving ends and thinking begins: The apprehension of objects in infancy. In A. Yonas (Ed.), *Perceptual development in infancy: The Minnesota symposia on child psychology* (Vol. 20, pp. 197–234). Hillsdale, NJ: Erlbaum.

Spelke, E. S. (2000). Core knowledge. *American Psychologist, 55,* 1233–1243.

Spelke, E. S., Breinlinger, K., Jacobson, K., & Phillips. A. (1993). Gestalt relations and object perception: A developmental study. *Perception, 22,* 1483–1501.

Spelke, E. S., Breinlinger, K., Macomber, J., & Jacobson, K. (1992). Origins of knowledge. *Psychological Review, 99,* 605–632.

Spelke, E. S., Katz, G., Purcell, S. E., Ehrlich, S. M., & Breinlinger, K. (1994). Early knowledge of object motion: Continuity and inertia. *Cognition, 51,* 131–176.

Spelke, E. S., & Kinzler, K. D. (2007). Core knowledge. *Developmental Science, 10,* 89–96.

Spelke, E. S., & von Hofsten, C. (2001). Predictive reaching for occluded objects by 6-month-old infants. *Journal of Cognition and Development, 2,* 261–281.

Spence, M., & Moore, D. S. (2003). Categorization of infant-directed speech: Development from 4 to 6 months. *Developmental Psychobiology, 42,* 97–109.

Spence, M. J., & Freeman, M. S. (1996). Newborn infants prefer the maternal low-pass filtered voice, but not the maternal whispered voice. *Infant Behavior and Development, 19,* 199–212.

St. Georges, C., Cassel, R. S., Cohen, D., Chetouani, M., Laznik, M., Maestro, S., & Muratori, F. (2010). What studies of family movies can teach us about autistic infants: A literature review. *Research in Autism Spectrum Disorders, 4,* 355–366.

Starkey, P., & Cooper, R. G. (1980). Perception of numbers by human infants. *Science, 210,* 1033–1035.

Starkey, P., Spelke, E. S., & Gelman, R. (1983). Detection of intermodal numerical correspondences by human infants. *Science, 222,* 179–181.

Starkey, P., Spelke, E. S., & Gelman, R. (1990). Numerical abstraction by human infants. *Cognition, 36,* 97–127.

Stavros, K. A., & Kiorpes, L. (2008). Behavior measurement of temporal contrast sensivitity development in macaque monkeys (*Macaca nemestrina*). *Vision Research, 48,* 1335–1344.

Stein, B. E., Meredith, M. A., & Wallace, M. T. (1994). Development and neural basis of multisensory integration. In D. J. Lewkowicz & R. Litckliter (Eds.), *The development of intersensory perception: Comparative perspectives* (pp. 81–105). Hillsdale, NJ: Erlbaum.

Stein, B. E., & Stanford, T. R. (2008). Multisensory integration: current issues from the perspective of the single neuron. Nature Reviews Neuroscience, 9, 255–266.

Stern, D. N. (1985). *The interpersonal world of the infant.* New York, NY: Basic Books.

Sternberg, G. (2013). Do 12-month-old infants trust a competent adult? *Infancy, 18,* 873–904.

Stevens, B., & Johnston. C. C. (1993). Pain in the infant: Theoretical and conceptual issues. *Maternal–Child Nursing Journal, 21,* 3–14.

Stiles, J., Brown, T. T., Haist, F., & Jernigan, T. L. (2015). Brain and cognitive development. In L. S. Liben & U. Muller (Eds.), *Handbook of child psychology and developmental science* (Vol. 2: Cognitive Processes, pp. 9–62). New York, NY: Wiley.

Stoffregen, T. A. (1985). Flow structure versus retinal location in the optical control of stance. *Journal of Experimental Psychology: Human Perception & Performance, 11,* 554–565.

Stoffregen, T. A (1986). The role of optical velocity in the control of stance. *Perception & Psychophysics, 39,* 355–360.

Stoffregen, T. A., Schmuckler, M. A., & Gibson, E. J. (1987). Use of central and peripheral optical flow in stance and locomotion in young walkers. *Perception, 16,* 113–119.

Strauss, M. S., & Curtis, L. E. (1981). Infant perception of numerosity. *Child Development, 52,* 1146–1152.

Streri, A. (1987). Tactile discrimination of shape and intermodal transfer in two- to three-month-old infants. *British Journal of Developmental Psychology, 5,* 213–220.

Streri, A. (1993). *Seeing, reaching, touching,* Cambridge, MA: MIT Press.

Streri, A., Gentaz, E., Spelke, E., & van de Walle, G. (2004). Infants' haptic perception of object unity in rotating displays. *Quarterly Journal of Experimental Psychology, 57A,* 523–538.

Streri, A. & Spelke, E. S. (1988). Haptic perception of objects in infancy. *Cognitive Psychology, 20,* 1–23.

Streri, A., & Spelke, E. S. (1989). Effects of motion and figural goodness on haptic object perception in infancy. *Child Development, 60,* 1111–1125.

Streri, A., Spelke, E., & Rameix, E. (1993). Modality-specific and amodal aspects of object perception in infancy: The case of active touch. *Cognition, 47,* 251–279.

Striano, T., & Bushnell, E. W. (2005). Haptic perception of material properties by 3-month-old infants. *Infant Behavior and Development, 28,* 266–289.

Studdert-Kennedy, M., Liberman, A. M., Harris, K. S., & Cooper, F. S. (1970). Motor theory of speech perception: A reply to Lane's critical review. *Psychological Review, 77,* 234–249.

Sugarman, S. (1978). Some organizational aspects of preverbal communication. In I. Markova (Ed.), *The social context of language* (pp. 49–66). New York, NY: Wiley.

Sumby, W. H., & Pollack, I. (1954). Visual contribution to speech intelligibility in noise. *Journal of the Acoustical Society of America, 26,* 212–215.

Sumi, S. (1984). Upside-down presentation of the Johansson moving light-spot pattern. *Perception, 13,* 283–286.

Sutherland, N. S. (1961). *The methods and findings of experiments on the visual discrimination of shape by animals.* Cambridge, England: Heifer.

Suttle, C. M., Banks, M. S., & Graf, E. W. (2002). FPL and sweep VEP to tritan stimuli in young infants. *Vision Research, 42,* 2879–2891.

Tajfel, H. (1981). *Human groups and social categories: Studies in social psychology.* New York, NY: Cambridge University Press.

Tauber, E., & Koffler, S. (1966). Optomotor response in human infants to apparent motion: Evidence of innateness. *Science, 152,* 382–383.

Trauble, B., & Pauen, S. (2007). The role of functional information for infant categorization. *Cognition, 105,* 362–379.

Taylor, C., Schloss, K., Palmer, S. E., & Franklin, A. (2013). Color preferences in infants and adults are different. *Psychonomics Bulletin and Review, 20,* 916–922.

Teinonen, T., Fellman, V., Naatanen, R., Alku, P., & Huotilainen, M. (2009). Statistical language learning in neonates revealed by event-related brain potentials. *BMC Neuroscience, 10,* ArtID 21.

Teller, D. Y., & Bornstein, M. H. (1987). Infant color vision and color perception. In P. Salapatek & L. Cohen (Eds.), *Handbook of infant perception: Vol. 1. From sensation to perception* (pp. 185–236). Orlando, FL: Academic Press.

Teller, D. Y., Civan, A., & Bronson-Castain, K. (2004). Infants' spontaneous color preferences are not due to adult-like brightness variations. *Visual Neuroscience, 21,* 397–401.

Teller, D. Y., Lindsey, D. T., Mar, C. M., Succop, A., & Mahal, M. R. (1992). Infant temporal contrast sensitivity at low temporal frequencies. *Vision Research, 32,* 1157–1162.

Teller, D. Y., Peeples, D. R., & Sekel, M. (1978). Discrimination of chromatic from white light by two-month-old human infants. *Vision Research, 18,* 41–48.

Thiessen, E. D., Hill, E. A., & Saffran, J. R. (2005). Infant-directed speech facilitates word segmentation. *Infancy, 7,* 53–71.

Tincoff, R., & Jusczyk, P. W. (2012). Six-month-olds comprehend words that refer to parts of the body. *Infancy, 17,* 432–444.

Titchener, E. B. (1902). *A textbook of psychology.* New York, NY: Macmillan.

Todd, J. T. (1982). Visual information about rigid and nonrigid motion: A geometric analysis. *Journal of Experimental Psychology Human Perception & Performance, 8,* 238–252,

Todd, J. T. (1984). The perception of three-dimensional structure from rigid and nonrigid motion. *Perception and Psychophysics, 36,* 97–103.

Tomasello, M., Carpenter, M., & Liszkowski, U. (2007). A new look at infant pointing. *Child Development, 78,* 705–722.

Tondel, G. M., & Candy, T. R. (2008). Accommodation and vergence latencies in human infants. *Vision Research, 48,* 564–576.

Trainor, L. J., Austin, C. M., & Desjardins, R. N. (2000). Is infant-directed speech prosody a result of the vocal expression of emotion? *Psychological Science, 11,* 188–195.

Trainor, L. J., Samuel, S. S., Desjardins, R. N., & Sonnadara, R. R. (2001). Measuring temporal resolution in infants using mismatch negativity. *Neuroreport, 12,* 2443–2448.

Trehub, S. E. (1976). The discrimination of foreign speech contrasts by infants and adults. *Child Development, 47,* 466–472.

Trehub, S. E., Schneider, B. A., & Henderson, J. L. (1995). Gap detection in infants, children and adults. *Journal of the Acoustical Society of America, 98,* 2532–2541.

Tremblay, H., & Rovira, K. (2007). Joint visual attention and social triangular engagement at 3 and 6 months. *Infant Behavior and Development, 30,* 366–379.

Trevarthen, C. (1975). Growth of visuomotor coordination in infants. *Journal of Movement Studies, 1,* 57.

Trevarthen, C. (1979). Communication and cooperation in early infancy: A description of primary intersubjectivity. In M. Bullowa (Ed.), *Before speech: The beginning of interpersonal communication.* Cambridge, England: Cambridge University Press.

Trevarthen, C. (2011). What is it like to be a person who knows nothing? Defining the active intersubjective mind of a newborn human being. *Infant and Child Development, 20,* 119–135.

Tsuji, S., & Cristia, A. (2014). Perceptual attunement in vowels: A meta-analysis. *Developmental Psychobiology, 56,* 179–191.

Turkewitz, G., Lewkowicz, D., & Gardner, J. (1966). Effect of intensity of auditory stimulation on directional eye movements in the human neonate. *Animal Behaviour, 14,* 93–101.

Turvey, M. T., Shaw, R. E., Reed, E. S., & Mace, W. M. (1981). Ecological laws of perceiving and acting: In reply to Fodor and Pylyshyn. *Cognition, 9,* 237–304.

Uchiyama, I., Anderson, D. I., Campos, J. J., Witherington, D., Frankel, C. B., Lejeune, L., & Barbu-Roth, M. (2008). Locomotor experience affects self and emotion. *Developmental Psychology, 44,* 1225–1231.

Ullman, S. (1979). *The interpretation of visual motion.* Cambridge, MA: MIT Press.

Ungerleider, L. G., & Mishkin, M. (1982). Two cortical visual systems. In D. J. Ingle, M. A. Goodale, & R. J. W. Mansfield (Eds.), *Analysis of visual behavior* (pp. 549–586). Cambridge, MA: MIT Press.

Vaillant-Molina, M., Bahrick, L. E., & Flom, R. (2013). Young infants match facial and vocal emotional expressions of other infants. *Infancy, 18,* E97–E111.

Valentine, T. (1988). Upside-down faces: A review of the effect of inversion upon face recognition. *British Journal of Psychology, 79,* 471–491.

Valenza, E., & Bulf, H. (2007). The role of kinetic information in newborns' perception of illusory contours. *Developmental Science, 10,* 492–501.

Valenza, E., Leo, I., Gava, L., & Simion, F. (2006). Perceptual completion in newborn infants. *Child Development, 77,* 1810–1821.

Valenza, E., Simion, F., Cassia, V. M., & Umilta, C. (1996). Face preference at birth. *Journal of Experimental Psychology: Human Perception and Performance, 22,* 892–903.

van der Meer, A. L. H. (1997). Keeping the arm in the limelight: Advanced visual control of arm movements in neonates. *European Journal of Paediatric Neurology, 4,* 103–108.

van der Meer, A. L. H., Svantesson, M., & van der Weel, F. R. R. (2012). Longitudinal study of looming in infants with high-density EEG. *Developmental Neuroscience, 34,* 488–501.

van der Meer, A. L. H., van der Weel, F. R., & Lee, D. N. (1994). Prospective control in catching by infants. *Perception, 23,* 287–302.

van der Meer, A. L. H., van der Weel, F. R., & Lee, D. N. (1995). The functional significance of arm movements in neonates. *Science, 267,* 693–695.

van de Walle, G. A., & Spelke, E. S. (1996). Spatiotemporal integration and object perception in infancy: Perceiving unity versus form. *Child Development, 67,* 2621–2640.

van de Walle, G. A., Carey, S., & Prevor, M. (2000). Bases for object individuation in infancy: Evidence from manual search. *Journal of Cognition and Development, 1,* 249–280.

Van Essen, D. C., & Maunsell, J. H. R. (1983). Hierarchical organization and functional streams in the visual cortex. *Trends in Neurosciences, 6,* 370–375.

van Hof, P., van der Kamp, J., & Savelsbergh, G. J. P. (2006). Three- to eight-month-old infants' catching under monocular and binocular vision. *Human Movement Science, 25,* 18–36.

van Hof, P., van der Kamp, J., & Savelsbergh, G. J. P. (2008). The relation between infants' perception of catchableness and the control of catching. *Developmental Psychology, 44,* 182–194.

Van Wermeskerken, M., van der Kamp, J., Savelsbergh, G. J. P., & von Hofsten, C. (2013). Getting the closer object? An information-based dissociation between vision for perception and vision for movement in early infancy. *Developmental Science, 16,* 91–100.

VanMarle, K., & Wynn, K. (2009). Infants' auditory enumeration: Evidence for analog magnitudes in the small number range. *Cognition, 111,* 302–316.

Virtala, P., Huotilainen, M., Partanen, E., Fellman, V., & Tervaniemi, M. (2013). Newborn infants' auditory system is sensitive to Western music chord categories. *Frontiers in Psychology, 4,* Article 492.

Vishton, P. M., Ware, E. A., & Badger, A. N. (2005). Different Gestalt processing for different actions? Comparing object-directed reaching and looking time measures. *Journal of Experimental Child Psychology, 90,* 89–113.

Voegtline, K. M., Costigan, K. A., Pater, H. A., & DiPietro, J. A. (2013). Near-term fetal response to maternal spoken voice. *Infant Behavior and Development, 36,* 526–533.

Volkmann, F. C., & Dobson, M. V. (1976). Infant responses of ocular fixation to moving visual stimuli. *Journal of Experimental Child Psychology, 22,* 86–99.

von der Heydt, R., Peterhans, E., & Baumgartner, G. (1984). Illusory contours and cortical neuron responses. *Science, 224,* 1260–1262.

von Hofsten, C. (1974). Proximal velocity change as a determinant of space perception. *Perception & Psychophysics, 15,* 488–494.

von Hofsten, C. (1976). The role of convergence in visual space perception. *Vision Research, 16,* 193–198.

von Hofsten, C. (1982). Eye–hand coordination in the newborn. *Developmental Psychology, 18,* 450–461.

von Hofsten, C. (1983). Catching skills in infancy. *Journal of Experimental Psychology: Human Perception & Performance, 9,* 75–85.

von Hofsten, C. (1980). Predictive reaching for moving objects by human infants. *Journal of Experimental Child Psychology, 30,* 369–382.

von Hofsten, C. (1990). Early development of grasping an object in space–time. In M. A. Goodale (Ed.), *Vision and action: The control of grasping. The Canadian Institute for Advanced Research series in artificial intelligence and robotics* (pp. 65–79). Norwood, NJ: Ablex.

von Hofsten, C. (2004). An action perspective on motor development. *Trends in Cognitive Sciences, 8,* 266–272.

von Hofsten, C., Kellman, P., & Putaansuu, J. (1992). Young infants' sensitivity to motion parallax. *Infant Behavior and Development, 15,* 245–264.

von Hofsten, C., & Ronnqvist, L. (1993). The structuring of neonatal arm movements. *Child Development, 64,* 1046–1057.

von Hofsten, C., & Rosander, K. (1996). The development of gaze control and predictive tracking in young infants. *Vision Research, 36,* 81–96.

von Hofsten, C., & Rosander, K. (1997). Development of smooth pursuit tracking in young infants. *Vision Research, 37,* 1799–1810.

von Hofsten, C., & Siddiqui, A. (1993). Using the mother's actions as a reference for object exploration in six- and twelve-month-old infants. *British Journal of Developmental Psychology, 11*, 61–74.

von Hofsten, C., & Spelke, E. S. (1985). Object perception and object-directed reaching in infancy. *Journal of Experimental Psychology: General, 114*, 198–212.

von Hofsten, O., von Hofsten, C., Sulutvedt, U., Laeng, B., Brennen, T., & Magnussen, S. (2014). Simulating newborn face perception. *Journal of Vision, 14*, 1–9.

Von Hornbostel, E. M. (1927). The unity of the senses (E. Koffka & W. Vinton, Trans.). *Psyche, 7*, 83–89.

Vouloumanos, A., Hauser, M. D., Werker, J. F., & Martin, A. (2010). The tuning of human neonates' preference for speech. *Child Development, 81*, 517–527.

Walk, R. D., & Gibson, E. J. (1961). A comparative and analytical study of visual depth perception. *Psychological Monographs, 75*(519).

Walker, A. S., Owsley, C. J., Megaw-Nyce, J., Gibson, E. J., & Bahrick, L. E. (1980). Detection of elasticity as an invariant property of objects by young infants. *Perception, 9*, 713–718.

Walker-Andrews, A. S. (1997). Infants' perception of expressive behaviors: Differentiation of multimodal information. *Psychological Bulletin, 121*, 437–456.

Walker-Andrews, A. S., Krogh-Jespersen, S., Mayhew, E. M., & Coffield, C. N. (2011). Young infants' generalization of emotional expressions: Effects of familiarity. *Emotion, 11*, 842–851.

Wallach, H. (1985). Learned stimulation in space and motion perception. *American Psychologist, 40*, 399–404.

Wallach, H., & Floor, L. (1971). The use of size matching to demonstrate the effectiveness of accommodation and convergence as cues for distance. *Perception & Psychophysics, 10*, 423–428.

Wallach, H., Newman, E. B., & Rosenzweig, M. R. (1949). The precedence effect in sound localization. *American Journal of Psychology, 62*, 315–336.

Wallach, H., & O'Connell, D. N. (1953). The kinetic depth effect. *Journal of Experimental Psychology, 45*, 205–217.

Wallach, H., & O'Leary, A. (1982). Slope of regard as a distance cue. *Perception & Psychophysics, 31*, 145–148.

Wallach, H., & Zuckerman, C. (1963). The constancy of stereoscopic depth. *American journal of Psychology, 76*, 404–412.

Wandell, B. A. (1995). *Foundations of vision*. Sunderland, MA: Sinauer.

Wang, Y., Seidl, A., & Cristia, A. (2015). Acoustic–phonetic differences between infant- and adult-directed speech: The role of stress and utterance position. *Journal of Child Language, 42*, 821–842

Warren, R., & Wertheim, A. H. (1990). *Perception and control of self-motion*. Hillsdale, NJ: Erlbaum.

Warren, W. H., & Verbrugge, R. R. (1984). Auditory perception of breaking and bouncing events: A case study in ecological acoustics. *Journal of Experimental Psychology: Human Perception and Performance, 10*, 704–712.

Wattam-Bell, J. (1992). The development of maximum displacement limits for discrimination of motion direction. *Vision Research, 32*, 621–630.

Wattarn-Bell, J. (1996a). Visual motion processing in one-month-old infants: Preferential looking experiments. *Vision Research, 36*, 1671–1677.

Wattam-Bell, J. (1996b). Visual motion processing in one-month-old infants: Habituation experiments. *Vision Research, 36*, 1679–1685.

Wattam-Bell, J. (2009). Stereo and motion D_{max} in infants. *Journal of Vision, 9*, 1–9.

Wattam-Bell, J., Birtles, D., Nystrom, P., von Hofsten, C., Rosander, K., Anker, S., . . . Braddick, O. (2010). Reorganization of global form and motion processing during human visual development. *Current Biology, 20*, 411–415.

Webb, J. A., & Aggarwal, J. K. (1982). Structure from motion of rigid and jointed objects. *Artificial Intelligence, 19*, 107–130.

Weikum, W. M., Vouloumanos, A., Navarra, J., Soto-Faraco, S., Sebastian-Gilles, N., & Werker, J. F. (2007). Visual language discrimination in infancy. *Science, 316*, 1159.

Weisleder, A., & Fernald, A. (2013). Talking to children matters: Early language experience strengthens processing and building vocabulary. *Psychological Science, 24*, 2143–2152.

Werker, J. F., Gilbert, J. H., Humphrey, K., & Tees, R. C. (1981). Developmental aspects of cross-language speech perception. *Child Development, 52*, 349–355.

Werker, J. F., & Tees, R. C. (1983). Developmental changes across childhood in the perception of non-native speech sounds. *Canadian Journal of Psychology, 37*, 278–286.

Werker, J. F., & Tees, R. C. (1984). Cross-language speech perception: Evidence for perceptual reorganization during the first year of life. *Infant Behavior and Development, 7*, 49–63.

Werker, J. F., Yeung, H. H., & Yoshida, K. A. (2012). How do infants become experts at native-speech recognition? *Current Directions in Psychological Science, 21*, 221–226.

Werner, L. A., & Bargones, J. Y. (1992). Psychoacoustic development of human infants. *Advances in Infancy Research, 7*, 103–145.

Werner, L. A., Folsom, R. C., Mancl, L. R., & Syapin, C. L. (2001). Human auditory brainstem response to temporal gaps in noise. *Journal of Speech, Language, and Hearing Research, 44*, 737–750.

Werner, L. A., Marean, G. C., Halpin, C. F., Spetner, N. B., & Gillenwater, J. M. (1992). Infant auditory temporal acuity: Gap detection. *Child Development, 63*, 260–272.

Wertheimer, M. (1912). Experimentelle Studien uber das Sehen von Beuegung. *Zeitschrift* fuer *Psyrhologie, 61, 161–265.*

Wertheimer, M. (1958). Untersunchungen zur Lehre der Gestalt. *Psychologische Forschung, 4*, 301–350. (Original work published 1923)

Wertheimer, M. (1961). Psychomotor coordination of auditory and visual space at birth. *Science, 134*, 1692,

Wheeler, A., Anzures, G., Quinn, P. C., Pascalis, O., Omrin, D. S., & Lee, K. (2011). Caucasian infants scan own- and other-race faces differently. *PLoS One, 6*, e18621.

Whitfield, I. C., Cranford, J., Ravizza, R., & Diamond, I. T. (1972). Effects of unilateral ablation of auditory cortex in cat on complex sound localization. *Journal of Neurophysiology, 35, 718–731.*

Whyatt, C., & Craig, C. (2013). Sensory-motor problems in autism. *Frontiers in Integrative Neuroscience, 7*, 1–12.

Whyte, V. A., McDonald, P. V., Baillargeon, R., & Newell, K. M. (1994). Mouthing and grasping of objects by young infants. *Ecological Psychology, 6*, 205–218.

Wilcox, T., & Schweinle, A. (2003). Infants' use of speed information to individuate objects in occlusion events. *Infant Behavior and Development, 26*, 253–282.

Wilcox, T., Smith, T., & Woods, R. (2011). Priming infants to use pattern information in an object individuation task: The role of comparison. *Developmental Psychology, 47*, 886–897.

Wilcox, T., Woods, R., & Chapa, C. (2008). Color-function categories that prime infants to use color information in an object individuation task. *Cognitive Psychology, 57*, 220–261.

Wilcox, T., Woods, R., Tuggy, L., & Napoli, R. (2006). Shake, rattle, and ... one or two objects? Young infants' use of auditory information to individuate objects. *Infancy, 9*, 97–123.

Wilkinson, N., Paikan, A., Gredeback, G., Rea, R., & Metta, G. (2014). Staring us in the face? An embodied theory of innate face preference. *Developmental Science, 17,* 809–825.

Witherington, D. C. (2005). The development of prospective grasping control between 5 and 7 months: A longitudinal study. *Infancy, 7,* 143–161.

Witherington, D. C., Campos, J. J., Harriger, J. A., Bryan, C., & Margett, T. E. (2010). Emotion and its development in infancy. In G. Bremner & T. D. Wachs (Eds.), *The Wiley-Blackwell handbook of infant development* (2nd ed., Vol. 1, pp. 568–591). Cambridge, England: Blackwell.

Woods, R. J., & Wilcox, T. (2006). Infants' ability to use luminance information to individuate objects. *Cognition, 99,* B43–B52.

Woods, R. J., & Wilcox, T. (2010). Covariation of color and luminance facilitate object individuation in infancy. *Developmental Psychology, 46,* 681–690.

Woodward, A. L. (1998). Infants selectively encode the goal object of an actor's reach. *Cognition, 69,* 1–34.

Woodward, A. L. (1999). Infants' ability to distinguish between purposeful and non-purposeful behaviors. *Infant Behavior and Development, 22,* 145–160.

Woodward, A. L. (2009). Infants' grasp of others' intentions. *Current Directions in Psychological Science, 18,* 53–57.

Wörmann, V., Holodynski, M., Kärtner, J., & Keller, H. (2012). A cross-cultural comparison of the development of the social smile: A longitudinal study of maternal and infant imitation in 6- and 12-week-old infants. *Infant Behavior and Development, 35,* 335–347.

Wundt, W. (1862). *Beitrage zur Theorie der Sinneswahrnehmung.* Leipzig, Germany: Winter.

Wynn, K. (1992). Addition and subtraction by human infants. *Nature, 358,* 749–750.

Xu, F. (1999). Object individuation and object identity in infancy: The role of spatiotemporal information, object property information, and language. *Acta Psychologica, 102,* 113–136.

Xu, F., & Baker, A. (2005). Object individuation in 10-month-old infants using a simplified manual search method. *Journal of Cognition and Development, 6,* 307–323.

Xu, F., & Carey, S. (1996). Infants' metaphysics: The case of numerical identity. *Cognitive Psychology, 30,* 111–153.

Xu, N., Burnham, D., Kitamura, C., & Vollmer-Conna, U. (2013). Vowel hyperarticulation in parrot-, dog-, and infant-directed speech. *Anthrozoös, 26,* 373–380.

Yang, J., Kanazawa, S., Yamaguchi, M. K., & Kuriki, I. (2013). Investigation of color constancy in 4.5-month-old infants under a strict luminance contrast for individual participants. *Journal of Experimental Child Psychology, 115,* 126–136.

Yeung, H. H., Chen, K. H., & Werker, J. F. (2013). When does native language input affect phonetic perception? The precocious case of lexical tone. *Journal of Memory and Language, 68,* 123–139.

Yirmiya, N., Gamliel, I., Pilowsky, T., Feldman, R., Baron-Cohen, S., & Sigman, M. (2006). The development of siblings of children with autism at 4 and 14 months: Social engagement, communication, and cognition. *Journal of Child Psychology and Psychiatry, 47,* 511–523.

Yonas, A., & Arterberry, M. E. (1994). Infants' perceive spatial structure specified by line junctions. *Perception, 23,* 1427–1435.

Yonas, A., Arterberry, M. E., & Granrud, C. E. (1987). Four-month-old infants' sensitivity to binocular and kinetic information for three-dimensional object shape. *Child Development, 58,* 910–917.

Yonas, A., Cleaves, W. T., & Pettersen, L. (1978). Development of sensitivity to pictorial depth. *Science, 200,* 77–79.

Yonas, A., Elieff, C. A., & Arterberry, M. E. (2002). Emergence of sensitivity to pictorial depth cues: Charting development in individual infants. *Infant Behavior and Development, 25,* 495–514.

Yonas, A., & Granrud, C. A. (1985a). Reaching as a measure of infants' spatial perception. In G. Gottlieb & N. A. Krasnegor (Eds.), *Measurement of audition and vision in the first year of postnatal life: A methodological overview* (pp. 301–322). Westport, CT: Ablex.

Yonas, A., & Granrud, C. E. (1985b). Development of visual space perception in young infants. In J. Mehler & R. Fox (Eds.), *Neonate cognition: Beyond the blooming buzzing confusion* (pp. 45–67). Hillsdale, NJ: Erlbaum.

Yonas A., & Granrud, C. E. (2006). Infants' perception of depth from cast shadows. *Perception and Psychophysics, 68,* 154–160.

Yonas, A., Granrud, C. E., Arterberry, M. E., & Hanson, B. L. (1986). Distance perception from linear perspective and texture gradients. *Infant Behavior and Development, 9,* 247–256.

Yonas, A., Granrud, C. E., & Pettersen, L. (1985). Infants' sensitivity to relative size information for distance. *Developmental Psychology, 21,* 161–167.

Yonas, A., & Hartman, B. (1993). Perceiving the affordance of contact in four- and five-month-old infants. *Child Development, 64,* 298–308.

Yonas, A., Pettersen, L., & Granrud, C. E. (1982). Infants' sensitivity to familiar size as information for distance. *Child Development, 53,* 1285–1290.

Younger, B. A., & Cohen, L. B. (1986). Developmental change in infants' perception of correlations among attributes. *Child Development, 57,* 803–815.

Younger, B. A., & Fearing, D. D. (1998). Detecting correlations among form attributes: An object-examining test with infants. *Infant Behavior and Development, 21,* 289–297.

Younger, B. A., & Gotlieb, S. (1988). Development of categorization skills: Changes in the nature or structure of infant form categories? *Developmental Psychology, 24,* 611–619.

Yuodelis, C., & Hendrickson, A. (1986). A qualitative and quantitative analysis of the human fovea during development. *Vision Research, 26,* 847–855.

Zanker, J., Mohn, G., Weber, U., Zeitler-Driess, K., & Fahle, M. (1992). The development of Vernier acuity in human infants. *Vision Research, 32,* 1557–1564.

Zelazo, P. R., Weiss, M. J. S., & Tarquinio, N. (1991). Habituation and recovery of neonatal orienting to auditory stimuli. In J. S. Weiss & P. R. Zelazo (Eds.), *Newborn attention: Biological constraints and the influence of experience* (pp. 120–141). Norwood, NJ: Ablex.

Zemach, I., Chang, S., & Teller, D. Y. (2007). Infant color vision: Prediction of infants' spontaneous color preferences. *Vision Research, 47,* 1368–1381.

Author Index

Page numbers followed by *f* and *t* indicate figures and tables respectively.

Subject Index

Page numbers followed by *f* and *t* indicate figures and tables respectively.

Made in United States
North Haven, CT
21 March 2023